DELHI REBORN

ROTEM GEVA

DELHI
REBORN

Partition and Nation Building in India's Capital

STANFORD UNIVERSITY PRESS

STANFORD, CALIFORNIA

Stanford University Press

Stanford, California

©2022 by Rotem Geva. All rights reserved.

Printed in the United States of America on acid-free, archival-quality paper

Library of Congress Cataloging-in-Publication Data

Names: Geva, Rotem, author.
Title: Delhi reborn : partition and nation building in India's capital / Rotem Geva.
Other titles: South Asia in motion.
Description: Stanford, California : Stanford University Press, 2022. | Series: South Asia in motion | Includes bibliographical references and index.
Identifiers: LCCN 2021051794 (print) | LCCN 2021051795 (ebook) | ISBN 9781503631199 (cloth) | ISBN 9781503632110 (paperback) | ISBN 9781503632127 (ebook)
Subjects: LCSH: Decolonization—India—Delhi. | Delhi (India)—Politics and government—20th century. | Delhi (India)—History—20th century. | India—History—Partition, 1947.
Classification: LCC DS486.D3 G385 2022 (print) | LCC DS486.D3 (ebook) | DDC 954/.56—dc23/eng/20211210
LC record available at https://lccn.loc.gov/2021051794
LC ebook record available at https://lccn.loc.gov/2021051795

Cover photograph: India independence ceremony, Dehli, August 16, 1947. Photo Division, Press Information Bureau, Ministry of Information and Broadcasting, Government of India.

Cover design: Rob Ehle

Typeset by Newgen in Adobe Caslon Pro 10.75/15

CONTENTS

ILLUSTRATIONS

ACKNOWLEDGMENTS

This book has been many years in the making and incurred countless debts along the way. Its seed was sown at the New School for Social Research, which proved formative for my intellectual development. I thank Oz Frankel, Hugh Raffles, Vyjayanthi Rao, Sanjay Ruparelia, Hylton White, and Ann Stoler for the knowledge and advice they shared at that early and foundational stage. Claudio Lomnitz's commitment to bringing together history and anthropology, and his attentiveness to people's experience of temporality as a historical force, have stayed with me throughout the years, animating the analytical perspective of this book.

I conducted research and developed the ideas in this book at Princeton University, where I am especially indebted to Gyan Prakash, who taught me so much on South Asian and urban history, and whose unique approach to history writing, with its emphasis on everyday life and attention to narrativization, has deeply influenced me. As a mentor, Gyan struck a fine balance between guiding his students and giving them space and freedom to explore and pursue their own interests—never imposing his way of thinking and always there to comment and refine the argument. I was fortunate to have his help at critical junctures of my academic trajectory. Allison Busch is sadly no longer with us, and she is sorely missed by her colleagues and students. She was a gifted teacher, and I am grateful for her generosity and her thoughtful comments on my drafts. Bhavani Raman's imagination and analytical rigor always gave a fresh perspective and enriched my scholarship, and I am also deeply thankful for her kindness and encouragement. Frances Pritchett's Urdu classes at Columbia University were a delight.

This book would not have been possible without the institutional and financial support I received at Princeton. Reagan Campbell, Kristy

Novak, Lauren Kane, and Jackie Wasneski addressed every request attentively and promptly. My archival research in India was funded by the Graduate School, the Department of History, and the Princeton Institute for International and Regional Studies. The Childbirth Accommodation Program and Student Childcare Assistance Program enabled me to juggle motherhood and writing. The American Institute of Indian Studies (AIIS) supported two periods of Hindi study in Jaipur that were great fun and advanced my language proficiency. I am also thankful to Elise Auerbach, Purnima Mehta, and Deepak Bhalla, whose help in obtaining a research visa to India and overcoming bureaucratic hurdles made possible my extensive research in Delhi. The staff and librarians at the National Archives of India, the Nehru Memorial Museum and Library, and the Delhi State Archives were all helpful. Special thanks go to Jyoti Luthra at NMML and to Sanjay Garg and the personnel at the Delhi State Archives for creating an environment conducive to research, and for their extra efforts in tracing records. I thank the Department of History at Delhi University, which provided me with affiliation.

In Delhi, I was fortunate to meet scholars, fiction writers, and other *Dilliwallas* who kindly related their experiences of, and reflections on, post-partition Delhi. Special thanks go to Alok Bhalla, who was generous with his time and materials. His reminiscences of his childhood in Delhi and his insights on partition—the fruit of long years of research—have been invaluable. I thank Veena and Philip Oldenburg for their hospitality and advice. Philip kindly shared his knowledge of Delhi's history and his memories of fieldwork during the Emergency. Shahid Amin offered some unexpected research leads. I am grateful to Aslam Parvez, whose recollections brought Delhi of the late 1940s and early 1950s to life. I am fortunate to have met the late eminent Hindi writer Krishna Sobti, who recounted her memories of the city. For sharing their knowledge, materials, and thoughts, I would also like to thank Mridula Garg, Vishwa Bandhu Gupta, Nirmala Jain, Ali Javed, Anjum Khaliq, Ajit Kumar, Prem Gopal Mittal, Joginder Paul, Rajee Seth, Ravikant Sharma, Shahid Siddiqui, Raman Sinha, Ravi Sundaram, Navin Suri, Noor Zaheer, and the late Mushirul Hasan. Sayeed Ayub's and Irshad Naiyyer's help with reading Urdu materials was indispensable.

I am thankful to my colleagues at the Hebrew University in Jerusalem, whose intellectual rigor, keen sense of history, and genuine interest in India's partition helped me to paint the story of Delhi on the broader canvas of modern history. For their companionship and help, in different ways, I thank Ofer Ashkenazi, Sivan Balslev, Raz Chen-Morris, Aya Elyada, Ayelet Even-Ezra, Yanay Israeli, Claudia Kedar, Kinneret Levi, Orna Naftali, Danny Orbach, Nissim Otmazgin, Sara Parnasa, Yuri Pines, Ronny Regev, Marina Rimscha, Hanoch Roniger, Gideon Shelach-Lavi, David Shulman, Eviatar Shulman, Marina Shusterman, Moshe Sluhovsky, Dror Wahrman, Yfaat Weiss, and Alex Yakobson. My deep gratitude goes to Yigal Bronner and Ronit Ricci, who gave me unwavering support and constant guidance as I struggled to combine teaching, writing, and parenting. It was Yigal's courses that sparked my passion for South Asia many years ago, and I am thankful that he encouraged me to pursue my interest in modern history, far removed as it is from his expertise in Sanskrit poetry, and for guiding me through challenges from afar. Ronit, whose superb scholarship and extraordinary accomplishments are matched only by her modesty and kindness, is truly a role model.

I am indebted to Dan Diner, my mentor in the European Research Council (ERC) project "JudgingHistories: Experience, Judgement, and Representation of World War II in an Age of Globalization." The extraordinary breadth and depth of his scholarship and his original mind opened historiographical terrains unfamiliar to me and helped me to understand how profoundly the war shaped the history of Delhi. The ERC generously supported my research on wartime Delhi. My reading sessions, workshops, and coffee breaks with Samir Ben-Layashi, Lutz Fiedler, Lior Hadar, Kobi Kabalek, Jonathan Matthews, and Iris Nachum broadened my knowledge, helped me develop my ideas, and offered many laughs along the way. Incredibly sharp and organized, Jenia Yudkevich provided indispensable administrative assistance.

This book was published with the support of the Israel Science Foundation (grant No. 85/22). Additionally, research for Chapter 5 was supported by the Israel Science Foundation (grant No. 887/20). I also benefitted from participating in the research group on "Twentieth Century Partitions," funded by the Van Leer Jerusalem Institute and the

University of Haifa. I thank Eitan Bar-Yosef, Ayelet Ben-Yishai, Yael Berda, Arie Dubnov, Sandy Kedar, Moriel Ram, Tséla Rubel, Ornit Shani, Ran Shauli, and Mahmoud Yazbak for illuminating discussions. Further exchanges with Arie contributed significantly to my understanding of the global history of partitions. Ayelet has become a dear friend and I thank her for reading my work and for helping me navigate the intricacies of academic life. Her sharp mind and unfailing sense of humor have been a blessing. My students, especially those who participated in the course on transnational and comparative histories of partitions, challenged me with their questions to learn more and elucidate my thinking. I presented portions of this book in various forums and conferences, and I thank participants for their questions and comments.

Colleagues and friends around the world helped this project along the way. At Princeton I greatly benefited from the friendship of, and academic conversations with, Nimisha Barton, Yael Berda, Ritwik Bhattacharyya, Nabaparna Ghosh, Rohit Lamba, Nikhil Menon, Arijeet Pal, and Nishtha Singh. The friendship of Franziska Exeler, Yulia Frumer, and Ronny Regev meant a great deal to me. Arudra Burra prompted me to think seriously about citizenship. I thank Rohit De, Radha Kumar, and Nurfadzilah Yahaya for their friendship, lively discussions, and feedback on my early drafts. I am obliged to both Radha and Rohit for extending advice and help at crucial moments over the years.

Rakesh Ankit has always been unbelievably generous, sending along every document and research lead he thought might help. His admirable memory and command of high politics helped me situate my findings in the largest context of South Asian history. Michal Erlich and Khinvraj Jangid opened their home in Delhi and helped with the bureaucratic intricacies of research. Vikas Rathee was great company when he stayed in Jerusalem and has generously provided assistance several times since his return to India. Hadas Weiss was exceptionally helpful whenever I needed her help. I thank Isabel Huacuja Alonso for fruitful exchanges and clearheaded advice over the years. Oded Rabinovitch offered his perceptive comments on my work in several academic forums and was always willing to place his academic experience at my disposal.

I am grateful to Andrew Amstutz, Ayelet Ben-Yishai, Rohit De, and Kalyani Ramnath for reading portions of this book and giving insightful comments. Gilly Nadel carefully edited this book, and I have greatly benefitted from her keen intellect, incisive comments, and friendship. Anubhav Roy and Swathi Taduru meticulously located and processed additional archival materials. Sharing my enthusiasm for this period, Anubhav eagerly traced critical photos for the book.

I thank the anonymous reviewers at Stanford University Press, who provided valuable and supportive comments. Marcela Maxfield, Sunna Juhn, Dylan Kyung-lim White, and Susan Karani have been consummate professionals, and caring and supportive to boot.

My father, Avraham Geva, who passed away while the book was in the making, and my mother, Nechama Geva, encouraged me to pursue my academic interests. My mother's insatiable love of books, endless intellectual curiosity, and resilience in the face of everyday hardships have shaped who I am. She never had a desk of her own, let alone a room, and she encouraged me to strive for mine. Bracha and Yossi Halperin have been pillars of strength, and I cannot thank them enough for their unconditional love, warmth, and support. For sharing the important moments, I thank Yifat, Adi, Michal, Lihu, Yuval, and Yoav, as well as my wonderful nieces and nephews, Shira, Amit, Omer, and Lior.

My deepest gratitude is to Udi Halperin, who has been with me through the ups and downs. His wisdom, sacrifices, and unbeatable optimism have made this book, and everything else, possible. Our daughter Noya is my happiness and pride. I dedicate this book to both of them.

NOTE ON TERMS AND TRANSLITERATION

I have restricted transliteration to direct quotations and titles of books and articles. Otherwise, I used the most common spelling for South Asian places, names, and terms, but I retained contemporary spelling when citing directly from the sources. Nouns are pluralized with an s, e.g., *mohallas*. I generally transliterated according to John T. Platts, *A Dictionary of Urdu, Classical Hindi, and English*, omitting most diacritical marks, and replacing ć with ch, ćh with chh, ś with sh, and g̠ and gh. I standardized the names of Delhi's localities, following their current spelling, but I kept the contemporary spelling when citing directly from the sources. The British India province of the "United Provinces" was renamed "Uttar Pradesh" in 1950. The book uses United Provinces and Uttar Pradesh when discussing the pre-1950 and post-1950 periods respectively. Translations are mine unless stated otherwise.

ABBREVIATIONS

AIML	All-India Muslim League
AIR	All India Reporter
CSAS	Cambridge Centre for South Asian Studies Oral History Collection
CC	Chief Commissioner
CID	Criminal Investigation Department
CPI	Communist Party of India
DC	Deputy Commissioner
DPCC	Delhi Provincial Congress Committee
DPR	Delhi Police Records
DSA	Delhi State Archives
IB	Intelligence Bureau
ICS	Indian Civil Service
INA	Indian National Army
MHA	Ministry of Home Affairs
MLA	Member of Legislative Assembly
MSP	Mridula Sarabhai Papers
NAI	National Archives of India
NMML	Nehru Memorial Museum and Library
RSS	Rashtriya Swayamsevak Sangh
SWJN	Selected Works of Jawaharlal Nehru, Second Series
SP	Superintendent of Police
SSP	Senior Superintendent of Police
SPO	Special Police Officer

Now, when I recall this scene, my mind travels even further back in time. During the doomsday of 1857 the people of Delhi were also forced to leave. When the temper of the British rulers somewhat cooled down, they permitted the people of Delhi to return. Yet so many did not have the fortune to return to their city. So many spent the rest of their lives missing Delhi and crying for Delhi. Delhi has always, repeatedly, made her children cry. Having been wrenched from her protective lap, they spend the rest of their lives wandering and wailing. Drenched in dust and blood, [Delhi] comes to life again. She changes her dress, embraces the newcomers, and is filled with renewed happiness. When Maulana Hali was telling the story of the late Delhi, a new Delhi was awakening from the earth, and when here [in Pakistan], Shahid Ahmad Dehlvi was crying over the destruction of his forefathers' Delhi . . . over there, Delhi opened her empty lap for the new, uprooted people.[1]

THIS PARAGRAPH WAS written by Intizar Husain, the celebrated Urdu writer, who was born and raised in United Provinces and migrated to Pakistan following partition. Husain depicts Delhi as a woman who has been devastated yet comes to life again with renewed vigor and vitality, drawing on a familiar trope—the city's history as a cycle of massive destruction and regeneration. Delhi's long and intimate association with political power resulted in an eventful history of conquests and wars, grand power, ruination and death, displacement and loss. As historian Robert Frykenberg notes, Delhi "has been the site for a succession of cities, each of which served as the capital or citadel or centre of a vast domain. This has been so for a thousand years, at the very least.... the ruins of almost all previous cities of Delhi are still visible."[2]

This eventful history was determined by Delhi's strategic location between the Punjab and the plains of north India: the "Ridge" to its west, which is the northern extension of the Aravalli Range, together with the Yamuna River, protected Delhi and allowed it to dominate the Gangetic plain. The river also supplied water for drinking, irrigation, and commerce. Yet once a regime had weakened and could no longer deploy the necessary resources, the city's position of strength could very easily turn into a point of weakness, rendering Delhi vulnerable to attack from both sides. Thus, "Delhi could also quickly become the 'graveyard of empires,'"[3] and, as historian Narayani Gupta says, "Delhi has died so many deaths."[4] Furthermore, Delhi's political importance had a cumulative effect, as the city gradually gained prestige and cast a spell on succeeding rulers who set off to conquer it. It was not merely its strategic location but also, and increasingly over time, its association with power that made it attractive to successive conquerors.

Accordingly, Delhi is often referred to as "the Seven Cities" (and sometimes eight, nine, or ten), referring to different locations in proximity to each other in which different regimes ruled, leaving grand monuments behind—the eleventh-century Qila Rai Pithora; the fourteenth-century Siri, Tughlaqabad, Jahanpanah, and Firozabad; the sixteenth-century Dinpanah (where Purana Qila is located); the seventeenth-century Mughal capital Shahjahanabad (known as Old Delhi); and the imposing colonial New Delhi, inaugurated in 1931, only sixteen years before colonial rule crumbled.[5] If we go even further back in time, to the gray area where history and legend are blurred, we will find that Delhi (specifically the Purana Qila site) is also identified with Indraprastha—the magnificent city of the Pandavas of the great epic *Mahabharata*, with its association with a colossal war.[6]

In the epigraph above, Husain draws on this familiar repertoire of images and associations, and locates the events of 1947 within the violent cycle of the rise and fall of empires. This latest political shift that Delhi experienced—from the seat of a colonial state to the capital of a nation-state—is at the heart of this book. Decolonization brought about its own share of violence and destruction, for independence was accompanied by partition. In 1947, while Delhi was the stage for the solemn public rituals celebrating the transfer of power, it also experienced mass violence and demographic transformation, with more than half a million Hindu and Sikh refugees arriving from Pakistan and 350,000 Muslims fleeing in the opposite direction. Accordingly, in the epigraph above, Husain alludes to the havoc that partition wrought on Delhi's Muslims. He portrays Delhi not simply as a woman, but specifically as a mother who welcomes new children with open arms while abandoning her own.

What evoked this powerful metaphor in Husain's imagination was a gathering of former "Dilliwallas" in Lahore in 1948. As Husain recounts in his memoir, Shahid Ahmad Dehlvi, the eminent writer, editor, and grandson of the first Urdu novelist, Deputy Nazir Ahmad, had gone to Delhi for a short visit to collect papers and books that he had left behind eight months earlier, when the city was engulfed in brutal violence. Dehlvi longed to see Delhi again, because, as he put it, for a Dilliwalla, the separation from Delhi was akin to separating nails from flesh.[7] However, once there, he found his beloved city utterly transformed. When he returned to Pakistan, he wrote a painful reportage of the violence, his uprooting from the city, and the grieved and uncanny feeling that possessed him when visiting an intimate yet estranged home.

Dehlvi read this chronicle aloud in the gathering that Husain attended. Several *muhajirs* from Delhi and the United Provinces met at the house of Hakim Muhammad Nabi Khan, grandson of the famous physician and influential political leader of Delhi Hakim Ajmal Khan, who had joined with Gandhi during the Khilafat movement.[8] They listened intently, but Dehlvi broke down crying and could not finish, and the party turned into a gathering of mourning. To express the shock and pain of his violent exile, Dehlvi likens himself in his reportage to a child whose mother has hit him, yet whose affection he still desperately seeks. He sees Delhi as a cruel mother, but his mother nonetheless.

DELHI REBORN

Delhi Reborn revisits one of the most dramatic moments in the modern history of Delhi—the megalopolis capital of India and one of the world's largest cities—tracing the momentous challenges of the present to the formative period of India's decolonization. It tells how the twin events of partition and independence remade Delhi.

As a center of Muslim life, Delhi bore the brunt of partition violence and its attendant mass migrations most convulsively. As India's capital, it was the arena for nation and state formation, with all their attendant struggles. Focusing on the late 1930s to the mid-1950s, this book both de-lineates the structural shifts of this period and teases out their emotional dimensions and impact on people's lives.

The book explores the period's most urgent questions, still central to understanding the city and nation today. How did World War II stimu-late the fight for independence, and what impact did it have on the city? Why did the demand for Pakistan take root in Delhi during the war, given that its most ardent supporters would eventually remain outside its borders and be devastated by its formation? How did the relatively lim-ited interreligious riots that the city experienced in the 1920s and 1930s transform into mass violence of an altogether different scale in 1947? How did such ethnic cleansing and its attendant demographic transformation reshape the city? Finally, what does the national government's response to this crisis in the capital reveal about the architects of independent India and about their visions for a postcolonial regime?

At the heart of the book are two stories. First, it traces how two nation-states—India and Pakistan—became increasingly territorialized in the imagination and practice of Delhi's residents, how violence and displacement were central to this process, and how tensions over be-longing and citizenship lingered in the city and the nation. Second, the book chronicles the post-1947 struggle, between the urge to democratize political life in the new republic and the authoritarian legacy of colonial rule, augmented by the imperative to maintain law and order in the face of the partition crisis. As the political nerve center of the country and the seat of national government, Delhi was where India's national leaders most directly negotiated these two fundamental tensions—between a secular democracy and a religion-based partition, between civil liberties and authoritarian impulses.

Throughout the analysis, we will see again and again Delhi's intimate association with the nation and with political power, and hence, with the shift from colonial order to nation-state. We will see that this shift was a twilight time, combining features of the imperial framework and the independent republic, and we will try to capture the lived experience of this liminality. To introduce the book's main arguments, let us return to Intizar Husain's epigraph above.

1947 AS A REPETITION AND CULMINATION OF 1857

For Intizar Husain, the catastrophe of 1947 was part of a cycle of pivotal events that had destroyed and rebuilt Delhi throughout history. Even more so, it is tied to the catastrophe of 1857—the *ghadar* (revolt) and its colonial suppression, which brought about the final dissolution of the Mughal Empire. The year 1857 indeed prevails in the memories and political imaginations of the historical actors of our story, and its relationship to 1947 is key to the interpretation of this book. It is worth elucidating this critical reference point.

Delhi had been the political center of Muslim dynasties that ruled over large parts of India since the early days of the Delhi Sultanate, in the thirteenth century. Its association with the rise of Islam in India left behind countless physical monuments, including the Qutab Minar, fortresses and mosques, graves and Sufi shrines. In the seventeenth century, the Mughal emperor Shah Jahan left his mark on the city's landscape with the construction of Shahjahanabad—a planned city named after him, whose grandeur was meant to project the empire's strength. Shahjahanabad, as Eckart Ehlers and Thomas Krafft conclude, was planned as a typical Islamic city, which, despite its transformation over time, remained the heart of Delhi's sociopolitical life during the period that interests us. (See Figure o.1.)

Shahjahanabad's eastern side was built along the bank of the Yamuna River and was dominated by the imposing palace complex known today as the Red Fort, which was, in essence, "a city within city."⁹ The magnificent and enormous Jama Masjid (Friday Mosque) was built on a hilltop about half a kilometer southwest of the palace. The city was surrounded by a wall, and the two main boulevards that radiated from the palace connected it to the city's gates. The elegant Chandni Chowk ran east-west from the Lahori Gate of the fort to Fatehpuri Mosque, then north toward the city's Lahori Gate. The second boulevard, Faiz Bazar, ran north-south from the fort's Delhi Gate to the city's Delhi Gate. Along the boulevards were gardens, mosques, bazaars, and the palaces of the nobility. Outside the city's wall were gardens watered by a sophisticated system of water channels that ran around the city and inside it, with a tree-lined canal flowing right at the center of Chandni Chowk. Over time, lands were allocated to members of the nobility who constructed *havelis*, or courtyard mansions, and these became the focal points of the city's main *mohallas*, or neighborhoods. The *mohallas* functioned as complex political, residential, and economic units, consisting of bazaars, workshops, and residential quarters for military men, servants, and artisans. The *mohallas* formed administrative subdivisions of the city's twelve wards, each under the control of the *thanadar*.¹⁰ In addition to the Jama Masjid, hundreds of mosques were spread around the city, the most important of which were located in the two main boulevards. Thus, Fatehpuri Mosque, the second most important mosque after the Jama Masjid, built of the same red sandstone used for the latter and for the palace, was located at the western end of Chandni Chowk. Like the Jama Masjid, it will be the setting for many events in this book.

With the decline of the Mughal Empire in the eighteenth century, Delhi was ransacked by a series of plunderers—from the Persian Nadir Shah, who carried off the famous peacock throne (1739), to the Afghan Ahmad Shah Abdali (1757) and the Rohilla Ghulam Qadir, who blinded the Mughal emperor Shah Alam II (1788). The weak emperor accepted the Marathas' protection, and they formed the real power behind his

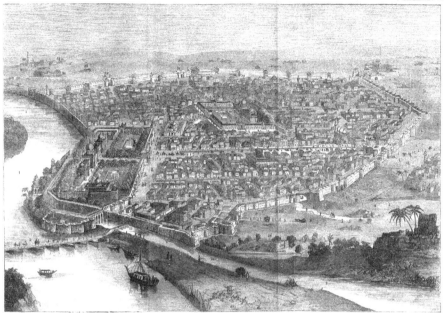

FIGURE 0.1 *The City of Delhi before the siege. A detailed engraving of the walled city of Shahjahanabad before the 1857 revolt. The palace (Red Fort) is on the left, on the bank of the Yamuna River. To its southwest is the Jama Masjid. The main road of Chandni Chowk stretches westward from the palace. Toward its end is the Fatehpuri Mosque. Source:* Illustrated London News, *1858.*

throne until 1803. Finally, the British East India Company took over Delhi in 1803, but historians agree that the disruptive impact of colonial modernity was not felt until the Revolt of 1857, which brought about the true colonial break with the past.

The story is well known. The rebellious Indian troops of the East India Company's Bengal army arrived in the city and asked the elderly Mughal emperor Bahadaur Shah Zafar to patronize the rebellion. British authority completely collapsed, and the rebels took over the city, bringing about the breakdown of law and order and basic services, destroying, looting, and killing. When the British recaptured Delhi several months later, they wrought havoc on the city. They executed the emperor's sons at what came to be known as *Khooni Darwaza* (The Gate of Blood), exiled the emperor himself to Burma, expelled the bulk of the population, and razed vast areas of the city. Hindu residents of the city were not allowed to return before 1858, and Muslim residents much later. The few who were allowed to stay, such as Delhi's quintessential nineteenth-century poet Mirza Ghalib, were subjected to strict curfews and rarely ventured outside their homes.

The city was utterly transformed through the construction of a railway, large-scale demolitions around the fort, and the conversion of the latter into a military garrison. Property ownership was restructured and social hierarchy upset, as the *havelis* and mansions of the Muslim aristocracy were transferred to loyalist bankers and merchants, mostly Hindus and Jains. While many members of the old nobility became impoverished, a new moneyed elite arose.[11] Concomitantly, the British began to "de-Mughalize" themselves, discrediting the Persianate etiquette, culture, and literature surrounding the Mughal court, notably the Urdu *ghazal* (love lyric).[12] Yet, once they overcame the initial trauma of the revolt, the British cultivated the Muslim well-born as a privileged group, both in Delhi and in other parts of India.[13] Hence, until 1947, Delhi's Muslim elite would be dominant in government employment and the municipal committee, a point to which we shall return later on.[14]

Administratively, Delhi became a district of the Punjab until 1911. The construction of the railway, which turned Delhi into a commercial center, spurred its expansion westward, outside the city wall, to the settlements of Kishan Ganj, Pahari Dhiraj, and Paharganj, and the new area of Sadar Bazar, which attracted people displaced by the large-scale demolitions and laborers building the railway. Sadar Bazar's proximity to the new railway on the Grand Trunk Road made it attractive also for merchants of the Punjabi Muslim community, who established their wholesale shops there. Toward the end of the nineteenth century, with the establishment of the Delhi Cloth Mills, flour mills, and other factories, Sadar Bazar and Sabzi Mandi became the centers of mechanized industry, attracting migrant labor to Delhi. These areas developed mostly haphazardly and were home to mostly low-income workers, but with the construction of the new imperial capital and the expansion of the population, they became attractive. Karol Bagh, another lower-class area, also began to draw educational institutions and well-off residents.[15]

Colonial architecture left its imprint through the construction of wide vehicular roads and a new civic square at the center of Chandni Chowk, whose focal point was the neoclassical Delhi Institute Building, later known as Town Hall (See Figure 0.2.). Town Hall hosted the recently formed Delhi Municipal Committee, as well as a college, a library, a museum, a "Darbar" hall for the British administrators' public audiences, and halls for social functions. The Mughal Jahanara gardens surrounding it were redesigned and renamed Queen's Gardens. A statue of Queen Victoria stood at the entrance, and at the center of the square was the tall Victoria Clock Tower (which would stand there until its sudden collapse in 1951). In time, this central square would become the hub of nationalist and other popular protests, subverting the intention of its colonial builders.[16] Other new public buildings included the railway station, hospitals, schools, bridges, post offices, clubs, and banks.

Simultaneously, a growing racial segregation was reflected in, and effectuated through, the construction of the Civil Lines, a European

FIGURE 0.2 *Clock Tower (Ghanta Ghar) and Town Hall, Chandni Chowk, Delhi, c. 1910–1920, unidentified photographer. Source: Image © Sarmaya Arts Foundation. Accession No. 2019.51.4 (b)*

quarter to the north of the walled city. Informed by contemporary European notions of a rational, clean, airy environment, it had broad streets, and its spacious bungalows were isolated from the streets and from each other by gardens. In the early twentieth century the Delhi administration, headed by the chief commissioner and deputy commissioner, moved to Civil Lines, and a new cantonment was established for the army in the Ridge. The ultimate colonial imprint on Delhi's landscape came with the transfer of British India's capital from Calcutta to Delhi in 1911, and the ensuing construction, south to Shahjahanabad on Raisina Hill, of a new planned capital city, featuring grandiose, monumental architecture, broad avenues and circles, large bungalows for the bureaucratic elite, and the high-end shopping center of Connaught Place.[17] (See Figure o.3.) The completion of New Delhi in 1931 also finalized the transformation of the erstwhile capital of the Mughal Empire into Old Delhi—the irrational, congested, chaotic, and unsanitary city, "an uncivilized 'slum.'"[18]

All these transformations could be traced to the events of 1857, which became an emblematic catastrophe—almost an obsession—in the memory of Delhi's Muslim well-born, who returned to it again and again in their writings. In fact, soon after the events there was a surge of texts mourning the destruction of the city and its culture, anchored in the genre of Urdu verse known as *shahr-e ashob* (city of misfortune), which had developed in the eighteenth century, when Persians and Afghans had ravaged the city. Thus, the last Mughal emperor Bahadur Shah "Zafar," who was also a gifted poet, wrote of "ruined habitation" (*ujra dayar*), echoing a famous verse ascribed to the eighteenth-century poet Mir Taqi Mir. Mirza Ghalib lamented the devastation of Delhi,[19] and the poet Khwaja Altaf Husain "Hali" wrote an elegy that opens with the words, "Dear friends, I beseech you, speak not of the Delhi that is no more, I cannot bear to listen to the sad story of this city."[20]

The weight of 1857 and the melancholic literature surrounding it came to define the Muslim elite's perception and experience of Delhi in the first half of the twentieth century. This notion of a declining world is perhaps best captured in the well-known lyrical novel *Twilight in Delhi*, published by the progressive writer Ahmed Ali in 1940. Set in Shahjahanabad and centered on a Muslim aristocratic family in decline during

FIGURE 0.3 *An aerial view of New Delhi, c. 1930. At the center are the Central Secretariat Buildings. Above and to their right is India's parliament building. Source: Central Press/Getty Images.*

1911–19, after the colonial capital shifted to Delhi, the novel seeks to capture the world of Old Delhi as it was fading, and it is suffused with wistful citations of Ghalib and Urdu ghazals.[21]

In hindsight, the novel becomes even more poignant, because Ali, who was in China when partition took place, was not allowed to return to India and had to move to Pakistan instead. It was, as he reflected years later, "a living repetition of history ninety years after the banishment of my grandparents and the Muslim citizens from the vanquished city by the British. Yet while their exile was temporary, mine was permanent, and the loss not only of my home and whatever I possessed, but also my birthright."[22]

Thus, 1857, which had been a formative experience in the collective memory of Delhi's Muslims, was a frame of reference through which 1947 was later understood. As Ali notes here, 1947 repeated 1857 and even went beyond it, completing the ruination of Muslim Delhi that had begun with 1857. Accordingly, in the epigraph above, Intizar Husain draws an explicit parallel between Khwaja Altaf Husain "Hali," who recited his *marsiya* about Delhi in Lahore in 1874, and Shahid Ahmad Dehlvi, who recited his own reportage of Delhi in Lahore in 1948. Dehlvi himself, gesturing toward Mir Taqi Mir and the last Mughal emperor, named one of his memoirs about Delhi *Ujra Dayar*,[23] and he opens his account of partition with the words:

> I often heard about the events of the *ghadar* from the elders, and read all that Khwaja Hasan Nizami wrote about the topic, and I used to think that such destruction had never befallen Delhi, and would never befall it again. But after the devastation of September, the ruin of 1857 seemed negligible. Such great destruction was never seen in world history.[24]

THE NATION-STATE AND THE MUSLIM QUESTION

These personal and emotional ruminations on the connection, and difference, between 1857 and 1947 are worth pondering and developing more analytically. As Ahmed Ali observes, unlike the banishment of his forefathers from the city, his own exile was permanent, and he lost his very birthright to the city. If the upheavals of 1857 took place under the pressures of empire, 1947 was caused by its dissolution. Hence, 1947 went further and consummated the colonial decline of the Delhi Muslim community, but simultaneously manifested an entirely new logic—the logic of the nation-state, carried out through a territorial partition and new citizenship regimes. This is why Ali's exile was permanent.

Nationalism emerged from within the colonial order itself, several decades after 1857, when an English-educated Indian elite established the Indian National Congress to advance its interests vis-à-vis the colonial regime. This story has been recounted countless times in history books.

Suffice it to state that, over time, the modest demand for increased access to government employment and limited political representation developed into a full-fledged nationalist, anticolonial movement that encompassed large sections of Indian society. Indian nationalism gathered momentum with the meteoric rise of Mohandas Karamchand Gandhi after World War I, resulting in mass movements in the early 1920s and early 1930s, which accelerated under the pressures of World War II.

Simultaneously, tensions developed between Hindus and Muslims, and these came to be known as the "communal problem" and the "Muslim question." Broadly speaking, the exposure of nineteenth-century Indians to Orientalist knowledge, Western science, colonial policies, and Christian missionaries sparked an epistemological crisis and a great deal of introspection. In response, religious "revivalist" and "reform" movements—both Hindu and Muslim—emerged, placing religious identities at center stage, thereby sharpening the boundaries between communities.[25] Moreover, endeavors to "purify" both religions and facilitate a return to an alleged golden age brought about attacks on popular syncretic religious practices and widened the rift between religious communities. From the middle of the nineteenth century, cities in India experienced periodic outbreaks of "communal riots," usually during religious festivals and processions.

The establishment of self-representation, even if limited, intensified competition over employment, education, and representation in local bodies. This competition coincided with, and was propelled by, colonial practices of governmentality that systematically mapped and enumerated the Indian population according to religion and caste, rigidifying and politicizing these identities. Educated Muslim elites, as epitomized in Sir Syed Ahmad Khan, felt increasingly anxious about the Congress Party's push for greater representation of Indians in local bodies on the basis of numerical strength and competitive exams, as this threatened Muslims' customary dominance disproportionate to their numbers.[26] The establishment of the Muslim League in 1906 as a Muslim organization parallel to the Congress and devoted exclusively to advancing the interests of Muslim elites represented a landmark in the politicization of religious identity. The colonial government consented to the Muslim League's demand

and granted separate electorates to Muslims in local bodies. This decision helped forge diverse regional, sectarian, class, and caste identities into "Indian Muslims" as a unified, all-India political and administrative category.

Certainly, partition at this point was not a foregone conclusion. Far from a linear separation, the relationship between Muslims and the nationalist movement in the first half of the twentieth century entailed cooperation and identification as well as alienation, depending on the particular moment in time and the specific historical actor.[27] Yet an overall trajectory is discernible. The language of self-determination, popularized by Woodrow Wilson during World War I, permeated Indian politics.[28] Once the principle that national groups had a right to territorial self-determination became entrenched, the nation took center stage in people's political imagination, along with growing efforts to define its contours. Additionally, experience with representative politics converted religious communities into "majority" and "minority" groups, defined in national and ethnic terms.

The working assumption framing the analysis in this book is that this trajectory was largely inevitable, a dynamic intrinsic to the dissolution of multiethnic and multireligious empires into nation-states, as evident in other parts of the globe, notably in the Ottoman, Austro-Hungarian, and Russian empires.[29] Historian Eric Weitz describes this process as the long transition from the "Vienna System," emblematized in the Vienna Congress of 1815, to the "Paris System," encapsulated in the post–World War I Paris Peace Settlements. The Vienna System

> centered on dynastic legitimacy and state sovereignty within clearly defined borders. Paris focused on populations and an ideal of state sovereignty rooted in national homogeneity. The move from one to the other marks the shift from traditional diplomacy to population politics, from mere territorial adjustments to the handling of entire population groups categorized by ethnicity, nationality, or race, or some combination thereof.[30]

The principle of self-determination brought with it an assumed ideal overlap between nation and territory, and an attendant drive for ethnic or religious homogenization, turning some religious communities into "problematic" minorities that required a solution.[31] As Hannah Arendt perceptively observed in her study of the post–World War I Minority Treaties, which sought to protect minorities in the newly established states in central and eastern Europe, "minorities within nation-states must sooner or later be either assimilated or liquidated."[32] For this reason, minorities could very easily become "stateless people," subject to forcible removal, with a very thin line separating removal through deportation from removal through genocide. Armenians and Jews are paradigmatic; without a national territory to flee to, they suffered the exclusion and most extreme form of violence inherent to the rise of the nation-state and its homogenizing impulse.

In India, as the idea of the nation took hold, the post-1857 decline of Muslim elites gradually metamorphosed into minoritization. Shabnum Tejani pinpoints the intense debates surrounding the structure of political representation in the 1909 constitutional reforms as the key historical juncture at which Muslims transformed from a mere "religious community" to a "communal minority."[33] As Aamir Mufti points out, there are striking similarities between the "Jewish Question" in Europe and the "Muslim Question" in India.[34] In both cases, efforts to address minoritization brought about the foundation of twin nation-states, unleashing great violence and mass expulsions. The process of Muslim minoritization in India, which culminated in partition and its aftermath, is a running thread throughout the book.

PAKISTAN IN DELHI: THE DEMAND FOR MUSLIM SELF-DETERMINATION

The Muslim League's demand for Muslim self-determination in the subcontinent, in its Lahore Resolution of 1940, was an anxious attempt to escape the trap of minority status. It was anchored in the two-nation theory, asserting that Muslims were not a minority but a nation akin to Hindus, hence the Muslim question was not communal but national, requiring an international solution. But, as contemporaries and later historians have noted, the Lahore Resolution and its ensuing clarifications were far from clear. Historian Ayesha Jalal has famously argued that Muhammad Ali Jinnah intentionally kept the concept of Pakistan vague over the course of an elaborate negotiating game he played with the Congress and the colonial government, in reality striving not for territorial partition but for equal political representation, above and beyond Muslims' numerical strength, in a future unified India.[35] Whether or not this is the case, Jinnah did not elucidate Pakistan in territorial terms. As historian David Gilmartin demonstrates, the Muslim League's definition of Pakistan was vague, uneasily combining a utopian interpretation of Pakistan as an ideal moral community and as a concrete, territorial reality. While Jinnah's mobilization strategy relied more on the former, it was the latter that most brutally unfolded in 1947.[36]

Examining what the idea of Pakistan meant for Muslim League supporters in the capital, my analysis builds on and buttresses the thesis about the territorial ambiguity of Pakistan.[37] We will see that the notion of Pakistan was so territorially open-ended, and the identification of Delhi with Indian Islam so robust, that many of Pakistan's supporters in the capital expected, until the very last minute, that Delhi would be part of Pakistan, and never contemplated migration.

This flexibility was not unique to India but anchored in a wider political territorial imagination of the interwar period in the British Empire and Europe. After all, the Paris System was a politics of populations, born in the transition from empire to nation-states, and during the interwar period it displayed the liminality of a transformational moment. The imperial powers tried to harness the principle of self-determination to resolve the tension between ambitious imperial expansion and the challenge of popular aspirations. Arie Dubnov and Laura Robson explain:

> The wartime collapse of the old central European and Ottoman empires and the emergence of new notions of the nation-state highlighted an essential paradox: the rise of new anticolonial nationalisms and a formidable discourse of national sovereignty at precisely the same moment that the power, authority, and ambition of the British and French empires were reaching their zenith. Facing this difficulty, the political and diplomatic leadership of the old "Great Powers" began envisioning a new global order comprising self-consciously modern, sovereign, more-or-less ethnically homogenous states under the continued economic authority of the old imperial players. The

multiple treaties of the immediate post–World War I era . . . collectively articulated a new "internationalist" vision that bore the imprint of both nationalist discourse and imperial ambition, with the unspoken intention of
containing the former and extending the latter. These agreements promoted
a new political language of ethnic separatism as a central aspect of national
self-determination, while protecting and disguising continuities and even ex-
pansions of French and, especially, British imperial power.[38]

Thus, territorial partitions—alongside population transfers, minority protection treaties, and mandates—were practices that spoke the language of
national self-determination while attempting to co-opt it.

This meshing of empire with nationalism led to a wide spectrum of
schemes for decolonization, many of which assumed different forms of
power sharing, layered sovereignty, and autonomous "free states," reflecting a federal-imperial horizon of expectations.[39] Faisal Devji and Arie
Dubnov, who both bring Pakistani nationalism and Zionism into the
same analytical field, show striking similarities between the political-
territorial formulas these movements floated around during the interwar
period—a broad range of schemes for limited national self-determination
within an imperial framework, shying away from complete national separation and sovereignty.[40] Such a flexible political imagination involved a
great deal of ambiguity, and it is no coincidence that both Zionists and
Pakistani nationalists liked the vague term "national home."

Thus, the liminality of the interwar period meant that the politics of
self-determination was much more open-ended than we realize today,
producing a protean political imagination. It is in this context that we
place the vagueness of the Pakistan idea, which easily accommodated visions of Delhi as a semi-autonomous territory, a shared capital of Hindustan and Pakistan, or an integral part of Pakistan. As late as July 1946,
the Cabinet Mission plan envisaged a decentralized Indian federation
composed of autonomous Muslim and Hindu provinces, whose center
would be Delhi.[41]

Such territorial open-endedness and wishful thinking was com-
pounded by the distinctly utopian qualities of Pakistan, nourished by the
memory of Muslims' past hegemony. Historian Farzana Shaikh makes

the suggestive claim that well-born Muslims had a profound belief in their preeminent claim to power: "By the time the Mughal empire came to dominate vast swathes of India in the 1550s, the force of Muslim over-lordship had been so firmly projected onto the collective memory that it sustained the myth of power as a Muslim birthright."[42] This notion fueled the early politics of the Muslim League, which sought to maintain the privileged position of the Muslim elites in the face of a growing representative politics through separate electorates and weighing. As the transfer of power neared and the threat of minoritization became acutely tangible, the familiar politics developed into a demand for self-determination.

In Muslim Leaguers' imagination, Delhi, the historical center of Muslim dynasties, would necessarily be part of Pakistan, whatever form the latter would take. This conviction was strengthened by Muslims' relative numerical strength in the city (over 30 percent) and their dominance in the city's police, administration, and Municipal Committee—a consequence of the colonial government's strategic cultivation of the Muslim elite as a counterweight to Hindu influence. This explosive combination of territorial ambiguity and utopianism shaped the politics of Pakistan in Delhi. Exploring this politics, the book traces how the captivating yet ambiguous idea of Pakistan gained momentum in Delhi during World War II, and how it then transformed from a nebulous, utopian concept to a concrete, territorial reality, ushering in a period of great violence, displacement, and uncertainty about belonging in the city and the nation.

NATION BUILDING AND STATE FORMATION

Shifting its gaze to the post-1947 years, the book delves into Muslim dispossession and spatial segregation, the politics of rehabilitating Sikh and Hindu refugees, the rise of the Jana Sangh Party as a political force in the city, and the role of the Urdu public sphere in voicing, interpreting, and shaping these structural changes on the ground. Debates over Indian secularism and citizenship loomed large in these formative days, shaping the contours of Indian democracy and delineating its lingering challenges. A contradiction underlay the 1947 moment—India was formed as a democracy committed to secularism, pluralism, and citizenship by birthplace (jus soli), yet it emerged from a partition along religious lines, which was implicitly undergirded by a notion of citizenship by blood descent (jus sanguinis) and involved horrid sectarian violence. As the analysis shows, this fundamental contradiction gave birth to competing articulations of the nation, minority rights, and citizenship, which clashed on the streets and in the cabinet, and occasionally within Jawaharlal Nehru's own mind and actions. A fundamental tension remained between individual rights and community rights, between national integration and minority protection, which mirrored the difficulty besetting the League of Nations' minority protection regime in interwar Europe. Muslims were caught between the contradictory pulls of assimilation and ghettoization.

The other issue that proved central to contemporary debates about democracy and citizenship was the confrontation between civil liberties and the legacy of colonial sovereignty—which was inscribed into the legal, administrative, and policing structures of the postcolonial state. The two imperatives clashed forcefully in Delhi, whose transformation from a viceregal center to a visible theater of national politics gathered momentum during World War II and reached full fruition after independence. Delhi's status as the nation's capital made it a pivot for national leaders, opposition parties, and mass movements, while simultaneously bolstering the authoritarian colonial concern with law and order, geared to restrain exactly such mobilizations. Thus, early postcolonial Delhi witnessed surveillance, restrictions on people's political freedoms, and even a surge of preventive detentions, all of which were holdovers from the colonial regime. Yet these abuses catalyzed a backlash from opposition leaders and activists, who advanced a vibrant discourse of civil liberties as part and parcel of citizens' rights.

In probing the intersection of partition with nation building and state formation, the analysis pursues recent studies, which have shown that the crisis that India and Pakistan had to address at the very moment of their birth generated state formation and the creation of national subjects, and shaped the political trajectories of the cities, states, and provinces where refugees settled.[43] Yet Delhi offers a special vantage point on this intersection because, as the center of national power, it was governed directly by the top echelons and served as the arena where they most squarely faced the period's upheavals and challenges. We thus see how the architects of independent India negotiated colonial legacies, the partition crisis, and their own clashing visions over the contours of the nation, citizenship, and democracy.

The book reveals state formation as a contest at various levels of power, from the ministries to the street corner. Prime Minister Jawaharlal Nehru advocated a secular, multireligious Indian nation with an inclusive citizenship based on birth in a territory. Another camp, associated with Home Minister Sardar Patel, doubted that Muslims belonged in the nation and the city. The book reveals how this uppermost level of political struggle connected to frictions down the line among bureaucrats, policing forces, and nonstate actors. It reveals that the state itself, far from a unified agent acting on society, was itself in the making. In charting the links between different levels of political struggle and mobilization, the book also integrates high politics with subaltern studies, overcoming the prevalent dichotomy between political elites as generating events and ordinary people as enduring them.

The book's political angle extends to the neighborhood level, finding that forms of urban citizenship that characterize contemporary India developed amid the crisis of partition. It traces how ideological uncertainties intersected with the more mundane scramble for material resources. It provides thick descriptions of local struggles over Muslim evacuee property and refugee rehabilitation, and of key players—local political leaders, social workers, press editors, and neighborhood "bosses" and "tough men" who emerged as intermediaries between vulnerable residents and state agents, foreshadowing modes of urban citizenship that are associated with the Emergency and the present day.

BOOK OUTLINE

The current literature on the partition crisis in Delhi mostly takes as its point of departure the year 1947.[44] Chapter 1 expands this temporal framework and provides the alleged rupture of 1947 with historical depth, by beginning in the late 1930s and exploring the transformation of Delhi's political culture under the pressures of World War II, which precipitated a crisis of the colonial state. Becoming a major military supply base for the Allies, Delhi underwent demographic, territorial, and industrial growth during the war, allowing some to get richer while subjecting others to requisitioning, extreme congestion, rising prices, and hoarding. Simultaneously, British defeats and the scare of Japanese invasion made the empire suddenly appear fragile. The result was a millenarian historicity, landing the politics of self-determination in the streets and in the public sphere of the capital with full force. An increasingly assertive and volatile political mobilization precipitated both the outbreak of anticolonial disturbances and the utopian politics of Pakistan, transforming the Muslim League of Delhi from a small and insignificant group to a preeminent political force. The chapter underscores the malleability of the political imagination and orientation during the war years. Pakistan entailed different possible arrangements that did not necessarily mean a clear-cut separation, much less Muslim migration from Delhi. Initially, both anticolonial and pro-Pakistan politics operated in tandem in defining Muslim mass politics, but from mid-1946 onward, it would congeal ever more firmly around Pakistan.

Chapter 2 is centered on the partition violence that erupted in Delhi in September 1947. It traces how the relatively limited form of "traditional" intercommunal riots in the city transformed into deadly violence whose scale and brutality fit the definition of ethnic cleansing. The chapter tracks this process through a careful reconstruction of events from 1946 onward, showing how the increasing territorialization of Pakistan was central to it, along with subtle but steady changes in the balance of power, both in the realm of high politics and at the lower levels of political mobilization. The chapter bridges a major gap in the historiography of partition violence—between the allegedly rational and calculated decision making of politicians and the emotions and inexplicable violence of society. By integrating the voices of several of the city's residents—both Muslim and Hindu—the chapter sheds light on how people experienced the intensifying violence.

Chapters 3 and 4 explore how the crisis of secularism and the contradictory pulls of minority protection and assimilation unfolded spatially and in the vernacular public sphere, respectively. Chapter 3 analyzes the conflicts over Muslim property in Delhi, considering them as an index of the great uncertainties over Muslim belonging in the years after partition. The chapter minutely traces the encroachment on, and shrinking of, "Muslim zones," thereby outlining the spatial expression of Muslim minoritization. It finds that, contrary to the prevalent assumption that Muslim zones were outside the jurisdiction of the Custodian of Evacuee Property, a great deal of the custodian's intervention took place precisely in these areas. The analysis reveals Delhi to be a deeply political space in which profound ideological divisions and power struggles at the uppermost levels of national government fed, and were fed by, conflicts among bureaucrats, local political leaders, social workers, neighborhood bosses, and policing forces. Putting together fragments of evidence scattered in several archives, the chapter reconstructs a microhistory of one locality, Phatak Habash Khan, showing how the indeterminate position of Delhi's Muslims turned their houses into semi-legal gray zones. In the shadow of the partition crisis, shady neighborhood bosses and informants emerged who negotiated the rights of the city's vulnerable residents—a pattern that remains central in contemporary urban India. By foregrounding the role of socioeconomic difference in Muslim dispossession, the chapter also unpacks the categories of *Muslims* and *refugees* and investigates the intersection of religious community with class.

Chapter 4 demonstrates how the demographic transformation of Delhi was mirrored and negotiated in its press world. The territorial vagueness of the idea of Pakistan shaped an expectation among Muslim editors, whose papers played a leading role in the Pakistan movement, that they would keep publishing from Delhi. However, most of them hastily left for Karachi after their offices were attacked in late 1947, and their place was taken by numerous publications of Hindu and Sikh refugees from the Punjab. While the minoritization of India's Muslims is often associated with the marginalization of Urdu, this chapter reveals the decade after independence as a twilight during which Urdu was the main journalistic medium forging the two rival publics in the city—Muslims and refugees—and their competing claims to the city. The extensive and intense editorial exchanges between Muslim and refugee editors, which centered on secularism and minority rights, created an extremely aggressive yet shared vernacular public sphere, traced to a time when Urdu served as a lingua franca, thereby pointing to the gradual and deferred nature of partition. Furthermore, that the editors of the former newspapers of Delhi, now based in Pakistan, frequently reported on and fueled these editorial exchanges shows how communities across the new borders remained bound together.

Chapter 5 centers on the tension between the democratization of political life and the authoritarian legacy left by colonial rule. With Delhi's politics now nationalized, the city became an emblem of the nation, a hub of national institutions, and a magnet for all organizations and politicians seeking national recognition. Thus, as the anticolonial agitators of yesterday became the postcolonial rulers of today, they faced the mayhem of partition and the challenge of mass protests, both peaceful and violent, by disgruntled refugees, Hindu nationalist organizations, Sikh Akalis, and communist and socialist workers. The chapter demonstrates that the persistent colonial restrictions and structures of surveillance, on the one hand, and an assertive clamor for civil liberties, on the other, acted as twin forces that fashioned a complex set of beliefs and practices around democracy and citizenship, in Delhi and India more broadly.

The epilogue describes the recent protests and violence surrounding the Citizenship Amendment Act and the farm laws, which shook Delhi, demonstrating how it continues to function as a theater of national politics staging the fundamental tensions that have beset India's democracy since the intertwining of independence and partition. Reflecting on these developments, the epilogue considers the interplay between deep structures and human agency and contingency in the history narrated in this book.

A NOTE ON THE UNIT OF ANALYSIS

When British India moved its capital to Delhi in 1912, it separated the urban core of Delhi and the surrounding villages from Punjab and turned them into a separate province, centrally controlled by the government of India through a chief commissioner. A portion of the Ghaziabad *tehsil* across the Yamuna on the east, including Shahdara town and the surrounding villages, was transferred to Delhi from the United Provinces, and in 1941 Delhi Province's territory stood at nearly 1,500 sq km. The population of Delhi in 1941 was about 917,000, three-quarters of which

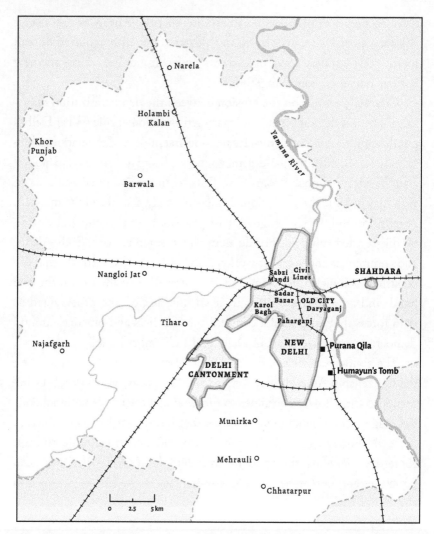

MAP 0.1 *Delhi Province, c. 1940. Its area comprised an urban core surrounded by a rural area of roughly 300 villages. The map shows only those villages mentioned in the book. The boundary of the urban area, marked in gray, is approximate.*

were concentrated in the urban area (695,686). A quarter of the population (222,253 people) lived in roughly 300 villages surrounding the urban area. (See Map 0.1.) In 1950, the chief commissioners' province of Delhi was redefined as a Part C State, and in 1956, as a Union Territory.[45] All these arrangements maintained strong central control over Delhi.

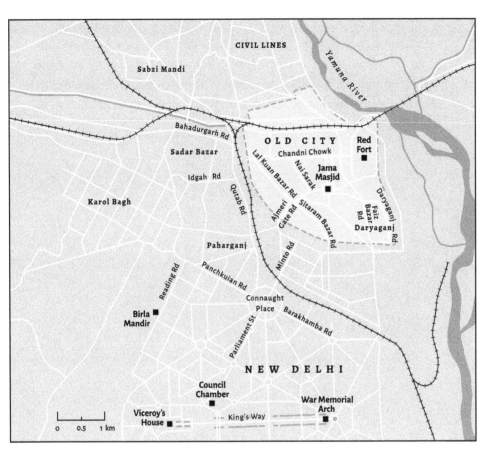

MAP 0.2 *The urban core of Delhi Province, c. 1940.*

This book focuses on the urban core: Shahjahanabad, or the old city; the localities to its west: Sadar Bazar, Paharganj, and Sabzi Mandi and Karol Bagh; the older "European quarter" of Civil Lines, where the Delhi Administration was located, and the adjacent university campus to the north of the old city; and, to the south, New Delhi, the well-planned and spacious capital complex with the surrounding residences of civil servants and the elite. (See Map 0.2.)

The bulk of the population in the period under investigation lived in the old city and the western extensions. These areas turned into geographies of violence in 1947. They also initially bore the brunt of migration. An influx of people during World War II and after independence resulted in a dramatic population increase, from 0.7 million people in 1940 to 1.8 million in 1956.[46] Accordingly, in 1961, the census zone of City-Sadar-Paharganj featured a density of 55,256 people per sq km, one of the highest in the world.[47] They experienced the sociopolitical pressures of the early postcolonial period most acutely, and they center the analysis of this book.[48]

CHAPTER 1

DREAMING INDEPENDENCE IN THE COLONIAL CAPITAL

It is generally said that if the British soldiers are so brave and gallant fighters why did they not fight in Malaya and Burma. . . . They know only how to shoot innocent and unarmed people by entering their houses.[1]

There was such force, such attraction in the name [Pakistan] itself that none of us ever bothered to find out its real meaning: whether it was the name of a country outside India, like Afghanistan or something out of a fairy-tale book. The name had gained wide currency just the same and we all talked non-stop about it.[2]

ABDUL RAHMAN SIDDIQI was a quintessential member of Delhi's Muslim educated public. Born to a Punjabi Muslim family, he grew up in Haveli Hissamuddin Haider, an affluent area of Punjabi Muslims in Ballimaran, the neighborhood where the nineteenth-century poet Ghalib had lived. When World War II broke out, Siddiqi was a high school adolescent, and by its end, he was a college graduate and a young man dedicated to the goal of Pakistan. Reflecting back on these years of collective and individual transition in the city of his forefathers, Siddiqi makes fascinating observations about the historicity of this particular time and place—historicity in the sense that past experiences and future expectations at a specific juncture shape the political orientations and actions of the historical actors—in our case, Delhi's Muslim Leaguers.[3]

Siddiqi suggests that the glorious past of Delhi as the seat of Indo-Muslim empires and its decline under British rule, culminating in the brutal suppression of the 1857 rebellion and the humiliating banishment of the last Mughal emperor, defined the mental makeup, political horizon, and actions of Muslim *Dilliwallas.* "For practically half a century after the Ghadar of 1857, Delhi had gone into a deep slumber, close to a coma."[4] It woke up in the aftermath of World War I with the rise of the Khilafat movement, when the city became the hub of all-India politics. "The city and its people would be wide awake only when dreaming of distant lands of grand sultanates and empires, of which the Ottoman Caliphate was the last living symbol."[5]

With the collapse of the Khilafat movement, Muslim Delhi again "lapsed into the deep post-Mutiny coma,"[6] as the Ali brothers who had led the Khilafat movement withdrew from national politics, and Abul Kalam Azad, Hakim Ajmal Khan, and Dr. Mukhtar Ahmed Ansari took up secular nationalism in the Congress.[7] The public awoke again only in the late 1930s, when Muslim League leader Muhammad Ali Jinnah promised "yet another distant land: a land that was not even there, which existed only in their dreams, hence was more real."[8] The post-Khilafat coma gave way to daydreaming about the promised land of Pakistan.

It is no wonder that such a political awakening, with its distinctly utopian qualities, took place during World War II. The war propelled a crisis of the colonial order, inducing diverse, intense, and competing dreams of independence in the capital of the British Raj. The war transformed India's relationship with Britain and precipitated the end of the Raj. As historian Indivar Kamtekar explains, the war triggered a crisis of the colonial state:

> A crisis may be defined as a period when old institutional arrangements have proved inadequate and new ones have not been established. A period of disorder and instability during which the state searches for a new relationship with society. It is a moment of transition, in which something that held together does not hold any longer and there is not yet something new. The problems which have arisen can no longer be solved within the old framework of politics. As there is no solution within the old framework, politics go

out of the negotiating chamber into the street, or (looking at it the other way around), the politics of the street burst into the negotiating chamber.[9]

How did this crisis come about? The war's insatiable hunger for resources necessitated a committed society prepared to make sacrifices. It thereby lay bare the difference between independent states and colonies. A black-and-white division of the world into Allies and Axis, good guys and bad guys, was complicated in the colonial context. Indians could not undertake the burden of blood and sweat as wholeheartedly as citizens of the metropole did.

The war forced the colonial state to mobilize Indian manpower and resources in an unprecedented manner, suspend the Government of India Act (1935) and the provincial autonomy that went along with it, and impose wartime emergency rule through the Defence of India Acts. At the same time that Britain imposed such extraordinary regulation on India's social, economic, and political life, its humiliating defeats in Southeast Asia eradicated its prestige. Thus, popular resentment of the state's intrusion into society coincided with the state's apparent vulnerability.

When Japan took over Burma and threatened to invade India, Britain was forced to negotiate with the Congress and the Muslim League for their continued cooperation, sending Sir Stafford Cripps in 1942 for this purpose. Cripps offered complete independence after the war in exchange for support for the duration. Although the Cripps Mission failed, its implications were profound. In offering full independence, England abandoned its vision of gradual constitutional reforms with a vague promise of dominion status sometime in the future. The colonial "illusion of permanence"[10] was shaken, and the end of colonial rule suddenly seemed imminent.

Crucially, the Cripps offer also allowed for the secession of provinces. The Muslim League had already shifted its agenda from communal representation to self-determination, articulating this goal in the Lahore Resolution of March 1940, and it now seemed to receive official British sanction for this goal. Although we shall see that the meaning of self-determination was not clear, and partition was not its inevitable outcome, the word *partition*, alongside *Pakistan*, entered India's political lexicon during the war. Thus, the twin events of 1947—independence and partition—emerged from the crisis of the war.

With empire exposed as both oppressive and assailable, the failure of the Cripps Mission ignited Indians' simmering resentment, resulting in the Quit India movement of August 1942—the most violent and extensive, even if short-lived, rebellion after 1857. Even while the entire all-India Congress leadership was jailed, people across the country engaged in mass demonstrations, attacked government personnel, and destroyed police stations, government offices, and other manifestations of the British Raj. Life in the capital was temporarily brought to a halt, and factories, schools, colleges, and transportation were paralyzed. Armed with its wartime emergency legislation and wielding fifty-seven army battalions, the colonial state suppressed the movement with full force.

It is noteworthy that the Quit India rebellion took place at a moment when the threat of a Japanese invasion into India was palpable, at a critical time before the tide of the war turned. Both the rebellion and its violent suppression drove home the point that the colonial state was ruling by force, not consent. They also exposed the fact that Indian government employees in New Delhi were assisting the anticolonial movement. When most of the Congress leaders were arrested, the underground movement was taken over by a younger and more radical generation, which ventured outside the familiar Gandhian paradigm of nonviolent civil disobedience. Anti-British sentiment would explode again after the war.

Both Quit India and the Pakistan movement tell us something about the historicity of the war years. As the colonial order was shuddering, and a new one had not yet taken shape, the future seemed open-ended and full of possibilities. Diverse and conflicting invocations of *Swaraj* (self-rule), independence, and Pakistan were in circulation, capturing people's imaginations and driving them to the streets.

The millenarian historicity of the war years was evident in the intensity and violence of the Quit India disturbances. It was even more clearly manifest in the Pakistan movement, centered as it was on an idea as captivating as it was territorially ambiguous. This idea, derived from a federative-imperial imagination that was prevalent in the interwar period more globally, gave birth to an array of schemes for the future—a territorially maximalist Pakistan stretching east of the Yamuna river (and hence encompassing Delhi), autonomous Muslim provinces within "Hindustan," territorial corridors, free cities, and "nations in minority." Their differences notwithstanding, most of these schemes drew a rather fuzzy connection between nationhood and territory, assuming that Delhi would be part of Pakistan, given its status as British India's capital and its robust identification with Indian Islam. The result was an emotionally intense movement whose tragic consequences its supporters never envisaged. Pakistan's vagueness indicates there was something open-ended and malleable about political orientation in this period. From mid-1946 onward, Muslim mass politics would congeal ever more firmly around Pakistan, but during the war, both anticolonial and pro-Pakistan politics could operate in tandem in defining Muslim mass politics.

Delhi underwent demographic, territorial, and industrial growth during the war. The 1941 census counted 917,939 people living in the city, an increase of over 44 percent compared with 1931, and the population continued to grow in subsequent years.[11] Delhi's role as a major military supply base for the Allies occasioned an expansion of the government secretariat and government employment, the arrival of troops to the capital, and an industrial boom. The two big textile factories in Sabzi Mandi—Delhi Cloth Mills and Birla Spinning and Weaving Mills—increased their production, and many other factories opened up, supplying the army with uniforms, tents, canvas articles, and leather work. The increase in military personnel, from three units in 1939 to twenty-six in 1944, and the opening of the Central Ordnance Depot in 1940, also led to an influx of civilians—service givers and laborers.[12] Industrialists and businessmen made a fortune from war-related contracts, and commerce also thrived. In the rural vicinity of Delhi, recruitment to the army was high. The affluence that the war brought to these sections of society is evident in the large amount of mortgaged land that was redeemed during the war, and in the repayment of over half the sums owed to the central cooperative bank.[13] Yet the economic boom did not reach everyone equally, and alongside demographic and spatial expansion, houses were requisitioned, essential commodities became scarce, prices of food and housing shot up, and social discontent was on the rise.[14]

Concomitantly, the nationalization of the city's political life, which began in 1911 when Delhi became the capital of the Raj, gained momentum, and Delhi lived up to its status as the hub of all-India politics. Sessions of the Legislative Assembly, high-corridor negotiations between the viceroy and Indian leaders, the Cripps Mission and, after the war, the contentious Indian National Army trials,[15] all took place in Delhi. National leaders of all parties organized mass meetings, and while some frequently shuttled between their home provinces and Delhi, others, including Jinnah, relocated to Delhi. As the politics of city and nation became ever more intertwined, the politics of self-determination landed with a vengeance on the city's streets, resulting in both the Quit India movement and the phenomenal rise of the Muslim League. The Delhi Muslim League transformed from a small and insignificant group to a tremendous political force, which, by the end of the war, held mammoth public meetings of 100,000 people, clamoring for Pakistan.

This chapter shows how both the Quit India rebellion and the mass mobilization for Pakistan emerged from the crisis of the colonial state and the collapse of the prewar constitutional framework, which resulted from World War II. The analysis starts at the height of the crisis.

1942: DELHI SHIVERS AND QUITS

In August 1942, a pamphlet printed in Hindi and Urdu was distributed in Delhi. Entitled "Blood Revenge" (Khun ka Badla Khun), it calls on Delhi's college students to attack the "tommie soldiers" who violated their women, shot their fellow citizens, and burned their flag. The pamphlet establishes the solidarity of Delhi's Hindu and Muslim residents by speaking of sexual assaults on women of both religions, alluding to grave incidents that allegedly happened near the Yamuna River and at the Lal Qila (Red Fort)—the Mughal palace that had become a military camp after the 1857 revolt.[16] The text is preoccupied with humiliation and the recovery of masculine honor, calling on Delhi's youth to be men, heroes, lions, like the German and Japanese soldiers. It urges them to assault the tommies in public, snatch their guns, tear off their uniforms, strip them naked, blacken their faces, seat them on donkeys, and shove them back into the Lal Qila:

Burn down their houses, burn down the station, then move on to New Delhi, put each and every house on fire, especially the viceroy's office. Kill these impure deceitful whites, snatch their cars, enter their houses and set them on fire, so much fire that would avenge 150 years. Oust these dogs from Hindustan. Don't be afraid of these monkeys.[17]

The focus on the sexual exploitation and violation of Indian women had become a dominant theme in the Indian press in the months preceding Quit India and prominent in underground literature. In Delhi, as in other places, it was a major catalyst of political mobilization and violence.[18] The text communicates immense rage and calls for arson. This is exactly what transpired on the streets of Delhi in August 1942, when the Quit India disturbances broke out, centered on incendiarism. Before we delve into these events, let us go back in time and explore how this outrage emerged from the "shiver of 1942."[19]

Delhi Shivers

The year 1942 was decisive in the history of World War II. Churchill called it the Hinge of Fate, because "in it we turn from almost uninterrupted disaster to almost unbroken success."[20] In the first six months, Rommel's forces approached Egypt, the German army advanced in the Caucasus, and Japan occupied Singapore, Malaysia, Burma, the Philippines, and the Dutch East Indies. This was also India's most dangerous hour, because the war "caught the colonial state looking the wrong way."[21] For decades Britain had focused on preventing a Russian attack on India from the northwest, and it was unprepared for an attack from the east. Japan's rapid advance in southeast Asia caught it by surprise.

When Singapore, the British "fortress" in the Indian Ocean, fell to the Japanese, it was a shocking and humiliating capitulation, on the order of magnitude of Dunkirk. "For the British, it was the end of a world that was never to be recreated, despite a second occupation after 1945 of nearly twenty years."[22] A garrison of over 85,000 men surrendered to a Japanese force of roughly 30,000 troops. About 45,000 Indian troops were turned over to the Japanese as prisoners of war, and many Indian soldiers, feeling betrayed, joined the new Indian National Army (INA, Azad Hindi Fauj), which would later fight the British Indian Army under the Japanese flag and become a symbol of Indian nationalism.

The fall of Singapore left the Bay of Bengal suddenly exposed to Japanese warships, and India vulnerable to Japanese invasion. Japan took over the Andaman and Nicobar Islands in March, and in April bombed Ceylon and the Indian coastline towns Vizagapatam and Cocanada. Then arrived trainloads of demoralized soldiers returning to India from the Burmese front, along with hundreds of thousands of weary refugees who had barely survived the journey from Burma. "For the refugees the outcome of the war was not in doubt, a Japanese victory was certain. They had witnessed the Allied defeat; they *knew* the empire was to end."[23]

Such an unprecedented threat sent shock waves throughout India—a mixture of anxiety, loss of faith in the colonial government, and anger.[24] Most important, people felt that the colonial order, which had seemed stable and enduring, might soon collapse. The government's attempts to cover up the army's blunders in the east and pass them off as a planned withdrawal merely augmented the loss of confidence in the state. British propaganda—rather effective at home—floundered in India, exposing the wide gap between state and society in the colony. This was the shiver of 1942—both the fear of Japanese invasion and the cracks that appeared in the colonial order. Kamtekar finds traces of it in the fantastic rumors that circulated in 1942, in the exodus of people—both elite and laborers—from the big coastline cities, and in a financial disinvestment in the state.

Though Delhi was far from the eastern coastline and the immediate threat, the capital did not escape the shiver of 1942. From that year onward, Delhi was filled with expectant tension.[25] An array of Air Raid Precaution shelters (ARPs) sprang up along Chandni Chowk, and residents of different *mohallas* (neighborhoods) sent applications to the municipality for permission to close alleys by erecting gates—a clear symptom of public nervousness. The Delhi press chastised Britain for not preparing India for war militarily and economically. Speeches in public meetings were more acid than usual and drew larger crowds. In April, after Japanese planes bombed Ceylon and India's southeast coastline cities, a large number of poor migrant laborers left Delhi and headed back to their villages, as did many upper-class families, including those of the Marwari merchants. The chief commissioner speculated that those who left were not so anxious about air raids as they were about the civil commotion that might take place in case of Japanese invasion.

Abdul Rahman Siddiqi, with whom we opened this chapter, was a high school student when the war broke out. He recalls that alongside ARPs, loudspeakers appeared at the city's major intersections, broadcasting war news and songs. An improvised radio station (Delhi Microphone Service) was set up in Hardinge Library in Chandni Chowk. It invited young Indians to "join the army and see the world."[26] Contemporary Indian journalists commented on the failure of such propaganda, which focused solely on the "mercenary motive"—on four meals a day and the opportunity to discover the world, rather than on patriotism. It was bound to fail, ruminated the nationalist press, as long as India remained colonized. "Once India is free and mobilised under a national Government there would be no need for all these insipid, stupid posters."[27] War propaganda posters were soon covered with red *paan* stains, and the ARPs in Chandni Chowk turned into filthy urinals.

Loss of confidence in official channels of information, coupled with ambivalence toward the war, made Axis radio propaganda popular. Siddiqi remembers the magic spell of the new radio set which his older brother, like many others, purchased for the first time during the war. Many people listened to Axis broadcasts half secretly at shops and restaurants in the lanes of the old city. Already in early June 1940, when the state attempted to conceal the unfolding fiasco at Dunkirk, the Criminal Investigation Department (CID) reported that radio dealers and restaurant owners in the old city were broadcasting the German radio to their customers.[28] From October 1941 the Azad Hind radio started broadcasting from Berlin, and after the fall of Singapore Indians became accustomed to hearing the voice of nationalist leader Subhas Chandra Bose, who had joined the Axis in order to oust the British from India.[29]

The absence of reliable information in the critical year of 1942 gave rise to a plethora of rumors that circulated in the bazaars and newspapers. Headlines in Delhi's Urdu newspaper *Tej* claimed that Bombay had been bombed. According to another rumor, which precipitated an exodus from the city in April, certain parts of Delhi were going to be declared military zones, and women and children would be evacuated from them. There were scare stories about people kidnapped at night to serve as recruits in the army or to have their blood drawn for transfusion. Another rumor that persisted, in spite of recurrent official refutation, anticipated that India would be handed over to the Americans and that the king's brother, the Duke of Gloucester, who was to visit in June, would announce this transfer.[30]

Such rumors give us insight into public interpretations of the crisis, and the rumored transfer of power to the Americans is especially noteworthy. It reveals public cognizance of the shifting balance of power between the British and the Americans during the war—namely, the decline of the British Empire and rise of the United States as the main global power. Siddiqi's recollections illustrate how this major international political shift was felt by Delhi's residents through the growing presence of American troops. Siddiqi's memory of the Americans is largely rosy, as he associated them with wartime prosperity. The influx of American soldiers made the city livelier. Their favorite rendezvous point was the Indian Coffee House near the fountain at Chandni Chowk. Soon, a bigger and glitzier branch opened for them at Scindia House in New Delhi, along with other restaurants catering to American tastes. They would come to the old city in tongas and go on shopping sprees. They liked spending money and would happily pay the tonga drivers eight times the accepted rate.[31]

Significantly, popular approval of the Americans emerged specifically in contrast with dislike of the British, carrying a subversive political message. The Yankees' generosity, cheerfulness, and informal friendliness contrasted with the stinginess of the British tommies, who would haggle over a single *anna* using foul language. The Yankees were said to outshine the tommies in all respects: they were tall and handsome in their shining uniforms and smart side caps, while the tommies looked shabby in their faded olive-green uniforms and soiled, unflattering berets. The British authorities were aware of the potential impact of their soldiers' poor appearance, and an internal military circular stated, "The conditions under which troops are living in the city at present make a high standard of turn out and dress difficult. There is no need, however, for post garrisons to appear as if they had just returned from the Burmese jungle."[32]

Indian audiences stopped showing due respect to the British anthem at New Delhi's cinemas, leaving the halls while the anthem played at the end of the movie. Siddiqi remembers an incident when a couple of tommies tried physically to stop Indians from leaving the hall, calling them "savages":

> The Indians—quite a few of them—pounced upon the tommies. The tommies—rum sodden, like always—lost their balance and fell down. 'Leave them alone, Leave them alone, these bastards. They would soon be out of India with blackened faces!' Voices were heard as the lights came back on. . . . India was free and independent already: The British might still be there, but the Americans were there too. And the Americans were . . . absolutely free from imperial hang-ups.[33]

The tommies, concludes Siddiqi, were "unwelcome strangers in their own imperial domain."[34] Rumors about an imminent transfer of power to the Americans expressed this prevalent feeling that America was the rising power and that it had already told Britain to quit India.

High Politics and Popular Politics
The overall uncertainty and loss of faith in the British Empire induced a politically charged atmosphere, amplified in the capital by high-profile negotiations between the government and Indian leaders. Back in 1939, Congress leaders had considered it a blow when Viceroy Linlithgow declared India's entry into the war without consulting them, given that they governed seven provinces of British India under the Government of India Act 1935. The Congress demanded immediate independence and the establishment of a constituent assembly, asserting that it was committed to the war against fascism, but that Indians could not fight for the liberty of other nations as long as they themselves were colonized, and that only a truly representative national government could mobilize the people for the war effort. When these demands were rejected, Congress provincial governments resigned.

Now, in 1942, the deadlock between the government and the Congress became pressing. At a time when India's collaboration with the war effort became vital for China's survival, the Chinese leader, General Chiang Kai-shek, came to Delhi, desperate to reconcile them.[35] A month later Sir Stafford Cripps arrived with a proposal from the British cabinet. The proposal's most contentious clause (aside from partition) involved the Viceroy's Executive Council, which would be Indianized, become a politically representative body, and function as a quasi-cabinet. Congress negotiators Jawaharlal Nehru and Maulana Abul Kalam Azad (the Congress president) expected that the Executive Council would function as a national government with power to control the army, but for Churchill, shifting power away from the British commander-in-chief was out of the question. Thus the high expectations and ultimate failure of the Cripps Mission reflected the fundamental contradictions underlying the colony's position in the Allied war camp. Delhi's nationalist papers reacted to the negotiations' failure with rage, echoing Congress's statement that the last opportunity to turn the war into a popular one was lost.[36]

Against the backdrop of the Chinese premier's visit and the drama of the Cripps Mission, Delhi bustled with political activity. The negotiations coincided with the annual winter session of the Legislative Assembly, which drew princes and leaders from across the country and was a politically stormy time to begin with. The gravitational center of high-corridor politics was New Delhi: negotiations with Cripps took place in a typical bungalow on Victoria Road; Congress Working Committee meetings were held at Birla House, where Gandhi stayed; Hindu Mahasabha meetings were held at the Hindu Mahasabha Bhavan, also built by the Birla family; and the Muslim League met at the palatial Gul-e Rana, the residence of Muslin League General Secretary Liaquat Ali Khan on Hardinge Avenue (today Tilak Marg).[37]

Simultaneously, the old city was the epicenter of popular politics. The civic square in Chandni Chowk that centered on Town Hall was constructed in the 1860s to project a Victorian ethos and colonial command over the battered city (see Figure 0.2). By the 1940s, after two decades of Gandhian nationalism, this area, especially the Queen's Gardens north of Town Hall, had become the main space for public agitation. In 1942, public meetings where Azad and Nehru spoke attracted tens of thousands of people, and local and provincial leaders from across the country held many meetings in Queen's Gardens.[38] The largest of these meetings took place a day after Cripps released his offer, and was meant to commemorate the martyrs of the first Gandhian movement, who had been shot by police on that day in 1919, and to mourn Bose, who was mistakenly reported to have died in a plane crash. Public mourning showed the prevailing popularity of this man who had joined the Axis to fight colonial rule, thereby expressing the contradictory pulls of anticolonialism and antifascism. Congress leaders from outside Delhi who spoke at the meeting mocked Britain's efforts to present defeats in the east as a planned withdrawal, stating that British generals were experts in just one thing—retreat. The large audience responded with laughter and clapping.

Kamtekar suggests that the shiver of 1942 and the attendant popular perception, delusional as it may have been, that the Raj was about to collapse, was the condition of possibility for Quit India. The audience's laughter in Queen's Gardens indicates that, even in Delhi—filled as it was with British institutions, symbols of power, and troops—the almighty state seemed fragile. As Delhi's chief commissioner commented at the end of May, it was vain to pretend that public confidence in the stability of British administration was anything near what it had been six months earlier.[39] News of Allied losses in North Africa further corroded public credence. In the weeks immediately preceding the disturbances of August 1942, the German army was advancing in southern Russia, and word on the street was that Russia's resistance would soon collapse and Japan would most likely invade India.[40] The vernacular press sneaked in Axis radio reports on German victory in the Kerch Peninsula and on an alleged meeting between Hitler and Bose in the Russian front.[41]

Throughout 1942 labor and social unrest further damaged the state's image. In February, after long spells of quiet on Delhi's labor front and just days before the fall of Singapore, ten thousand laborers of the Delhi Cloth Mills went on strike. The strike turned violent, the police resorted to a *lathi* (wooden baton) charge, and one of the laborers died of his injuries, provoking anger. Five thousand laborers of Birla Mills went on strike next, and employees of the Central Ordnance Depot in the cantonment and other war-related factories followed with strikes of their own. It was during this time that rumors of a likely Japanese invasion impelled thousands of laborers to leave Delhi and return to their villages. Thus growing labor unrest coincided with British defeats in the east, fear of Japanese invasion, and the disappointment of political negotiations.

Concurrently, crime was on the rise in 1942 and Delhi experienced severe wheat shortages. Authorities were surprised to learn that under-the-radar grain hoarding had begun in November 1941, even before the Japanese entry into the war.[42] Shortages were exacerbated in 1942 by Punjab and the United Provinces' intermittent decisions to reserve their stocks and restrict exports. From March 1942 onward, authorities reported that the concept of "scorched earth" defense used in Bengal aroused strong feelings among the public, and even the old-fashioned Hindu bankers and merchants were furious over this issue.

Amid this volatile atmosphere, and in response to the failure of the Cripps Mission, the Congress started a feverish campaign to enroll volunteers for the upcoming mass movement of Quit India, building up suspense. Nehru and Azad, who often came to Delhi, explained the Congress's Quit India resolution to the huge crowds who gathered to hear them.[43] Young cadres repeatedly announced that India would become a free country on August 9. Street corner meetings, consisting of hostile anti-British speeches and flag salutations, were a daily feature, and in one such meeting in Connaught Place, a large Congress flag was left flying for several hours before it was removed. A seemingly minor detail, it points to the millenarian historicity that sustained the outbreak of violence a couple of days later.

Delhi Quits

On the morning of August 9, news arrived that Gandhi and the Congress high command had been arrested in Bombay after passing the Quit India resolution. The Congress was declared an unlawful organization, and throughout the day local Congress leaders were rounded up and detained under the Defence of India Act. Others absconded and went underground. The government took possession of the Congress office in Chandni Chowk (House No. 161) and the Gandhi ashrams in the countryside. A public meeting of ten thousand people was held that evening at Queen's Gardens, where Musamat Parbati Devi and the communist Muqimuddin Farooqi, an impassioned young student leader, delivered strong speeches in support of the movement. They were later arrested. Thus, although the Communist Party of India (CPI) officially supported the Allied war effort and opposed Quit India after Germany attacked the Soviet Union, in reality, Delhi communists participated in the movement. Moreover, among the audience, noted the CID, were both Hindus and Muslims, including government employees.[44]

The following morning, the army held a flag march of two infantry battalions through the city. A clear demonstration of state power geared to discourage resistance, the march did not make much of an impression, because a few hours after it, a mass demonstration took place.[45] When it reached the Clock Tower, it dispersed into groups, which stormed through the bazaars, forcing shopkeepers to close their shops. In Chandni Chowk and adjacent alleys, the crowd threw brickbats and stones on British people, trams, and tramways. Alarmingly for the administration, the disturbances spread to New Delhi when a crowd managed to break its way through the police posts at Ajmeri gate. On reaching Connaught Place, the men smashed electric street lamps and threw stones through the windows of Lloyds Bank, nearby shops, and a bus of the Convent of Jesus & Mary. They threw stones at the V sign inside the park, and flew the Congress flag on it.[46] The crowd reportedly consisted mostly of students coming straight from meetings organized by communist leaders Muqimuddin Farooqi and Yag Dutt Sharma.[47]

Over the next several days, thousands of people violently attacked state officials, policemen, soldiers, and state institutions, especially those essential to law and order and the war effort. Laborers suspended production in the mills, and students—mostly from Hindu College and Ramjas College—suspended studies and participated in the mayhem. Early in the morning of August 11, a crowd of mill hands attacked British sergeants while trying to break into the Delhi Cloth Mills in Sabzi Mandi. In Chandni Chowk, about eight thousand men gathered near Fatehpuri Mosque. According to police reports, the crowd seemed to wait for leaders to guide a planned procession and became confused when the leaders did

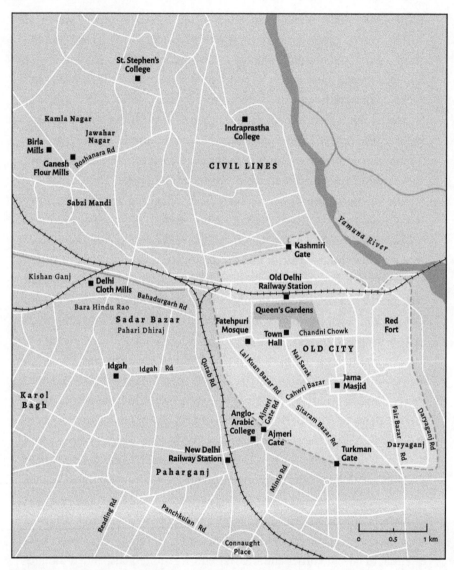

MAP 1.1 *The Old City and the western localities, c. 1940.*

not show up (they had probably been arrested). Incidents of "mischief" followed. Some assaulted shopkeepers who had kept their businesses open. Others set fire to the first-class compartments of three trams outside the Central Bank. A procession of about five hundred people attacked a patrol car of sergeants and policemen, then continued to the Clock Tower and on to the Kotwali—the central police station in Chandni Chowk. Deputy Commissioner and District Magistrate Le Bailey ordered the people to disperse, but they did not budge. A police *lathi* charge failed to scatter the crowd, which now threw stones, brickbats, and broken bottles at Le Bailey and high-level police officers. As the crowd tried to force its way into the Kotwali itself, and only when police officers opened fire were they able to contain the situation. A section of the crowd encircled the Town Hall and set fire to the building. When the municipal fire brigade arrived, the crowd stoned the firemen and destroyed their engines.

In the face of such open and violent defiance of authority, and with violent attacks against British and military vehicles taking place,[48] the military was called in to take command of Delhi's defense. Over the next two days, the police and army opened fire on 47 occasions, killing 19 people and wounding 45.[49]

Nevertheless, the violence continued. Shops along the bazaar were shattered and burnt, and the smell of burning rubber tires filled the air, and the clock on the clock tower opposite Town Hall stopped. The ladder leading to it was burnt and there was no way of reaching it and stopping the siren, which kept wailing for hours.[50] A crowd broke into the main railway station, torched the cabins, destroyed electrical instruments, and then moved on to do the same in the New Delhi and Kishan Ganj railway stations. The Railway Clearing Accounts office near the Dufferin Bridge was set on fire and continued to burn for days.[51] Other government buildings were set alight and wrecked in different parts of the city, including the newly constructed fire station; the Income Tax Office on the Grand Trunk Road, where records were destroyed; and the Ceremonial Platform at New Delhi Railway Station. Crowds in different localities cut electric and telephone wires, smashed electric lamps and petrol pumps, and burned signboards and mailboxes. People looted the Ganesh Flour Mills in Sabzi Mandi—a politically charged spot, given the severe shortage of wheat and the hike in prices—and torched a factory in Teliwara producing military uniforms. (See Map. 1.1 for the main locations mentioned in this account.)

On the evening of August 11, the deputy commissioner imposed an order prohibiting the assembly of five or more persons in the urban area (under Section 144 of Criminal Procedure Code). A curfew was imposed in several localities. Yet the trouble continued with widespread arson and destruction in the area of Karol Bagh and Panchkuian Road, and with violent attacks on city magistrates, police officers, and constables.[52]

Incidents decreased over the following days, and the emergency subsided. Disturbances broke out again in the third week of August, but by the end of the month it was safe enough to release the army and let the police retake charge of law and order.[53] Still, schools, shops, banks, trams, and war-related factories remained shut for days—most importantly, from the perspective of the British war effort—the Central Ordnance Depot, the Birla Mills, the Delhi Cloth Mills, and the Ganesh Flour Mills. About 20,000 to 30,000 people, mainly laborers, left Delhi, further hampering production for the war effort.[54]

It is worth pausing here to reflect on the outbreak of Quit India in Delhi. Evidence suggests that it was spontaneous and without clear guidance. While Congress workers had undoubtedly prepared the ground for the movement in the preceding weeks, most of the local leaders were either arrested on August 9 or had left Delhi several days earlier to attend the All-India Congress Committee session in Bombay.[55] The movement spun out of the leadership's control and took on a violent life of its own.

The historical agents of this outbreak were the crowds. While it is difficult to pinpoint specific individuals, reports suggest the involvement of students, laborers, and trade unions. Most oral history accounts claim that the Muslim public, on the whole, stayed away from the movement, an indication of the growing rift between the Congress and Muslim League, to be discussed below.[56] Yet lists of the people arrested include quite a significant number of Muslims.[57] It is not clear who they were—perhaps Congress workers, Jamiat Ulama-e Hind members, or mill laborers. Official reports claim that many of the participants, whether Muslim or Hindu, were "*goondas*" (thugs) and "loafers" or just young men drawn to the thrill and drama. Even if attraction to the *tamasha* (spectacle) played a role, the crowds' actions were clearly political, calculated to harm the symbols and institutions of the state and the war effort. Their actions amount to a language of resistance, articulated more explicitly in the posters and pamphlets that circulated at the time, which, like the one quoted at the beginning of this section, expressed sheer hatred of the British—especially the "tommies," who, we must remember, became unprecedentedly prominent in the landscape of wartime Delhi.[58]

In the weeks and months after the initial violence was curbed, the movement in Delhi went underground. Congress distributed illegal literature in English, Hindi, and Urdu. Processions and demonstrations sprang up in defiance of Section 144, usually dispersing upon the appearance of police. And there was picketing of schools, colleges, mills, government offices, and the residences of members of the Executive Council in New Delhi.[59] As in other cities, students were at the vanguard of the movement.[60] The government also suspected that strikes at the Delhi Cloth Mills and the Birla Mills were secretly financed by the mills' owners, Lala Shri Ram and G. D. Birla, their assurances notwithstanding. Alongside such traditional Gandhian acts of civil disobedience were isolated but persistent cases of sabotage aimed at factories, railways, mailboxes, and telegraphs.

The few prominent local leaders who managed to avoid an early arrest or to escape led the movement in Delhi from their places in hiding.[61] They included Jugal Kishore Khanna, general secretary of the Delhi Pradesh Congress Committee (DPCC); Congress leader C. Krishna Nair; and Aruna Asaf Ali—wife of imprisoned Congress leader Asaf Ali—who became a legend when she escaped the authorities in Delhi.[62] Jayaprakash Narayan (called JP), leader of the Congress Socialist Party, grew a flowing beard and a big mustache, so that he was impossible to recognize. He wandered freely, bringing newspapers and books from Connaught Place, while Khanna and others did not see the light of day.

Khanna and his associates moved every evening to a new hideout, where they would meet with their trusted workers to plan next steps. Urdu journalists Ram Lal Verma and Gopi Nath Aman, who worked for *Tej*, edited the Congress underground publications. We shall meet them again in this book, standing on the other side of the fence in their capacity as regulators of press censorship after independence. Lakshmi Chand Jain, then a student at the Hindu College, the son of imprisoned Congress leader Phool Chand Jain, served as the movement's main messenger.[63]

The movement also rested on the complicity of government officials, indicating that the Raj was losing its legitimacy among Indian bureaucrats, who became more prominent due to wartime Indianization. Authorities noted the extensive circulation of Congress literature among government employees. Clerks leaked information from secret government circulars to Khanna,[64] and Congress literature was often printed on government stationery and used government service stamps.[65] The underground movement was in fact sustained by high-level government officials, who provided shelter to the absconders at their homes in New Delhi and lent their cars to move them from one hideout to another. One of Khanna's hosts, a deputy director of chemicals, even taught them how to derail trains by mixing Vaseline with other substances.

Indeed, toward the end of December and in early 1943, the movement assumed a more violent orientation. Grave incidents became more frequent. There was arson in the post office in Chandni Chowk and in the Hardinge Library, where an improvised radio station broadcast wartime British propaganda. A group of people armed with a pistol, a gun, and spears entered a railway station, fired on the railway staff, set fire to the station office, and burned down its records and railway tickets. Similar incidents took place in other stations. Crude bombs exploded or were found in several places, including the Birla Mills, the railway between Kishan Ganj and Sarai Rohila, and outside Odeon Cinema in New Delhi. Telegraph wires and telephone junction boxes were burned.

Intelligence reports claimed that behind such activities were Khanna and Aruna Asaf Ali, along with Devdas Gandhi, son of Mahatma Gandhi and editor of the nationalist daily *Hindustan Times*.[66] Khanna affirms that the group operating from Delhi had a huge supply of arms, ammunition, hand grenades, and pistols. While claiming that Devdas Gandhi "was in the thick and thin of it" and helped finance the violence, he denies his own connection. The center of gravity shifted to a more radical group, and Khanna was marginalized when he argued that such acts were futile.

The Quit India movement followed the same pattern in other regions, as a younger, more impatient, more socialist generation took over. A worker named M. M. Shah appears in the CID records as a member of the underground movement. He was arrested in January 1943 and gave a statement in which he named several people, most unknown figures whom we won't encounter again in Delhi's subsequent history, who belonged to five groups operating from Delhi and engaged in sabotage.[67] Whereas one group, led by Girwar Narain Ved, an expert in making bombs and hand grenades, was directly financed by the Delhi Congress, the others were working independently, with no coordination between them and without consulting the high command. Aruna Asaf Ali occasionally lent them her support whenever she could.

In the Aftermath of Quit India

Aruna Asaf Ali, who left Delhi by March 1943, evaded arrest until the war's end, but she was an exception. By the end of October 1943, most of the underground movement leaders had been arrested, including Khanna and JP Narayan, and the movement fizzled out. Chaudhury Brahm Prakash, a young worker from rural Delhi who would rise in the Congress hierarchy to become Delhi's first chief minister after independence, recalls this period. He was arrested in 1942 and released in 1943. When he went to the bazaar and handed five *paisa* to a shopkeeper, the latter laughed out loud. While Prakash had been in jail, inflation was rampant, and the money had lost its value. Scarcity of wheat and even "inferior" food grains became acute. Severe fuel shortages soon followed, alongside hoarding of small coins.

The crisis was exacerbated by the continuous arrival of military personnel. In August 1943, the Allies established a new Southeast Asia Command under Lord Admiral Louis Mountbatten, locating its headquarters in New Delhi. Mountbatten's arrival in September caused great perturbation across classes. Rumors circulated that Mountbatten was bringing along a gigantic staff of 350,000 people, both British and American, which would result in a fresh and aggressive wave of house requisitioning and food shortages. Americans' appetite for beef, it was said, was already driving up prices.[68]

While officials dismissed the rumors as fantastic, they reflected undeniable distress. Military units continued to arrive in the city, and government departments—both military and civil—continued to expand,

increasing the population of an already overcrowded city. Housing shortages were acute, and rents rose to extortionate levels.[69] The Hoarding and
Profiteering Prevention Ordinance of 1943 succeeded only partially, and
while prices of food grains were somewhat reduced, other commodities
disappeared from the shelves. Rationing, belatedly introduced in mid-
1944, aroused its own anxieties and social tensions.[70] Growing discontent
among lower-paid officials in May 1944 worried the authorities, who recognized that wild inflation made those living on fixed incomes distressed
and restless.[71]

Despite the growing frustrations, Brahm Prakash noticed in dismay
that people, by and large, accepted their suffering submissively, saying
that the Congress had no prospects and the Raj would never end.[72] Quit
India was effectively and brutally suppressed, and concomitantly, starting
in late 1942, the tide of the war began to turn in favor of the Allies. The
military crisis was over, and the shiver of 1942 long gone.[73] Under the
circumstances, economic hardships did not catalyze mass protests, but
rather drew people's attention further away from news of battlefronts
outside India and political agitation within, toward the material stuff of
everyday existence.[74]

The Congress was banned outright, and anticolonial agitation came to
a standstill. It would erupt again, as we shall see, after the war's end, but
for now the Muslim League thrived on the political vacuum, spreading
the message of Pakistan. We now turn to an examination of how the politics of Muslim self-determination developed and played out in Delhi.[75]

THE 1930S: DAWN OF THE PAKISTAN DEMAND

In order to understand the Pakistan demand, we step back in time to the
beginnings of communal tensions in the city. Siddiqi clearly remembers
recurrent riots and the communalization of urban space in the late 1930s,
with Hindu and Muslim *mohallas* occasionally becoming forbidden territories for each other.[76] Delhi's politics became ever more imbricated with
the nation's, and the intensification of communal riots in the city was
linked to the larger political shift taking place in the late 1930s.

A catalyst and expression of the accentuated polarization was the
entrenchment in 1937 of both Hindu nationalist organizations and the

Muslim League in the city. The Arya Samaj movement, which arrived in Delhi in the late nineteenth century, had prepared the ground for Hindu organizations, as it did in Punjab. Established in 1875 by Swami Dayananda, the Arya Samaj, like other socioreligious reform movements in nineteenth-century India, was established in response to the encounter with colonial modernity and the cultural crisis it precipitated. Dayananda reinterpreted the ancient Vedic age of the Aryans in light of colonial and Christian criticism, cleansing Hinduism of polytheism and the oppressive caste system. The movement adopted a militant approach toward Christians and Muslims, and was the main harbinger of Hindu nationalist organizations in India.[77]

The Arya Samaj spread in Delhi through the work of Swami Shraddhanand (born as Munshi Ram). Shraddhanand took part in the Hindu-Muslim Noncooperation-Khilafat movements, but when this collaboration collapsed, he contributed to the straining of Hindu-Muslim relationships and the breakout of communal riots. Shraddhanand entangled his anticolonial sentiments with the Hindu nationalist agenda of cow protection, promotion of Hindi, and *Shuddhi* (purification), which aimed at (re-)converting Muslims and uplifting "untouchables," considered vulnerable to the missionary efforts of Christians and Muslims. Shraddhanand was killed in 1926 in his house in the Hindu *mohalla* of Naya Bazar by a young Muslim, Abdul Rashid, following the controversial conversion of a Muslim woman.[78]

By 1931 there were more than 50,000 Arya Samajis among the 400,000 Hindus in Delhi. The political party Hindu Mahasabha also expanded its offices and activities throughout the decade, founded the English weekly *Hindu Outlook*, and built a large headquarters building, the Hindu Mahasabha Bhavan, on Reading Road in New Delhi. Near the party's headquarters, it erected the Lakshmi Narayan Temple. Popularly named the "Birla Mandir" after the industrialist Baldeo Das Birla, who financed it, the temple became the first important pilgrimage site for Hindus in Delhi (see Map 0.2, Figure 1.1). A city hitherto considered "non-Hindu" now became the hub of organized Hinduism.[79]

The Arya Samaji entanglement of nationalism with Hinduism remained a central feature of the Congress in Punjab, where the Congress

FIGURE 1.1 *The Laxminarayan Temple (Birla Mandir) on Reading Road (today Mandir Marg). Source: Photo Division, Press Information Bureau, Ministry of Information and Broadcasting, Government of India.*

had a particularly Hindu slant, and in some circles of the Delhi Congress.[80] Both the Hindi daily *Arjun* and the Urdu daily *Tej*, aligned with the Congress, were owned and edited by Arya Samaji followers of Swami Shraddhanand—his son Pandit Indra Vidyavachaspati and his spiritual disciple, Lala Deshbandhu Gupta, a leading member of the Delhi Congress. Both papers fueled communal tensions in the city.[81]

It was also during the 1930s that the most aggressive Hindu-right organization—the Rashtriya Swayamsevak Sangh (RSS, or Association of National Volunteers) took root in Delhi.[82] The first Delhi branch was established in 1936 within the Hindu Mahasabha headquarters building, close to the Birla Mandir, by Vasant Rao Oak, an RSS *pracharak* (propagator) from Nagpur. Jugal Kishore Birla, Baldeo Das's elder son, who patronized both the temple and the Mahasabha Bhavan, extended his help to the RSS, and the RSS found its first recruits among the young

men who hung out in and around the temple.[83] Within a year after opening its first branch, it already had six branches in the city. By the time of
independence in 1947, there would be one hundred. The RSS was especially successful among government servants, students from the three big
colleges of Delhi University, and the *Banias* (Hindu merchant castes).
Hindu businessmen, industrialists, and traders financed the organization.

The Muslim League began to strengthen its presence in the city during this time as well, with the establishment in 1937 of a local branch—
Muslim League Delhi. It established its office in Lal Kuan Bazaar.[84]
Many of the founders were merchants, and the organization did not have
mass appeal at this early stage, as evident in the meager attendance at its
meetings.[85]

The provincial elections held in 1937 were pivotal to polarization
along communal lines. Two years earlier, the 1935 Government of India
Act extended the franchise to nearly 35 million Indians and granted the
provinces a large degree of autonomy while keeping tight control over
the center.[86] The elections that were subsequently held in 1937 resulted
in a stunning success for the Congress, which won the majority of open
(non-Muslim) seats and formed governments in seven provinces. For the
Muslim League the election proved a humiliating defeat, as it won less
than 5 percent of total Muslim votes and was almost nonexistent in the
Muslim-majority provinces that would form the cornerstone of Pakistan
a decade later. It was relatively strong in the Muslim-minority provinces,
notably the United Provinces, but even there the Congress famously shut
the door on the League's offer to form a coalition. Relations between the
Muslim League and the Congress were strained even more as a result of
Hindu majoritarian policies under Congress provincial governments in
the next two years. Muslims accused the Congress ministries of aggressively enforcing cow protection, advancing Hindi at the expense of Urdu,
excluding Muslims from government employment and local organizations, and precipitating anti-Muslim riots. The Muslim public began to
fear a future India in which Congress "secularism" would secure Hindu
majoritarian tyranny.[87]

The Muslims of Delhi did not actually experience Congress rule. As a
central charge overseen by the government of India through an appointed

chief commissioner, Delhi was not granted provincial autonomy. Delhi had one seat in the Central Legislative Assembly, which in 1934 was won by Congress Muslim leader Asaf Ali.[88] Delhi's limited electoral politics was confined to the Municipal Committee, where half of elected seats were reserved for Muslims, elected by separate electorates.[89] Compared with Muslim-minority provinces, the city had a much more substantial Muslim population, amounting to roughly a third of the total population, and Muslims were dominant in the police and the judicial bureaucracy.[90] Nonetheless, the bitter experience in the United Provinces gradually influenced Delhi as well.

Over the next two years, the Delhi Muslim League actively sought emotive topics around which it could mobilize support in the city. It tried to rally support around international commitment to the Arab revolt against the British Mandate and Jewish immigration in Palestine. But this issue was distant and symbolic, and was shared by all Muslim organizations. A much more effective rallying point was the oppression of the Muslim minority in adjacent provinces under Congress governments. By early 1939, the Delhi Muslim League was comparing the alleged atrocities against Muslims under Congress ministries to Nazi policies against the Jews.

It effectively entwined this broader issue with local disputes over space between Hindus and Muslims in the city itself. One was a legal dispute that arose in 1936 between the managing committee of the Fatehpuri Mosque and Seth Gadodia, the Hindu owner of the adjacent property. Second in its importance only to Jama Masjid, the Fatehpuri Mosque, established in 1650 by Fatehpuri Begum of the Mughal royal family, is located at the end of Chandni Chowk, near the wholesale market of Khari Baoli.[91] Allegedly, construction of what is now known as the Gadodia Market damaged one of the mosque's walls.[92] Although the parties to the lawsuit reached a compromise, many other Muslims opposed it.[93] The dispute erupted into a wider communal controversy between Muslims and Hindus, and Urdu posters appeared in the city tying construction on Gadodia's land to the anti-Muslim tyranny of Congress ministries in other provinces. Typical titles were "The Fatehpuri Mosque raided in broad daylight," "The cry of the Jama Masjid: save the small domes of my

FIGURE 1.2 *The Fatehpuri Mosque, 1995, with the rooftop of the Gadodia Market behind it. Source: Photo by Sondeep Shankar/Getty Images.*

sister the Fatehpuri Mosque from the clutches of Congress Hindus and traitors," and "the Bande Mataram flag over the Fatehpuri Mosque."[94] The dispute also pitted the mosque's managing committee against other Muslims, who accused it of criminal negligence and sued and even physically attacked its members. (See Figure 1.2.)

The newly formed Delhi Muslim League played a central role in the agitation, using the issue to catapult itself to prominence. Defying the rules of the mosque, it held regular mass meetings inside the building on Fridays after prayers, delivering insulting speeches against the committee. Uniformed volunteers with *lathis* attacked the mosque's students. In July 1938, following the Friday prayer, the Muslim League led a procession of five thousand people from the Fatehpuri Mosque through the main streets of the city, concluding with a public meeting in Queen's Gardens and a collective burning of Gandhi caps.[95]

Throughout the war years, the Muslim League would continue to use the Fatehpuri Mosque for its mass meetings. Significantly, its speeches and pamphlets targeted not only the Congress, but also leaders of the

Jamiat Ulama-e Hind and Congressi Muslims, whom it depicted as traitors and paid agents of the Congress, working against the Muslim cause. The Jamiat Ulama-e Hind (Association of Islamic Scholars) was established in 1919 by a group of ulama, mostly from Deoband, who were actively involved in the Khilafat movement. The organization continued to support the Congress nationalist struggle after the collapse of the noncooperation movement, amid the growing the communal rift. Along with other Muslim leaders aligned with the Congress, most prominently Maulana Abul Kalam Azad, they were called "nationalist Muslims."[96] The Fatehpuri Mosque land dispute is where we can discern the beginning of concerted attacks by the Muslim League on the "nationalist Muslims," the transformation of the former from a small, elite body into a political force gathering mass support, and the decline of nationalist Muslim leadership.[97]

Other large-scale disturbances arose over similarly local disputes. One day in early August 1938, a large crowd of Hindus collected in the southeastern corner of Queen's Gardens, where a sadhu (Hindu holy man) had built a prayer platform, bringing materials with them to build a Shiva temple. An open-air Muslim mosque already existed on the western side of Queen's Gardens, close to where a mosque had stood decades earlier. The following days saw clashes between Hindu crowds throwing stones and policemen executing *lathi* charges. Hindu Mahasabha and Congress members with Arya Samaji inclinations, notably Swami Shraddhanand's follower Deshbandhu Gupta, were apparently behind the movement.

Siddiqi recalls that Deshbandhu Gupta's *Tej*, alongside the Delhi Muslim Urdu dailies *Wahdat*, *Al Aman*, and *Watan*, "made capital of the episode, splashing it across their front pages day after day to make the Shiv Mandir case the rage of the city."[98] Imams called for jihad, as they saw the new temple as violating the sacred space of the Muslim temple. The Muslim League was quite visible in this dispute as well. Finally, a Muslim high school student from the Ajmeri Gate Anglo-Arabic school stabbed and injured the sadhu. The incident kindled explosive communal tensions, a riot broke out, and quite a few neighboring Hindu and Muslim *mohallas* turned into warring fortresses. The city was filled with rumors, *hartals* (strikes), and calls for boycotting along religious lines.[99]

Siddiqi recounts that people had to take roundabout routes to avoid walking through a *mohalla* of the other religion. He also talks about *binot* (*lathi* fights) becoming "an almost regular feature of the city life. They were at once a live *tamasha*, hugely enjoyed by the spectators as well as sort of a catharsis—a release of so much pent-up communal anger."[100] The Muslim *bandhanis* (coolies) of Paharganj featured recurrently in such riots.[101]

Such communal battles over space in Delhi became a part of the growing rift, throughout India, between the Muslim League and the nationalist Muslims.[102] Jinnah and the Muslim League sought to be recognized as the sole representatives of a divided and heterogeneous Muslim public. Hence, their attacks on Muslim rivals—Maulana Abul Kalam Azad and leaders of the Jamiat Ulama and the Majlis-e Ahrarul-Islam—became even more vociferous than their attacks on the Congress.[103] The Urdu newspapers *Al Aman* and *Wahdat*, which were edited by Muslim League member Maulana Mazhar Uddin, accused the Jamiat leaders of complicity in the death of Muslims in riots in the United Provinces. In revenge, on March 14, 1939, two young Muslims associated with the Jamiat murdered Uddin.[104] The Muslim League called for the retaliatory murder of Jamiat Ulama leaders Mufti Kifayatullah and Maulana Ahmad Seed.[105]

The League also engaged in heated debate with the nationalist Ahrars. Each side published pamphlets and posters claiming that membership in the other party was haram. The League obtained fatwas from anti-Congress ulama against the Jamiat for collaborating with infidels, forcing the Jamiat's top leaders to formulate a theological justification for their support of the Congress.

In the late 1930s Muslim League mass meetings took place in the Fatehpuri Mosque, while the Ahrars dominated Jama Masjid. We shall see that, as the Muslim League gathered momentum during the war, it would come to dominate both spaces. The parties took their rivalry to the city's youth, setting up competitive voluntary youth organizations, each with ritual uniformed flag salutations held regularly on Fridays.[106] These competitive demonstrations of power in different localities led to skirmishes when, for example, Muslim butchers, who followed the Ahrars, attacked Muslim Leaguers attempting to perform a flag salutation.

Tensions grew in Churiwalan and Farash Khana, where local branches of the Muslim League and the Ahrars competed.

In August 1939, the Muslim League held an impressive fifteen-day program of public meetings and flag salutations, drawing large crowds and featuring speakers from across the country. On the eve of the war, it had completed its transformation into a major political force. The meeting signified another development of the war years. While speakers made the usual references to Muslims being oppressed in the minority provinces, a new theme loomed large—a call to revise India's federal structure.[107] It was indeed at this time that a meeting of the All-India Muslim League in Delhi formed the All-India Pakistan Committee to investigate the diverse schemes for a future Pakistan.[108] Its deliberations would yield, a few months into the war, an explicit demand for an independent Muslim territory in the Indian subcontinent. Concomitantly, many Muslims continued to move away from leaders associated with the Congress, toward the Muslim League.

Let us go back to Siddiqi, who was studying at the Daryaganj branch of the Anglo-Arabic school. His initiation into the Pakistan movement took place soon after the war's outbreak, when the Congress ministries resigned and the Muslim League celebrated a day of deliverance and thanksgiving throughout the country. The Delhi Muslim League organized flag salutation ceremonies and meetings, and Siddiqi remembers walking with most of the school's students to a public meeting of the Muslim Students Federation at Queen's Gardens, chanting, "Mr. Jinnah *zindabad*, Muslim League *zindabad*."[109] The atmosphere was less that of a political gathering than of a festival, and Siddiqi spent the day gossiping with his friends and munching all the spicy snacks his pocket money could afford. Soon, however, Siddiqi became a truly "committed Pakistani."

DREAMING OF PAKISTAN

Several months after the war began, the Muslim League officially declared the right to Muslim self-determination as its main agenda. The famous Lahore Resolution of March 1940, declared at the All-India Muslim League annual session, is considered the decisive moment at which the League embarked on the political mission of forming a separate Muslim state. The resolution rested upon the two-nation theory, claiming that Muslims were not a minority but a nation, and that the Muslim question was thus an international problem. Its most discussed and debated paragraph argued that

> no constitutional plan would be workable in this country or acceptable to the Muslims unless it is designed on the following basic principles, viz. that geographically contiguous units are demarcated into regions which should be so constituted, with such territorial readjustments as may be necessary, that the areas in which the Muslims are numerically in a majority, as in the North-Western and Eastern zones of India, should be grouped to constitute Independent States in which the constituent units shall be autonomous and sovereign.[110]

Long considered the Pakistan Resolution, the Lahore Resolution did not mention the word *Pakistan*, let alone *partition*. Furthermore, as contemporaries and later historians have remarked, the crucial paragraph quoted above did not specify the territorial boundaries of the Muslim states, the precise connection of these states to each other, or the connection between them and the rest of India. Apparently, the Lahore Resolution attempted to reconcile through ambiguity the different and contradictory imaginations of Muslim leaders from minority and majority provinces. Indeed, it was the product of a year and a half of deliberations over these various proposals.[111] This vagueness, which lasted almost until partition itself, was a crucial factor that, as historian David Gilmartin claims, enabled Muslims of different backgrounds and conflicting interests to rally behind the Pakistan demand, for Pakistan meant different things to different people.[112]

Building on Gilmartin's argument, I suggest that Pakistan's ambiguity is indeed critical for understanding the growing support for Pakistan among Delhi's Muslims. Evidence suggests that many did not comprehend, until the very last moment, the grave implications of Pakistan politics. They believed that Delhi would be part of Pakistan, and they never contemplated having to migrate. Today Delhi is located 400 kilometers from the India-Pakistan border—an international border between two rival nation-states that have fought four wars and maintain strict control over movement between them. It is thus difficult to conceive how Delhi's Muslim Leaguers, who ardently supported the idea of Pakistan during the war, imagined that Delhi would be part of it. In order to grasp this, we need to embark on an exercise in imagination and reconstruct the territorial-political horizon of expectations held by India's residents during the twilight of empire. We can reconstruct it from the different schemes that circulated at the close of the 1930s, which interpreted the concept of Pakistan in diverse ways. Such schemes reflected Muslims' anxieties over the prospect of living as a minority under Hindu-majority rule following the troubled experience of the Congress ministries in 1937–39.

Among the schemes floating around, some were federative or confederative, assuming an all-India center shared by Muslim and Hindu political divisions. Others ruled out a shared center, envisioning complete sovereignty for the Muslim areas. Some assumed the continuity of the British Empire as a necessary framework, while others expected total independence. Some were territorially maximalist, preferring large tracts that would include a large number of non-Muslim minorities, while others were territorially minimalist and more "purist," envisioning smaller, more homogenous Muslim territories. The schemes included various degrees of power sharing and layered sovereignty, and many visualized an intricate web of territorial corridors connecting the various parts of the subcontinent, anticipating a free movement of people across Muslim and non-Muslim territories. Moreover, these plans did not necessarily contemplate an overlap between territorial residence and national belonging. Notably, most of them dismissed demographic unification through population exchange as totally impractical. As we shall see in the next chapter, the ethnic cleansing that eventually took place was beyond the conceivable until it abruptly took place.

Let us analyze some of these schemes, teasing out what they implied about Delhi's place in the future arrangements contemplated at the time. I shall put forward two claims. First, most schemes were shaped by a federal-imperial horizon of expectations, which was shared by political leaders and thinkers in the interwar era more globally, both colonizers and colonized, and emerged from the imperial experience and the attempt to reconcile imperial continuity with the language of national self-determination.[113] Significantly, a complete separation between parts of the subcontinent was beyond the framework of this kind of thinking. Second, many of the schemes visualized Delhi, and often even western United Provinces, as part of a future Pakistan.

Delhi in the Pakistan Schemes

Some plans, being straightforwardly federative or confederative, exemplified the federal-imperial horizon. They go back to Muhammad Iqbal, who is considered the father of the Pakistan idea and who thought of a Muslim homeland as part of an all-India federation.[114] They assumed both the continuity of British rule and a shared center for "Hindu India" and "Muslim India." Thus, *A Scheme for a Confederacy of India* (1939) by "A Punjabi" envisioned India as a confederation of five federations of provinces, two Muslim and three non-Muslim, which would share a center dealing with defense, external relations, and water supply issues. The scheme assumed that British rule would continue with a British viceroy, governor-general, and governors. While it suggested giving up some of the non-Muslim districts of Punjab, thereby making the Muslim federation in the northwest more homogenously Muslim, it explicitly ruled out an exchange of populations, calculating that a substantial Muslim minority of 37 percent would be left in the Hindu federations. The scheme provided for several corridors to connect different zones.[115] Although it was not explicitly mentioned, we may assume that the all-India center was to be located in Delhi, conferring special status on this territory.

This is also the case in Sir Sikander Hayat Khan's scheme, as delineated in his pamphlet "Outline of a Scheme of Indian Federation" (1941). The scheme, which is closest in spirit to the 1935 Government of India Act, amalgamates both British Indian provinces and princely states into seven zones confederated under British rule. Each zone would have an autonomous legislature, and Muslims would enjoy one-third representation at the center and in the zonal ministries. Thus schemes like these two contemplate not a territorial-political separation but a redistribution of power within India as a whole. For the Muslims of Delhi and minority provinces, the future envisioned in these schemes seemed to flow almost seamlessly from the present, with no major break.

I suggest that the mark of this idea is evident even in plans that were not strictly federative, indicating a federative mindset that shaped people's imaginings of the future. For example, the recommendations of Sir Abdullah Haroon's committee, formulated at the behest of the Muslim League's Foreign Committee and leaked to the press in February 1941, emphasized that safeguards for minorities could not be guaranteed without a center, which would coordinate policy on foreign affairs, defense, communications, customs, and minorities, at least for a transitional period.[116] Likewise, the first interpretations and clarifications of the Lahore Resolution by Muslim Leaguers from the United Provinces were confederative. Chaudhry Khaliquzzaman stated in a press conference in late March 1940 that the media misunderstood the Lahore Resolution, that the latter did not mean a partition but the establishment of three autonomous states within an all-India confederation.[117] Again, in December 1940, Nawab Isamil Khan, president of the United Provinces Muslim League, gave a confederative interpretation of the Lahore Resolution and stressed that no population migrations were contemplated.[118]

Other federative schemes are important for explicitly including Delhi inside Pakistan. For example, Dr. Syed Latif, a professor of English at Osmania University, Hyderabad, proposed an Indian federation with an all-India center but with Muslim and non-Muslim blocks exercising the highest degree of autonomy possible and connected by corridors. Like the schemes by "A Punjabi" and Khan, it also assumed that this federation would remain within the British Empire. To achieve religious homogeneity within these blocks, Latif proposed an exchange of populations; this is one of only two well-known proposals that did so.[119] Important to our concern, among the four Muslim zones was a Delhi-Lucknow block, "extending in a line from the eastern border of Patiala to Lucknow rounding up Rampur and including Agra, Delhi, Cawnpore and Lucknow but leaving out great Hindu religious centres like Benares, Hardwar, Allahabad and Muttra."[120] The plan also supposed a rather flexible link between national belonging, citizenship, and territory, promising free

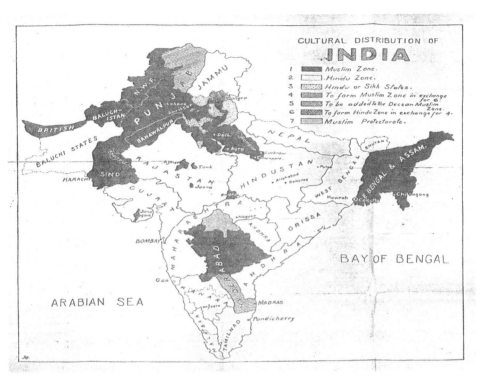

FIGURE 1.3 *Dr. Syed Latif's scheme of a future Pakistan in an all-India federation. Delhi (in black) is part of the Muslim zone called Delhi–Lucknow Block. Source: Latif,* Muslim Problem in India.

movement of people to other zones, where they would be granted citizenship rights. (See Figure 1.3.)

A different approach was envisioned in "The Problem of Indian Muslims and Its Solution" (1939), a scheme outlined by Aligarh University professors Mohammed Afzal Husain Qadri (officially the signer of it) and Syed Zafrul Hasan. It is especially noteworthy because, unlike the schemes discussed above, it nominally ruled out a shared political center. Because it originated from Aligarh—the bedrock of the Pakistan movement in the Muslim-minority province of the United Provinces—it reflects an acute concern with the predicament of Muslims in places like Delhi, in which Muslims were a minority and which could be left outside the territorial core of Pakistan. The plan divided India into three independent and sovereign states: Pakistan (including Kashmir), Bengal (including the Muslim-majority districts of Bihar and Assam), and Hindustan. Significantly, the scheme contemplated the creation of two new autonomous provinces inside Hindustan—Delhi in the north and Malabar in the south—in which Muslims would be a "nation in minority," part of a larger nation inhabiting Pakistan and Bengal. Delhi would include, in addition to Delhi proper, districts of the United Provinces with a substantial Muslim population, including Aligarh. Muslims would comprise 28 percent of Delhi's population and hence still be a minority, but, "Being highly cultured and educated as the Muslims of these parts are, and having their boundaries close to the Muslim Federation of Pakistan, they will be in much stronger position to guard their interests than otherwise."[121] (See Figure 1.4.)

Given that Muslims in the territory of Hindustan would live mainly in cities, the scheme also attempted to eliminate interference from provincial and central Hindu governments by turning all towns with a population of fifty thousand or more into "free cities" with a great degree of autonomy, apparently modeled on Danzig. Moreover, within these cities, Muslims would enjoy separate police and judicial arrangements. Muslims scattered in rural areas of Hindustan would be encouraged to aggregate in Muslim-majority villages. The plan promised minorities political representation proportional to their populations, separate electorates, and religious and cultural rights—in exchange for religious minorities within Pakistan receiving these same protections. Indeed, although the scheme moved away from federal models, it left room for a joint court of arbitration to settle disputes, alongside defensive and offensive alliances.

Thus, even when intellectuals at the forefront of the Pakistan movement in the United Provinces ruled out a shared federal center, not only did they not imagine complete separation, they also envisioned multiple layers of sovereignty, and sought to grant Delhi and other Muslim centers special autonomous status.[122] Furthermore, since Pakistan was to include the whole of Punjab, they expected territorial contiguity between the autonomous province of Delhi and Pakistan proper. Interestingly, the proposed map designates the city of Delhi with the same markings as Pakistan. The writers emphasized that Aligarh, as the center of Muslim

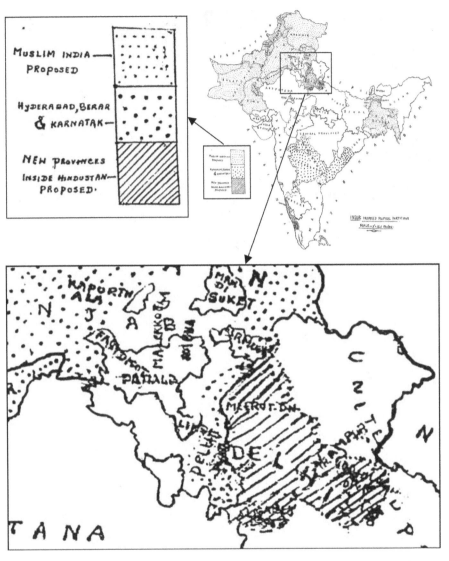

FIGURE 1.4 *The scheme of a future Pakistan outlined by Aligarh University professors Mohammed Afzal Husain Qadri and Syed Zafrul Hasan (1939). The scheme envisions a Muslim Delhi Province, with a special autonomous status, inside Hindustan and contiguous with Pakistan proper. While Delhi Province is marked in diagonal lines, the city of Delhi is marked in the same dots as Pakistan. At the upper right corner is the original map. To the left is an enlargement of the legend. Below is an enlargement of the area of Delhi. Source: File 42, Delhi Police Records, Second Installment, NMML.*

education, must be included in the autonomous province of Delhi, for it could not be left unprotected inside the overwhelmingly Hindu portion of the United Provinces. Unsurprisingly, eight more professors of Aligarh endorsed this plan.[123]

The Aligarh professors' scheme may have reflected—and influenced— a territorial-political imagination shared by Muslims in Delhi and western United Provinces in the years before partition. Such imagination was the root cause of their utter shock in the face of the clear-cut partition and large-scale migrations that took place in 1947, as we shall see in the next chapter. The imprint of the Aligarh scheme's line of thinking can be traced in the Lahore Resolution itself. Liaquat Ali Khan, for instance, insisted on keeping unnamed the provinces that would go into Pakistan, and on including the vague promise of "territorial readjustments," specifically in order to leave room for the inclusion of Aligarh and Delhi.[124] Similarly, Haroon's committee planned a Delhi province that would encompass western United Provinces, including Aligarh. Jinnah himself echoed the Aligarh scheme with his idea of a corridor via the United Provinces connecting the western Muslim state with the eastern one.[125]

Another example is a pamphlet published in the *Aligarh Muslim University Gazette* in December 1943 by Kazi Saiduddin Ahmad, a geographer at the university. He envisioned the division of the subcontinent into four "commune-regional states"—Pakistan, Hindustan, Dravidastan, and Bengalistan—along with a fifth Rajasthan state. Pakistan would include a Delhi province stretching over the Ghaggar Plain, between Sutlej and Yamuna Rivers, and encompassing eastern Punjab.[126] Though he explicitly ruled out a confederation, he envisaged an India Council to coordinate defense and foreign relations, functioning within the framework of the British Empire, with the viceroy serving as a link between the different political units.

Similar ideas were everywhere. A treatise published just before the Lahore Resolution by Anis Al Din Ahmad Rizvi, a graduate of Aligarh Muslim University, argued that Delhi and western United Provinces must be part of an independent Pakistan, since they formed the very center of Islamic culture in India.[127] Another plan, by Rahmat Ali, the first to coin the word *Pakistan*, envisioned a commonwealth of Muslim states, including Pakistan (which would encompass Delhi), Bangistan, and Usmanistan (Hyderabad). This plan exemplifies the flexibility of the territorial-political imagination of this period: Ali imagined a distinct national status and even separate territory for Muslim minorities within India that would form part of the Pak Commonwealth. Ali's proposed maps include Delhi in a territorially maximalist Pakistan.[128]

Historian Venkat Dhulipala discusses at length Anis Al Din's and Kazi Saiduddin Ahmad's treatises in the framework of his elaborate analysis of Pakistan discourse among the United Provinces Muslims in the 1940s. Dhulipala claims that, contrary to the common historiographical wisdom, Pakistan was in fact clearly imagined. Yet the rich materials that Dhulipala provides run against the thrust of his argument, affirming that people's imaginings were devoted to Pakistan as an Islamic utopia, and neglected its more concrete territorial aspects. Anis Al Din himself stated in his text that he did not delve too deeply into the territorial aspects of Muslim states, as he was more concerned with their Islamic nature. Further, there is a discrepancy between his textual discussion—his suggestion to create homogenous Muslim states by letting go of eastern Punjab—and the maximalist visualization of Pakistan in his map, which includes Punjab in its entirety, alongside Delhi and the western United Provinces.

Contrary to Dhulipala's argument, what emerges from the different schemes for Pakistan circulating in the 1940s is far from a coherent picture, territorially speaking. Furthermore, it appears that the different dreams of Pakistan were molded by people's present experiences and did not entail a major rupture with it. Many of the schemes implicitly or explicitly assumed at least some shared center and ongoing British presence in one form or another. Even those that did not still imagined that the subcontinent would continue to function as a whole through territorial corridors, autonomous regions of "nations in minority," and relatively free movement of people. One Musavvir Khan, who gave a speech in support of the Lahore Resolution in 1940, assured the audience that

> All provinces would remain in their current place and would not go flying in separate directions. Just as one could go from U.P. to Punjab on Frontier Mail today, one could continue to do so in the future as well. Similarly, one

FIGURE 1.5 *A map of future Pakistan from the mid-1940s. Delhi, on the bank of the Yamuna, is at the eastern end of Pakistan. Source: Ahmed,* Jinnah, Pakistan and Islamic Identity, *112.*

could take the train from Allahabad to Calcutta in the future as was being done presently.[129]

Taken together, these schemes convey a fluid, flexible, and open-ended political-territorial imagination rather than rigid model of a nation-state with full sovereignty, clearly demarcated international borders, and defined regimes of citizenship—much less a precise overlap between religious-ethnic composition and territory. Such a flexible imagination enabled the inclusion of Delhi within a future Pakistan, either as part of West Pakistan or as an autonomous area contiguous with it. See, for instance, Figure 1.5 for a map from the mid-1940s. This map may not be as maximalist, but it includes Delhi in Pakistan.

The Territorial Amorphousness and Emotional Intensity of Pakistan in Delhi
Siddiqi's recollections confirm that territorial ambiguity marked the idea of Pakistan in Delhi. The movement had a distinctly utopian quality—Pakistan was a dreamland and an ideal rather than a concrete program. During the war, Siddiqi enrolled in the Anglo-Arabic College (previously Delhi College) outside Ajmeri Gate, which was in the vanguard of the Pakistan movement, second only to Aligarh Muslim University in the United Provinces, and he became part of a group of committed Pakistanis on campus.[130] He observes with retrospective astonishment that their animated discussions about Pakistan were devoid of any real substance about its shape, geography, and demographic composition.[131] Siddiqi and his friends did not truly conceive that the establishment of Pakistan might mean an exodus from Delhi. When a *karkhandar* (artisan) raised a question about the place of Delhi in Pakistan, people replied, "Well, where else could Delhi go [but Pakistan]? Delhi is where the Dilliwallas are. Can fingernails be ever separated from the flesh?"[132] During these years, Siddiqi made some inquiries regarding the true meaning of Pakistan, but never received a straightforward answer. People would say, "Must we know what Allah Almighty is all about? Nobody has ever seen Allah. And yet everyone believes in him."[133]

An interview that historian Nazima Parveen conducted with an elderly Muslim who, like Siddiqi, belonged to an educated family and took part in the Pakistan movement in his youth, buttresses Siddiqi's argument that Muslim Leaguers in the capital did not explore Pakistan's territoriality.[134] Similarly, Shaista Suhrawardy Ikramullah, one of the few women to take part in the Pakistan movement and later a member of the Pakistan Constituent Assembly, made the same point. She lived in Delhi during World War II and was enamored by it: "The frontiers of

Pakistan had not been defined and it never entered our heads that Delhi would not be included within it. How sure we were that Delhi was ours and would come to us."[135] When a conversation about the place of Delhi in a future Pakistan took place and someone raised doubts, Ikramullah's husband pointed to the domed and turreted skyline of Delhi, to its essentially Muslim character, asserting it belonged with the Muslims and hence with Pakistan. As Nishtha Singh suggests, we need "to acknowledge the dominant personality of places as contemporaries viewed them. How people viewed places impacted the politics they adopted."[136] In the case of Delhi, its perceived Muslimness and strong identification with Muslim political dynasties and the historical domination of well-born Muslims as a ruling elite shaped the expectation that it would be part of Pakistan, in one form or another.

From late 1941 the notion of Pakistan, amorphous as it may have been, became the League's main rallying point in Delhi. The move to focus solely on Pakistan can be traced to a flag salutation ceremony in the open area opposite the Jama Masjid, held on Eid in October 1941. Jinnah unfurled the Muslim League flag and asked the Muslims to reaffirm with all their enthusiasm on the holy day of Eid that they would stand for Pakistan and Pakistan alone with all unity and discipline, and stand firmly by the Muslim League flag.[137] Jinnah and Liaquat Ali Khan were now based in New Delhi, living in spacious bungalows, and Ali Khan closely watched over and guided the Delhi branch of the party. Dilliwallas became familiar with Muslim League leaders from other provinces, who came to the city often, frequented Chandni Chowk and Ballimaran, and delivered speeches in public meetings, drawing the Delhi Muslim audience ever closer to the all-India politics of Pakistan. Gradually, remembers Siddiqi, *Pakistan* permeated everyday life in the city—the Jinnah cap came into prominence, mosques filled up even on weekdays, especially Fatehpuri Mosque and Jama Masjid, and Delhi's eunuchs and "cheap *qawwals*" (Sufi devotional singers) would sing songs in praise of Jinnah.[138]

True, Siddiqi's above-cited reference to the skeptic *karkhandar* implies that there was a class division between supporters of Pakistan, who belonged to the educated middle and upper classes, and poorer Muslims,

who remained aloof. Nazima Parveen has likewise found a class difference in her interviews, concluding that the Muslim League's Pakistan
movement in Delhi was narrow. As we shall see, the evidence suggests a
more complex picture. It appears that the hard core of Muslim Leaguers in Delhi was indeed the educated middle classes, yet Muslim League
meetings gained a popular dimension during the war. The sources do not
divulge who, exactly, took part in them, but the numbers are impressive.[139]
The question of the reach and demographic composition of the Pakistan
movement in Delhi remains inconclusive.

In 1941 the League started to challenge the dominance of the nationalist Ahrars in the politically important space-time of Jama Masjid after
Friday prayers, when tens of thousands of Muslims would congregate
there. Henceforth, Muslim League meetings would take place both in
Fatehpuri Mosque and in Jama Masjid, as well as in Urdu Park opposite
the Jama Masjid.[140] It was also during the war that Jinnah established in
Delhi the party's English-language daily newspaper, *Dawn*, which became a powerful mouthpiece of the Pakistan movement.

While the Congress was banned, the League received full recognition
and support from the Delhi administration throughout the war. Members
of the Congress and the Ahrars state that the Muslim League's policy
during these years was shaped by the directives of Delhi's chief commissioner and deputy commissioner who, conversely, ran the administration
practically in collaboration with the League.[141] Such close cooperation
meant that, while Delhi's streets were emptied of Congress activities until
mid-1945, they saw mass mobilization of the Muslim League, especially
on Pakistan Day, held annually on March 23.[142]

Pakistan Day celebrations were performative, demonstrating the
League's growing power through meetings, flag salutations, processions, and speeches by local leaders from Delhi and other provinces, as
well as national leaders such as Jinnah and Ali Khan.[143] Leading thousands through the city's streets, shouting Pakistan slogans, and deliberately halting at sensitive spots such as the Sikh Gurudwara Sis Gang
and the Congress office, the Muslim League asserted its claim on public
spaces against those of rival communities, and often provoked communal tensions. These parades mimicked the familiar pattern of religious

processions, but they carried a new politics surrounding the territorial demand for self-determination.[144]

As Sandria Freitag notes with regard to nineteenth-century religious processions, "processional activities provide particularly appropriate venues for incorporating new expressions of popular values."[145] The Muslim League processions featured its youth volunteers, the Muslim National Guards, wearing gray coats and trousers, and sometimes carrying spears and swords. In the 1945 Pakistan Day events, the volunteers were mounted on horses, camels, a bullock cart, and a tonga bearing loudspeakers. They shouted Pakistan slogans, recited Pakistan poems, carried placards, and sold lapel pins of the Muslim League flag. A bullock cart bore a Pakistan map as well as population statistics for the projected eastern and western zones of Pakistan and various European and Middle Eastern countries, probably to make the case that Pakistan would have a substantial population as compared with other countries.[146] Thus, while Muslim League processions were modelled on religious-communal processions and asserted control over an urban space, they were infused with a new kind of political language associated with the nation-state. Against the backdrop of the Shiver of 1942 and an impending transfer of power, the fanfare around Pakistan Days showcased the Muslim League's strength, signaling that it was a force to reckon with in any future negotiation.

POSTWAR CONVULSIONS

When the defeat of Germany was announced on May 8, 1945, the response in Delhi was lukewarm, driving Indian newspapers to contrast the apathy in India's capital with the euphoric scenes in London. But, the chief commissioner noted with satisfaction, tens of thousands turned up to watch the official victory celebrations, which included a military march from Connaught Circus via Chandni Chowk to the Red Fort, the feeding of forty thousand poor residents, nighttime illumination of the Red Fort and government buildings, and fireworks in the Ramlila ground outside Ajmeri Gate.[147] Siddiqi recalls the celebrations, the splendid appearance of the Clock Tower decorated from top to bottom with multicolored lights, and the dazzling lights of the shops lining Chandni Chowk. Yet he remembers that, in contrast with the celebration of King

George's Silver Jubilee in 1935, there was no spontaneous enthusiasm in the crowd. "People partook of the festivities more as free *tamasha* . . . than as a part of the victory celebration."[148]

Within a few months, public reaction turned from lukewarm to outright violent. As we saw, the decline of the colonial state during the war precipitated politicization and mass mobilization. This became all the more blatant after the war, with the Labour Party's victory in Britain, the release of Congress leaders and workers from prison, and the resumption of negotiations over a transfer of power.[149] Amid these high-politics events, there were extraordinary popular outbursts: a movement for the release of INA prisoners, a mutiny in the Royal Indian Navy, a massive strike wave, the Tebhaga (sharecropper) movement in Bengal, the Punnapra-Vayalar communist uprising in Travancore, and the Telangana armed peasant rebellion in Hyderabad. The fall and winter of 1945–46 were described by contemporaries as "the edge of a volcano."[150]

In Delhi, as we shall see in the next chapter, Pakistan would come to eclipse all other issues from mid-1946 onward. But in the months from the end of the war until roughly mid-1946, mass politics was more malleable, defined by anticolonial agitation as much as by growing communalization over the Pakistan question. The war had led to food and fuel shortages, and an influx of government and military personnel had driven rents and food prices even higher. Now retrenchment may have begun, but from 1945 onward, Delhi saw the arrival of ex-soldiers from other provinces in search of employment.[151] Economic distress intersected with political developments. Anticolonial sentiment, suppressed for more than two years after the brutal crushing of Quit India, came to the surface again. Concomitantly, the Pakistan movement continued with full force.

In the winter of 1945–46, after Congress leaders were released and the ban on the party was removed, elections were held to the Central Legislative Assembly and the Provincial Legislative Assemblies. The stakes were high, and both the Congress and the Muslim League utilized emotional, even violent rhetoric in their campaigns. The Congress campaign had overt anticolonial tones, glorifying Quit India and the INA—two forms of extreme and militant anticolonialism, one that had slipped out of the control of the Congress high command and one that directly contravened Congress policy, especially Nehru's. On the Muslim League side, the elections were presented as a referendum on Pakistan and proved an important catalyst for the party's mass mobilization in all parts of the country.[152]

As a central charge, Delhi did not hold provincial elections. Hence, elections amounted to the one seat allocated to Delhi in the Central Legislative Assembly under a joint electorate, which Congress leader Asaf Ali won again, as he had in 1934. Yet the capital did not escape the election frenzy.[153] The Delhi Muslim League continued its public meetings, flag-raising ceremonies, and speeches by leaders from outside Delhi.[154] Like their counterparts at the Aligarh Muslim University, students of the Anglo-Arabic College harnessed themselves to the campaign, organizing a Pakistan Club and raising money for the Muslim League election fund. The Delhi Muslim League escalated its campaign against Congressi Muslims, and attacks on Maulana Azad became more vicious by the day. When Azad and Asaf Ali returned to Delhi, shopkeepers displayed black flags, and students shouted anti-Azad slogans at Kucha Chelan in the old city, where he was staying. Azad avoided addressing a public meeting, claiming ill health but apparently fearing disturbances.[155] Siddiqi remembers how Azad, with his trimmed beard and elegantly tailored, homespun *sherwani* (long-sleeved coat), steadfastly warned the Muslims against the horrific consequences of partition. But Jinnah denounced him as the Congress "show boy," and Siddiqi and his friends, "youthful Jinnahites," echoed and reechoed Jinnah.[156]

Yet the Muslim League campaign shows that, despite the emotional intensity attached to Pakistan as an ideal Islamic order, and despite the vicious attacks on everyone who opposed it, territorial vagueness continued to underlie the movement. This is clearly evident in Urdu campaign pamphlets that the League distributed in Delhi on Eid-ul-Zuha in November 1945. They strengthen Gilmartin's findings with regard to electioneering flyers in Punjab—namely, that they rarely explored the territorial meaning of Pakistan and the basic features of its statehood.[157] In the pamphlets, Quaid-e Azam (great leader) Jinnah appeals to the Muslims of India on the occasion of Eid that they put aside their differences, unite in the name of God behind the Muslim League, and be willing to make sacrifices for the ultimate goal of India's Muslims—Pakistan. Pakistan is the only guarantee of Muslim security, freedom, and salvation, of Muslim political, economic, moral, and educational progress. The one sentence in the pamphlets that alludes to the concrete aspects of Pakistan reads, "And we want an independent Pakistan in an independent India" (aur ham azad Hindustan mein azad Pakistan chahte hein)—a statement that could easily be understood as an autonomous state within India, rather than an independent country outside it, echoing Iqbal's 1930 demand for "a Muslim India within India."[158] The pamphlet includes a map marking Punjab and Bengal as Pakistan provinces, and excluding Delhi and the United Provinces.

Similarly, in response to Jamiat Ulama's claim that Pakistan would unite the Muslims in the majority provinces at the expense of those from minority provinces, *Dawn* replied that Jinnah wanted to unite Muslims in the majority provinces specifically so that they could take up and defend the cause of Muslims in the minority provinces. To Nehru's charge that Pakistan was unclear, *Dawn* answered that it was simple and straightforward—yet it explained it in abstract and emotional language: "Pakistan is the pointer 'Hands off the Muslims.' Pakistan is the warning that the Muslims are awake. . . . Pakistan is unity—unity in thought, unity in action, unity in movement."[159] The most concrete description that *Dawn* offered was metaphoric and could easily have pointed to an autonomous arrangement:

[Pakistan means] to have our own Government in provinces where we are in majority. The same may be granted to the Hindus. We have no objection. . . . If you live in a common house with some other people, who are not supposed to be interested in your welfare in any case, it is likely that some day some harm may come to you from them. They may steal your luggage or pack your bag and baggage out of the house. How would you like if you are given a separate room to yourself, where you can keep your luggage safely and live in perfect security. This allotment of a separate room to you makes all the difference between Pakistan and Akhand Hindustan.[160]

Ultimately, the Muslim League failed to win seats under joint electorates (including the Delhi seat), but it won all thirty Muslim constituencies. The Delhi Muslim League celebrated the occasion on February 11, 1946. Many Muslims kept their shops and houses illuminated, and fireworks displays took place in various Muslim localities. In Urdu Park, Jinnah attracted an audience of 100,000 people, who cheered and set off firecrackers on his arrival. Jinnah was presented with a silver football, a silver shield inscribed with the names of the thirty successful candidates, and a gold bullet in a chest on which a map of Pakistan was engraved. Jinnah thanked the Delhi public for their warm support and stressed the now-familiar claim that Muslims would not rest until they achieved the goal of Pakistan, for without Pakistan, Islam and the Muslims would cease to exist. The other, no less central, theme was the need for unity and sacrifice.[161]

Yet, on the very same day, younger, more radical members of the Muslim League marched in anticolonial protests over the trial of Muslim INA officer Abdul Rashid. They were arrested at the conclusion of the procession for defying the Defence of India Act. Both the trial and the arrests unleashed Muslim agitation with anti-British overtones, which split the local Muslim League, revealing a gap between the leadership, focused on Pakistan, and popular sentiment, apparently more connected to the anticolonial mood engulfing the country. Before further examining this gap, let us attend to the INA trials and the resentment they aroused.

The INA Trials

After the war, Britain decided to court-martial INA soldiers captured in Southeast Asia. The first and most high-profile trial, against three top-level INA officers who had operated under Subhas Chandra Bose, opened in early November 1945 and seriously backfired.[162] Intended to win over public sentiment, the trial instead encapsulated the contradictory experiences and understandings of the war in the metropole and the colony—what the British saw as treason, Indians saw as anticolonial patriotism. The decision to conduct the trials in Delhi's symbolically resonant Red Fort, from which the last Mughal emperor had been exiled after the 1857 rebellion, combined with the fact that the officers belonged to all three religious communities, prompted a popular patriotic reaction cutting across communal lines. A wave of demonstrations, public meetings, and strikes swept across the country. Protests became extremely violent in some areas, especially Calcutta.[163]

Although Nehru had grave reservations about Bose's collaboration with the Axis, the Congress sensed the extent of popular resentment and fully capitalized on the INA cause. It set up an INA Defence Committee office in Daryaganj, and about fifteen lawyers volunteered their services for the defense, most notably Nehru himself.[164] The defense's main argument was that the Provisional Government of Free India that Bose had established in Southeast Asia was a recognized government of a recognized sovereign state, whose army legitimately fought under international law to liberate India.[165] The court-martial proceedings were covered extensively by the Indian press and proved an opportunity to report on the INA's deeds. The newspapers also quoted Bose's patriotic speeches, reiterating his famous slogan, "Dilli Chalo" (On to Delhi) and his promise to raise the tricolor flag above the Red Fort.

In January 1946, the three officers were found guilty of waging war against the king-emperor (the equivalent of treason). They were sentenced to exile for life, but in the face of the INA release movement, commander in chief of the Indian Army Claude Auchinleck decided to commute their sentences. The released officers were taken on procession through the streets of Old Delhi, cheered and carried on supporters' shoulders. Congress politicians rushed to the scene of congratulate them.[166]

Soon after, *Hindustan Times* reporter Moti Ram published an account of the trial in a book with a foreword by Nehru. The book helped spread the patriotic discourse surrounding the INA by reporting on, among other things, the three officers' accounts of their political awakening in light of British racism in the Indian army, their abandonment by British officers in Singapore, and Bose's charisma. Significantly, the book juxtaposed the INA trials with the historic trial of the last Mughal emperor, which had also taken place in the Red Fort. It thereby enhanced the link between 1857 and the INA as a harbinger of India's independence, and centered the story in Delhi, the historical capital of Indian empires before the British. In the following months, different presses in Delhi followed suit and unleashed a flood of books and pamphlets in English, Hindi, and Urdu, describing the feats of the INA and spreading the myth of Netaji and his legendary patriotic army.[167]

Though the INA release movement was integrated into the Congress's election campaign, it was a spontaneous and enthusiastic outpouring of emotion that, just like the earlier Quit India movement, exceeded the Congress leaders' expectations and escaped their control. Nehru's reflections on the movement certainly echoed his understanding of Quit India: "significant signs of the fires below the surface. A spark lights them. In a sense the Congress represents these forces but they are stronger than any organisation and can be controlled only to a limited extent and provided conditions are favourable."[168] Frustrations, pent up for several years after Quit India, came to the surface all of a sudden.

Discontent did not die down with the release of the three officers but continued throughout the second and third INA trials. The main accused in these trials were Abdul Rashid, whose defense was undertaken by the Muslim League, and Shinghara Singh and Fateh Khan, whose defense was undertaken by the Congress. Lessons from the first trial learned, the British decided to move these trials to a less symbolically charged location and to shift the focus from treason to brutality and the perpetration of atrocities in wartime camps, where Indian prisoners of war had been pressured to join the INA. The accused in these two trials were sentenced to seven years and fourteen years, respectively, of rigorous imprisonment.[169]

It was in protest against Abdul Rashid's trial that the young Muslim Leaguers marched on February 11, the day of the mammoth, 100,000-strong Muslim League celebration. That the two events were condensed within the same day indicates the malleability of Muslim mass politics in this period, and the operation of the Pakistan movement alongside a push for decolonization that transcended the Hindu-Muslim divide.

The following day, Muslim cloth merchants closed their shops to protest the arrest of the young Muslim League members, and a crowd gathered outside the Karol Bagh police *thana* to demand their release. It formed a procession shouting pro–Muslim League and antigovernment slogans. In a scene that epitomized the protean times, communist leader Sarla Gupta demonstrated with burqa-clad Muslim women in front of the council chamber, shouting slogans for both Pakistan and Hindu-Muslim unity.[170] Speeches in Muslim League public meetings condemned the trial of Abdul Rashid, the arrest of Muslim League leaders, and the continuation of the wartime Defence of India Act, which forbade public processions. They deployed the anti-British discourse of the INA release movement, condemning the British for abandoning Indian soldiers to the mercy of the Japanese in 1942 and linking the INA to the rebellion of 1857 in Delhi. The fire of hatred kindled in Muslim hearts in 1857 was still burning, said the speakers, and the people still remembered how the British had presented the last Mughal emperor with the heads of his three sons. Master-slave relationships must end, declared one speaker, while another asserted that an independence uprising was imminent.[171]

Like the Congress, however, the Muslim League was not in full command of the situation and seemed to chase popular sentiment rather than shape it. In a private meeting, Muslim League leaders rejected a resolution to hold processions in defiance of the Defence of India Act, instead settling for the more limited method of peaceful demonstrations. Leaders resolved to pacify the Muslim crowds and to ask them to wait several more weeks until Pakistan Day on March 23, when the All-India Muslim League would launch a concerted agitation for the formation of Pakistan. A British officer commented that the "more responsible members" of the local Muslim League sought to reserve the people's energies for the bigger issue of Pakistan but had no control over their "volatile and irresponsible" followers, who were more concerned about the INA trials. "Much of the agitation is not Muslim League and really shows how unstable the Muslim crowds are."[172]

Victory Week Disturbances, March 1946

The split in the local League reached a peak with the approach of Victory Week, scheduled to begin on March 7. Victory Week was organized by the government and the army to celebrate the successes of the British Indian Army in the war, in an effort to divert attention away from the INA trials—a move that backfired, like the trials themselves. The Congress called for a boycott of the celebrations, and the younger, more radical branch within the Muslim League joined in. Leaders of this faction, including Anis Ahmed Hashmi (general secretary of the Provincial Muslim League), criticized the police firing on crowds in Calcutta and Meerut, demanded the release of Abdul Rashid and other INA men, and called for anti-British actions during Victory Week, beginning with a *hartal* and the raising of black flags. The more conservative elements in the Delhi Muslim League were afraid of mass demonstrations and wished to conserve energies for the Pakistan movement. A sharp controversy ensued, and members decided to refer the matter to the high command, specifically to Liaquat Ali Khan. When he expressed reservations about defying the government of India's orders, Hashmi resigned. Younger and "less restrained elements" within the Muslim League protested outside the Muslim league office, shouting against the "toadies" and "traitors" who collaborated with the British.

On the eve of Victory Week celebrations—amid disturbances elsewhere in India, including the Royal Indian Navy mutiny—the superintendent of police estimated that "responsible members of the Congress and the Muslim League are not expected to do more than advocate non-cooperation or boycott, but the rowdy elements . . . have been talking about active counter-demonstrations." By "rowdy elements" he meant "the *goonda* elements and rowdy students of this town as well as a few congress socialists . . . and some assorted communists."[173] CID files and the recollections of Delhi's communists confirm that communists and students—specifically those associated with the communist-dominated Delhi Provincial Students Federation—were indeed involved.[174]

On the appointed day of the victory parade, as soldiers marched through Connaught Place, the public booed and jeered. Viceroy Archibald Wavell was shaken, lamenting that the Indian soldiers who had fought so gallantly during the war and defended India were insulted, while a bunch of INA traitors and cowards were exalted.[175] (See Figure 1.6.)

Disturbances soon escalated into a replay of the violence that had engulfed the city in 1942. A huge crowd collected in Chandni Chowk and the adjacent lanes on the morning of March 7. "Rowdy elements" attacked the victory arches, the scaffolding on the Clock Tower, and other

FIGURE 1.6 *Indian Army mountain guns carried by pack mules pass the saluting base during the Victory Parade in Delhi, March 1946. Source: @ Imperial War Museum (IND 5040).*

decorations connected with the victory celebrations. They lit fires on the roads and erected roadblocks. The crowd reportedly attempted as much destruction as possible, adopting the technique of incendiarism that had become prominent in 1942. A thousand men or more, armed with *lathis* and stones, entered the Town Hall, smashed the windowpanes, and set fire to several rooms. They stoned the fire brigade that arrived on the spot. The fire station on Queen's Road was torched next, along with a Terminal Tax Post and a Rationing Enquiry kiosk, a private car, a ration shop, a police van, and a railway grain shop. The same group of people apparently moved down Pul Bangash toward Rohtak Road and set the Railway Clearing Accounts office at Kishan Ganj on fire.[176] The roughly eighty people put on trial for these disturbances included both Hindus and Muslims, and their occupations were listed as follows: communist workers, (few) Congress members, laborers, artisans, masons, petty shopkeepers, *goondas*, "bad characters" and "history sheeter," coolies, tailors, taxi drivers, milk sellers, *chaprasis* (peons), and lower-level clerks.[177]

The greatest wave of strikes and labor unrest in the history of colonial India ensued.[178] In Delhi, a police mutiny broke out on March 20–23, led by two hundred of the young and, in official eyes, "ill-disciplined" recruits of the Delhi police, but gaining the sympathy of many constables.[179] Further strikes followed among postal employees, tramway employees, municipal sweepers, milk sellers, and Birla Mills workers.[180] Delhi's most important communists and labor organizers were arrested and detained, as they would be after independence.[181]

Labor strikes continued throughout the summer of 1946, but one can discern a shift in the city's politics starting in April of that year: anticolonial agitation receded, while competition over the "day after" took center stage. The annual Pakistan Day was celebrated, as usual, on March 23, and in his speech Liaquat Ali Khan stressed the familiar claim that Muslims were willing to sacrifice their lives to achieve Pakistan. A day after, the Cabinet Mission arrived from Britain to resolve the political deadlock.

CODA

Siddiqi recollects that, when he was general secretary of the Anglo-Arabic College Students Union, he and his friend Arif, who was vice president of the student union, used to visit Liaquat Ali Khan at his palatial bungalow, Gul-e-Rana, on Hardinge Road. Liaquat was warm and affectionate and would paint an alluring picture of Pakistan as a land of promise that would offer the young Muslims dignity, pride, independence, and abundant employment and business opportunities. When they raised questions about whether they would need to leave Delhi, he responded vaguely, "[W]ho knows? Remember one thing . . . that is no matter where you might be after Pakistan—whether here in Delhi as most of us would indeed be or in Lahore or Karachi—we could still serve Pakistan. For Pakistan is and shall be the only goal and ultimate destiny of Muslim India regardless of where one might be."[182] Siddiqi would leave these meetings galvanized, resolved to get Pakistan at any cost.

In the summer of 1945, Siddiqi graduated and undertook graduate studies in history at the prestigious St. Stephen's College, situated in the new campus of Delhi University, north of the city walls near the Ridge. Bitter arguments over the question of Pakistan divided even this apolitical institution. The head of the history department and dean of the faculty of arts was Dr. Ishtiaq Hussain Qureshi, a proclaimed Pakistani.[183] Qureshi, recalls Siddiqi, "couldn't think the emergence of Pakistan would in any way compromise the basic oneness and unity of India." He thought that "Partition would in no way mean the partition of either the body or the soul of India. It would be purely an administrative arrangement . . . political re-definition of the subcontinent to let the two communities live in peace and shape their lives in their own 'Indian' way. . . . And he would still be teaching at the Delhi University—his home and alma mater."[184]

In his own *mohalla* of Ballimaran, the bazaar resounded with chants of "We shall take Pakistan by dividing Hindustan" (Leke rahenge Pakistan: Bat ke rahega Hindustan). The few remaining nationalist Muslims warned of the consequences of Pakistan, but their admonitions went unheard. The Jamiat Ulama leaders Mufti Kifayatullah, Maulana Ahmad Saeed, and Maulana Hussain Ahmad Madani lost their hold over the public.

Siddiqi read the English Muslim League paper, *Dawn*, every day, avidly memorizing Potham Joseph's popular column "Over a Cup of Tea" and the provocative, vitriolic editorials of Altaf Hussain, who was on a warpath, engaged in a war of words with the city's "Hindu papers." The "*Dawn* boys" seemed larger than life, heroically facing the powerful Hindu papers and representing the Pakistan cause. Siddiqi joined this club in 1947 as an unpaid apprentice sub-editor, working under News Editor Mahmud Hussain. His enthusiasm knew no bounds as he walked every day to the editorial offices at the far end of a narrow, twisting lane in Faiz bazaar in Daryaganj.

CHAPTER 2

PARTITION VIOLENCE SHATTERS UTOPIA

The road itself seemed to be moving even faster than the commuters: it left little time even for a short break to catch their breath. By advancing the date for the transfer of power from June 1948 to August 1947, Mountbatten had taken all of us by surprise. We were not quite prepared for our journey to Pakistan in so abrupt and hasty a manner. We were not even sure if we really would have Pakistan as a country in brick and mortar. . . . For once, we thought of the frightening possibility of migration: of leaving Delhi—the seat and symbol of Muslim culture, art and architecture, and the city where lay buried the bones of our ancestors.[1]

MASSACRE AND MIGRATION: SEPTEMBER 1947

Friday, September 5, 1947, was a fateful day. Abdul Rahman Siddiqi, then twenty-three years old, was at *Dawn*'s news desk when, around 3 p.m., the teleprinter came alive: "Bomb explosion inside the Fatehpuri Mosque during the Juma prayers. Several wounded. City under curfew.' 'Good Lord, it has started. The war is on!' we exclaimed, almost in the same breath."[2] Shahid Ahmad Dehlvi heard the explosion from his office in Khari Baoli—a Hindu locality and wholesale grain market near the mosque. He saw hundreds of pigeons flying up in the air from Fatehpuri Mosque, accompanied by startled exclamations of "Allah O Akbar." Then there was a dead silence, and Hindus were seen running across the roof of Gadodia Market (See Figure 1.2).

Dehlvi embodied the Muslim intellectual milieu of pre-partition Delhi. He was an accomplished writer, literary editor, and grandson of Deputy Nazir Ahmad—a prominent figure in the nineteenth-century Delhi Renaissance. Dehlvi's reportage of the September violence, entitled *Dilli Ki Bipta* (The Calamity of Delhi), was written soon after; it was published in 1950 in Pakistan, where he migrated immediately after the events.

On witnessing the explosion, Dehlvi felt great danger, since his office was located at the heart of the Hindu locality. The few Muslims residing in the area all gathered in his mother's house, holding knives, wood logs, stones, and a gun in anticipation of an attack. Some men began collecting large bricks, empty bottles, and peppers. The Hindu houses around them, however, remained quiet, and Dehlvi, along with three aides, left the locality and set off toward his home in Jama Masjid—a Muslim neighborhood, hence a safe haven. The walk, which was a relatively short distance, seemed long route, full of pitfalls and dangers, as every turn, shortcut, and lane they took was a fateful decision. The short and abrupt sentences that tell of their escape convey the feeling of urgency, unraveling Shahjahanabad as a space of fear, totally underwritten by communal logic. The streets were desolate apart from groups of young men—Hindus in Hindu alleys and Muslims in Muslim ones—who might be either standing idle or on the lookout for victims. Dehlvi bore witness to the stabbing of a Hindu man. On finally reaching Jama Masjid, he sighed in relief. He thought he would return the following day to his office to collect essential documents, but a curfew was imposed for many days, and the next time he visited the office was a month later, before departing for Pakistan.[3]

The first week of September marked a turn from sporadic stabbings and shootings to organized attacks on Muslim life and property on a massive scale, in both the city and its rural surrounding. In the villages, hundreds of Muslims were killed, mosques burned down, property looted, and many forced to choose between death and conversion.[4] In the jurisdiction of Narela, northwest of the city, fifty-five bodies were found in Holambi Kalan village, and more than three hundred Muslims were killed in Barwala village. Violence spread to villages west of the city in the jurisdiction of Najafgarh, Nangloi, and Mehrauli. In Mehrauli village, near the historic minaret of Qutab Minar, dozens were killed, the bazaar was burned down, and the remaining three thousand Muslims were huddled in one place and later evacuated. The villages of Chhatarpur, Tihar, and Punjab Khor turned into improvised refuges for rural Muslims.[5] (See Map 0.1.)

In the city, the violence reached all quarters, albeit unevenly: the old city of Shahjahanabad, the localities west of it, Civil Lines north of it, and even the posh areas of New Delhi to its south. The fashionable shopping area of Connaught Place became chaotic, as rioters looted Muslim shops in broad daylight, and it is told that Prime Minister Nehru, touring the city, stepped out of his car outraged, snatched a gun from one of the soldiers passively standing by, and threatened the looters.[6] Groups of attackers roamed around New Delhi's residential areas, where houses of diplomats were also located, entering bungalows, looting, and killing Muslim domestic servants, to the embarrassment of the Indian government.[7]

But the neighborhoods struck by the bloodiest violence were the three "mixed localities" of Karol Bagh, Sabzi Mandi, and Paharganj, west of the walled city. (See Maps 0.2, 1.1). Their mixed habitation rendered their Muslim population especially vulnerable, since they could not set up gates and other forms of protection as did Muslims in the Muslim-majority neighborhoods. In Sadar Bazar, the fourth main locality to the west of the old city, some neighborhoods were attacked—including Bara Hindu Rao, Bahadurgarh Road, and Kishan Ganj—while others remained strongholds of Muslim presence. Another locality of mixed habitation that suffered greatly was the government employees' neighborhood of Lodi Colony in New Delhi. In addition, Turkman Gate at the outskirts of the old city was one of the worst-hit localities. Throughout September, the violence extended to other localities in the old city—Faiz Bazar in Daryaganj, Kalan Masjid near Turkman Gate, Ajmeri Gate, and Phatak Habash Khan. Large fires burned in various parts of the city, and smoke hovered above. Sweepers did not work for weeks, and the streets

FIGURE 2.1 *A soldier manning a Bren gun at the entrance to Paharganj bazaar, September 1947. The destroyed buildings testify to the severe violence that took place in this locality. Source: Keystone/Stringer/Getty Images.*

were cluttered with garbage and rotting corpses. Internal transport and phone communications broke down.

In Karol Bagh, reported the chief commissioner, "Hindus and Sikhs were definitely the aggressors," and, according to Dehlvi, Muslim houses had been marked out in advance of the riots. Karol Bagh was a stronghold of Congress-supporting nationalist Muslims, who were adamant about staying put and prevented others from leaving for the Muslim-majority areas as well. The attack on the locality, when it came, was disastrous. One of the city's most gruesome assaults was in this locality, when a group of Muslim high school students sitting for the matriculation exam were separated from the rest and butchered by Sikhs with *talwars* (sabers).[8] Jamia Millia University, a stronghold of nationalist Muslims, was attacked and its library burned down, along with hundreds of thousands of books.[9] In

Ajmeri Gate, the Anglo-Arabic College, the hub of the Pakistan movement, met a similar fate. Ebadat Barelvi, then at the college, recalls how Pakistan's high commissioner, Zahid Hussain, sent a wagon to rescue the college's students at the very last minute and gave them refuge in his house.[10] Tragically for the nationalist Muslims who opposed Pakistan, attackers did not distinguish between nationalist Muslim institutions and those associated with the Muslim League.

In Paharganj, Sabzi Mandi, and Turkman Gate, Muslims apparently fought hard to defend themselves, and reports mention Sten guns and Bren guns. In Paharganj, Muslims were massacred in large numbers and Muslim women were paraded naked on the street.[11] Among the first victims in Sabzi Mandi, according to Dehlvi, were the laborers in the cotton mills area.[12] Anis Kidwai—sister-in-law of Cabinet Member Rafi Ahmed Kidwai, who participated in the rehabilitation efforts in Delhi—pinpoints the Birla Mills, owned by the wealthy Birla family, as the place where the carnage took place.[13]

Local Congress leader Phool Chand Jain and his son Lakshmi Chand Jain lived at the northern edge of Sabzi Mandi in Jawahar Nagar, close to the Delhi University campus. It was "a frontier territory, overgrown with trees and shrubbery, with the possibility of sighting the odd jackal, and almost totally uninhabited."[14] In an interview, Phool Chand Jain recalls:

In Subzimandi I, together with my son Lakshmi Chand and my brother Kastur Chand, lifted the dead bodies with our own hands. No one else went there. No one entered this area for three days. It was raining heavily. It was on the occasion of *Janmashtami*. So we went house by house and took away the dead bodies. We saw what kind of destruction befell each house. In these houses we also saw *gulel* [slingshots], which were prepared as weapons, lying there, like the catapults used in gardens to scare away birds. In preparation for the fighting, people also sharpened iron blades. Sticks were found in all houses. . . . In Arya Pura, Subzimandi, and in Lal Masjid we found bodies of three or four women who were totally naked. I cannot say for certain what happened to them before they were killed. There was one school, a big building in which many women were hiding. There, as well, perhaps one woman had a shred of cloth on her body, the rest were totally naked. They were killed in that very place. We lifted about 700–750 dead bodies just from Subzi-mandi. Other people cleared away a similar number in Paharganj.[15]

His son recalls:

> Dead bodies were littered all over the place around the University area es-pecially Subzi Mandi and Roshanara Road. P. N. Dhar . . . whom I knew from Hindu College and I got together a group to clear the bodies from the streets. The group included some 40 students from the University, mainly those from . . . the University Officers Training Group, who were like Home Guards; they had dummy rifles given to them for training. We needed some sort of protection because the people who had killed the residents of that area would not allow anybody to remove those bodies. They said, let them rot there. So we decided to go in a force of 40 to persuade the residents who were watching from their balconies. We told them that if the bodies rotted there, disease would spread into their homes and they would risk infection. After one or two hours of argument, we started clearing away the corpses. The September rains, which were fierce in Delhi in 1947, had soaked the bodies . . . the stench was unbearable. My father arranged for two trucks from the Municipality to be made available to us. Over 15 days, we removed 3000 dead bodies which were carted away by the Municipal trucks to a place designated by the Municipal Committee. There were more dead bodies to be removed, but we could not do it. We used to get nightmares. We had to wash our hands 3–4 times before we ate.[16]

Jawahar Nagar, claims Ishtiaq Husain Qureshi, was a bastion of the RSS (Rashtriya Swayamsevak Sangh, the Hindu nationalist organiza-tion), and camps for the refugees from Punjab had been established in the area. A Muslim League member who moved to Pakistan and be-came the rehabilitation minister and an important historian of Pakistan, Qureshi was the dean of Delhi University's Arts Faculty back in 1947. The university was surrounded by fruit orchards, and the fruit trade was a Muslim monopoly. He heard screams throughout the night as Muslims were murdered in the orchards—probably the *Arains* (Muslim gardeners) surrounding Sabzi Mandi—and began to pour into the university cam-pus. The next morning, the campus was attacked. There was no loss of life, but all Muslim houses were looted. Muslim students and teachers fled by car to Pakistan's High Commission.[17]

As in cities across Punjab, Delhi's railway stations—the New Delhi Railway Station near Paharganj and the Old Delhi Railway Station in Chandni Chowk—turned into death traps. Around New Delhi Railway Station, the *bandhani* (coolies) community was targeted.[18] Jugal Kishore Khanna, a member of the Delhi Congress and deputy secretary of the Constituent Assembly of India, was appointed a special magistrate during the crisis, and was posted at the Old Delhi train station. Muslims from Delhi, and those who fled the United Provinces and disembarked in Delhi on the way to Pakistan, found themselves face to face with vengeful Hindu and Sikh refugees who had just barely survived the journey from Pakistan. They were also easy targets for the gangs of Sikh rioters who traveled across north India, killing and looting Muslims:

> Almost daily I used to obtain an order taking out the bodies, of course, mostly of Muslims on average 30 to 35 bodies a day from this Frontier Mail and there was no question of going into formalities. We could not get any names or any post mortem, not even counting was there. They were put on the Municipal refuse trucks and dumped into the Jamuna.[19]

> Once when I was on duty I saw a Muslim running about to catch the special train. He had with him a girl of about 10 or 11 years of age. The train had not reached the platform but before that the girl and the man came by crossing the railway line. Instantly I heard a shot, I ran towards the line and I saw the girl lying in a pool of blood; I noticed a stab wound on the side of her ear. About the same time I noticed that the old man . . . ran towards the platform and when I came back I saw that the old man was lying dead. Similar incidents were witnessed by me on several occasions.[20]

> At the railway station, there was an office of the Government Railway Police. Behind that office there was a waiting room and a bathroom and some sort of an enclosure. And one day news was brought to me that when Muslims came to the G.R.P. office they sought police protection, but their luggage used to be kept in the office and they were asked to go at the back of that

enclosure and there they were butchered, of course, with the assistance of the police, it may be connivance, it should be really the assistance of the police. I detected some bodies there. I came to Panditji [Jawaharlal Nehru] and said, "This is the state of affairs. I am helpless." In a worried mood he listened to me and then rushed to the spot to see things with his own eyes and then gave a bit of his mind to Randhawa [Delhi's Deputy Commissioner] who had come by that time. . . . But the administration, of course, on account of circumstances also was very loose and demoralized.[21]

In his broadcast to the nation on September 9, Nehru asserted that the government intended to deal with the crisis "on a war basis in every sense of the word."[22] It was also on September 9 that Gandhi arrived in Delhi. While he had planned to stop in Delhi for only a few days on his way to riot-stricken Punjab, by the time he arrived, the city was already in flames, and he decided to stay in order to restore peace in the capital. Until his assassination on January 30, 1948, Gandhi addressed the people of Delhi in his daily prayer meetings, preaching for communal harmony and reproaching those engaged in violence and hatred.[23]

As in other cases of mass killing, it is difficult to know for certain how many people were massacred.[24] There was no police registration, no counting, and certainly no post mortem or proper burial—the bodies were simply collected on municipal trucks and thrown in dumping grounds or in the Yamuna River. Congress social workers who volunteered in the relief work estimated the total deaths to be ten thousand,[25] while the local Muslim League gave a higher estimate of twenty-five thousand.[26] The riots drove the Muslims who survived out of their neighborhoods, in search of safer places. Abdul Rahman Siddiqi recalls how the survivors from Phatak Habash Khan came trickling into his Muslim-majority locality of Ballimaran. Dehlvi witnessed his neighborhood of Jama Masjid turning into an improvised refugee camp. Those who managed to flee the violence in the mixed localities stayed with their relatives and friends. Every house hosted a dozen or two dozen guests, and those who could not be accommodated spent their days and nights in the by-lanes of the *mohalla* (neighborhood). Jama Masjid's population doubled

within a few days. Congestion became unbearable and verged on hazard-
ous, since there were no sanitary arrangements for cleaning. The *mehtar*
(sweepers) stopped cleaning the *mohalla*, and cholera broke out.

Other temporary refugee centers for Muslims were set up in Idgah
(Sadar Bazar) and in a by-lane on Qutab Road (the main road running
north-south through both Sadar Bazar and Paharganj).[27] As these swelled
with people, Muslim refugees were transferred to the two large refugee
camps opened for them south of New Delhi, in the ruins of Humayun's
Tomb and the medieval fort Purana Qila, which served as an internment camp for Japanese during World War II.[28] (See Map 0.1.) By mid-
September, there were as many as 120,000 Muslim refugees in the camps,
living in horrid conditions without sanitation.[29] By late October most
of them were evacuated by trains to Pakistan, while others—thousands
according to some, hundreds according to others—returned to the city.

BLOODSHED AS BATTLE: THE OFFICIAL NARRATIVE

"Traditional" communal riots in the city, as we saw in the previous chapter, were restricted to public spaces, involved rival groups of men wielding
lathis (wooden batons) and brick bats, resulted in a limited number of casualties, and remained confined within specific *mohallas*. What transpired
in September 1947, on the other hand, was of an altogether different scale
and order: the violence targeted people's homes along with women and
children, and was accompanied by sexual brutality, large-scale arson, mass
killings, and expulsions, effectuating the "purification" of whole neighborhoods. Consequently, the city as a whole underwent an enormous demographic transformation: roughly 350,000 Muslims—about two-thirds of
Delhi's Muslim population—fled to Pakistan, while half a million Hindu
and Sikh refugees settled in their place.[30] In its form and consequences,
the violence of September fits the definition of ethnic cleansing—namely,
an ethnic or religious group targeting another group in order to drive it
out from a certain territory.[31] In Delhi, as in other parts of India during partition, violence was no longer merely about "renegotiating status
and power within the symbolic framework of a local order," but about
"moral appropriation and purification of territory."[32] It was specifically

connected to British withdrawal and the contest for power and territory that accompanied it.

The account given above draws the general contours of the ethnic cleansing that took place in Delhi. In what follows I will delve deeper into its roots, structure, and main agents. To what extent was it a spontaneous outbreak, and to what extent was it planned in advance? Who were the main agents perpetrating the violence—the bitter and traumatized Hindu and Sikh refugees, as so many accounts suggest, or local residents and the victims' old neighbors? Were agents of the state complicit in it? At what levels? Addressing these questions will help us to unpack the fundamental question that looms large over the event: how did the relatively limited form of communal riots transform into deadly violence of a novel kind?

The official, nationalist narrative, which developed during the time of the violence and congealed afterward, tends to minimize the September violence and to blur responsibility for it. The violence is often presented as a spontaneous, uncontrolled outbreak of anger following atrocities committed in Pakistan and the arrival of Hindu and Sikh refugees from there. The first chief commissioner's report on the violence, for example, states, "The communal tension with which the city was surcharged owing to influx of refugees from West Punjab burst into an orgy of murder, loot and arson in the first week of this month."[33] The historical agents in the report are largely the emotions that took over the masses. Verbs such as "burst," "exploded," and "swept" often recur, giving the impression of a natural disaster that came all of a sudden and was beyond anyone's responsibility or control. An upshot of such narratives is an apparent disconnect between state and society: the state—especially its upper echelons—temporarily lost control over the rampaging mobs on the streets. As soon as it could, the state contained the crisis and used all its force to restore law and order.[34]

Note that while the emphasis on emotions obscures the perpetrators of the violence, responsibility is implicitly ascribed to the refugees—to the outside. Other sources point to the refugees more directly. R. N. Banerjee, who at that time was home secretary to Sardar Vallabhbhai Patel, later recalled, "What happened was that law and order practically ceased to exist on the 5th, 6th, and 7th of September 1947. A large number of Sikhs and Hindus drained out of Pakistan in conditions well known, came on to Delhi and practically began to kill every Muslim at sight."[35] Similarly, the *Delhi Gazetteer* notes that "The uprooted millions [*sic*] from West Pakistan who poured into the city were in a state of terrible mental tension. They had seen their near and dear ones hacked to pieces, women abducted, properties looted and houses consigned to flames. Their minds were filled with wrath and they were eager to wreck vengeance."[36] The violence is thus presented as a frenzied outbreak whose origin was, on the whole, external. Laying responsibility on the traumatized refugees helps justify the events as retaliation for atrocities elsewhere, and it also fits the motif of the lawless migratory element, prominent in nationalist historiography and official and media reports on communal riots.[37] The "migratory" element is likewise conspicuous in coverage of the Delhi violence in the English daily *Hindustan Times*, which blame refugees, servants, and textile mill laborers, many of whom were migrants.[38]

In fact, the *Hindustan Times* and its Hindi counterpart *Hindustan*, which were owned by Ghanshyam Das Birla and associated with the Congress, were important in shaping the standard narrative as the violence was still unfolding. It is therefore worth examining them more closely. Not only do these papers fudge responsibility, they also tend to depict Muslims as aggressors. Alongside reports and memoirs by bureaucrats working closely with Sardar Patel, these dailies helped disseminate Patel's view of the September violence as "a riot," in the sense of a balanced struggle between essentially equal rivals.[39] We shall return to Patel's position in greater detail in the next chapter. Here our purpose is to analyze how media and bureaucratic sources helped congeal a minimized interpretation of the events.

A close reading of coverage in the Congress-related daily papers reveals a huge discrepancy between the headlines, which understate the scale of the violence, and the bodies of the articles, which disclose a much graver picture of dozens of dead bodies found scattered in the city every day.[40] The overload of details creates the impression of violent chaos, composed of discrete, haphazard incidents, and the writing does not connect these into the overall picture of systematic violence targeting a particular community. The papers do provide such a clear and broad perspective in coverage of the violence against Hindus and Sikhs in West Pakistan. Furthermore, the papers selectively follow the ban on disclosure of the religious identities of victims and aggressors, which was meant to prevent inflaming passions. The papers disclose these identities only in cases in which Muslims were, or were thought to be, the aggressors.[41]

An important motif creating the impression of a symmetric battle between equal forces is the plethora of weapons that Delhi's Muslims allegedly held, along with recurrent reports on Muslim snipers in Sabzi Mandi and Turkman Gate.[42] With their extensive coverage of Sardar Patel's account of the September violence in the Lok Sabha, the dailies became important channels for disseminating his claim that Muslim-majority localities used firearms against non-Muslim residents and the army, and that searches in their houses revealed large quantities of illicit weapons and ammunition. Patel's report, echoed in the papers, presented the total cleansing of Karol Bagh from Muslims as a battle sparked by a bomb Muslims had implanted in the Hindu part of the *mohalla*.[43]

Muslim weapons are also central to framing official reports and the narratives of Indian bureaucrats who worked closely with Patel. Recurrent mentions of the Bren guns are especially prominent, perhaps because machine guns offer a minority the potential to overcome its numerical inferiority in battle.[44] This emphasis suffuses the events with an aura of a symmetrical struggle between rival groups, and implicitly justifies the use of violence by the army and police against the Muslims. The chief commissioner's fortnightly report notes that "In Subzimandi, Muslims, who were better armed and had a lot of illicit arms in their possession, caused a good deal of damage by firing with machine guns and Sten guns from their houses. A pitched battle was fought between the Military and the *Arains*, and it was after great difficulty that these pockets of resistance were cleared."[45] The term "pockets of resistance" represents what Ranajit Guha called, in another context, "Prose of Counterinsurgency"—the official discourse that justifies violence by the state against specific groups.[46]

The threat of Muslim insurgency is central to one of the most influential accounts of partition—Justice G. D. Khosla's government-commissioned book: *Stern Reckoning: A Survey of the Events Leading up to and Following the Partition of India.* Khosla emphasizes that Delhi was a Muslim League base and was threatened by underground activities of the Muslim National Guards. "An abortive attempt to create disorder in November 1946 failed, but Muslim preparations continued, and there was ample evidence of secret collection of arms by the Muslims."[47] Khosla defines the September violence as "riots," in which

> Muslims were found to be heavily armed. They used automatic weapons, country-made cannons, rifles, bombs, mortars and other missiles. . . . One Haji Obedullah played a prominent part in the riots in the area of Subzi-mandi, and he was responsible for importing large quantities of weapons into Delhi. The shops of Muslim blacksmiths and motor mechanics were converted into small arsenals where spears, mortars, and crude muzzle-loading guns were manufactured. After the riots, it was discovered that many Muslim localities had been provided with a wireless transmitter and receiving set. . . . In Subzimandi area a tunnel was discovered in which a large quantity of arms and ammunition had been stored.[48]

Khosla claims that Muslim provocation started the riots, and, like Patel, he pinpoints the explosion of a bomb in a Hindu locality in Karol Bagh on September 3 as the catalyst for the violence. He further highlights how Dr. Abdul Ghani Qureshi of the Delhi Muslim League murdered the famous surgeon Dr. N. G. Joshi in the same locality.[49] "There was constant firing by the Muslims in Paharganj, Subzimandi and Turkman Gate. . . . In the Subzimandi area a veritable battle between the Muslims and the police lasted for a whole day [until] Muslims surrendered and asked to be evacuated to a safe place."[50]

Khosla offers a considerably low estimate of the number of Muslim deaths as roughly one thousand and assures us that most of the Muslims who were evacuated to the camps returned to their homes. Although slightly more balanced, the memoirs of Secretary of States V. P. Menon, Home Secretary R. N. Banerjee, and V. Shankar, Patel's private secretary, echo the emphasis on Muslim arms dealers, weapons, and provocations.[51]

Thus the standard narrative that emerges from official reports, newspaper coverage, and bureaucrats' memoirs presents the violence as spontaneous and emotional, laying responsibility directly or indirectly on traumatized refugees. Some sources even downplay the havoc wreaked on the Muslim community, and some speak of counterinsurgency, laying the blame on Muslim aggression.

HISTORICIZING THE VIOLENCE

Recent secondary literature neither downplays the extent of the massacre nor presents Muslims as aggressors.[52] Gyanendra Pandey offers the most comprehensive historiographical reconstruction of the event to date, in a chapter on Delhi in his monograph *Remembering Partition*. Drawing on official reports and memoirs, mostly by Muslims, Pandey recounts the chain of events from the outbreak of violence to the evacuation of Muslims from the city. The Muslim voices combine into a powerful narrative that communicates shock at the extraordinary violence and the abrupt uprooting of the city's Muslim life. Pandey's analysis reflects the democratization of partition's historiography—the transition from high politics, focused on a few key players, to the experience of ordinary people. Indeed, Pandey has been a representative voice of this shift. He criticizes historians' preoccupation with the high politics of partition and the blame game for India's division as an offshoot of the nation-state's obsession with unity, a focus that excludes the violence itself, its experience, and its long-term implications.[53] Paradoxically, Pandey claims, "the history of violence is . . . almost always about context—about everything that happens around violence. The violence itself is taken as 'known.' Its contours and character . . . need no investigation."[54]

Yet the decision to reconstruct the violence in Delhi through the eyes of Muslims, and to begin the narrative with the outbreak of violence in September, reaffirms the event's inexplicability. The masses do not appear as agents but rather as victims of historical decisions taken elsewhere and beyond their control. It seems as if things just happen, and they happen so rapidly that they leave the main characters, and readers, bewildered in the face of the abrupt and violent rending of the city's social fabric. Indeed, one of the main challenges in the historiography of partition is a disconnect between high politics as a realm of rational and calculated decision making (partition's causes) and histories of the social realm as riddled with emotions and inexplicable violence (partition's implications).[55]

To address this interpretive challenge, we will begin our exploration of communal relations and violence in the city in 1946, thereby providing the events of September 1947 with historical depth and allowing us to see them as the culmination of profound shifts in the communal politics of the city, for which Muslim Leaguers were as responsible as Congress, Sikh, and Hindu-right organizations. This understanding builds on our exploration in the previous chapter of the Pakistan movement in Delhi, with its virulent attacks on rivals, paradoxical combination of emotional intensity and territorial ambiguity, and implicit wishful thinking that Delhi be part of Pakistan. Such emphasis is not meant to deny that Muslims were the victims of an atrocious massacre. Rather, it allows us to see Muslims, notably middle-class Muslims and students who supported the League, as agents rather than just passive victims. Like tragic heroes, Muslim Leaguers inadvertently contributed to bringing about their own and other Muslims' downfall. The tragedy lies in their inability to comprehend and anticipate the results of their actions. It lies in the gap between the political imagination that informed the politics of Pakistan and its actual consequences. The ambiguity of Pakistan is, of course, a key to this tragedy. The politics of Pakistan in Delhi was shaped by a federal horizon of expectations, an assumption that independence would bring about some form of power sharing, layered sovereignty, and territorial adjustments, which would enable Delhi's residents to be part of Pakistan. No one predicted the horrendous violence that took place when a partition into two sovereign nation-states necessitated a massive population exchange.

The chapter follows the tragic transformation of utopia into reality, tracing the transmutation of limited communal riots into ethnic cleansing, and revealing the graver form that communal riots in the city began to take in late 1946. Territory—or, more precisely, the increasing territorialization of the meaning of *Pakistan*—was central to this process. Bound up with such territorialization were subtle but steady changes in the balance of power against the Muslim League. We will see that the shift took place simultaneously at the lower levels of political mobilization and in the realm of high politics.

Our historical investigation will also reveal the preparations for a civil war that took place in the months immediately before September 1947, and enable us to reconstruct the structure and perpetrators of the violence in greater detail and precision than has been attempted previously.[56] We will follow the steady buildup of the RSS and its connections with the Hindu business community and Sikh organizations, as well as the Hinduization and Sikhization of the Delhi police effected by Home Minister Sardar Patel. Our analysis will show how these trends intersected with the arrival of refugees in the city from March 1947 onward. By contextualizing the violence in this way, we will be able to draw a nuanced picture of the September riots as a combination of preplanning and spontaneity, high politics and political mobilization on the ground, and local and refugee activity. It will also demonstrate that the deadly violence in Delhi did not emerge in isolation, but was bounded up with the territorialization of the meaning of Pakistan and the unfolding of partition politics in the rest of the country, especially in the Punjab.

A LIMINAL YEAR: 1946

Tracing the roots of the September violence takes us back to 1946 and the subtle changes that it brought. As we saw in the previous chapter, at the end of 1945 and the beginning of 1946, the city was rife with both anticolonial agitation and communal tensions, and the authorities were preoccupied with the disturbances on Victory Day and the police mutiny. Starting in April 1946, communal hostility increasingly took center stage. Retrospectively, the months from March to December 1946 appear to have possessed a liminal quality. We can locate in them the gradual transition from the older and more familiar pattern of communal riots to the much graver violence that would engulf Delhi after independence. By the end of the year, as we shall see, an imminent change was in the air, felt simultaneously on the street and in the corridors of political decision making. Concurrently—and here lies another aspect of this year's liminality—though polarization over the question of Pakistan became increasingly aggressive, the territorial implications of Pakistan had not yet come to the surface.

As discussed in the previous chapter, in March 1946, the British government sent to India the three-member Cabinet Mission of Frederick Pethick-Lawrence, Stafford Cripps, and A. V. Alexander. They proposed that India become a loose federation of three groups of provinces: Muslim-majority provinces in the west, Muslim-majority provinces in the east, and the bulk of Indian territory comprising Hindu-majority regions. The three groups would have a great deal of autonomy vis-à-vis an established center, which would be in sole charge of defense, foreign relations, and communications. In other words, this scheme provided for a Pakistan while interpreting it not as a separate, independent nation-state, but rather as two semi-autonomous groups of Muslim-majority provinces inside India. The plan was grounded in the more fluid territorial imagination of the early 1940s, which included a host of federative schemes, discussed in the previous chapter. At the same time, it gave provinces the option to secede after ten years. Initially, the Muslim League accepted the plan, and the Congress followed suit, but a controversial speech given by Nehru in July caused a stir, and both parties withdrew their acceptance.[57]

The collapse of the plan ended any possibility of a united India, driving home the prospect of a territorial division. It was also the first act in the partition violence, a year prior to the event. The League responded to the plan's failure by announcing a national Direct Action Day on August 16, 1946, with Muslims protesting for an independent Pakistan. This triggered the outbreak of violence in Calcutta, unprecedented in its brutality and scale. Riots, which took the lives of about four thousand people, came to be known as the Great Calcutta Killing.[58] In the following months, the violence spread to Bombay, eastern Bengal, Bihar, and the United Provinces. Jinnah, in one of the few statements he made on the topic in the 1940s, urged that population exchange be considered. While this statement was more emphatic than earlier ones, it did not offer any concrete elaboration and was dismissed by critics as hopelessly impractical and fantastic.[59] Nonetheless, the idea was in the air.

In the midst of this deteriorating situation, Britain established an interim Indian government headed by Nehru on September 2, 1946. Following failed negotiations between the two parties, it did not initially include Muslim League members. Important portfolios were held by

Nehru (External Affairs and Commonwealth Relations), Patel (Home, Information and Broadcasting), Baldev Singh (Defence), and John Matthai (Finance). Even after Muslim League members joined in late October, relations between the two parties were so strained that the Interim Government had trouble functioning properly.[60]

These developments left a strong impact on Delhi. Communal tensions gathered momentum against the background of the Cabinet Mission's arrival in India. On April 10, the Delhi Provincial Muslim League organized an impressive convention in Urdu Park opposite Jama Masjid, attended by one hundred thousand people and centered on the demand for Pakistan.[61] It lodged several hundred students from Aligarh Muslim University in the government clerks' locality of Lodi Colony and, according to Hindu inhabitants of the locality, these students roamed around in lorries, shouting provocative slogans. An especially inflammatory poster appeared in the neighborhood, claiming that the Cabinet Mission's objective was to crush the demand for Pakistan. It called on Muslim youths to respond to the call of the leader and, in case a Hindu state was formed without Pakistan, to prepare to sacrifice their lives for Pakistan and wage a war against their Hindu enemies. In practical terms, it called on people to enlist mujahidin, train in sabotage and fighting, collect weapons, gather intelligence, build connections with Muslim policemen and army men, destroy government and Hindu properties, cut wires, and destroy railway lines. With rumors of *goondas* (thugs) in nearby Nizamuddin village and of *lathis*, daggers, and knives collected by Muslim residents of the neighborhood, the Hindu residents panicked "so much so that for several nights they would not go to bed and remained outside their quarters in batches shouting at the pitch of their voices apparently to keep up their courage."[62] A fourteen-year-old Hindu boy was stabbed in Lodi Colony soon afterward, causing further alarm. Tensions had been simmering there long before. Interestingly, tensions had also been simmering in the government clerks' quarters in Karol Bagh, where Hindu and Muslim government clerks sent anxious letters about impending communal attacks, and enrolled enthusiastically in the paramilitary volunteer organizations.[63] As we may recall, both Lodi Colony and Karol Bagh would be among the worst-hit localities in September 1947.

When the League accepted the Cabinet Mission plan, the Delhi Muslim League organized a public meeting with an audience of twenty-five thousand people. The audience was apparently confused by developments, because speakers made great efforts to explain the reasons for accepting what seemed to be a nail in the coffin of Pakistan. Acknowledging that the plan seemed disappointing at first glance, they asserted that it would bring the Muslims closer to their desired goal of Pakistan. They assured the audience that the League still stood by the Lahore resolution, asking it to keep faith in Jinnah's acumen.[64]

When the plan finally failed, the provincial Muslim League of Delhi took part in the August 16 Direct Action Day. It organized flag salutation ceremonies in various localities; a strike in all Muslim schools and in the Anglo-Arabic College, which was at the forefront of the Pakistan movement; and a public meeting in Jama Masjid following Friday prayers. The Delhi Provincial Muslim Students Federation organized a meeting at the Anglo-Arabic College, inviting speakers from Delhi and elsewhere. The Direct Action Resolution was read out and fiery speeches were delivered. The Hindus finally proved themselves *banias* (Hindu merchants, used here pejoratively as greedy moneylenders), claimed Qazi Muhammad Isa of Baluchistan, to the applause of the audience. In a spirited speech that received frequent applause from the students, Isa further asserted that the meaning of Direct Action Day was "goodbye constitutionalism," and that Muslims did not believe in nonviolence, but rather in "eye for an eye." "Could the Muslims ever tolerate a Hindu raj?" He asked. The audience answered in the negative. He struck a note of warning to nationalist Muslims, saying that Islam enjoins a severe punishment for traitors.[65]

Significantly, while the Pakistan movement intensified in Delhi after the plan's failure, the future contours of Pakistan and their implications for Delhi were still shrouded in fog. We can see the intertwining of emotionally intense political mobilization and territorial uncertainty in *Dawn's* issue on Direct Action Day of August 16. The paper called on each and every Muslim to follow Jinnah and pledge to sacrifice himself in the cause of national freedom, stating in bold headlines that "Pakistan is ours by right of nationhood, by right of majority, by right of national

FIGURE 2.2 *A map of future Pakistan, published by* Dawn *on August 16, 1946. The map, which includes the whole of Punjab and Delhi within Pakistan, is very similar to the one in Figure 1.5. Source: File DC 601/1946, DSA.*

justice and right popular verdict," and that "we shall fight for it, we shall die for it, take it we must—or perish." In the middle of the page is a map of Pakistan that includes the Muslim-majority provinces, Punjab, Bengal, and Assam in their entirety, and Delhi itself.[66] The map emerged from the various imaginations of Pakistan circulating throughout the 1940s, which assumed that Delhi belonged in it. It tells us of the liminality of 1946, located between the utopian vision of Pakistan in the 1940s and the territorial meaning of partition that would come to the fore in 1947.

The violence that broke out in Calcutta on Direct Action Day left its mark on Delhi. The city's press became more polarized, and its tone deteriorated from August 1946 onward. All papers described the Great Calcutta Killing as premeditated mass slaughter, the worst in India's history, while providing graphic descriptions of the carnage and, in some cases, pictures of dead bodies lying in the streets. But they strongly disagreed over the massacre's source, perpetrators, and victims. *Tej, Hindustan Times, National Call,* and *Statesman* repeatedly stated that the Muslim League bore responsibility. A powerful cartoon in the *National Call* showed a sack full of human skulls, presented to Jinnah by Suhrawardy as "The First Offering of Direct Action!" *Dawn* rejoined by describing such coverage as the power of an organized Hindu propaganda to make night appear as day. The "week of long knives" in Calcutta, it claimed, was orchestrated in advance by Congress and Hindu circles, as proven by the fact that the overwhelming majority of victims was Muslim. The battle lines of the Delhi press were drawn ever more clearly along communal lines: Muslim versus Hindu.[67]

Polarization deepened even more after the establishment of the Congress-led Interim Government on September 2. Muslim League supporters observed it as a day of mourning, hoisted black flags on their shops and houses, and demonstrated at the residence of Mr. Asaf Ali, now Congress member of Railway and Transport, calling him a traitor to Islam. A procession of Muslim League supporters marched through Chawri Bazar toward Hauz Qazi, shouting, "With our blood we shall have Pakistan," "Death to Nehru," and "Hindus should be destroyed."[68] There were reports of Muslim clerks in the imperial secretariat who absented themselves from their offices for two hours on that day, hoisted black flags on their quarters, and wore black armbands to protest the formation of a Congress government.[69] The bitterness permeated the Delhi Municipal Committee, where Congress member Jugal Kishore Khanna attempted to move a resolution congratulating the Interim Government.[70]

THE YEAR ENDS IN VIOLENCE: NOVEMBER 1946

These growing tensions broke out in disturbances in the city on November 7. These disturbances possessed a liminal quality, situated at a threshold between the familiar pattern of communal riots and the violence of partition.

On November 6, on the occasion of Eid-ul-Zuha, some Muslims in Paharganj led three cows to slaughter at the Idgah in Sadar Bazar. After a group of Hindus released one of the cows, Hindus, represented by Deshbandhu Gupta, and Sikhs demanded that the Muslims take the remaining cows a different way, not through Hindu *mohallas*. Police high officials were called to the spot to negotiate, but the two sides did not reach a compromise, and, in the midst of the discussions, someone brought one of the two cows to the spot. As the cow stood at the crossroads of Paharganj Bazaar and Chuna Mandi, angry crowds gathered on each side. The senior superintendent of police (SSP) decided to take the cow to Idgah through the less contentious route, but the procession was nevertheless attacked by huge crowds of angry Hindus and Sikhs, who threw stones and brickbats. The police used tear gas, and, when it failed, opened fire.[71]

Taking cows to slaughter from Paharganj to Sadar Bazar was a conflict-prone event that took place annually during Eid-ul-Zuha, often triggering clashes.[72] In this sense, the conflict followed the familiar pattern of communal riots in the city and could be understood as yet another instance of symbolic struggle over public space in the city. But soon enough, the localized conflict turned into a wave of deadly stabbings that began in Paharganj, spread to other localities in the city, and lasted for almost ten days, resulting in twenty-eight deaths and fifty-four people being seriously wounded. There were also several cases of arson. Sadar Bazar and its localities of Pahari Dhiraj and the Bara Hindu Rao, we should note, would also see ethnic cleansing ten months later.

A curfew was imposed; schools, colleges, and shops remained closed; and the city wore a deserted look. Foreshadowing the rumor-infused atmosphere that would characterize Delhi several months later, the nights were filled with shouts of communal slogans that began somewhere in Sadar Bazar and were picked up and spread to other localities, keeping people in different localities on the housetops, awake and watchful.[73]

The disturbances of November were more limited in their scope and intensity than the brutal violence that unfolded in other parts of India at the time, and that would engulf Delhi ten months later. Yet the stabbings were deadlier and more severe than the brick batting and *lathi* fighting that Delhi's streets had known in the past. They led to a high number of casualties and were accompanied by nerve-wracking panic. As the recently appointed Deputy Commissioner M. S. Randhawa emphasized, the serious turn that events took was connected to the violence erupting elsewhere in India at the time.[74] Indeed, the wave of stabbings must have resulted from the rival volunteer organizations' efforts to recruit and train young men in *lathi* and knife fighting. Muslim National Guards reportedly provided training in knife fighting in various mosques and rooftops during the nights just before the disturbances.[75]

The preparations for civil war that preceded the November violence only accelerated afterward. As in other parts of India, these preparations were connected to postwar demobilization. At the end of World War II, demobilized soldiers roamed around, and large quantities of arms and ammunition left behind by the American army circulated on the black market.[76] Expecting imminent attacks in light of events elsewhere, Muslim League leaders spoke of an urgent need to strengthen the defense of Muslim *mohallas*, and organized branches of the National Muslim Guards in various areas. On the Hindu side, a private meeting of the RSS took place in Karol Bagh on November 23, soon after the disturbances. It was presided over by Vasant Rao Oak, the RSS *pracharak* (full-time propagandist and worker) who had established the first branch in Delhi in 1936, and was attended by 250 prominent RSS workers. They passed several resolutions: to make inquiries about the number of Muslims residing in Hindu areas and how many of them could take part in riots; to arm all the Hindus of Delhi and its surrounding areas; to carry out strong anti-Muslim propaganda; to methodically supply knives and daggers; to supply all the Sikhs in Delhi with *kirpans* (daggers) and to cultivate "sweet relations" with them; to import firearms from Gwalior state; to provide the Hindus in the adjacent United Provinces areas of Meerut and Bareilly with firearms from the factory of one Sudarshan Shukla; to store all firearms in temples; and to provide the aforementioned Shukla with financial assistance to prepare more arms and weapons in his factory.[77] The report reveals that the violence that erupted in September 1947 had long been brewing under the surface. At least nine months beforehand— and several months before refugees started arriving in Delhi—the local RSS and the Hindu business community were engaged in systematic preparation for a civil war.

It should be emphasized that, although both sides prepared for a civil war, power in the city started to tilt against the Muslim League. In December 1946, the Muslim National Guards numbered seven hundred men and were not well organized, while the RSS had three thousand volunteers who performed physical exercise regularly. "Their policy is claimed to be purely defensive, but they are obviously a potential menace to law and order."[78]

Changes in the power balance on the street were paralleled at the upper level of political decision making. The Interim Government, which operated during the turbulent months of September 1946 to August 1947, has not received enough historiographical attention.[79] Its implications for Delhi are especially significant. As a central charge, Delhi was controlled by the Home Department through an appointed chief commissioner. Home Member Patel thereby took direct responsibility over its affairs. Patel criticized the Delhi Police's handling of the dispute in Paharganj, which turned into a large-scale riot.[80] One of the first changes that Patel initiated soon after the event was a change in the communal composition of the Delhi police. He ordered a correction of what he deemed an over-representation of Britons, Anglo-Indians, and Muslims, replacing them with Hindu and Sikh policemen. Though the process was gradual and, to Patel's mind, too slow, it is clear that eight months before the riots, under the direction of one of the strongest national leaders of the Congress, the Delhi police began to undergo a purge of both European and Muslim elements.[81]

THE TERRITORIALIZATION OF PAKISTAN: 1947

In 1947 the territorial meaning of Pakistan began to surface. On February 20, 1947, British Prime Minister Clement Attlee announced that Britain would withdraw by June 1948, and appointed Lord Mountbatten as the last viceroy of India, who would oversee the withdrawal. The announcement made the transfer of power palpable and rendered the competition for it even more urgent.

This was especially true in Punjab. There, the Muslim League received more votes than the regional Unionist Party, which had dominated Punjabi politics since 1923, but it did not succeed in forming a coalition, and the much-weakened Unionist Party managed to cling to power by forming a coalition government with the Congress Party and the Akali Sikhs. Fearing that British withdrawal would catch the Muslim League out of office in the most important Muslim-majority province, the League intensified its campaign of civil disobedience against the coalition government, which it had begun even before Attlee's announcement, and which led to Premier Khizr Hayat Tiwana's resignation on March 2. The campaign and the fall of the coalition government led to the outbreak of grave riots against Hindus and Sikhs in the western districts of Punjab. In reaction, Hindus and Sikhs, followed on March 8 by the Congress Working Committee, demanded that Punjab be divided in any future settlement. The following morning the *Hindustan Times* published the CWC resolution alongside maps showing two Punjabs and two Bengals.[82]

The events in Punjab spilled over into Delhi, and from early 1947 events in Delhi became totally enmeshed with those in Punjab. In late January, the Delhi Muslim League initiated demonstrations in sympathy with the civil disobedience campaign in Punjab. In both Punjab and Delhi, the League's public actions reflected its transformation into a mass movement based on popular support.[83] On January 25 it organized a complete *hartal* (strike) of Muslim shopkeepers to protest the arrest of Muslim League leaders in Lahore, along with a meeting in Jama Masjid attended by 25,000 and a procession of 2,500 around the city. When the procession dwindled, those who remained arrived in the Muslim League office, shouted slogans against nationalist Muslims, and forced Muslim shopkeepers to close their shops. This repeated itself with the observations of Punjab Day on February 2 and again on February 24. The League held a public meeting of 30,000 people and a procession of 6,000 (including 70 women) carrying provocative banners and enacting mock funerals of Premier Tiwana.[84]

Ironically, even tragically, this moment when the Muslim League appeared to reach its peak, reaping the fruits of years of mass mobilization, was also the beginning of its downfall. Underlying changes in power relations would soon come to the surface. Because, at this same moment in March, Hindu and Sikh refugees began to pour into the city, fleeing the riots in western Punjab. Their desperate condition and tales of horror were covered extensively by the press. On March 9, the RSS held a mass demonstration of power, with one hundred thousand participants, half of them from Delhi, attending its annual procession across the city.[85] Two days later, Hindu and Sikh leaders organized an Anti-Pakistan Day with a general *hartal*.[86] On March 23—a day after Lord Mountbatten arrived in Delhi, and the same day that Nehru welcomed leaders from other countries to the Asian Relations Conference in Purana Qila[87]—the Muslim League celebrated the annual Pakistan Day, holding flag salutations in various wards of the city, and decorating streets in Muslim-majority neighborhoods with green bunting. It held a meeting attended by nine thousand at the Anglo-Arabic College and a mass public meeting in Urdu Park. Muslim League leaders recited poems and delivered speeches exhorting Muslims to enlist in the Muslim National Guards and make sacrifices for the cause of Pakistan. Volunteers of the Muslim National Guard were present in almost all these functions. Despite these displays of strength, Muslim League leaders expressed in their meetings a growing understanding of their precariousness, fearing retaliation over events in Punjab.[88]

Such apprehension proved well founded. Trouble started in front of Jama Masjid just before the public meeting across the street. A jeep and a lorry carrying Sikhs armed with *kirpans* collided with a Muslim cyclist and began to attack Muslims who were gathering for the meeting. Soon after, not far from there, near the Gurudwara Sis Ganj on Chandni Chowk, Sikhs armed with *kirpans* attacked Muslim National Guards, killing one and seriously injuring another.[89] Fights and stabbings spread to various localities in the old city and to the adjacent localities of Paharganj, Sadar Bazar, and Karol Bagh, and continued for more than a month. Stabbing cases and curfews became a regular feature of everyday life in the city, and by the end of April, twenty Muslims and nine Hindus had been killed.

The events indicate a turning point. First, as Chief Commissioner William Christie observed, whereas communal disturbances in the past were linked to certain religious festivals, and conditions usually returned to normal soon after, these disturbances were not sparked by any religious occasion. They were "political," to use Christie's term, and it was unclear when and how they would stop.[90] Second, all three communities in the city were involved in the stabbing attacks equally, and coverage by the Hindu press (including Congress newspapers) and the Muslim Leagui press was equally inflammatory. Newspapers on both sides disclosed the religious identity of people involved in the violence, in contravention of longstanding instructions.[91] Third, as in Punjab, the communalization of the police had eroded public trust in them: Muslims accused Sikh police officers of discriminatory treatment, while Sikhs and Hindus complained against Muslim police officers.

Fourth, though Muslims were equally involved in the numerous stabbings, a closer look reveals that the power balance between the communities had begun to tilt against them, as a result of the vigorous preparations by the RSS, the change in the demographic composition of the Delhi police ordered by Patel, and the arrival of Hindu and Sikh refugees from Punjab. With the arrival of refugees, militant Sikhs also became prominent.

Groups of Sikhs, who looked like patrols of armed troops, roamed the city in lorries and jeeps, armed with *kirpans*, creating panic in Muslim localities they passed through. It was such a group of armed Sikhs riding a jeep that ignited the disturbances on Pakistan Day.[92] The Sikhs carried *kirpans* on a religious pretext, despite a prohibition on carrying weapons in the city, and this became a major source of contention and apprehension for Muslims. The *kirpans* also seem to explain why, though members of all three communities took to stabbing attacks, Muslim injuries proved more fatal.[93] Many of the victims were vulnerable *tonga* drivers on the streets. Intelligence reports reveal that before the disturbances broke out, members of the Akali Dal had made elaborate defensive and offensive preparations and formed an organization called the Akal Regiment. Two thousand volunteers enlisted to defend the Sikh community in Delhi, and its leaders were said to be involved in the incident near the

Jama Masjid. Pakistan Day, which used to be an annual demonstration of Muslim League strength in the city during the war years, was seriously challenged. Muslim National Guards leader Manzur-ul-Haq was arrested, and some members became demoralized and were reluctant to appear in uniform.[94]

During this time, in the luxury area of Connaught Place (Block B), Muslim residents complained of mysterious visits by Sikhs who started to collect systematic information on Muslim houses in the neighborhood.[95] In the same month, apparently as part of Patel's initiative to change the demographic composition of the Delhi police, the Muslim deputy superintendent of police, Delhi City, was replaced by a Hindu officer. This important post was traditionally occupied by Muslim officers. Members of the Muslim League met with the chief commissioner to express their nervousness.[96] Subtle but significant changes were taking place simultaneously in power relations on the ground and at the level of high politics.

Police reports from April onward reveal worrying signs of an intensifying buildup toward "a savage civil war."[97] They disclose the use of firearms in several incidents, accidental explosions in improvised "arms factories," and recovery of explosive substances. Members of all three communities applied for gun licenses and collected firearms, knives and daggers, even crude weapons such as catapults and arrows. According to Chief Commissioner Christie, people were willing to pay fabulous sums for a weapon.

Youth organizations were increasingly active, with the inequality of power between them deepening further. Muslim National Guards were seen parading daily in various localities in the walled city and to its west, shouting slogans of Pakistan. They also sought guidance from Muslim National Guards in Lahore in manufacturing bombs.[98] But there were overall signs of confusion in the Muslim League. A rift opened between moderates and those defined by the Criminal Investigation Department (CID) as the "extremist members," such as Sheikh Shuja-ul-Haq, Dr. Abdul Ghani Qureshi, and Anis Hashmi, who pressed for civil disobedience to demand that Delhi's administration ban Sikh *kirpans*, increase the number of Muslims in the police, and release Muslim National Guards arrested during the disturbances, especially their leader Manzur-ul-Haq.

Muslim National Guards associated with the extremist elements seized the Provincial Muslim League office and barred entry to moderate members, forcing the All-India Muslim League to intervene. They sought to set up their own defense committees in the various *mohallas* instead of the committees established by the Muslim League, which they deemed ineffective.[99] Concomitantly, the number of Muslim National Guards in Delhi decreased.[100]

The RSS, on the other hand, strengthened its power. Its systematic preparations included military training in the camp in Gurgaon and large purchases of arms and first aid. A sample of weapons ordered from Lahore "consisted of a metal catapult fitted with a powerful rubber and [the] arrow had a sharp iron spear-head attached to its point. The point was to be dipped in a poisonous chemical before use."[101] Reports named specific people in the Hindu community who were involved, including Mr. Birla (it was not mentioned which member of this wealthy business family), who purchased a large number of helmets for the RSS.[102] The RSS simultaneously bolstered its collaboration with the newly formed Sikh Akal Regiment. Sikh volunteers, for their part, trained in *lathi* and sword fighting, and Sikhs also purchased jeeps, motorcycles, and lorries to enable their armed *jathas* (armed bands) to move about rapidly. A large number of Sikh *kirpans* were manufactured daily under the license of one Mohan Singh in the Central Public Works Department, and there were reports of Hindus converting to Sikhism in the rural area for the sole purpose of carrying *kirpans*.[103] Overall, the information confirms Nehru's later complaint to Patel that the writing was on the wall, and that intelligence reports even named the persons and groups, but nothing was done in the matter.[104]

WHEN REALITY CONFRONTS UTOPIA:
MAY–AUGUST 1947

Concurrently with these preparations, the Congress and the Muslim League held intensive negotiations over independence after Mountbatten's arrival in India on March 22. Debates on the pages of the Delhi press crystallized around Pakistan, indicating that people were coming to terms with the fact that Pakistan was bound to be formed in one form or

another. Newspapers were full of speculation about its borders and con-
jectures about the details of partition.

The possible partition of Bengal and Punjab was especially controversial. Sikhs and Hindus demanded that Punjab be divided, so that non-
Muslim areas escape Muslim rule.[105] Refugees from Punjab arriving in
Delhi were especially insistent on dividing Punjab. These demands drove
home, most acutely, the territorial implications of a prospective partition.
It is no coincidence that precisely at this point, Delhi Muslim Leaguers started to explicitly and vocally demand that Delhi become a part
of Pakistan. One, Mumtaz Fateh Ali from New Delhi, wrote to Jinnah,
"The Headquarters of Pakistan Republic should on no account be either
at Karachi or Lahore or Calcutta, but at Delhi, the seat of the Moghul
Empire, in the footsteps of which the Pakistan Republic is to go."[106] Ali
Asadullah Khan from Hyderabad was adamant that "Delhi will be the
capital of Pakistan and Bombay or Nagpur may be the capital of Hindustan."[107] Muhammad Yamin Khan of the United Provinces Muslim
League wrote to Jinnah that, if he was forced to accept a partition of
Punjab, he should demand in return portions of Ambala and Jullundur in
eastern Punjab, along with Delhi and parts of western United Provinces
(including Meerut, Rohilkhand, Aligarh, and the cities of Agra and Lucknow), based on population exchange.[108] This wishful thinking combined
elements of the Aligarh professors' and Latif's schemes, showing their
imprint on the territorial imagination of Muslim Leaguers in the minority provinces.

Siddiqi recalls a growing anxiety about the future of the city. The consensus in his milieu was that Delhi should function as the joint capital
of Hindustan Pakistan.[109] In a public meeting on May 9, attended by
between ten thousand and twelve thousand people after Friday prayers in
Jama Masjid, Shaib-ul Hassan Bakhtiari proposed a resolution condemning the Congress plan to partition Punjab and demanding that Delhi
be part of Pakistan. Giving an account of the Mughal period and of the
building of Jama Masjid, the Red Fort, the Quwwat-ul-Islam mosque,
and the Nizamuddin *dargah* (Sufi shrine), the speaker asked the audience whether they could tolerate the inclusion of Delhi, where their forefathers' remains were buried, in "Akhand Hindustan" (a united India).

The audience replied in the negative.[110] He stressed that Delhi, which had been ruled by Muslim kings for seven hundred years, was the seat of Muslim culture and civilization, as attested by the many mosques and tombs of Muslim divines. He further claimed that Muslims were the largest group in the city, numbering 450,000, whereas Hindus numbered 400,000 and "Achhut" (untouchables) 150,000. Syed Mohammad Taqi, editor of *Jang*, likewise justified the inclusion of Delhi in Pakistan on a demographic principle, claiming that the 1941 census, taken during World War II, did not truly reflect the number of Muslims in Delhi. Many of them refrained from registering, he said, for fear of being enlisted in the army. Two other speakers, Maulvi Zuber Ahmed and Maulana Abdul Ghaffar Khan Kheri, dwelt at length on the history of Muslim invasions and rulers, and exhorted the audience to be prepared to make sacrifices for the inclusion of Delhi in Pakistan.

Muslim League leader Abdul Salam voiced similar views a week earlier in a mass meeting of five thousand people following the Friday prayer in Fatehpuri Mosque. He warned the Muslims of Delhi that their opponents were openly saying that Delhi could not be part of Pakistan, and that if Muslims did not wake up, they would find themselves part of Akhand Hindustan. Such utterances bring to the surface longstanding, perhaps implicit, assumptions that Delhi would be part of Pakistan. Similarly, in the later part of May, some Muslim League members formed a Delhi Provincial Pakistan Committee with the object of securing the inclusion of Delhi in Pakistan.[111] That such a demand was voiced on the eve of the announcement of partition underscores the hold that the amorphous idea of Pakistan had on Muslim publics in the city, even at that late stage.

At the same time, doubts about the viability of a Pakistan cut in two by 2,000 kilometers of Indian territory also became pressing. On May 21, Jinnah famously demanded a corridor connecting East and West Pakistan.[112] The Delhi Hindu press described it as "fantastic and grotesque," but it was endorsed by the Muslim League press, which "did not bother to securitize its practicality."[113]

It is at this troubling time that Siddiqi locates the beginning of the end. Uncertain about the defensibility of such a corridor, he went to see the historian Ishtiaq Husain Qureshi at Delhi University, who assured him that Jinnah's demand was totally legitimate under the "Right of the Sealed Wagons" in international law. Siddiqi rushed to the India Coffee House, where his Hindu pals were waiting to taunt him about the absurdity of Jinnah's new demand, and he felt he overwhelmed them with the mysterious and innovative international law concept.[114] Notwithstanding, doubts began to creep in, as his friends asked him where he would live after partition. As reality confronted utopia, the troubling practical questions that he had avoided took center stage, and the frightening possibility of leaving Delhi arose.

On June 3 Mountbatten made his historic announcement that British withdrawal would take place much earlier, on August 15, 1947, and would effectuate the partition of India. Once Nehru, Jinnah, and the Sikh leader Baldev Singh publicly endorsed the plan, the way was paved for a rushed withdrawal. Mountbatten's decision to advance the transfer of power from June 1948 to August 1947 caught the Muslim League in Delhi unprepared. To Siddiqi, the two months preceding independence were like a speeding train. As the contours of Pakistan took clearer shape, doubts about it emerged, and the very air was filled with suspense.

Mountbatten's plan entailed the division of Punjab and Bengal, rather than transferring them to Pakistan intact. In accepting the plan on June 9, the League turned its back on Jinnah's longstanding insistence that he would never agree to a "maimed, mutilated and moth-eaten Pakistan."[115] Perhaps Jinnah was not such a superior political strategist after all, suggested Siddiqi's Hindu friends sarcastically, as they sat at the coffee house. Wasn't the Muslim League caught in its own trap?

It now became clear that the Muslim community would be divided between two nation-states. Delhi's Muslims, reported the chief commissioner, were not happy about living in Hindustan but were "apparently reconciling themselves to the decision taken by the leaders of the Muslim League."[116] This laconic statement merely hints at the emotional turmoil in which Siddiqi and others found themselves.

Nawab Siddiq Ali Khan, leader of the All-India Muslim National Guards, delivered a speech in a meeting of the Muslim National Guards in Jama Masjid on June 14, to an audience of twelve hundred people.

Khan, who would leave for Pakistan upon independence, emphasized that an exchange of population was not viable, and that Muslims in Hindustan would have to remain there. Invoking the hostage theory, he assured his listeners that their interests would be safeguarded by the presence of Hindus in Pakistan. He regretted that Delhi's Muslims would have to live in Hindustan but stressed this was not the fault of the Muslim League but of the Mughal emperors, who failed to convert the people in Delhi's vicinity to the Muslim faith.[117] Such a speech by the commander of the All-India Muslim National Guards was a blow to members of the Delhi branch. In a meeting held in a mosque in Sadar Bazar, they strongly denounced the decision to leave Delhi, Agra, and Ajmer Sharif outside Pakistan. They sent desperate messages to Muslim National Guards branches in other cities, asking them to send volunteers and ammunition to help them capture Delhi by force.

Khan also rejected their request to launch a civil disobedience campaign in Delhi to protest the conviction of their leader Manzur-ul-Haq. This request was in fact a major source of a rift between the Delhi Muslim National Guards and the moderate sections of the Delhi Muslim League, which were more cautious. The Delhi Muslim National Guards turned to All-India Muslim League leaders Jinnah, Liaquat Ali Khan, and Nawab Siddiq Ali Khan. But rather than backing them up, these leaders, who would all soon leave for Pakistan, gave them the cold shoulder. Launching a disruptive popular movement across Delhi's streets was out of the question now.

Pakistan was in sight, recalls Siddiqi, and "it had nothing of the gloss and glitter of the dream we had dreamt of, the vision we had projected . . . a wonderland with flowers blossoming and birds singing."[118] Admiration for the Muslim leaders was soon replaced by bitterness and betrayal. Siddiqi describes a scene that severely shook his confidence soon after partition was announced. A delegation of Muslim women went to Jinnah's house on Aurangzeb Road, shouting slogans in support of Pakistan. They were received very reluctantly by his sister. When Jinnah finally came out, he told them, "Those who could make it to Pakistan at all would be welcomed. Others would have to stay in India. Pakistan cannot accommodate all of you. As for your sacrifices, they had to be made for Pakistan in any case."[119]

Muslim League leaders departed for Pakistan, leaving behind a fearful public to face the consequences of Pakistan's establishment. Having sold his residence on 10 Aurangzeb Road to the Hindu businessman Seth Ramkrishna Dalmia, Jinnah departed for Karachi on August 7, asking his followers to leave old grudges behind and become loyal citizens of India.[120] Other prominent local Muslim Leaders would do the same. Habibur Rahman, at the time president of the Delhi Municipal Committee, who owned a lot of property, sold his building in Chandni Chowk to Punjab National Bank, and left for Pakistan.[121] Siddiqi, like many Muslims of Delhi, felt abandoned by the Muslim League leadership.

Maulana Azad recalled that many of the Muslim League leaders came to see him afterward, claiming that Jinnah had deceived them. He could not at first understand what they meant, but gradually he realized "that these men had formed a picture of partition which had no relevance to the real situation. . . . these Muslim Leaguers had been foolishly persuaded that once Pakistan was formed, Muslims, whether they came from a majority or a minority province, would be regarded as a separate nation and would enjoy the right of determining their own future."[122] Such expectations were reminiscent of ideas of Pakistan that circulated throughout the 1940s. Similarly, last-minute attempts by provincial Muslim Leaguers in the United Provinces and Bombay to advance proposals for creating "Pakistan pockets," "autonomous units," and even "sovereign independent Muslim states" inside India[123] echoed the Aligarh professors' scheme and the one formulated by Latif. Jinnah's departure shattered these expectations, and many turned now to Azad—the man who until not long before had been reviled as a traitor to Islam.[124]

Siddiqi felt that Delhi was no longer his home—it would be the capital city of independent India, where he would have no place as an ardent supporter of Pakistan. His Hindu interlocutors no longer asked him whether he would go to Pakistan, but when. A growing stream of Hindu and Sikh refugees, who settled everywhere they could, exerted terror on the Muslims, and Siddiqi, along with many others, replaced his Sherwani pajamas with a shirt and trousers. "We were all very, very afraid. The sight of the ferocious-looking, *kirpan*-carrying, dressed-in-black Sikh fanatics . . . struck terror in our hearts. We avoided their fiery stares as best we could: like a pigeon in the face of a wild cat."[125]

ON THE BRINK OF CATASTROPHE

Independence was declared on August 15. The streets were festive and the atmosphere celebratory, yet, as Nehru delivered his riveting "Tryst with Destiny" speech, the city was on the verge of crisis, packed with Hindu and Sikh refugees from West Punjab.[126] By August 5, there were already 80,000 refugees in the capital, and 4,000–5,000 refugees were arriving in Delhi every day. They brought with them tales of atrocities committed in Punjab—neighborhoods besieged, houses burned, and women abducted. News of the riots in the Punjab appeared in bold letters in the newspapers' front pages, inflaming communal resentment.

The refugees also exerted unprecedented pressure on the city's resources, and Delhi faced acute shortages of food, clothing, fuel, electricity, and, of course, housing.[127] The real estate market spiraled out of control. The refugees, argued Shahid Ahmed Dehlvi bitterly, were far from poor, hungry people. They frantically bought up property in the city, driving prices up.[128] A *Hindustan Times* article of August 21 claimed that the upper-class refugees were a disturbing factor, buying up firms and residential premises at fancy prices with money they had amassed in the black market during the war.[129] The first waves of refugees, which arrived before partition, were mostly of middle- and upper-class backgrounds. Wealthy Hindu and Sikh businessmen engaged in anticipatory migration to Delhi from June onward, transferring bank accounts, registering Punjabi companies, and opening offices in Connaught Place. By independence, the upscale locality of Model Town in Lahore had been emptied out of its non-Muslim residents.[130] On August 28, RSS members held a secret meeting, condemning Hindu refugees who, despite repeated warnings, purchased Muslim properties for enormous sums of money. The members resolved to set fire to all such buildings, commencing with the new branch of the Punjab National Bank in Civil Lines.[131]

Property was an important catalyst for the imminent upheaval. The refugees were divided into people of means, who bought up property and pushed up prices, and those who were excluded from the real estate market. Of the latter, some eventually resorted to violence, occupying Muslim houses by force during the September riots and afterwards. In Karol Bagh—which would be one of the worst-hit localities—Muslim houses were marked in advance. In fact, we know that, already in November 1946, the RSS in this *mohalla*, in the private meeting presided over by the *pracharak* Oak, decided to survey Muslim houses in the locality. Then house prices shot up. Dehlvi tells of a Muslim friend from Karol Bagh who bought his house there before the war for Rs. 8,000. When refugees started to arrive in the city, he decided to sell the house and leave for Pakistan. He initially asked Rs. 25,000 but, as prices kept rising, he increased his demand to Rs. 40,000 and then to Rs. 50,000. When a buyer agreed to the price, he demanded that they pay Rs. 60,000, then Rs. 75,000 and Rs. 80,000. At this point the riots in Karol Bagh broke out, and he lost everything apart from the clothes he wore. Just before he escaped, he entrusted the house key with a Hindu neighbor, asking him to protect the house until peace was restored. But even as he was escaping the house with his family, a group of refugees already burst in, disregarding the neighbor's protests.[132]

Who broke into the house? It is difficult to know for certain. Perhaps they were refugees of lesser means, left hungry and homeless by spiraling property prices and out-of-control rent.[133] Or perhaps they were members of the Sikh gangs that roamed around East Punjab and the princely states, taking over Muslim properties. Property was a driving force in the turmoil that took over the city in 1947–1950, as people bought, sold, rented out, and illegally occupied what came to be known as "evacuee property." The next chapter will attend to this issue in detail.

Concomitantly, disturbances in Gurgaon and Alwar pushed Muslim Meo refugees into Delhi, and the Delhi Provincial Muslim League settled about ten thousand Meos in two camps.[134] They gathered in the Urdu *maidan* (open area) in front of Jama Masjid. For the Muslims living in the Jama Masjid locality, as Dehlvi recalls, the Meo camp served as a buffer, protecting them from the Hindu localities and giving them a sense of security.[135]

Nirmala Jain recalls how the arrival of the Meos was experienced from the other side of this "buffer zone." The Jains' *haveli* (mansion) was situated in a sensitive location, facing the Jama Masjid, at the border between the Muslim *mohalla* and the Hindu one. As the Meos settled in the Urdu *maidan*, rumors of their excessively violent character intensified the anxieties of Hindu and Jain residents. Jain remembers her mother staying awake night after night, constantly investigating the various sounds and sights coming from the direction of the Meo camp. The Meos, Jain realizes retrospectively, were no less terrified—and thus would light up their lamps and patrol their camp throughout the night, further igniting her mother's fears.[136]

When examined side by side, Dehlvi's and Jain's accounts draw a troubling picture of the communalization of space, turning the city into a geography of fear, with clearly drawn boundaries between Hindu and Muslim territories. Accounts of this period convey a city ridden by unbearable tension. Iron gates were placed on the narrow alleys, turning neighborhoods into small fortifications.[137] Male residents organized into groups who patrolled the locality and guarded from the rooftops during long curfews and sleepless nights.

Phool Chand Jain recalls preparations in his locality of Jawahar Nagar:

> People were very passionate. Now it's difficult to recall names but the general perception was that these were RSS men. They told people in the different *mohallas* that we should all get organized, lest we all get killed. They said, "You should get weapons . . . collect *lathis*, enclose the *mohalla*, build fortifications." This kind of thing began on a regular basis two months before . . . even three. This activity began with great vengeance. . . . We in our homes also planned that first we'd kill our women, we'd set a fire, and then leave the house so that they wouldn't be dishonored. So, on one side were meetings of the Muslim League people, on the other side were meetings of people in the *mohallas*. All this infused people's hearts with great fervor.[138]

This recollection is intriguing, because Jain had been a longstanding member of the Gandhian movement in Delhi. In the aftermath of the riots, we may recall, he and his son volunteered in the relief work and gathered up the dead bodies of Muslims. Nevertheless, as he recollects preparations for a civil war, his language slips from "they" (RSS members) to "we in our homes," and moves to a chilling account of how "we" got prepared to kill "our" women, lest they be dishonored. It shows how, within the context of aggressive polarization and the brutalities that swept north India, distinctions between the Hindu right and Congress became blurred, and everything was congealed into Hindu or Muslim. Noteworthy is how central the patriarchal impulse to protect women's bodies was to this dynamic. The slip from "RSS people" to "we in our homes" might be a key to deciphering the violence as a product of pre-planning and a climate of fear sustained by rumors.

WHO IS RESPONSIBLE? SEPTEMBER 1947

As Gyanendra Pandey alerts us, the primary sources on mass violence are marked by the "signature of the rumor," and it is extremely difficult to identify specific faces in a crowd dynamic, let alone their motives.[139] Thus every attempt at a historical reconstruction of such events is doomed to be incomplete. Yet the evidence gathered here enables us to sketch out, even if partially, the overall structure and the main perpetrators of the September violence in Delhi. Rather than a spontaneous outbreak of passions on the part of disgruntled and traumatized refugees, we see a multilayered dynamic in which both locals and outsiders, preplanning and spontaneity, were in play.

The local RSS bears great responsibility for planning and orchestrating the violence. Let us consider the bomb explosion in Fatehpuri Mosque, which both Siddiqi and Dehlvi describe. Intelligence reports confirm that it was RSS members who threw the bomb from an apartment in the adjacent Gadodia Market. The location has symbolic resonance. We may recall the high-profile dispute between Gadodia and the Fatehpuri Mosque, discussed in the previous chapter. The dispute belonged in the "traditional" pattern of competition between communal groups over space in the city, which was more symbolic in nature and resulted in limited communal riots. But the dispute was also one of the first issues that enabled the small and insignificant Delhi branch of the

Muslim League to mobilize and gather support from the Muslim public. It was here that, throughout the war, the Muslim League voiced its demand for Pakistan in weekly post-prayer meetings—and it was here that the RSS threw the bomb that began its lethal attack on Delhi's Muslim.

RSS preparations began long in advance, in collusion with the local Hindu business community, which helped to finance the purchase of arms. Such collaboration happened in other cities, too, notably in Calcutta during the Great Killing of August 1946.[140] Importantly, the RSS and the Arya Samaj were the first to set up relief camps and aid for the refugees, long before the government stepped in.[141] Many of the refugees, especially those already belonging to the Hindu right in the Punjab, were absorbed into RSS networks and took part in the violence. It is no wonder that enrollment in the RSS increased dramatically in precisely those localities that were hit hardest in September, where refugees settled in Muslim homes. The clear-cut dichotomy between locals and outsiders that traditional sources describe must give way to a recognition of mutual relations.

There is also clear evidence that, from November 1946 onward, the RSS reached out to the Sikh community in Delhi and that, from March 1947, Sikhs had a more aggressive presence in the city. Again, it is difficult to identify who these Sikhs were. They comprised an amalgam of locals, newcomers from the Punjab who settled in Delhi, and outsiders, members of the Sikh gangs that roamed around East Punjab and the princely states at the time—offshoots of the demobilization drive at the end of the World War II, which, alongside the American weapon dumps, invested the partition violence with military material. Jugal Kishore Khanna recollects:

> Sikhs came in the Frontier Mail and they travelled without tickets. There was no question of buying tickets in those days. They came to Delhi and committed violence and put locks on the properties of the Muslims, went back, then came back and then they allotted those properties to Hindus and so on. That was a regular thing which went on for about two months.[142]

Nehru noted at the close of September that information had reached him from many sources, which indicates that the trouble in Delhi was caused by certain well-organised bands, some Sikh and some Hindu. Probably most of the murders were committed by one or more organized and well-armed Sikh bands which had come here especially for the purpose and which subsequently visited Simla and Kalka and other places. The Hindu bands seemed to owe allegiance to the R.S.S. It seems to me clear that the R.S.S. have had a great deal to do with the present disturbances, not only in Delhi but elsewhere. In Amritsar their activities have been very obvious.[143]

Other sources indicate the responsibility of certain local groups that took advantage of the situation to settle old scores or take control of Muslim areas. Dehlvi points to the *mehtar* and *chamar* sweepers of Kalan Masjid near Turkman Gate, where, we know, Muslim National Guards had a prominent presence, with daily parades and loud slogans throughout 1947. According to Dehlvi, *mehtars* set Muslim houses on fire. As these attacks became bolder, the Muslims responded fiercely. This, in turn, led to the intervention of RSS groups and, subsequently, of the military.

Clearly, policemen and parts of the military were complicit too. The Delhi police in the late colonial period was dominated by Muslims, who comprised roughly 75 percent of the force. Patel, as we saw, began to change the composition of the force. While he made progress at the upper level, it is not clear how far this change proceeded at the lower ranks by September.[144] According to Home Secretary R. N. Banerjee, unlike in other provinces, Muslim policemen in Delhi were not given the option to leave for Pakistan, and hence, when riots broke out, the police force remained predominantly Muslim. Many of them deserted in the midst of the crisis and fled to Purana Qila, along with their guns. When Patel heard of this, he instructed that all Muslim police leaving for Pakistan by railway be intercepted. Banerjee relates that he had the opportunity to question a few constables

and some of them were really very sensible. They said that they did not find anybody responsible to whom they could hand over their rifles and so they did not want to leave them. They threw away their rifles on me, asking me to take charge of them, adding that they were not interested in any rifles; they simply wanted to go away; they simply wanted to go away.[145]

The subtle change in the balance of power that had begun in the aftermath of the November 1946 riots thus reached its zenith in September 1947. This moment dramatically changed the composition of Delhi's police, turning it from a Muslim-dominated force into one in which Muslims are almost absent. Most of the vacancies were hastily filled by Hindu and Sikh refugees from the Punjab, who had "tainted sympathies" and apparently complicit in the violence.[146]

The army stationed in Delhi was also partisan, composed mostly of Hindus and Sikhs who did not prove reliable during the riots. One of the first steps taken by the Emergency Committee was to bring in the Madras troops from the south, who, according to various sources, were geographically and emotionally distanced from the experience of partition and played a key role in overcoming the initial crisis.[147] Yet policing forces—both official and voluntary—as we shall see in the next chapter, would continue to play a partisan role in the violence that lingered on until 1950.

The next chapter will also describe a clash within the Congress high command between Nehru and Patel over what transpired in Delhi. Nehru would accuse Patel of a communal outlook and of sponsoring communally minded officials, notably Deputy Commissioner Mohinder Singh Randhawa. To clarify, there is no direct link between Patel and the violence. Yet, as this chapter established, from November 1946 onward, Patel strengthened Hindu and Sikh elements in the local police just as the transfer of power drew near and the territorial implications of Pakistan gradually became clearer. Simultaneously, when he was asked in June to curtail volunteer paramilitary organizations all across India, Patel resisted: "So long as the ML [Muslim League] members are in the government and are not prepared to dissociate themselves from the activities of the MLNG [Muslim League National Guard], no action can be taken against [RSS]."[148] Internal correspondence of the Home Department reveals that Patel and his secretaries felt that, given the dysfunction of the police forces, it would be better to leave communities to fend for themselves through these voluntary youth organizations. Put differently, the high command decided to let the streets police themselves. Both Muslim and Hindu and Sikh residents of the city sensed this. As streams of refugees started to change the demographic composition of the city, even before partition, it became abundantly clear who would "own" Delhi.

Truly, during the September massacre, some of the Muslim quarters resisted, and some sections of the Delhi Muslim National Guards fought hard. They may have thrown bombs and used guns, even Bren guns. We may recall that Dr. Abdul Ghani Qureshi of the extremist faction of the Delhi Muslim League and the Delhi Muslim National Guards was charged with the murder of Dr. Joshi in Karol Bagh. Thus, the widely circulated rumors about a Delhi Muslim conspiracy to capture Delhi by force might have had a grain of truth: a core of Muslim National Guards hardliners, long harboring dreams of Pakistan, may have thought out an underground operation. If so, it was totally unrealistic.

The rumor of a Muslim attempted coup was blown out of proportion and justified the vicious attacks on Muslim neighborhoods, thereby linking the orchestrated aspects of the massacre with the more spontaneous ones. In times of crisis, when familiar reality rapidly transforms, rumors become the preferred medium of communication, inciting panic, and enabling the aggressive majority to experience itself as a victim. There is a strong resemblance between the rumors that emerge during crises and everyday mental structures, images, and stereotypes.[149] Thus, the rumors of Muslim conspiracy fed on and exaggerated longstanding patterns of thought in Delhi's forms of sociality—the longstanding claim Muslims had on Delhi as "a Muslim city," the strength of certain Muslim groups, such as the *bandhanis*, in street fights, the dominance of Muslims in the arms trade, and the militant and vocal presence of the Muslim National Guards.

Rumors thus had their share in what followed: a massacre of the Muslim population with clearly purificatory characteristics. The Muslim League became a nonentity in the city, and Muslims now gathered around the Jamiat Ulama-e Hind. September 1947 was the critical moment in which the minoritization of Delhi's Muslims took place. In October 1947 it was Maulana Azad's turn to deliver a speech in the Jama Masjid to a demoralized audience:

FIGURE 2.3 *Maulana Azad addressing a crowd to mark the first anniversary of independence, with the Jama Masjid in the backdrop. The photograph was taken in August, 1948, ten months after his famous speech in this setting. Source: Photo Division, Press Information Bureau, Ministry of Information and Broadcasting, Government of India.*

Today, when I see the agitation in your eyes and the desolation of your hearts, I suddenly recall all the forgotten stories of the last few years. Do you remember? I had called out to you, and you cut my tongue off; I raised my pen, and you cut off my hands; I tried to walk ahead, but you chopped off my feet; I tried to turn around and you broke my back; when the bitter politics of the past seven years, which have now abandoned you, were still in their infancy, I shook you on the road to peril, but you not only ignored my call, you renewed all the traditions of forgetfulness and denial. The result is well known, that today those very dangers have surrounded you whose fear had led you far away from the Straight Path.[150]

CODA

Dehlvi described how, with the opening of the Purana Qila refugee camp, the Meos were moved out of Urdu *maidan*. The "buffer zone" that had given the Jama Masjid residents some degree of confidence was eliminated, leaving the residents increasingly vulnerable to attacks that came closer and closer to the Muslim locality, as the houses surrounding them were taken over by refugees. Jama Masjid was located between two Hindu areas—Bazaar Sita Ram on the one side and Daryaganj on the other. When the Muslim residents of Kalan Masjid were driven away, Jama Masjid became even more exposed. Both Dehlvi and Siddiqi's recollections of these days are dominated by the sense of a noose tightening around their necks. This ushered in a period of great confusion and tension within the Muslim localities, as residents debated whether they should stay or migrate. Attempts to impose collective discipline on the residents failed, as more and more families started to sneak out of the localities.

Delhi's Muslims turned into refugees in their own city, like the Muslims who had fled in the aftermath of the 1857 Revolt and hidden in the ruins and villages surrounding Delhi. It is not surprising that Muslim memoirs describe the riots of 1947 as a repetition, even an extension, of 1857. Both were tragic events of epic proportions, involving massacres, destruction, and large-scale exodus. If 1857 was a brutal attack on Muslim Delhi, 1947 was its death blow.

To Ghalib, the quintessential Urdu poet of nineteenth-century Delhi, the city itself died in the aftermath of 1858: "Delhi was 'a city of the dead.' Did someone ask about Delhi? 'Yes, there was once a city of that name in the realm of India.'"[151] Almost a century later, Dehlvi concluded his reportage thus: "The scar of the separation from Delhi will remain forever. Delhi is still there, and Muslims still reside there, but where is that Delhi? Delhi died. . . . Long live Delhi."[152]

Dehlvi left for the Purana Qila camp and from there took a train for Lahore on September 19. Siddiqi left Delhi on October 9. It is to the expansion of the circle of violence and its persistent, lingering nature that we now turn.

CHAPTER 3

AN UNCERTAIN STATE CONFRONTS
"EVACUEE PROPERTY"

WHEN MADHUSUDAN, an aspiring Hindi writer and journalist, first arrived in Delhi in the early 1950s, he lived with a friend in Kasabpura, once a Muslim-majority neighborhood in Sadar Bazar. Madhusudan's endless excursions in search of employment in the big city exhausted him physically and emotionally. His only refuge from depression was the sitar music played by Ibadat Ali during the long, sleepless nights. Ali was nominally the owner of the house but, in reality, its most marginal inhabitant. The house in Kasabpura had been given to his forefathers many generations before by the Mughal court for their service as professional sitar musicians. Before partition, Ali had lived in the main portion of the house and rented out the other rooms to Muslim tenants. Then, during the September riots, all his tenants fled. Ali hesitated for a while but, one night, finally took his young daughter and quietly slipped out of the house. They left for Lahore in Pakistan. When they returned three months later, also in the middle of the night, they found that the house had been occupied by Hindu refugees in their absence. Ali applied to the Custodian of Evacuee Property and, after numerous petitions, somehow managed to clear the upper room on the rooftop. The refugees who remained in the house persistently harassed him and denied him access to the main water pump in the courtyard. While his assertive daughter would quarrel with them, the old man became submissive and slowly faded away, withdrawing into himself and his sitar playing.

Ibadat Ali is a touching minor character in Mohan Rakesh's *Andhere Band Kamre* (Dark closed rooms), a Hindi novel that takes place in Delhi in the 1950s. By depicting Ali as a scion of sitar players long patronized by the Mughal court, Rakesh comments on the disappearance of the social and cultural world of Mughal Delhi. More narrowly, this is a literary representation of the gradual encroachment of refugees on Muslim-majority areas such as Kasabpura—a process that will form the focus of this chapter. The shrinking presence of Ibadat Ali in his own house is symbolized by the faded letters of his name on the signboard at the house's entrance—his first name is totally erased, while the word Ali, a generic sign of Muslim identity, is faintly visible. Ten years later, when the protagonist returns to Delhi, he notices that the letters have gone forever.

The signboard as a symbol of Muslim marginalization in the city functions similarly in another post-partition Hindi novel about Delhi, perhaps the most famous one—*Jhutha Sach* (The false truth) by Yashpal. When the Punjabi businessman Pandit Girdharilal Datta moves to Delhi from Lahore in September 1947, he erases the name of the original Muslim owner of the house he comes to live in and writes his own name in its place. As in *Andhere Band Kamre*, this act stands for the demographic transformation accompanying partition and its broader ramifications.[1]

It is telling that both novels pay attention to the return of thousands of Muslims to Delhi during 1948. Like Ibadat Ali, who returns to Delhi from Lahore, Abdul Samad, the original owner of the house in Daryaganj depicted in *Jhutha Sach*, returns to Delhi and stakes a claim to his old house, initiating a property dispute between him and Pandit Girdharilal. As we will see, at the crux of the debates and struggles over Muslim property was the uncertainty of Muslim belonging in post-partition India. This uncertainty reflected conflicting visions of the Indian nation and the Muslim minority's place in it—and led to an unstable Muslim presence, as many of them moved back and forth across the border in the first years after partition.

Yet there are differences in the two stories. While Ibadat Ali's house in Kasabpura is illegally occupied during the riots, Samad's house in

Daryaganj is willingly exchanged, just before the riots break out, for Pandit Girdharilal's house in Lahore. This is a fictional representation of the other channel through which property ownership in Delhi was dramatically transformed in the context of partition and its aftermath—the many private transactions between Hindus and Muslims of the middle and upper classes.[2] As we noted in the previous chapter, Muhammad Ali Jinnah himself sold his house on Aurangzeb Road to the Hindu businessman Ramkrishan Dalmia before he left for Karachi.[3]

It is also noteworthy that Pandit Girdharilal needs to protect the house from the crowds of poor Punjabi refugees who threaten to break in at any moment, oblivious to his cries that this is no longer a Muslim residence but his own house, legally transferred to him. The hungry and tired crowd argues that it is unfair that such a large place houses only two old people, and that Pandit Girdharilal and his wife should make room for others.

Taken together, these two novels provide clues to the central place of evacuee property in the history of post-partition Delhi, and the dynamics through which ownership of houses was transferred from Muslim evacuees to Hindu and Sikh refugees. While the story of Ibadat Ali tells of the larger trend of Muslim dispossession and marginalization, *Jhutha Sach* complicates this picture by depicting the role of socioeconomic factors, which caused friction within religious communities while creating alliances across them. It is their similar economic class that allows Pandit Girdharilal to reach an agreement on property exchange with Abdul Samad, and class that separates him and the crowds of refugees of lesser means. Thus, alongside ideological and communal divisions, class will be central to this chapter. Let us begin by introducing the main features of the mayhem in 1947–50.

PERSISTENT VIOLENCE

After the violence of September 1947, Delhi was in a sorry state. Municipal services broke down and were slow to recover. It took a while to clear the streets of the dead bodies, and heaps of garbage continued to be a feature of everyday life.[4] While the municipality and local volunteers embarked on "cleaning days," the sanitary situation in the city was incessantly challenged by the stream of refugees from West Pakistan. Refugee camps were gradually set up; the biggest in Kingsway, north of Old Delhi, near Civil Lines and the university campus, where the 1911 Darbar announcing the shifting of the capital to Delhi took place. It consisted of four main World War II–era military barracks: Edward Line, Outram Line, Reeds Line, and Hudson Line. The barracks and tents that had housed the soldiers during the war now housed the refugees. The other three main refugee camps were in Rajinder Nagar, the Purana Qila (after it was emptied of Muslims), and Pul Bangash.[5] But the camps could not meet demand, and refugees occupied Muslim mosques and shrines as well as municipal schools. The city's education system shut down for a few months, leaving refugee and other children loitering in the streets.[6] The city was packed with homeless people conducting their domestic lives on railway platforms and every available street corner. The long queues of desperate refugees outside rationing offices became characteristic of the urban landscape, featuring prominently in fiction and memoir representations of the period.[7] By January 1948, four hundred thousand refugees had already registered in Delhi, and more people were living on the streets than in houses.[8] Outside the city, the mayhem was exacerbated by floods that dislocated whole villages across the Yamuna.[9]

Severe food and housing shortages, congestion, and squalor were accompanied by a prolonged crisis of law and order—a rise in crime in general, and violence targeting the Muslim minority in particular.[10] Standard nationalist narratives tend to delimit partition violence in Delhi to September 1947, but violence continued long after. Far from an event neatly bounded in a short time span, partition was a protracted process.

We concluded the previous chapter with Dehlvi's and Siddiqui's anxiety that the noose was tightening around their necks. While the violence of early September was concentrated in demographically mixed localities, the circle of violence expanded in the following weeks and came closer and closer to Muslim-majority localities within the walled city and in Sadar Bazar, with attacks on Bahadurgarh Road, Bara Hindu Rao, Pahari Dhiraj, and Pul Bangash. There were frequent cases of stabbing, stone throwing, looting of Muslim shops, sacking of mosques and burning of religious books, and forcible occupation of Muslim houses and shops.

To be sure, the chief commissioner heaved a sigh of relief when Bakr-Id passed off peacefully, thanks to Muslims' refraining from slaughtering cows in sensitive consideration of the feelings of the majority. Others saw it as an indication of the fearful state of mind to which the city's Muslims were reduced.[11] It was, indeed, a far cry from the disturbances that had broken out a year before on the same occasion.

Violence escalated as winter approached and more and more people found themselves on the streets, exposed to the cold. By November an increasing enrollment in the RSS (Rashtriya Swayamsevak Sangh, the Hindu nationalist organization) was reported in Sabzi Mandi, Karol Bagh, and Paharganj—the localities where the September violence had taken place and where approximately one hundred thousand refugees had settled. The growing strength of the RSS was evident in a well-attended procession that ranged over the entire city in December.[12]

In the meantime, Mahatma Gandhi pursued his unflagging efforts to bring peace to the city. His messages were broadcast on the radio and covered extensively in the daily newspapers. His prayer meetings had a powerful effect on the crowds, as described in reportages and memoirs of the period.[13] Yet Gandhi could not effect a miraculous transformation, and the prayer meetings were often interrupted by groups of bitter refugees who protested when Gandhi included verses from the Quran. They resented his insistence on Muslims' belonging in the city and his criticism of Sikh and Hindu refugees' disruptive effect. It was even reported that a group of refugees burst into one of his meetings and killed a Muslim in his presence.[14]

It was against this background that Gandhi undertook his final fast unto death on January 12, 1948. Gandhi conditioned the termination of his fast on a complete change of heart and restoration of peace, protection of Muslim life and property, and repairing of shrines and mosques, especially the *dargah* (Sufi shrine) of Qutbuddin Bakhtiyar Kaki in Mehrauli. Various Congress and socialist groups initiated peace meetings and processions in the city. After key bureaucrats, Congress leaders, nationalist Muslims, and even RSS leaders signed a pledge to restore peace and protect Muslims, Gandhi agreed to end his fast on January 18. A campaign to vacate mosques followed, along with a peaceful celebration of the *Urs* at Mehrauli, in which Muslims, Hindus, and Sikhs participated.[15]

Yet violence continued in the midst of the fast, targeting Muslims and Congress peace processions. The atmosphere in the city was highly polarized. Hindu-right circles resented the Indian government's decision to release Pakistan's share of British India's cash assets while the war in Kashmir raged on, and saw Gandhi's fast as political blackmail to achieve precisely this aim. Hindu Mahasabha leaders criticized the peace pledge and took action against members who signed it. A few days after Gandhi ended his fast, a first attempt on his life was made by Madan Lal. In the Arya Samaj procession that followed, Hindu Mahasabha leaders participated and six thousand people attended, shouting slogans against Gandhi and the Muslims and praising Madan Lal.[16]

On January 30, on his way to a prayer meeting in Birla House, Gandhi was shot dead by Nathuram Godse, who had a long association with the RSS and the Hindu Mahasabha. At the public funeral, Gandhi's bier was borne on a carriage and taken in procession from Birla House to the banks of the Yamuna River. The streets were packed with people expressing their reverence and grief. Crowds attacked the offices and residences of RSS and Hindu Mahasabha leaders and associated newspapers.[17] The shockwaves created by the assassination gave the Congress government and the Delhi administration momentum to take severe action against the RSS and other communal organizations, which were banned.[18] Yet, even after the assassination, and especially once the initial impact of Gandhi's martyrdom waned, violence erupted again. Delhi continued to experience waves of violence every several months, well into 1950. The violence that lingered in Delhi in these years caused anxiety and confusion among the remaining Muslims and prompted further waves of Muslim migration to Pakistan.

At the heart of the violence was the scramble for Muslim houses, resulting in further encroachment on Muslim neighborhoods in the city. This chapter analyzes the conflicts over Muslim property in Delhi as an index of the great uncertainties concerning Muslim belonging in the city and the nation in the first years after partition. This uncertainty was the

FIGURE 3.1 *A huge crowd gathers for the funeral procession of Mohandas Gandhi, Delhi, 1948. Prime Minister Nehru is seen at the center. Source: Bettmann/Getty Images*

product of a fundamental, structural contradiction between the secular, pluralistic vision underpinning Indian democracy, and a partition based on the logic of ethnic homogenization. While whole neighborhoods were emptied of Muslims, roughly a third of the Muslim population remained. Where did they belong? In the aftermath of a bloody partition, underwritten by the logic of ethnic cleansing, there was no consensus about the answer. Many of the Muslim inhabitants went back and forth across the border in these first years. As Niraja Gopal Jayal demonstrates, contrary to a prevalent notion that India started with an inclusive territorial definition of citizenship (jus soli) and only later shifted to an exclusionary definition based on blood-based descent (jus sanguinis), a tension between the two principles of citizenship was apparent from the very beginning.[19] This tension underlay the scramble for Muslim houses and the prolonged violence it propelled.

In illuminating the intimate connection between dispossession of property and dispossession of citizenship, this chapter builds on the work of Vazira Zamindar, which traces the impact of partition on Muslim families from Delhi who were divided on either side of the border. Zamindar argues that partition took effect through bureaucratic discourses and practices aimed at turning the residents of colonial India into national citizens and distinguishing Indians from Pakistanis. Delhi's Muslims posed a challenge to this classification, because their migration was contingent and incomplete. Thousands of Delhi's Muslims were caught in a complex bureaucratic net that intertwined evacuee property laws with regulation of people's movement across borders.

This analysis, however, also departs from Zamindar's in significant respects, and contributes a more nuanced account of how partition played out in the city. First, it meticulously maps encroachment on Muslim zones, considers the multiple forces involved in this dynamic, and demonstrates that the bureaucratic violence of the Custodian of Evacuee Property took place precisely in the Muslim zones that were supposed to be outside its purview. The chapter thereby delineates the spatial expression of Muslim minoritization—their ghettoization in specific neighborhoods and the gradual shrinking of such neighborhoods.

Second, rather than viewing bureaucratic discourse and practices as a sui generis field, the analysis contextualizes bureaucratic action within national politics, revealing Delhi in this period as an intensely political space, with profound ideological divisions and power struggles at all levels, from the uppermost tiers of national government to bureaucrats, local political leaders, social workers, neighborhood bosses, and policing forces. It thus unpacks the category of "the state" as a unified agent acting on society, and instead demonstrates the blurred boundaries between state and society.[20]

Third, the chapter unpacks the category of religious community. Rather than representing Muslims as a cohesive category—a minority rendered powerless by the Kafkaesque bureaucracy of the state—the chapter explores power dynamics within the Muslim zones. It shows how social class, the informal economy, and corruption all played a role in determining whose house would be occupied, by whom, and in what manner. Religious community intersected with class in producing the specificity of Muslim dispossession and spatial ghettoization. While recognizing the plight of propertied Muslims and their desperate attempts to save or at least sell their houses, this chapter foregrounds the predicament of Muslim tenants, and how their interests conflicted with those of propertied Muslims leaving for Pakistan. The chapter exposes a world of micropolitics within the Muslim zones, in which local "bosses" and "tough men" assumed the role of *mohalla* (neighborhood) representatives, who negotiated with the Custodian of Evacuee Property authorities, often to the detriment of poorer, more vulnerable residents. Thus the crisis of partition brought about forms of urban citizenship and urban political dynamics that have hitherto been explored mainly in the context of the Emergency of 1975–77 and in contemporary India.[21] What emerges is a graded picture of agency, victimhood, and culpability.

A STATE OF UNCERTAINTY: A DIVIDED POLITICAL LANDSCAPE

> The truth is that there was a difference of attitude between Sardar Patel on the one hand and Jawaharlal and me on the other. This was affecting local administration and it was becoming clear that the officers were divided into two groups. The large group looked up to Sardar Patel and acted in a way which they thought would please him. A smaller group looked to Jawaharlal and me and tried to carry out Jawaharlal's orders.[22]

The relationship between Jawaharlal Nehru and Sardar Patel, the two most powerful political leaders in this period, was fraught with tensions and profound ideological differences, going back to the division between left and right in the 1930s within the Congress high command. Their correspondence during the months following partition reveals a fundamental disagreement over their visions for independent India and the place of the Muslim minority in it. While Nehru advocated a secularist and pluralistic Indian nation, Patel represented the right-leaning wing of the Congress Party, closer in spirit to the Hindu right. He received strong support from colleagues such as Syama Prasad Mukherjee, N. V. Gadgil, and Sardar Baldev Singh, and drew further and further away from Nehru, Maulana Abul Kalam Azad, and Gopalaswami Ayyangar. Patel felt that the Nehruvian camp poisoned Gandhi's ears against him, and the latter, undeniably, became increasingly critical of Patel.[23]

In his public speeches, Patel warned of Muslim "dual loyalty," calling on Muslims to search their conscience and ascertain whether they were truly loyal to India. Especially controversial was a speech he delivered in Lucknow in early January 1948, in which he reminded the audience that the Muslims of that city had advocated the "two-nation theory." He told Muslims that mere declarations of loyalty were insufficient, and that they must provide practical proof by openly condemning the Pakistan-supported attack on Kashmir. "It is your duty now to sail in the same boat and sink or swim together. . . . you cannot ride on two horses. You select one horse, whichever you like best."[24]

To tag Patel as "communal" does not adequately explain the man and the larger trend he represented. There were deep divisions between secularist and communalist tendencies within the Congress top leadership, the Congress Party more generally, and society at large.[25] Patel spoke for many in the country when he voiced his suspicions of Muslim loyalty to India. These suspicions emerged after several years of poisonous politics for which the Muslim League was as responsible as the Hindu right, and against the backdrop of a bloody partition, war in Kashmir, and the uncertain status of Hyderabad. The indeterminate belonging of the Muslim minority in India inhered in a partition based on religion.[26] This was undoubtedly tragic, especially so for Muslims who did not participate in the Pakistan movement or even actively resisted it. Many of those who had drawn fire from the Muslim League during the 1940s for their criticism of Pakistan were now labelled "Muslim Leagui" and "Pakistani spies." As we shall see, these terms and the suspicion they reveal occasionally crept even into the language of Nehru and other left-leaning players in the city.

Delhi was an important battleground for Nehru's and Patel's conflicting visions. Tensions emerged soon after the September violence, as the

two differed greatly in their interpretation of the events. Nehru and Maulana Azad saw the September violence as a premeditated massacre executed with the collusion of the local administration and police. By contrast, Patel's extensive searches for arms in Muslim localities, which were
widely disseminated by the Birla-owned newspapers, helped to congeal
the theory of a widespread Muslim conspiracy and to justify the violence
as a response to Muslim aggression.[27]

Patel and Nehru constantly argued over Delhi's governance. Because
Delhi was a central charge governed by the Home Ministry through the
unelected chief commissioner, it was de facto governed by Home Minister Patel, who resented what he saw as Nehru's uncalled-for meddling,
especially when he gave direct orders that contradicted Patel's instructions or bypassed his authority. Both turned to Gandhi, each threatening
to resign and asking him to arbitrate.[28]

Their ongoing dispute about the proper division of authority between
the home minister and prime minister resulted in confused procedures,
as the bureaucratic and policing forces tried to carry out the orders of one
or the other. This was clearly visible at the top level of the Delhi administration in the ongoing frictions between Chief Commissioner Khurshid
Ahmad Khan and Deputy Commissioner and District Magistrate M. S.
Randhawa. The chief commissioner's Muslim identity rendered him especially vulnerable and occluded all other aspects of his identity. While
Khan himself was nationalist and non-communal,[29] his niece was married to the president of Delhi's Muslim League, and he had relatives who
left for Pakistan.[30] He thus embodied the indeterminate figure of the
Indian Muslim in the post-partition days and the suspicion it aroused.
"Nationalist Muslims" were intertwined in familial and friendly relations with "Muslim Leagui," fueling anxieties about their loyalty. Khan
was constantly sidestepped by Deputy Commissioner Randhawa, who
wielded the real authority. Randhawa was at least nominally a Punjabi
refugee, since he originated from Lyallpur in West Punjab. The relationship between the two represents, in a nutshell, the broader "Punjabization" of Delhi at the expense of its Muslim population.

Nehru and Patel were deeply implicated in the troubled relationship between Khan and Randhawa. Assessing Delhi's situation in early

October, Nehru wrote to Patel that the chief commissioner of Delhi exercised hardly any authority during the crisis.[31] In his reply, Patel pointed to Khan's relationships with Muslim League leaders—implicating them in weapons stockpiling—as a reason that his authority was undermined.[32]

Nehru and Patel's disagreement centered on Deputy Commissioner Randhawa. Many Muslims began to see him as an archenemy, an RSS man through and through. A poster demanding Randhawa's transfer was signed by three hundred Muslims from different localities and pasted on various walls in the old city.[33] Others expressed a more cautious view, suggesting that Randhawa had been an honest officer who was influenced by the dark turn of events.[34] In a letter to Patel, Nehru expressed concern over Randhawa's handling of the riots. Despite warnings, he had failed to arrest suspicious people and forestall the disturbances, and once violence broke out, he dismissed it as a spontaneous matter without any organizers. Nehru concluded that Randhawa's sympathies lay with the Hindu right, and that this led to laxity in arresting RSS and Sikh instigators—and thus to ongoing violence in the capital. In response, Patel claimed that Randhawa was a good and reliable officer doing his best under stressful conditions.[35]

By August 1948, both the chief commissioner and the deputy commissioner were removed. Khan was transferred to a lesser position and died a few years later, a heartbroken and bitter man.[36] Randhawa's subsequent career was long and successful, including positions in the Ministry of Food and Agriculture, in the Planning Commission, and as the chief commissioner of Chandigarh. His account of refugee rehabilitation in East Punjab is considered the standard narrative of the era, cited time and again in partition studies.[37] Shankar Prasad, then commissioner of Ajmer, was appointed Delhi's chief commissioner and remained in office until 1954. Together with the new deputy commissioner, Rameshwar Dayal, he restored the proper hierarchy between the two posts. Yet one of his greater challenges was to maneuver between the contradictory orders he received from Nehru and Patel.[38]

Conflicts at the uppermost levels of government and administration shaped the Special Police Force created to cope with the outbreak of violence. The Police Act of 1861 authorized an additional police force, made up of citizen-volunteers, to work alongside the regular police in emergency situations.[39] To deal with the partition emergency in Delhi, about two thousand men were enlisted and organized hierarchically as magistrates, officers, and constables.[40] Thus people who were not part of the state entered into state-like positions of power. Special Police forces were irregulars as well as activists from across the political spectrum, including rival factions within the local Congress party and rival organizations outside it, most notably the RSS.[41] These divisions further politicized the security forces operating on the street and fueled the contest for power between Patel and Nehru—and between Patel and the socialist-dominated Delhi Provincial Congress Committee (DPCC).

Government records disclose that the enrollment of Special Police officers was fraught with conflicts over who should be enlisted and who had the authority to make that decision. In fact, the dispute between Patel and Nehru was directly related to the recruitment of Special Police officers. Patel reproached Nehru for his and the DPCC's excessive intervention in the process, and stressed that cooperation between local authorities and the local Congress committee did not mean "running day-to-day administration on party lines."[42] Nehru claimed that Special Police members included suspected organizers of the riots, and that Deputy Commissioner Randhawa had totally bypassed Chief Commissioner Khan in the recruitment process. He wanted Randhawa to revise the list in consultation with the chief commissioner and local Congress leaders, in order to purge the ranks of RSS men who had behaved improperly. Muslim residents indeed complained that Randhawa enlisted RSS and Akali members who were terrorizing them.[43] Conflict also arose when policing forces undermined each other's authority. A group of Special Police officers aligned with the socialist wing of the Delhi Congress, and referred to as "Congress SPOs," sent daily reports on the Delhi situation to the DPCC and several government bodies, documenting anti-Muslim violence, including stabbing, abducting women (notably both Muslim and Hindu), snatching rickshaws from Muslim drivers, looting, and forcibly occupying Muslim houses and businesses. The reports contain frequent complaints against other forces—police officers, Special Police officers, and army *haveldars* (sergeants), who not only did not cooperate with the Special Police, but were often complicit in the violence. For example:

> About 20 persons while going on foot along the Delhi-Shahdara Rly. line were killed on 4th Oct. Mr. Lincoln A.S.P., who doubted the authenticity of the report [sent by us] was taken by Messrs. Thara Kan and A.V. Rao and Jagat Prakash headed by Ch. Sher Jung to the place of occurrence where they found, after some enigmatical obstruction on the part of the C.I.D. official, a Havildar and a constable, the ground besmeared with blood and blood-stained cloth at the edge of the bridge from where, as the Havildar confessed later on, the dead bodies had been thrown into the water.[44]

This report adds that the head constable questioned the SPOs' authority to investigate and eventually confessed that he had followed orders from the magistrate and other officials in covering up the murders.

When the Home Ministry opened an investigation into the Congress SPOs' reports, it was not interested in their grave accounts of violence or their charge of obstruction on the part of other policing forces. Instead, Home Minister Patel and his secretaries treated these reports as evidence of the Congress SPOs' insubordination. Patel was especially infuriated by their leader Chaudhury Sher Jung—in the past a member of Bhagat Singh's Hindustan Socialist Revolutionary Army, and now part of the leftist circles who volunteered in Delhi to restore peace.[45] In an interview, Sher Jung told the *Daily Worker* (London) that, during the September violence, "the regular Police were so active in looting and killing that the Hindu murderers were probably quite amazed they had been arrested."[46]

In October 1947 Captain Ranjit Singh, the officer commander of the Special Police, claimed that three Congress SPOs had fired indiscriminately at a Hindu crowd near Fatehpuri Mosque, disobeyed the orders of the Special Police magistrate and area commander, and insisted that they would not accept orders from anyone but Sher Jung. For his part, Sher Jung argued that these Congress SPOs had caught three Hindu boys looting and, when they tried to arrest the boys, "a mob" had gathered around them and attacked them, leaving them with no option but to fire in the air. As for the Special Police area commander on the spot,

Congress SPOs had disobeyed him because he had instigated the crowd in the first place.[47]

The Home Ministry adopted Captain Singh's claim against Sher Jung and his men. They were removed from the force, and the Home Ministry and Deputy Commissioner Randhawa sought to prosecute them in court. The DPCC, the chief commissioner, and Nehru himself all tried to intervene, but the Home Ministry remained adamant. In the end, many of the accused simply did not show up in court, and the cases against them fizzled out or concluded in light penalties. The Home Ministry was particularly upset that Sher Jung's case was time-barred; he could not attend court because he had been sent to Kashmir on a special mission by Nehru.[48]

Throughout 1948, Delhi saw periodic waves of violence, and each episode led to the enlistment of Special Police officers, resulting in ongoing conflicts over the selection process. After Gandhi's assassination, with the RSS delegitimized in official circles and among the public, Chief Commissioner Khan reorganized the Special Police and purged the regular police force of communal elements. By the end of March 1948, 127 RSS members were removed from the Special Police.[49] But the force was dissolved soon afterward, and a new body of Home Guards was established in June, enlisting many of the former Special Policemen and inciting further controversies.[50]

The ideological and political divisions that ran through different levels of state and society are central to the specific ways in which Muslim dispossession took place. Let us turn to the struggles over evacuee property.

ETHNIC CLEANSING ROUTINIZED

An estimated 100,000 refugees occupied Muslim houses in the mixed localities that were hit in September—Karol Bagh, Paharganj, and Sabzi Mandi.[51] The Muslim inhabitants of these localities escaped either to the predominantly Muslim areas or to the refugee camps in Purana Qila and Humayun's Tomb, which served as transit camps before setting off to Pakistan. A massive exodus took place within less than two months, as indicated by the demographic data for the two camps: at their peak in mid-September, they jointly hosted roughly 164,000 Muslim refugees.

Just a month and a half later, Purana Qila closed down, and the remaining 2,000 refugees were shifted to Humayun's Tomb, whose population had also drastically declined to 4,000.[52] The majority had left for Pakistan, but thousands returned to the city. Their return was the fruit of intense efforts by nationalist Muslim and Gandhian leaders and volunteers to convince the Muslims that they belonged, and would be safe, in Delhi. Maulana Azad's speech at the Jama Masjid after the Friday prayer on October 24 was reportedly a key moment that convinced many Muslims to return from the camps.[53]

Establishing "Muslim Zones"
In his correspondence with Patel, Nehru initially entertained the idea that some portion of the Muslims returning from the camps would be rehabilitated in the localities from which they had been driven out. In early October, he anticipated that half of the 120,000 Muslim refugees in the camps would go to Pakistan, while half would return to the city. He asked Patel:

> Where are the other half to go? . . . Some parts of Delhi which the Muslims did not evacuate, like Ballimaran, Faiz Bazar, etc., are already full and there is not much room for additional people. Where else then are they to go to except to certain areas from which they were evacuated. These areas thus cannot be considered as reserved completely for non-Muslims.[54]

Patel, however, expected that most of Delhi's Muslims would go to Pakistan;[55] in any event, their houses were already occupied by refugees, and the localities were too dangerous for Muslims to live in or even visit. In Gali Banduqwali (Ajmeri Gate), a gang threatened Muslims who tried to reoccupy their houses, and in Paharganj, Dr. F. H. Mufti, health officer of the Delhi Municipality who visited the locality to prevent cholera, was stabbed to death.[56] That Muslims could not return to their homes in the formerly mixed localities became a shared premise of the central government and the Delhi administration. This was an important juncture at which the violent cleansing of September was routinized by the state.

Most of the Muslims who stayed in the city or returned from the camps flocked to the Muslim-majority localities, now considered the

TABLE 3.1 *"Muslim Pockets" in Delhi in 1948 and 1952*

Area	Number of Muslim pockets 1948	Number of Muslim pockets 1952
Faiz Bazar	32	19
Sadar Bazar	17	6
Hauz Qazi	31	7
Kotwali	6	3
Kashmiri Gate	2	0
TOTAL	88	35

SOURCE: Files 117 and 118, Delhi Police Records, Sixth Installment, NMML.
NOTE: The Muslim urban population in October 1948 was estimated to be 92,480. The second list, from 1952, does not include a population estimate. All pockets, except for Sadar Bazar, are in the old city. The fifth area of Kashmiri Gate was negligent toward its Muslim population. In fact, it was one of the hardest-hit areas during the riots, and many of the inhabitants fled in September.

only safe places for Muslims. This spontaneous internal displacement was subsequently systematized by the state. By late November, Nehru reluctantly admitted that Muslims were not safe in predominantly non-Muslim areas and advocated turning the Muslim-majority areas into "Muslim zones." The All-India Congress Committee published a resolution in favor of Muslim zones, and henceforth, it was in these areas that efforts to rehabilitate Muslims were concentrated.[57]

Yet Muslim zones proved precarious. Different sources list different localities as Muslim at different times. This instability indicates the gradual encroachment on the Muslim zones. This is evident on comparing two lists of the main areas in which the Muslim urban population was concentrated, as well as the smaller units, or "pockets," of Muslim habitations within each of them. (See Table 3.1.)

By the end of October, an estimated 8,000 houses and 2,000 business premises had been evacuated by Muslims, and about two-thirds of these were already occupied by refugees. Less than a month afterward, the estimate had increased to 32,000 premises. Subhadra Joshi, a member of the Shanti Dal who will be discussed further below, later estimated 44,000 houses in the old city alone.[58] Hence, although there is no official final estimate, it is evident that a major shift in property ownership took place.

Moreover, it extended far beyond the initial forcible occupations within mixed localities during the September violence, into the Muslim zones themselves.

Civic Violence

The refugee crisis in the city was such that, even after the mixed localities were "cleansed" of Muslims and occupied by one hundred thousand refugees, the pressure for housing did not ease. By early November, the population in these localities had increased by 50 percent, and refugees were still pouring into the city.[59] The next waves of violence expanded to the Muslim zones, targeting both vacant houses whose residents had left in September and populated houses, with the intention of driving their residents out.[60] Pressures on the Muslim zones increased by the day, producing a spiral effect: more attacks drove more Muslims out, and the empty houses they left behind drew yet more attacks.

It is no surprise that the population of Muslim refugees in the Humayun's Tomb camp, which had dwindled to 4,000 by the end of October, swelled again to 25,000 in mid-November. About 30,500 Muslims left Delhi for Pakistan via the camp during January and February. While this is not stated explicitly in the reports, it is quite clear that most of them left the Muslim zones, whether they were originally inhabitants of these areas or had settled there after having been uprooted from the mixed localities in earlier waves of violence.[61]

The Custodian of Evacuee Property

The key state institution responsible for regularizing Muslims' dispossession was the Custodian of Evacuee Property. This position was established simultaneously in West Punjab (Pakistan) and East Punjab (India) following a Joint Defence Council meeting in Lahore on August 29, 1947, attended by the prime ministers of both dominions and by Lord Mountbatten. Based on a mutual promise that illegal seizure of property would not be recognized, both Pakistan and India entrusted abandoned properties to newly appointed custodians, who would protect and preserve them until their original owners could return. This agreement reflects the great bewilderment in government circles in the face of the massive exodus that took place, and their hope that the demographic transformation was still reversible.

Yet both governments faced an acute refugee crisis and large-scale forcible occupations of houses. Refugees kept pouring into cities and villages in desperate search of accommodation. The function of the custodians thus transformed rather quickly from protecting the rights of homeowners to dispossessing them. Pakistan authorized the Rehabilitation Commissioners (counterparts to India's Custodians of Evacuee Property) to utilize abandoned properties for rehabilitating refugees for a limited period of one year. India soon issued a similar ordinance and, over time, the two governments continued drafting retaliatory legislation that further restricted owners' rights to their properties. Meanwhile, as the partition violence spread to Delhi, the East Punjab Evacuee Property Ordinance was extended to Delhi, and a custodian was appointed there on September 20.

Lobo Prabhu, the first custodian of Delhi, recognized illegal occupations effected during the September riots, so long as the occupiers reported to the custodian and were refugees rather than local residents who had taken advantage of the mayhem to seize Muslims' property. Delhi was divided into thirteen sectors, each under the charge of an assistant custodian and an advisory committee. Their role was to examine the eligibility of those already in possession of houses and to find eligible tenants among the refugees for vacant (Muslim) houses.

In addition to legitimizing forcible occupations, the custodian allotted more vacant houses from November 1947 onward. To be clear, such allotment did not amount to transfer of ownership. Rather, it granted the right to occupy a house temporarily. Ownership of the properties was still nominally vested in the Muslim evacuees, and the custodian's possession of the houses extended only until the original owners would return or until an overall compensation settlement would be reached between the two dominions. In the meantime, refugees occupied these houses as tenants and paid rent to the custodian, to be held in the name of evacuee owners.

The evacuee property legislation placed numerous restrictions on the original owners' ability to reoccupy, rent out, sell, or exchange their properties.[62] These rules were geared to maximize the pool of evacuee property that the custodians could utilize to rehabilitate refugees, by preventing individuals from disposing of their property and thus narrowing the pool of evacuee property.

For the same reason, the definition of an evacuee was broad and open-ended. As Zamindar emphasizes, Some of the Muslims whose houses were declared evacuee property had never left Delhi, or had left and returned. When India amended its ordinance in January 1948, it extended the definition of *evacuee* to include not only those who left India starting on March 1, 1947, but also those who could not personally occupy or supervise their properties. This, in effect, enabled the custodian to take possession of Muslims' property as "evacuee property" even when they had moved only to another neighborhood in Delhi. Some of these "evacuees" settled in the empty houses left behind by other Muslims and became, just like the Hindu and Sikh refugees, tenants of the custodian.

The definition of evacuee was made even broader by the introduction of the category of "intending evacuee" into the new Evacuee Property Ordinance of October 1949. This language turned all of Delhi's Muslims into potential evacuees and, if the custodian declared a Muslim an "intending evacuee," the burden to prove otherwise fell on the person himself.[63] This enabled the eviction of people still living in their houses. Civil courts lacked jurisdiction to adjudicate whether a given property was an evacuee property or not and to determine the legality of the custodian's actions, allowing it to go "wholly unchecked."[64] Taken together, the expansive and vague definition of an evacuee; the severe restrictions on sales, exchanges, and mortgages of evacuee properties; and the discretionary power of the custodian meant that every member of the minority community was considered a potential evacuee and that the custodian was able to take control of many properties of Muslims in Delhi.[65]

Dispossession of property was thus bound up with dispossession of citizenship, underwritten by the logic of jus sanguinis rather than jus soli—the Muslim component of people's identities came to override their birth and long-term residence in Delhi. Let us consider how the custodian apparatus was complicit in the shrinking the Muslim zones. When the Muslim zones were declared, Jamiat Ulama-e Hind pressed to exclude them from the project of rehabilitating Hindu and Sikh refugees.[66] Anis Kidwai, member of the Shanti Dal, a religiously diverse organization that advocated for Muslim zones, explained the rationale:

> We requested [that no refugee be settled in Muslim neighborhoods] because whenever a refugee settled among them, ten Muslim households would pack up and head to the camp. . . . From the minute the refugees set foot in a locality, they devoted their energies to capturing the neighbourhood for friends and family, by hook or crook. Whether driven by need or vengeance or both, the result always was that the atmosphere got so charged that locals had to run for their lives.[67]

What has escaped scholarship thus far is that a great deal of the dispossession took place in the Muslim zones. A prevalent assumption at the time, expressed in the Constituent Assembly debates, was that Muslim zones were outside the jurisdiction of the custodian.[68] But it was precisely in Muslim zones that the custodian operated, resulting in their gradual shrinking.

This is evident in complaints written by Muslim residents in September 1948, compiled by the Group for the Reform of the Custodian (Jamaat-e Islah-e Custodian), established by veteran local Congress leaders and members of the Forward Block, Imdad Sabri, and Lala Shankar Lal.[69] All reveal that the custodian was confiscating properties and declaring them "evacuee property" even when the Muslim owners were still in Delhi. While some complainants in this report were driven from mixed localities in September, others are residents of the Muslim zones that came within the circle of violence only in 1948. Thus, nine petitioners from Nawabganj (Sadar Bazar) complain, not about the custodian seizing houses that had already been abandoned, but about the custodian actually evicting Muslim inhabitants, both owners and tenants, sealing the houses, and in some cases allotting them to non-Muslim refugees. Some of these houses were sealed while the owners were away on a trip;

others were forcibly vacated. One complainant claims that his house was forcibly taken in order to clear space for the local custodian's office. If a custodian office was opened in the *mohalla*, we can infer that the custodian was systematically confiscating houses in this Muslim zone. It is noteworthy that Nawabganj was included in the first Criminal Investigation Department (CID) list of Muslim pockets produced in 1948, but by 1952, it no longer made it onto the list.[70] The complaints provide a clue as to how this change came about—that is, how the pressure put on Muslim houses by refugee violence combined with the custodian's intervention in opening up this locality for refugees.

A similar picture arises in Pul Bangash, another Muslim-majority neighborhood in Sadar Bazar, which was cordoned off as a Muslim zone in late September 1947 and became a focal point of violence during the winter of 1947–48 and again in the summer of 1948.[71] In one complaint, a Muslim who once lived in a house in Pul Bangash while renting out several others begs that at least the upper floor be left for his family. His daughters, who live with their husbands and children in two of his other houses, are being forced to pay rent to the custodian, as is a Muslim family uprooted from Karol Bagh. One other tenant has been evicted, and two more are being evicted now.[72]

The Factionalized State and the Muslim Zones

Why did the custodian operate in the Muslim zones? After all, they were supposed to be cordoned off for Muslim rehabilitation in the city and excluded from the rehabilitation program for refugees. As we have seen, both the political leadership and the bureaucracy in India and its capital city were polarized on the question of Muslim belonging. Such a division directly bore upon the contradictory and incomplete implementation of Muslim zones. While Prime Minister Nehru and Chief Commissioner Khan wished to protect the zones solely for Delhi's Muslims, Home Minister Patel and Deputy Commissioner Randhawa supported the refugees' demand that these spaces be opened for their rehabilitation. They claimed that exclusively Muslim zones would only entrench communal suspicion and enmity between "miniature Pakistans and Hindustans in the whole city" and pose security risks.[73] Similarly divided were the police, the Special Police, the local Congress Party, and the various extra-governmental organizations operating in Delhi.

Shanti Dal (Peace Corps) was perhaps the main organization advocating for Muslim zones. During the winter of 1947, when violence in Delhi intensified, Hindu and Muslim social workers in Old Delhi's localities formed the Shanti Dal and worked relentlessly to restore peace in the *mohallas*.[74] Anis Kidwai, sister-in-law of Cabinet member Rafi Ahmed Kidwai, joined the rehabilitation efforts in Delhi and the Shanti Dal after her husband was killed in the partition violence in Mussoorie. Kidwai's reportage, published soon after the events, along with the numerous reports of the Shanti Dal, reveal the Shanti Dal's ongoing struggles with policemen and custodian officials, as well as involvement by the uppermost levels of government. For the Shanti Dal, the source of the problem was the ideological uncertainties marking the period of transition—that is, the deep differences within the Cabinet over a secular Indian state. Official statements never ruled unequivocally on the question of Muslim zones, leaving officers on the ground to interpret official policy as it suited them. Muslim zones were accordingly protected only partially and reluctantly.

A MICROHISTORY: THE SCRAMBLE FOR HOUSES IN PHATAK HABASH KHAN

In the absence of clear policy from above, circumstances within localities determined which localities and houses were encroached upon, by whom, and in what manner. The following microhistorical study of one locality—Phatak Habash Khan—utilizes fragments of sources scattered in different archives in order to reconstruct the process whereby this locality, which was included in the CID list of Muslim pockets in 1948, disappeared from the list by 1952.

The events leading up to this disappearance drew in Nehru, Patel, President Rajendra Prasad, and Minister of Rehabilitation Mohanlal Saksena, as well as Shanti Dal and the Muslim organization Jamiat Ulama-e Hind. As in the controversy over the Congress SPOs presented earlier, struggles at the uppermost levels of government over Muslim belonging were closely connected with tussles further down the ladder. Yet a closer look reveals that, where houses were involved, ideological and religious divisions intersected with class politics, further complicating the picture.

Phatak Habash Khan was a predominantly Muslim locality in Old Delhi, close to the famous Fatehpuri Mosque, the railway station, and several business centers. It was an affluent neighborhood of the Muslim Punjabi community, whose members owned shops and business firms in Chandni Chowk and Sadar Bazar. Its inhabitants' dispossession began, as always, with civic violence. The locality was attacked in the third week of September 1947, during curfew hours. The residents fled to the Muslim locality of Ballimaran. Abdul Rahman Siddiqui, recalls:

> It had been shocking to see them pouring into the haveli, old men with beards unattended, young men with faces unshaven, women even without their dupatta not to speak of the burqa. There were young girls, married and unmarried wailing and weeping, trying to cover their shame, with hardly anything to cover with.[75]

Three and a half months later, in early January 1948, the locality became the site of ongoing struggles between the police, which guarded vacant houses, and groups of refugees trying to break in. The refugees would send women to try to occupy the houses and, when the women were stopped by the police, they would gather a crowd of about a thousand people, pushing and shouting slogans against Gandhi, the Muslims, and Pakistan. On some occasions, the police used tear gas, shot in the air, and arrested people. This scene repeated itself several days in a row. Police reports place these incidents within the broader context of a flare-up of violence in the city, culminating in Gandhi's assassination at the end of the month.[76]

The reports reveal that some Muslims of the locality played a role in the refugees' occupation of vacant houses:

> One Mohd. Hussain who is running a hotel in Phatak Habash Khan is said to have given his hotel to a certain Hindu after getting a good sum as "Pugree." This has caused sensation amongst the refugees and now they are openly saying that these houses are not for poor people but those who can

pay a handsom [*sic*] amount as a good will. This behaviour of the Muslims of
the locality will result in aggravating the already high communal tension that
is flowing amongst the refugees at present.[77]

The following day, the Special Police reported that the same Mohammed
Hussain was arrested for receiving a *pugree* of Rs. 2,300, noting that Hussain gave Rs. 360 of the *pugree* to another Muslim of the locality, Sadiq
Karachiwala. Also arrested was Mohammed Hassan, who brokered deals
between refugees and Muslim owners.

Pugree (literally "turban") is an initial fee, paid illicitly by a prospective tenant. It developed during colonial rule to circumvent urban rent
restrictions and, during partition, became a means to circumvent restrictions on transfer of evacuee property. Old Delhi's property market in the
post-partition period continued to feature immense sums of money given
informally as *pugree* alongside relatively low rents.[78]

We will return to the system of *pugree* in greater detail. Suffice it to
note here that the scramble for Muslim houses set in motion an informal
economy based on transfers of *pugree* even before the outbreak of violence in September.[79] Most *pugrees* were demanded by Muslims, thereby
disrupting from within the endeavor to protect Muslim zones. Muslim
owners who could not hope to sell their houses took thousands of rupees as *pugree* and left for Pakistan, hoping to come back and sell the
property when things calmed down. Kidwai, who took part in the Shanti
Dal's Sisyphean endeavors to keep Muslim zones protected, discusses the
unfortunate results of this practice. Overnight, an affluent family would
take thousands of rupees as *pugree* and vanish, leaving poorer Muslims
at the mercy of their new refugee neighbors. In other cases, the servant,
relative, or neighbor entrusted with property when its Muslim owner left
for Pakistan was tempted by the opportunity to receive a *pugree* of Rs.
5,000–10,000.[80]

After a few months of relative calm, Phatak Habash Khan and other
Muslim localities again experienced increasing pressure. The impact of
Gandhi's assassination was beginning to wane, the summer heat reached
its peak, but construction of housing for refugees had not yet begun.
Tensions in the city and its rural surrounding were again growing. One

alleged cause for the tensions was the return of Muslims from Pakistan to the city and its villages. Simultaneously, Hindu far-right organizations began to resurface, as many RSS workers were released from jail and resumed physical training classes. Shooting and stabbing incidents resumed, and rumors circulated about looming communal violence to commence on June 15.[81]

To combat the deteriorating situation, Shanti Dal reorganized. The Shanti Dal was headed by Mridula Sarabhai, a Gandhian and Congress leader. The daughter of the wealthy mill owner and leading Congressman from Ahmedabad, Ambalal Sarabhai, she took to a life of simplicity early on and became a follower of Gandhi. She was particularly active during the crisis of partition and is known for her leading role in the recovery of abducted women.[82] By all accounts she was a formidable, defiant, and opinionated woman, fearlessly dedicated to idealistic causes, and

FIGURE 3.2 *Mridula Sarabhai working at her desk, 1948. Source: Photo Division, Press Information Bureau, Ministry of Information and Broadcasting, Government of India.*

she aroused mixed reactions. While Nehru relied on her resourcefulness, Patel overtly disliked her, seeing her as whispering against him in Gandhi's ears.[83]

Alongside Sarabhai worked Subhadra Joshi. Born as Subhadra Datta in Sialkot, she took part in the underground movement of 1942 and was imprisoned by the colonial government. She became associated with the socialist wing of the Delhi Congress and married socialist worker B. D. Joshi, who was among the Congress SPOs described above. She would later become president of the DPCC and a member of the Lok Sabha, representing a Muslim-inhabited constituency in Old Delhi for many years. In addition to Sarabhai and Joshi, prominent in the Shanti Dal were Shah Nawaz Khan of the Indian National Army; Sikander Bakht, who would become a prominent local Congress politician and, decades later, a Bharatiya Janata Party member; and Anis Kidwai. Their involvement in the Phatak Habash Khan affair throws light on the important role played by this social organization and the fascinating, yet understudied, female figures who headed it. Like the Special Police Officers, and neighborhood "tough men" to be discussed shortly, the Shanti Dal demonstrates the porous line between state and society and the participation of both state and nonstate actors in the factionalized landscape of the post-partition city.

In her reports, Mridula Sarabhai defined Shanti Dal as a cross-party organization that included Congress members, socialists, and Jamiat Ulama-e Hind members, who were "non-communal, non-sectarian and non-provincial,"[84] and sought to link its work with official efforts. She formed "vigilance committees" in each police *thana*, which would act as "information bureaus," provide a check on antisocial and antinational elements, and create confidence among the population. She requested that vigilance committee members be accepted as official through a press note.[85]

It should come as no surprise that this endeavor created bitter discord between Shanti Dal and the Home Ministry, replaying the controversy surrounding the Congress SPOs. Like Chaudhury Sher Jung and his men, Sarabhai and her workers were aligned with socialist elements in the local Congress and the city; were highly critical of the Delhi administration and police; and sent reports documenting violence and oppression in the various localities and villages of Delhi. Chief Commissioner Shankar Prasad later recalled this affair:

> One day, I received a very bulky file from the Ministry of Home Affairs. I discovered that at nearly all Police Stations, a tented camp had been put up by Mridula Sarabhai. Her excuse was that the old administration was partial to refugees and hostile to the Muslims and that in general, the Police could not be trusted. The Sardar [Patel] was very much opposed to this arrangement as he thought that the tented camps acting as rival Police Stations would undermine all constituted authority and that they should be dismantled. Nehru, on the other hand, thought that the activity was relatively harmless and that the social workers under Mridula Sarabhai could exercise a wholesome and salutary check on the activities of the Police. The controversy had gone on for a long time and it had not been settled when I arrived.[86]

Prasad also notes that Sarabhai used her own substantial means to gather intelligence and send reports to top government officials. Indeed, Sarabhai's papers include numerous intelligence reports issued by workers and informants of the Shanti Dal, whose scope and methods resembled those of the CID. It is noteworthy that many of them carry the address "to Panditji [Nehru] only."

Muslim zones were one of the main areas of dispute between Shanti Dal and the Home Ministry. Toward the summer of 1948, Randhawa warned that, if Muslim zones were not opened up, refugees' frustration would again explode. He called for the allotment of at least some houses in the Muslim zones for government employees and other "responsible elements" among the refugees. Finally, Rehabilitation Minister Mohanlal Saksena decided to eliminate the Muslim zones. The government would make no efforts to preserve houses for returning Muslims, but bona fide Muslim occupants would no longer be ejected. Shanti Dal decided to collaborate with the custodian in surveying the Muslim zones, sealing off all vacant houses and allocating them to Muslims and refugees, in order to ease pressures on these areas and ensure the process was justly carried out.[87] Shanti Dal's vigilance committees prepared lists of houses and shops belonging to evacuees, specifying which of these were occupied by locals and which were occupied by refugees. They also identified refugees who occupied more than one property and refugees who occupied property beyond their status and means. The custodian used this information to seal and allot houses in Phatak Habash Khan and other Muslim zones in August 1948.

The collaboration between and Shanti Dal and the custodian, however, was soon disrupted. Affluent residents of Phatak Habash Khan, led by Sadiq Karachiwala—the same person mentioned a few months earlier as involved in a *pugree* deal—reached a settlement with the assistant custodian. The vacant houses in Phatak Habash Khan would be saved, and *all* houses in the adjacent *mohalla* of Katra Shafi, where poor Muslim day laborers resided, would be vacated, sealed, and allotted to refugees.

Shanti Dal workers interfered forcefully to counter this eviction, removing the seals from the Katra Shafi houses. Subhadra Joshi personally supervised the reoccupation of the houses by the tenants who had been evicted. She claimed that the deal involved bribery, contravened the earlier agreement that bona fide occupants would not be ejected, and was deeply unjust: it meant the wholesale forcible evacuation of vulnerable people from their homes in order to save a few empty houses owned by rich Muslims, which were undeniably evacuee property. The poor tenants of Katra Shafi were evicted without any prior notice and were left to the mercy of Sadiq and his men, who handled them roughly. Furthermore, Sadiq had been a staunch Muslim Leaguer prior to partition—a claim verified by pre-partition CID reports—and he was a neighborhood bully who used his influence, connections, and strong arm to terrorize poorer Muslims.[88]

The assistant custodian filed a police report against Joshi for house trespass, and the custodian of Delhi, Uma Shankar Dikshit, who backed up the assistant custodian, sent a strong report to all concerned, including Nehru and the new chief commissioner Shankar Prasad, condemning Joshi for taking the law into her own hands. Nehru reproached Mridula Sarabhai in a similar vein, saying that leaving the merits of the case aside, Joshi and the Shanti Dal could not simply circumvent the responsible bureaucrats. Nehru expressed concern that such acts would reflect badly on the organization and endanger it.[89] Harsher letters by Rajendra Prasad and Sardar Patel followed, claiming that Shanti Dal operated as a virtu-ally parallel organization to the government and should be closed down.[90] The Shanti Dal succumbed to the pressure and asked the residents of Katra Shafi to vacate their houses again.

Mridula Sarabhai's and Subhadra Joshi's extensive reports on the case tease out several elements that shed light on how the scramble for Muslim houses played out. What becomes clear is that the houses in both Phatak Habash Khan and Katra Shafi were evacuee property, in the sense that their owners had left for Pakistan. The Muslim laborers at Katra Shafi were immigrants from the United Provinces who had been uprooted from other localities of Delhi during the disturbances of September and subsequently occupied these houses. Strictly speaking, they had no legal right to the houses, like many occupants of such houses at the time—whether they were Muslims driven out of mixed localities or Hindu and Sikh refugees from Pakistan. But while government policy was commit-ted to refugee rehabilitation and generally regularized refugee tenants, it left Muslim tenants unprotected. The custodian in this case did not feel obligated to provide the evicted tenants of Katra Shafi with alternative accommodation. Thus Muslim tenants remained in a zone of illegality that rendered them vulnerable to evictions when circumstances changed.

Such illegality opened up space for locality bosses and strongmen to operate, in collusion with the Custodian of Evacuee Property officials. While Sadiq Karachiwala had been the one to settle the poorer laborers in Katra Shafi in the first place—most probably to save this area from the custodian and refugee intrusion—once the custodian resolved to allot houses in his own locality, priorities changed and Sadiq decided to drive the tenants out of the houses. The assistant custodian officials may or may not have received a bribe, as Joshi claimed. But she and Sarabhai made a more fundamental observation—namely, that since the custodian resolved to get the maximum number of houses in the locality at any cost, its officials resorted to working through such shady persons as Sadiq Ka-rachiwala, who could deliver the goods without being restricted to legal means.[91]

This dynamic fits a later theorization of urban citizenship in con-temporary India, framed within "political society," as distinct from "civil society."[92] The most subaltern populations occupy illegal urban spaces, where they stake their claims to the space and the state's services not as right-bearing individuals but through political pressures and negotiations in which locality bosses play a key role as intermediaries. Emma Tarlo shows how moments of crisis, such as the Emergency of 1975–77, disrupt such fragile, unwritten agreements and render subaltern existence in the city especially vulnerable, effectuating large-scale evictions of slum dwellers.[93] Further, the Emergency's high-handed family planning program involved enormous pressures by political leadership on government employees to produce as many sterilization certificates as possible. Pressures extended from the top bureaucrats through lower-level employees into poor neighborhoods, turning sterilization certificates into a means of negotiating citizens' access to land and government services. A graded structure of coercion was set in place, in which the most vulnerable were the ones to undergo operations. The case of Phatak Habash Khan shows how the partition crisis operated in the same way and may even have helped to shape such dynamic of urban citizenship. The equivocal policy of the authorities with regard to Muslim zones and the unauthorized—and therefore unprotected—occupation of houses there turned them into zones of political society, in which the broad discretionary power of the custodian, working alongside local bosses, dispossessed poor Muslims.

Shanti Dal records on Phatak Habash Khan and other Muslim zones forefront the class element. Muslim house owners who, leaving for Pakistan, disposed of their property disturbed the effort to protect Muslim zones and maintain Muslim existence in the city. The house owner either transferred the house to non-Muslim refugees in exchange for a high *pugree*, or sold it to non-Muslims when legal policy allowed it. Such property transfers almost always resulted in the eviction of Muslim tenants by the new non-Muslim owners. As a result, the Shanti Dal pursued a policy that may seem, at first glance, counterintuitive. The organization most dedicated to a secularist vision and protection of the Muslim minority was among the most vocal proponents of banning exchanges of property by Muslim evacuees, thereby taking part in their dispossession. Together with members of the Jamiat Ulama, the Shanti Dal insisted that Muslim evacuees leaving for Pakistan should not be allowed to sell their houses, and reported Muslims who returned to India on a temporary permit to dispose of their property.[94] Criticizing the imminent (and eventually temporary) decision to allow private exchanges of property, Sarabhai stressed that such transactions should not take place in the Muslim localities of Delhi: "In Delhi purchase of a building by non-Muslim in a predominantly Muslim area results in ousting of the Muslim tenant who does not get any alternative accommodation in other areas due to the existing atmosphere."[95] We should keep in mind that the categories "propertied" and "tenants" were not neatly separated; in the contemporary state of flux, people who had once been house owners were dispossessed by civic and bureaucratic violence and were now subject to eviction. Nevertheless, the general contours of migration had a class element. The better off left for Pakistan. Nationalist Muslim political leaders remained, safe in their homes. And the poorest remained as well, dispossessed. They were gradually joined by migrants from the United Provinces.

Pressures on Phatak Habash Khan became pressing again toward the end of 1949, with numerous refugees attempting to occupy houses forcefully.[96] Renewed violence in 1950 in East and West Bengal spilled over into Uttar Pradesh and Delhi, setting off another massive migration from North India to West Pakistan and again triggering the all-too-familiar dynamic of pressure on Muslim areas in Delhi.[97] On March 19, 1950, there was a serious outbreak of violence in Delhi, and thousands of Muslims left the city, leaving behind empty houses that were occupied by refugees, either through *pugree* or by force, and by local Muslims—probably those who fled neighborhoods under attack, such as Bara Hindu Rao.[98]

The deputy commissioner issued an order declaring all such occupations illegal, and the police started evicting both refugees and Muslims. The custodian sealed two thousand vacant houses, increasing tension in the city. Muslim grievances voiced on *Al Jamiat*, as well as other sources, testify that the Custodian of Evacuee Property operated with a vengeance in this period, enacting the discretionary powers at its disposal with full force and moving extremely fast in taking possession of houses. Muslims who had already been cleared as non-evacuees were again asked to prove they were not, numerous times.[99]

Shanti Dal's alarmed reports on the rapid and deepening encroachment on Phatak Habash Khan in this period reveal how this bureaucratic violence worked in tandem with the informal economy of *pugree*, and with the "enterprise" of self-appointed *mohalla* leaders. It is noteworthy that reports from September 1949 onward begin to refer to Phatak Habash Khan as a "mixed area," thereby reflecting yet another stage in its disappearance from the list of "Muslim pockets."

A series of reports by an informant of Shanti Dal inside the *mohalla* sheds light on this dynamic. The reports stressed that Phatak Habash Khan was an area of strategic importance for Muslims' sense of security in the city. It was inhabited by longstanding residents, mostly well-to-do and influential people, as well as many people displaced from other parts of Delhi and the United Provinces, and it served as a check on incursions into Ballimaran. The latter, the reports stated, was the target of refugees who had already encroached into Pul Bangash and adjacent localities. There had been many attacks on Phatak Habash Khan, as well as transfers through *pugree*, in the past but the locality by and large endured. The present situation, emphasized the informer, was different. Disintegration of the area was taking place exceptionally fast, and if this continued, the whole area would be swept clean of Muslims soon. More than half a dozen attempts of forcible occupation of Muslim and a few non-Muslim houses had been reported in the previous month. While the police acted fairly and speedily in these cases, it was helpless when it came to *pugree*.

There was a rapid increase at this time of *pugree* as an antisocial practice, tearing the *mohalla* asunder from within. In addition to homeowners who disposed of their property in exchange for *pugree*, now many tenants occupying evacuee houses vacated them in exchange of for *pugree*. This resulted in part from the growing pressures of Custodian Department officials on Muslim tenants. The custodians started to demand arrears of rent in lump sums, and many tenants—mostly Muslims—were unable to pay and quietly surrendered the house on payment of *pugree* to others—mostly refugees.[100] In other cases, Muslim tenants may have been able to pay the rent but preferred to make a profit from *pugree* and relocate to Muslim wards where other family members lived. Still other tenants complained of sheer harassment by gangs of *pugree dalals* (brokers) who forced them to leave their houses. Hence, houses that were mostly evacuee properties were transferred by the tenants themselves, and no action could be taken by the police without an order from the Custodian Department, which moved extremely slowly. *Pugree*, concluded the informer, operated through a combination of greed, financial difficulties, harassment, threats, and fear.

The reports named specific individuals—refugees, Muslims, and Custodian Department officials—who colluded in this "game." These included self-appointed leaders of refugees in the locality, one Tara Chand of the Tara Press for instance, who intimidated impoverished Muslims, offered them some money to vacate, and then transferred their houses to others for a profitable *pugree*. On the Muslim side, there were two rival groups—one led by Sadiq Karachiwala, who is familiar to us by now, and who presented himself as a champion of Muslim interests, the other by Abdul Fakhir Siddique, who aligned with non-Muslim refugees.

Fakhir Siddique came from Meerut in the United Provinces, where he had practiced many professions. According to a Shanti Dal report, he had at various times been a propagandist for the British war efforts, a propagandist for the Muslim League, and a pro-refugee extremist. He was expelled from Meerut because of some shady dealings and, after transferring his house in Meerut on *pugree*, he came to Delhi to try his luck. When Siddique entered the business of evacuee property *pugree*, he clashed with local Muslims already engaged in that, mainly Sadiq Karachiwala. While the latter operated under extreme pro-Muslim pretensions, Abdul Fakhir assumed extreme pro-refugee pretensions. He approached the refugee association led by Mr. Gidwani, expressed anti-Muslim ideas, and thus made connections in the Ministry of Rehabilitation. He also became a secret correspondent of the refugee daily *Vir Bharat*, promising to supply it with information on Muslims concealing evacuee property. He used his popularity with the refugee press as leverage in the locality and to blackmail both Muslims and refugees. The rival group, led by Sadiq Karachiwala, turned to the Muslim press. The atmosphere in Phatak Habash Khan became agitated, and there was danger of an outbreak of violence.

The Delhi administration ordered both rivals to leave the city for three months, on charges of activities prejudicial to peace. On his return to Delhi, Siddique offered his services as an informant to the Custodian Department officials. According to an official in this area, Siddique was thrust upon them by the Ministry of Rehabilitation and the custodian-general. He became intimate with a circle within the Custodian Department that was known for harassing Muslims, including Assistant Custodian J. S. Tyagi, who was related to the Tyagi-Gidwani's refugee association. The Shanti Dal reports described how Tyagi, using misinformation and false witnesses supplied by Siddique, would evict Muslims and declare them evacuees by using false witnesses and covering legal loopholes. Together, they had evicted practically all the Muslims in Pul Bangash, and were now working in Ballimaran. While the custodian of Delhi was aware of what was going on, Siddique had support within the Ministry of Rehabilitation, allegedly from the custodian-general of India himself, and there was little he could do.[101]

Siddique soon became overconfident and started abusing his powers. He assumed the powers of Custodian Department officials, illegally evicting occupants, sealing houses, and allotting properties. The Shanti Dal reports were transferred to Nehru, and a short while afterward, Siddique's services with the Custodian Department were terminated and the police registered a case against him for illegally assuming powers he did not have in evicting Muslims. Siddique's is another example of how "enterprising" Muslim individuals operating from within the *mohallas* took part in their disintegration. It also shows how such individuals could tap into and utilize the larger ideological-political conflict—between secularists and communalists, Muslims and refugees—to advance their own interests, determining a *mohalla's* fate. The large-scale national political questions of this period intersected with the day-to-day scramble for resources in the city, and often acted as a channel for it. We can also see, yet again, how, in the divided political landscape of this period, the uppermost level of national government—in this case Nehru—intervened in the micropolitical affairs of Delhi's localities. Political players close to him, both within government and outside it, such as the Shanti Dal, directly turned to him to force the hand of "corrupt" or "communal" officials. The state is thereby revealed as an intensely politicized body, with rival factions operating at cross-purposes, in collusion with nonstate actors.

By 1952 Phatak Habash Khan had disappeared from the list of Muslim pockets. Later, it was even renamed after Tilak, further suppressing its Muslim history.[102] Our close reconstruction of this process reveals how a Muslim locality could be taken over by refugees as a result of the combined pressure of violence, *pugree*, and the collusion of officials and *mohalla* bullies—a messy and politically saturated dynamic grounded in the indeterminate status of the Muslim zones.

WINDING UP EVACUEE PROPERTY

The grave conditions across North India and East Pakistan led to negotiations between the prime ministers of the two countries, resulting in the Nehru-Liaquat Ali (Delhi) Pact of April 8, 1950. The agreement was meant to halt the exodus of people and ensure the security of minorities in both countries.[103] In this context, Nehru sent several letters to Minister of Rehabilitation Saksena, insisting that the evacuee property legislation must be reformed. Nehru was critical of the new Evacuee Bill, prepared by Saksena and being discussed in parliament, saying that it would exacerbate the situation just when renewed violence was pushing many Muslims to leave India, and when India had undertaken to prevent such fears. Nehru was also critical of the law as interpreted and implemented by the Custodian of Evacuee Property. His harsh evaluation was based on numerous complaints by Muslims that had accumulated on his desk, convincing him that the law had become an engine of oppression in the hands of the custodian: the proceedings were inquisitorial, and the assistant custodians functioned more like prosecutors than judges, taking pains to prove people guilty of some offence; cases went on interminably without a final decision; the burden of proof lay on the accused, in violation of all canons of justice; people who had already been proven to be non-evacuees were asked again and again to show cause why they should not be declared evacuees; sometimes people were declared non-evacuees and still their property was seized.[104] "Although the evacuee property laws deal with property as such, the effect of their application may well be the deprivation of citizenship or nationality and this is a serious matter," Nehru concluded.[105]

The appointment of a new rehabilitation minister marked the beginning of a shift in the government's policy. The new minister, A. P. Jain, was identified with secularists within the Congress Party, and Nehru pushed for his appointment against Patel's wishes.[106] Patel died a few months later, and ultimately Nehru asserted his authority over the Congress. In August 1952, Jain pushed for the deletion of the "intending evacuee" category against strong opposition in parliament.[107] In November 1953, Nehru wrote to Jain that it was time to rethink their position on evacuee property. These laws were a response to an emergency situation and could not be prolonged forever. It was high time that India lift the sword of Damocles hanging over its Muslim citizens and preventing them from conducting normal business and life.[108]

India made several more attempts to resolve the evacuee property deadlock with Pakistan. It sent a detailed offer in October 1952, according to which both countries would take over evacuee properties and compensate their owners. Pakistan turned down the offer, insisting on solving the problem through private transactions. In May 1954, Nehru informed Pakistani prime minister Mohammad Ali that, since six years had passed and no progress had been made, India was taking unilateral steps. First, it abrogated the legislation with regard to future cases that may arise—that is, no more properties could be declared evacuee. Second, it permanently acquired title to properties that the Custodian of Evacuee Property had already taken possession of, and would utilize them to compensate displaced persons. Evacuee owners would be compensated for the value of these properties; the amount and manner of compensation would be based on a settlement with Pakistan, should one be reached.[109] In October of that year, India enacted the Administration of Evacuee Property (Amendment) Act 1954 and the Displaced Persons (Compensation and Rehabilitation) Act, providing for just these terms. Since no mutual agreement was ever reached with Pakistan, Muslim evacuee property was, in effect, seized permanently without compensation to its owners, whether they had left for Pakistan or remained citizens of India. And so, seven months later, in May 1955, Nehru was astonished that over 130,000 judicial cases of evacuee property were still pending or under adjudication. "These are staggering figures. . . . These very figures indicate the terrible pressure on the Muslims of India. I had absolutely no idea that so many months after the ending of the Evacuee Property Law, we shall be pursued by this nightmare."[110]

Throughout the 1950s, Muslim tenants in Delhi continued to experience pressure from refugees. As late as 1954, a local Hindu Mahasabha leader, Professor Ram Singh, appealed to refugees to drive out Muslim tenants living in evacuee properties, claiming that this could make room for forty thousand refugees.[111] They were also continually subjected to the Custodian Department's draconian rent collecting methods, especially the habit of collecting all installments at once, leading to evictions.[112]

In their letters to Nehru, Joshi and Sarabhai emphasized that, in fact, most of the Muslims of Delhi were now tenants. Some of them had owned houses in the mixed localities of Delhi or in other areas of north India, but they had been driven out and could neither take possession of their houses nor realize rent from them.[113] Although they were as much victims of the partition disturbances as the city's Hindu and Sikh refugees, they were totally neglected by the government's rehabilitation policy. Joshi requested that rehabilitation measures be extended to them by allotting the remaining sealed, vacant evacuee houses or making their existing occupancy of such property official.

After the government's unilateral decision in 1954 to take over the property rights of evacuees, the Rehabilitation Ministry auctioned off evacuee property, resulting in large-scale evictions of unauthorized occupants, many of whom were Muslim tenants.[114]

A SPACE OF SUSPICION

The predicament of Delhi's Muslims in the aftermath of partition was encapsulated in the history of Muslim zones. Maintaining and protecting Muslim zones was a policy advocated by those most committed to an inclusionary and pluralistic India. Randhawa's challenge to this policy, that there was no room for religious zoning of citizens in a secular country, was only lip service. He was not so interested in intermingling as to suggest the rehabilitation of Muslims in their homes in the previously mixed neighborhoods of Paharganj, Karol Bagh, and Sabzi Mandi. Patel himself, we may recall, decisively rejected this option when Nehru raised it in October. For Patel and Randhawa, mixed neighborhoods meant settlement in only one direction, with refugees increasingly taking over Muslim neighborhoods. Yet this argument cannot be dismissed easily. The Nehruvian policy of Muslim zones, although possibly the only option, authorized and perpetuated the process of ghettoization that began with the September violence.

Ghettoization was the spatial dimension of Muslim minoritization—the tragic outcome of the two-nation theory and partition. If, before August 1947, nationalist Muslims such as Maulana Azad could claim that Muslims were not a minority in the sense of being a weak group, after partition, the significant decline in their numbers, the loss of the Muslim-majority provinces, and the exodus of Muslim elites left the remaining Muslims a truly vulnerable minority. Their precarious existence could be maintained only by such "ghettoes."

And protecting them proved a challenge, as their ongoing diminution attests.[115] The debate over Muslim zones reflected the equivocal attitude toward the Muslims of India in those critical years. Patel, Randhawa, and others in the administration, police, and society who objected to this policy doubted that Muslims could be trusted as equal and loyal citizens. Were these Muslims Indians or Pakistanis? Nationalist Muslims or Muslim Leagui? The troubled history of Muslim zones reflects the ideological and political conflicts between secularist forces—with their inclusive, territorial model of citizenship—and those inclined to a Hindu majoritarian state—with their exclusive, ethnoreligious model. The conflict enmeshed the Congress top leadership, multiple levels of government, and a host of unofficial and semiofficial organizations that straddled the line between state and society—as well as multifarious alliances among these players. What emerges is an everyday life saturated with political mobilization. Such a factionalized, messy, and intensely politicized everyday belies abstract conceptualizations of a monolithic state.

Growing competition over resources in a city sinking under the burden of refugees produced ever-deeper suspicions. At a time when Delhi absorbed hundreds of thousands of refugees who had survived the violence inflicted by Muslims elsewhere, many felt that it was unfair for refugees to be denied access to empty houses merely to protect Muslim zones. Evacuee property and economic considerations were embroiled in questions of citizenship and security. As Nehru perceptively put it in his letter to Saksena on the draconian evacuee legislation and its implementation, "We try to punish people who in law and effect are our citizens, but who we suspect might perhaps transfer their allegiance."[116]

Indeed, in May 1950 the superintendent of the CID reported that Muslims set guards to watch all entrances to their *mohallas* and prevent any non-Muslim from entering, and even equipped these entrances with locking gates. The report did not treat this as a response to violence and dispossession, but as a sign of sectarianism. It concluded, "So long as this mentality prevails and is tolerated, the claim of the Muslims of their being nationalists and true subjects of the Indian Dominion is but farce and cannot obviate the 'danger' of turning their faces on the Indian Dominion at any time of 'Emergency.'"[117]

Such mistrust also led to restrictions on the movement of Muslims across the borders. Starting in March 1948, thousands of Muslims who had fled to Pakistan returned to Delhi and either reoccupied their old houses in the Muslim zones or occupied other vacant houses in these areas.[118] Others visited Delhi with the aim of disposing of their property and going back to Pakistan. The refugee papers responded with panicky reports on the arrival of Pakistani spies. The city's administration and police were also alarmed and reported on the infiltration of "spies" and other "undesirable elements" sent from Pakistan to create trouble in Delhi. From April 1948 onward, the CID sent regular reports on arrests of Muslims in Delhi under the Punjab Public Safety Act for reasons as vague as loitering, "cutting pranks with Hindu girls," impersonating Hindus, and engaging in subversive activities.[119]

In order to check such entry, India introduced a permit system in July 1948, requiring Muslims to apply to the Indian High Commissioner in

Pakistan for a permit to enter India. It followed with the passport system of 1952. The permit and passport systems were coordinated with the bureaucracy of the Custodian of Evacuee Property and the evacuee property legislation, which also began to fix citizenship through its categories of "evacuee" and "intending evacuee."[120]

The prevailing suspicion was built into the situation. It emerged out of the increasingly poisonous atmosphere prior to partition, the traumatic violence, and the sudden need to distinguish between Indians and Pakistanis in the context of a mass exodus that no one had predicted. A revealing correspondence between the Custodian Department and the CID illustrates the resulting anxiety. In January 1952 an assistant custodian asked the CID about a Muslim woman who had testified in the Custodian's court that she had never left Delhi. The assistant custodian wrote that he had strong reason to believe that the lady who gave the statement was not the woman whose property was at stake. The CID admitted that it had no way to verify who had given the statement in court and whether the property owner had left for Pakistan or not, since many people crossed through the eastern border, where there was no permit system or any control.[121] This is an important reminder that the CID was not an all-knowing body, and that the aspiration for complete knowledge of society was, more often than not, a fantasy. But it was exactly this aspiration for total surveillance—and its constant failure—that perpetuated suspicions. The semiporous condition of the borders, together with the vague definition of an evacuee, fed the uncertainty about Muslim belonging, which in turn propelled the CID's efforts to draw clear lines between Indians and Pakistanis, non-evacuees and evacuees, in accordance with the emerging taxonomy of the new nation-state.

Even in Nehru's letters, which confirm time and again his commitment to protecting Muslim life and property, suspicion creeps in. In one note, for instance, he asks his secretary for a comprehensive report on the number of Muslims returning from Pakistan under the Nehru-Liaquat Pact of April 1950, saying that he has been informed that Pakistan was sending some troublemakers among these people. There is no need to open up this issue with Pakistan, he says, but the people returning on permits should be scrutinized.[122]

The many pressures on Muslim localities wreaked havoc on the social fabric and mutual trust of such neighborhoods. Shahid Ahmed Dehlvi, the author we met in the previous chapter, visited his old *mohalla* in April 1948, after seven months in Pakistan. He found that the area south of Jama Masjid had become a Muslim zone, packed with all those who had been uprooted from other neighborhoods. The Muslim traders and shop-keepers from Chandni Chowk had all moved to this area. It was so congested that one could not cross the street. This demographic transformation tore the old social fabric asunder. Dehlvi writes:

> Those I saw seemed scared, speaking in hushed tones while constantly look-ing to both sides. They did not trust each other. Every person could be a *jasus* [spy, agent]. There were several people who were trained by the police, who would make false or true complaints against their brothers and have them ar-rested. This is how they earned their money, by making threats [against other people that they would have them arrested].[123]

Indeed, the sources tell us of numerous such informants—Hindu refugees as well as Muslims who were employed by the CID, the Custo-dian Department, and organizations such as the Shanti Dal, all of which infused these localities with political machinations, rumors, and allega-tions. We have seen that state ambivalence toward Muslim zones left these areas vulnerable to the workings of a host of internal factors—informants as well as class difference, the informal economy of *pugree*, the operation of local bosses, connections, and bribery. A case in point is a complaint submitted to Delhi's chief commissioner by a group of Muslim residents of Kalan Masjid in December 1948.[124] The petition-ers write about one Muslim of the locality, Ghulam Mohammad, who used to belong to the Muslim League and the Muslim National Guards. Mohammad had been arrested a few months earlier under the Punjab Public Safety Act and detained for three months. Upon his return, he took revenge on the local residents (who apparently had brought about his arrest) by making false allegations that led to the arrest of several innocent people. In their absence he demanded Rs100 from their wives and threatened those who failed to pay. When his Muslim tenants were out of the house, he broke their locks, threw their belongings in an alley, and in their place settled refugees, who were paying fourfold rents and high *pugrees*.

Mohammad is another illustration of local "entrepreneurs," like Sadiq Karachiwala and Fakhir Siddique in Phatak Habash Khan, men who were quick to adjust to, and take advantage of, the new circumstances. His story also exemplifies how the economy of *pugree* became embroiled with class divisions and internal disputes within Muslim localities, and demonstrates that such internal disputes resulted from, or were at least exacerbated by, the pressures faced by Muslim localities in this period. After all, the complaint against Mohammad arose against the back-ground of numerous arrests of Muslims from the neighborhood in mid-1948. What is also noteworthy is the language of loyalty through which the petitioners frame their case. They conclude their letter by noting that Mohammad has recently started to dress like a Hindu, keep a *choti* (braid) on his head (like a Hindu), befriend Hindus, and present himself as such. This last piece of information was clearly intended to arouse the authorities' suspicion toward Mohammad at a moment when Muslims were often arrested for roaming Hindu localities dressed like Hindus. In fact, the petitioners assert, not only is he a Muslim Leagui, but his whole family has left for Pakistan. They thus tie together allegations about his Muslim Leagui leanings before partition with insinuations that he is an "intending evacuee." Local disputes such as this one were often presented to authorities in the language of national loyalty, echoing how the is-sues of Muslim property and (dis-)loyalty were interconnected in the discourse of the Custodian Department bureaucracy, the police, and the CID.[125] The CID investigation of the matter determined that Ghulam Mohammad had indeed been a Muslim Leagui and a member of the Na-tional Guards, but had changed his allegiance and joined the nationalist Muslims in 1946, helping Asaf Ali in the elections. Clearly the boundary between the categories of "nationalist Muslim" and "Muslim Leagui" was a slippery one, as people could easily move from one to the other. This propelled the politics of suspicion in the post-partition period, both to-ward and among Muslims.

After independence, most of Delhi's Muslims lived within the walled city of Shahjahanabad, and very few dared to venture outside these areas for several decades. They tended to live contiguously in two main concentrations, "one extending southward from the Jama Masjid into Suiwalan and up to the Turkaman Gate, the other extending from Chandni Chowk and Ballimaran westwards through the area south of the Fatehpuri Mosque to Farash Khana and Kucha Pandit."[126] To these we should add a few localities in Sadar Bazar, the small enclave of Nizamuddin, and the area of Okhla in New Delhi, where Jamiat Millia University is located. Certainly, as this chapter has shown, the number of Muslim neighborhoods in these areas declined as refugees advanced into the Muslim zones. The ghettoization of Muslims and ongoing encroachment into these localities produced, especially in Sadar Bazar, "small concentrations of Hindu [mostly refugee] and Muslim population, at once segregated and living in close proximity with each other."[127] By the late 1960s, Muslims began to move out of the old city and its surroundings to Jamia Nagar in Okhla and to Seelampur, across the Yamuna River.[128] During the demolition drive of the Emergency, thousands were uprooted from the Jama Masjid, Turkman Gate, and other parts of the old city and resettled in Seelampur and Welcome across the Yamuna.[129] It is noteworthy that Subhadra Joshi, then a member of parliament representing a Muslim-populated constituency of the old city, was among the sole voices protesting the violence and forced evictions.[130] Her social and political work is yet another thread connecting the crises of partition and the Emergency.

Muslims who lived in Delhi through partition report that its repercussions lasted for many years. The atmosphere of hostility and the inability to find employment or residence in non-Muslim areas bred a sense of instability and thoughts of migration. A Muslim who lived in the old city during partition tells that in the 1960s "this continued and you should note, only after the 1971 war, the borders were closed finally and the option to leave was no longer there." Another person says: "After the 1965 war, Muslims were jolted badly . . . but many still continued to believe that they'd have to leave India. It was only after the 1971 war with Pakistan that it became clear to everyone that they would be here for good; it was only then that these people put serious effort into establishing business."[131]

CHAPTER 4

CLAIMING THE CITY AND NATION
IN THE URDU PRESS

LET US RETURN to Pandit Girdharilal Datta from the novel *Jhutha Sach*. We recall he arrives in Delhi in August 1947 and exchanges his Lahore property for a house in Daryaganj. Unlike the indigent refugees on the streets, Panditji is well off, and he has transferred some of his life savings to his bank's branch in Delhi before his arrival in the city. Back in Lahore, he started as a young proofreader working for 20 rupees a month and gradually built himself up, opening a small bookshop and then publishing a weekly Urdu magazine. By the time of partition in 1947, he was an established and well-respected figure in the press world of Lahore—the owner of a successful Urdu printing press and a spacious house in Gawalmandi. After independence, Panditji's daughter Kanak joins her parents in Daryaganj and finds a job in one of the Punjabi Urdu dailies that recently moved from Lahore to Delhi. But the editor makes shameless advances to her and constantly rewrites her articles to suit the newspaper's anti-Muslim agenda, so when she finally tracks down her sweetheart, Jaidev Puri, she follows him to Jalandhar in East Punjab.

In Lahore, Puri was a poor but promising young writer, earning a meager income as a journalist for an Urdu daily. In August 1947 he flees Lahore and arrives, destitute and exhausted, in a refugee camp in Jalandhar. His fortune quickly changes when he encounters Vishwanath Sood, an influential local Congress leader with whom he was imprisoned during the war. Sood hands over to Puri an Urdu printing press left behind by one Isaac Mohammed. Mohammed was a nationalist Muslim who objected to the Pakistan movement, but amid the violence had no recourse but to flee to Pakistan. He entrusted the keys to his house and printing press to Sood, asking him to keep them safe until he could return in a few months. Now, Sood not only lets Puri run the press but also uses his political connections to provide him with an abundance of printing orders from government offices and private businesses. The press becomes a profitable business, and Puri uses his new earnings to fulfill an old dream—starting his own Urdu weekly, which supports Sood's political faction and receives his patronage. When Kanak arrives, she marries Puri, and the two invest their energies in this exciting new enterprise.

Thus the quintessential Hindi novel about independence and partition centers on Urdu writers, journalists, and publishers. At the outset, this choice appears peculiar, considering the intimate connection between the nationalist movement and Hindi, and between the nation and the genre of the novel. Independence, after all, marked the final triumph of Hindi over Urdu—the outcome of the long Hindi-Urdu conflict that had begun in the second half of the nineteenth century, and that was intertwined with worsening communal relations between Hindus and Muslims.[1] The recognition of Hindi and the Nagari script as the official language of lower-level legal and civil administration in Bihar (1881) and in the North-Western Provinces (1900) was the first stage in the "inexorable advance of Hindi."[2] During the Constituent Assembly debates (1946–1950), the language question emerged as one of the most acrimonious issues. The Hindi camp led a campaign against Urdu and Hindustani, which it presented as Urdu in disguise, and eventually the Constitution named Hindi, not Hindustani, as the Union's official language.[3] Although Hindi eventually gave way to English, which has remained the language of law and administration, it has received strong state patronage, including extensive public resources for the promotion of Hindi literature and the production of Hindi books.[4] In Uttar Pradesh (formerly the United Provinces), Urdu's historical heartland, the government has recognized Hindi as the sole language of administration and suspended aid to Urdu schools. Urdu has increasingly become a minority language—marginalized and associated exclusively with the Muslim minority.[5]

This trend was evident in Delhi, whose history had been intertwined with Urdu from the Mughal period. The term *Urdu*, after all, was originally the name of the city itself.[6] By the 1961 census, only 5.8 percent of the population identified Urdu as their mother tongue—a number that correlated almost perfectly with the Muslim population remaining in Delhi.[7] Moreover, the Nehruvian government turned Delhi into the cultural hub of the new nation by establishing various media and cultural institutions there, including the *Akashvani* (radio), the *Doordarshan* (national television), and the three national Academies—for literature, art and music, and dance and drama. For all their attempts to fulfill the Nehruvian ideal of "unity in diversity," these institutions eventually entrenched the national hegemony of English and Hindi, turning Delhi into a center of Hindi literature and a magnet for Hindi writers.[8]

Because Hindi had been a defining component of Indian nationalism and the Indian nation-state, the Hindi novel tends to narrate the nation and represent national themes.[9] Hence, one would expect *Jhutha Sach*—the monumental Hindi novel chronicling the Indian nation coming into its own in its capital city—to focus on Hindi. Yet Yashpal chose instead to foreground the world of the Urdu press. Why? Illuminating the vanishing sociocultural landscape of Urdu, rather than the victorious, forward-looking sphere of Hindi, fits the novel's anti-triumphalist message and its focus on the darker aspects of independence—partition violence, the exploitation of women, and corruption. But the novel also reflects the resilience of Urdu in Punjab and Delhi during the early postcolonial period. A realistic novel, which meticulously reconstructs the social currents of the time, *Jhutha Sach* accurately depicts the Urdu-centered Punjabi world as it was uprooted and resettled in Delhi.

The novel draws attention to two facts that we will investigate in this chapter. First, the city's publishing and press world was demographically transformed, mirroring the demographic upheavals of the city at large. While Muslim presses, publications, editors, and writers disappeared from the city, new ones from Punjab took their place. Second, amid this rupture, and for almost two decades after independence, Urdu continued to occupy a central role in the city's public sphere. The novel, in other words, draws attention to the gradual and deferred nature of partition.

Indeed, even in 1961, when only a tiny minority of people claimed Urdu as their primary language in the census, most newspapers and periodicals published in Delhi were in Urdu. Nearly a decade and a half after independence, Delhi still featured 16 Urdu dailies, as compared with 13 in English and 3 in Hindi. Similarly, there were 54 Urdu weeklies, as compared with 38 English weeklies and 20 Hindi ones.[10] True, the English and Hindi publications, although they were fewer, reached a larger readership and showed a greater concentration of ownership, attesting to their growing importance at the expense of Urdu.[11] Nevertheless, a few Urdu dailies also had a circulation as high as 14,000, and taken together, they had a substantial readership.[12]

Aslam Parvez, an eminent Urdu scholar, a biographer of the last Mughal emperor, and a *Dilliwalla* born and raised near Turkman Gate, remembers how Urdu print dominated everyday life in Delhi in the 1950s. While independence and partition eventually resulted in the decline of Urdu, their immediate impact was to make Urdu even more conspicuous in Delhi's streets. Thanks to the newcomers from Punjab, Urdu was everywhere—on the signboards of shops and trollies, in newspapers and magazines, and in the private schools and colleges set up by the refugees. This continued for almost two decades after partition.[13]

Literary critic Aijaz Ahmad similarly suggests that the division of language, like other aspects of partition, did not correspond neatly to the division of territory, but was a long and protracted process that matured fully only in the 1960s, especially after the Indo-Pakistan War of 1965, which "stabilized a different kind of literary map."[14]

Adjustment to what India became after Partition has required enormous and entirely willed *losses* of memory. Few historians, literary historians included, care to remember that since Urdu had become the language of cultural literacy for large numbers of Punjabi intellectuals, for whom Lahore was the main centre, the Partition of the country meant that large numbers of Urdu writers moved not only from India to Pakistan but also from Pakistan to India. . . . There were . . . thousands, perhaps hundreds of thousands, who were Hindus and Sikhs, for whom Punjabi was the spoken language, but Urdu the language of reading and writing, and who then reconciled themselves to the new realities in all sorts of painful and impoverishing ways.[15]

While Ahmad focuses on the cosmopolitan and pluralistic literary world of progressive writers,[16] this chapter delves into another legacy that lingered in the post-partition years—the legacy of Urdu journalism as a public arena in late-colonial Punjab, mediating and performing the political mayhem and the increasingly toxic communal polarization. It is this legacy and its workings in post-partition Delhi that Yashpal brings to light in *Jhutha Sach* and that we excavate here.

Urdu journalism holds the key to social realities in the streets of post-partition Delhi. Urdu was the main political language through which the two most liminal groups in the city—the Muslims who remained and the Hindu and Sikh refugees who were newly arrived—interpreted and renegotiated their right to the city and the nation at a moment when belonging and citizenship were in flux. It is no wonder that the first press officer appointed in Delhi to monitor newspapers after independence was Gopi Nath Aman, an Urdu writer and journalist who had been the editor of the daily Urdu *Tej* during the Quit India movement.[17] His selection may have been determined by the association of the Urdu press with communal trouble.

A robust language with a rich literary tradition, Urdu served as a powerful tool for an argumentative and polemic journalism. Unlike mainstream English and Hindi dailies, such as the *Hindustan Times* and *Hindustan*, where editorials were unsigned and written in a neutral and dry tone, in Urdu newspapers the editorials were signed by the owner-editors and clearly marked by their personal views and writing styles. They wielded melodrama and sarcasm, addressed the readers directly, and overwhelmed them with an excess of images, metaphors, and motifs, doggedly repeated. "There are cases in which it appears there is more poetry than journalism," complained Delhi's chief commissioner.[18]

Through their lengthy, emotive, and combative editorials, Urdu newspapers forged two main rival publics in the city: "the Muslims" and "the refugees." Indeed, if the previous chapter revealed the socioeconomic divisions that complicated such communal categories, this chapter moves to the realm of discursive representation and performance, where class differences were glossed over in order to construct more essentialized and normative publics. The newspapers of each public—Muslim and refugee—narrativized recent history, and in doing so, helped to create a unified public, interpret its position in the present, and stake its claims to the future.

The editorials demonstrate how concrete struggles over space and resources in the city were imbricated with more abstract political arguments about the categories of "minority" and "majority," the proper relationship between them, and the practical meaning of secularism. While the Constitution and Nehru's government forged a secular India, there remained a fundamental tension between community rights and individual rights, between the need to protect religious minorities and the urge to render religious identity irrelevant in political life for the sake of national integration. The Urdu press processed and concretized this dilemma through debates on everyday disputes in the city, debates that coalesced around Muslims' belonging and demands for their assimilation. The aggressive Hindutva ideology espoused by the refugee press sustained the ascendency of the Bharatiya Jana Sangh in the political life of Delhi. For their part, Muslims may have undergone marginalization and dispossession, but they were not voiceless. This chapter's analysis diverges from Zamindar's assessment that the Delhi Muslim press was "remarkably cautious" in its criticism of the government lest its loyalty be questioned.[19] The Muslim press assertively commented on the problem of minoritization and fiercely attacked the government for its inability or unwillingness to protect Muslims' lives and property. Its writings give us some access to how local Muslim public figures made sense of the secular state and minority rights, and the blind spots and tensions that beset their own positions.

In this chapter I chart the demographic transformation of Delhi's press world, as well as its narrativization of the recent past and claims to the future. Considering first the Muslim press and then the Hindu refugee publications, I analyze the main arguments and tropes in each, and point to the affective and expressive qualities of Urdu journalism, which made it a powerful tool for identity politics. Both narratives revolved around victimhood and grievances against the government, but whereas the refugee narrative represented an assertive public on the offensive, the Muslim one represented a public in withdrawal.

The chapter then moves to the "editorial wars" between these newspapers, foregrounding their performative qualities and the problem of Muslim assimilation that stood at their center. These controversies also reveal that, while partition and the cultural and linguistic policies of the newly independent state deepened the division between Hindi and Urdu and the conflation of Urdu with the minority community, closer to the ground, in the vernacular arena that leaders and officials contemptuously called the "gutter press" or "communal press," Urdu continued to function as an intimate language of communication between Muslims and Hindus. It was, no doubt, a hurtful and contentious communication, one that drew these publics further apart. Thus, Markus Daechsel's observation about late-colonial Lahore applies to our case: "Instead of a shared public sphere, Urdu constituted, perhaps more than religiously exclusive languages, a shared linguistic battleground."[20] Furthermore, we shall see that Delhi's former Muslim Leagui papers, which left for Pakistan, took an interest in the editorial controversies from across the border, fueling questions about Muslim belonging and demonstrating how connected urban spaces in India and Pakistan continued to be throughout their bitter separation. As Sarah Ansari and William Gould emphasize, India and Pakistan in the early post-independence period were "relational spaces," shaped by close connections and movement between them.[21]

A PRESS WORLD TORN ASUNDER

Before partition, Abdul Rahman Siddiqi worked for the most important Muslim League news organ—the English daily *Dawn*.[22] Siddiqui recalls how, after the June 3 announcement of partition, Altaf Hussain, the legendary editor of *Dawn*, was on top of the world. The management decided to publish the newspaper simultaneously from Delhi and Karachi, starting with a solemn edition on August 15.[23] In retrospect, this was a fanciful aspiration, another indication that important Muslim Leaguers did not yet fathom the full implications of a division into two states, even at this late stage. The Bombay-based writer Dosabhai Framji Karaka reported that, when he met Hussain in Delhi in June 1947, the latter "visualized no difficulties about the future of Pakistan. He was also sure the link with India would continue. 'Trains still run from Dacca to Delhi,' he said. 'There is no reason why they should not continue to do so in the future.'"[24]

But as partition drew near, such dreams dissolved. Hussain and other senior staff left for Karachi, and there was a growing rift between them and the team that stayed in Delhi, overcome by a gnawing uncertainty about the future. The Delhi office barely managed to function—"It was a like an abandoned ship, left to sink or swim on its own."[25] Siddiqi remembers that Altaf Hussain's vitriolic editorials felt out of place in the changing context, and the Delhi edition started writing its own editorials. The bitter editorial of August 18 declared:

> Is it not true that one of the reasons which led the Muslims of the minority provinces to throw themselves whole-heartedly, almost recklessly, in the vanguard of the battle for Pakistan was the hope and assurance that when such a state was established, it would be able to protect them also against injustice and tyranny? Now that Pakistan has come into, that promise must be honoured and hope fulfilled.[26]

Describing the Independence Day celebrations in Delhi, another item in the same issue depicted the Indian flag flying above the *Dawn* office as the most beautiful in the whole area. Such an attempt to fit into a new India was awkward and doomed. On September 9, Deputy Commissioner Mohinder Singh Randhawa, in his capacity as district magistrate, served a prepublication censorship order on *Dawn* for publishing inflammatory accounts of the partition violence.[27] A couple of days later, *Dawn's* office in Daryaganj was ransacked and the building set on fire.[28] Any dreams of maintaining the Muslim Leagui paper in India shattered. After October 1947, the paper was published solely from Karachi, and circulation of it in Delhi was, in fact, banned.[29]

The Urdu daily *Jang* (Battle) continued to function in Delhi for a while longer, and the editor, Mohammed Suleiman Sabir, harbored hopes similar to Hussain's, as evident in a letter he sent to Prime Minister

Nehru four months after partition, accusing Randhawa of persecuting the paper, proclaiming his complete loyalty to the Indian Union, and emphasizing that the staff and proprietor of the paper had changed after Independence Day. The proprietor and publisher Khalil-ur Rahman had indeed departed for Karachi, leaving the paper's legal status doubtful. Randhawa, for his part, explained that the paper had published scurrilous material on communal disturbances and continued to do so despite recurrent warnings and a prepublication censorship order. By February 1948, publication of the paper was banned, and *Jang* was published solely from Karachi.[30] *Anjam* (End, Fulfilment) lasted a little longer, but by 1952, it appeared in the press files, alongside *Al Aman* (Peace), as a "Pakistani newspaper."[31] Many other Muslim publishers, editors, and press owners left as well.[32] The Muslim press of post-partition Delhi was a broken world. The few papers that stayed behind had a limited circulation and were in a very precarious financial position, always on the verge of closure. The Delhi administration aggravated their vulnerability by using the colonial measures of demanding and forfeiting securities from newspapers and presses.

Maulana Abdul Waheed Siddiqui, who founded *Nayi Duniya* (New World) as a daily paper in 1951, was constantly shadowed by the CID.[33] Like many other Urdu newspapers, *Nayi Duniya* was a family-run business, and the office was located on the first floor of the family house in Haveli Hissamuddin Haider—a residential area within Ballimaran, where Abdul Rahman Siddiqi also lived until his departure for Pakistan. Their residence was an "open house," a social hub where people constantly came and went, often staying overnight. The CID paid some of the poorer visitors and office employees to report regularly on the goings-on in the place. CID files on *Nayi Duniya* through 1960 confirm that it was under close watch, intermittently characterized as a pro-Pakistan, pro-communist, or pro-American paper.[34] Simultaneously, recurring government demands for securities destabilized the family's already-insecure finances, and Siddiqui had to close down the paper in 1963.

Other Muslim-owned publications, even strong supporters of a "nationalist Muslim," pro-Congress stance, experienced similar hardship. Take, for example, Aziz Hasan Baqai, a veteran Delhi journalist associated with the anti-British Khilafat movement. His weekly *Hurriyat* (Liberty) was a ferocious critic of Pakistan and the Muslim League in the 1940s, calling its leaders "terrorists" and accusing them of conspiring to poison Congress leaders.[35] Celebrated Congress leaders, including Vijaya Lakshmi Pandit, Govind Ballabh Pant, Rajendra Prasad, and Maulana Azad, to name a few, wrote letters in 1946–1947 attesting to Baqai's unflagging and fearless support of India's freedom and unity, in an effort to help *Hurriyat* secure advertisements from commercial firms.[36] In 1948 Deputy Commissioner Randhawa vouched for Baqai's unflinching service to the Indian Union and his loyalty to the Congress, which had even led to threats on his life and attempted arson by Muslim League *goondas* (thugs). Yet, after independence, the paper experienced financial difficulties, suspicions of Pakistani ties, and close CID surveillance, and it closed down in 1949. Baqai felt betrayed, and his health deteriorated. His daughter, now living in Pakistan, wished to visit him, but the Indian High Commissioner in Pakistan denied her application; when she was finally granted permission and arrived in Delhi, it was too late.[37] Baqai's family represents the predicament of Muslims divided across the border, and of nationalist Muslims who had opposed the Muslim League before partition and now remained to pick up the pieces it left behind. Another example is Abdullah Farooqi, proprietor of Farooqi Press. He had been imprisoned by the British for his role in the noncooperation and civil disobedience movements, and he was a member of the Ahrars, who had opposed the Muslim League and Pakistan. Nevertheless, he was arrested after partition for publishing a poster criticizing Randhawa, police officers, and Special Police officers for their role in communal violence.[38]

The insecure position of Muslim newspapers after independence is most glaring in the case of the Urdu daily *Al Jamiat* (The Association)— the official organ of the Jamiat Ulama-e Hind (Association of Islamic Scholars).[39] As discussed in Chapter 1, the Jamiat Ulama was established in 1919 by a group of ulama, mostly from Deoband, who participated in the pan-Islamic, anti-British Khilafat movement. The organization subsequently supported the Congress nationalist struggle for independence and situated itself in opposition to the Muslim League's two-nation theory. Its headquarters was in Delhi, and after independence, when many Muslim

League leaders left for Pakistan, the Jamiat Ulama sought to become the new mouthpiece for the shattered Muslim public in the city and the nation. Maulana Azad supported it, and in his famous speech at Jama Masjid in October 1947, he told his Muslim audience that the Jamiat Ulama was now the only body to safeguard their interests.[40] At its 1948 conference in Lucknow, the organization reiterated its alliance with the Congress, endorsed the secular constitution that was in the making, and condemned separate electorates and reservations for Muslims. It also renounced its political functions and declared itself a purely socioreligious organization, though in practice its leaders continued to operate in the political arena and even vie for seats on the Congress ticket.[41] As a major broker of Muslim votes, it had a strong alliance with the Congress, which provided it with government resources to maintain its social and educational network.

Yet official correspondence on *Al Jamiat* by press offices in the Delhi secretariat and the CID reveals that officers' perception of the paper was equivocal. It oscillated between representing *Al Jamiat* as a "nationalist" paper with a sober tone, considered legitimate for publishing government advertisements, and a "communal" paper that "has indulged in insidious propaganda of a dangerous type against the Indian Union."[42] One CID officer went so far as to state that *Al Jamiat*'s abundant criticism poisoned the political atmosphere and stood "as a living and open danger to the internal as well as external, security of Bharat."[43] Another claimed, "'Al Jamiat' is still playing on its communal siren of creating another Pakistan in India of today."[44]

That even the Muslim newspaper closest to the Congress experienced such an inconsistent official attitude indicates that the predicament of the Muslim press and public was structurally embedded in the political situation that emerged from partition. What the *Al Jamiat* articles that officers found so objectionable all had in common was a preoccupation with the status of Muslims as a minority (*aqaliyat*), specifically with its oppression and victimhood. Officers deemed this a "communal" approach that reinforced the separateness of Muslims as a community, curbed their assimilation into the national body, and played into the hands of Pakistan at a time when the two states were trying to regularize the protection of minorities. We shall see that *Al Jamiat*'s writings on the minority's predicament antagonized not only a few officers, who may have been biased, but Nehru himself. His ambivalent attitude to *Al Jamiat* points to the tensions that underlay his own efforts at forming a secular state against the backdrop of partition.

WHAT SHOULD THE MUSLIMS DO?
MINORITIZATION ON THE PAGES OF *AL JAMIAT*

> What Should the Muslims Do? Conditions have changed fast. After August 15, every morning and every evening have brought a new upheaval.
>
> Probably no community in this century has faced such hefty troubles as the Muslim minority in India, so abruptly and rapidly. The greatest wound was inflicted on the Muslims by their own leaders. Having crippled the community, they fled and abandoned it in the midst of the cyclone.
>
> If our leaders were brave like the leaders of other communities, having failed, they would have stayed among us and struggled, or at least borne with the community the very troubles they created. They did not have the courage to do either. The unsuccessful leaders of other communities commit suicide. This path probably would have been better than fleeing, both for them and for the community.
>
> The disasters that befell the Indian Muslims have broken mountains, and just the thought of them causes one to quiver. But the courage and firmness with which they have tolerated these problems teach us that they have the ability to survive. Now the question remains as to what the Muslims should do in order to cross this river of blood.[45]
>
> You are on the bank of the river and I am standing in its depths. I can say with full responsibility that conditions in the country are improving.[46]

Al Jamiat, like *Nayi Duniya*, was published from the Muslim locality of Ballimaran, at Gali Qasim Jan. Its circulation, estimated in 1951 at 5,000, was lower than those of the refugee papers but higher than those of most other Muslim publications.[47] As letters to the editor indicate, its readership consisted mainly of north Indian Muslims from Uttar Pradesh and Delhi. It conveyed the Jamiat Ulama's concern with the spread of Islam and with the moral, spiritual, and educational uplift of Muslims, and extensively covered the organization's social work among Muslims and the activities and speeches of its leadership. Its editorial page featured, alongside the leading article, a regular column on the cultivation of a moral daily life guided by the Quran. The paper also used a relatively Arabicized Urdu, which distinguished it not only from the Hindu papers but also from *Nayi Duniya*, whose language was simpler and more accessible.

As the epigraphs above signal, crisis was an overarching theme in *Al Jamiat* in the period immediately after partition. The first quote is taken from an editorial published in February 1948. The second, published exactly a year later, cites a speech delivered by Maulana Azad to a Muslim public.[48] The image of the Muslim community standing on the bank of a river is present in both, capturing the experience of this period as a cataclysm and expressing the Muslim public's apprehensions about the future. This anxiety is conveyed by the titles of editorials from this period, which often end with a question mark: "What Should the Muslims Do?," "Why Are the Muslims Leaving?," "What Is Happening?" They all point to one fundamental question—what are the position and prospects of the religious minority in an independent state that is formally committed to democracy and secularism, yet has just emerged from a partition along religious lines entailing horrific sectarian violence?

The question was asked against the background of mounting pressures on Muslim zones and the uncertain movement of Muslims across the India-Pakistan border.[49] These hardships are detailed both in the paper's articles and in letters to the editor. Letters from Uttar Pradesh and Hyderabad refer to grievous riots—more accurately pogroms—especially during the annual *Holi* festival, and to the continuing outflow of Muslims to Pakistan.[50] Letters from Delhi refer to small-scale violence and, more often, to a daily experience of harassment, dispossession by the Custodian of Evacuee Property, and boycotts of Muslim businesses. In the summer of 1948, when Delhi was suffused with communal tensions following the return of thousands of Muslims rumored to be Pakistani spies, *Al Jamiat* reported that Muslim travelers on trams faced daily abuse and were repeatedly asked, "Why didn't you just go to Pakistan? Why do we still see your face here?" Even if injured, they would not report the incident to the police knowing they would be dismissed.[51] The following summer, the newspaper reported on tensions escalating around Muslim evacuee property, allegations that Muslim men were molesting Hindu women, and business competition in Sabzi Mandi, where Muslims from Pakistan arrived on temporary permits to sell mangoes during the summer season.[52] While mainstream papers like the *Times of India* downplayed these incidents as "minor,"[53] *Al Jamiat* claimed they were grave and the result of a deep RSS (Rashtriya Swayamsevak Sangh, the Hindu nationalist organization) conspiracy ignored by police officers.[54]

Reports of persecution became pressing in 1950, when violence targeting minorities on both sides of the border escalated to worrisome proportions. As discussed in Chapter 3, riots in East Pakistan were reciprocated in West Bengal and, subsequently, in Uttar Pradesh and Delhi, setting in motion another wave of Muslim emigration. *Al Jamiat*'s leading editorial from May 5, 1950, entitled "Why Are the Muslims Leaving?" included a sampling of purported letters from readers, who described growing fear and isolation.[55] One person reported that refugees from Karol Bagh had ordered goods from him but then refused to pay and even threatened to kill him, taking advantage of Muslims' vulnerability. Another letter, entitled "Why Shouldn't the Muslims Leave?," complained that one merely needed to go shopping in Delhi's markets in Khari Baoli to get a sense of the majority's mindset:

> Go to a Hindu shopkeeper and ask for something. The minute he sees your beard, he will turn his face away. If you request twice or thrice more, he will reply in such a way that will clarify he does not want to sell anything to us. . . . If such things reach the ears of the officers, they do not listen. Muslims are helpless. What shall they do but migrate?[56]

Another item described a new phenomenon of "communal begging": Beggars, mostly refugees, roamed Delhi's train stations and bazaars, targeting Muslims. Shoving a small Congress flag in their hands, they asked for money in return, creating a *tamasha* (spectacle) to pressure their targets, who feared the accusation of disloyalty if they refused.[57]

The events of 1950 harshly exposed the uncertain fate of minorities in both countries and, concomitantly, brought to a boiling point the simmering tensions between *Al Jamiat* and state authorities in charge of the press. *Al Jamiat* was preoccupied with violence against Muslims and, increasingly, with the Nehru-Liaquat Pact—also known as the "Delhi pact" or "minorities pact"—signed between the prime ministers of both countries on April 8, 1950, in New Delhi. We mentioned this pact briefly in Chapter 3. It is time to analyze its implications more fully, because it became a contentious issue on the pages of *Al Jamiat*, one that distills the contradictory conceptions of citizenship in this period of flux.

The pact made the two governments accountable to each other with respect to protecting their minorities in Bengal. Each government agreed to ensure to its minority

> complete equality of citizenship, irrespective of religion, a full sense of se-
> curity in respect of life, culture, property and personal honour, freedom of
> movement within each country and freedom of occupation, speech and wor-
> ship, subject to law and morality. Members of the minorities shall have equal
> opportunity with members of the majority community to participate in the
> public life of their country, to hold political or other office, and to serve in
> their country's civil and armed forces.[58]

The pressing matter was to curb the exodus of refugees and to enable those who had fled to return. Accordingly, the agreement emphasized the urgent need to restore normal conditions and to inspire confidence among the minorities. Significantly, it underscored the role of the press, and both sides agreed to "prevent the dissemination of news and mischievous opinion calculated to rouse communal passions by press or radio or any individual or organisation."[59] Allegations and counterallegations of violating the pact followed.[60]

In this charged atmosphere, *Al Jamiat* editorials and readers' letters dwelt at length on the Indian government's failure to fulfill its part of the deal. They claimed that India's police officers, Custodian Department officials, and newspapers did nothing to restore the minority's confidence, but instead induced fear and migration to Pakistan. Instead of compensating Muslims for their looted property, punishing perpetrators of riots, and expelling communal police officers—measures specified in the agreement—the government signaled to Muslims that their lives and

property were unsafe in India. Editorials and letters repeated these complaints again and again, forming a discourse of victimhood that, justified
as it may have been, annoyed press officers, who claimed that *Al Jamiat*
was tarnishing India's reputation and serving as Pakistani propaganda.
In its effort to illuminate the dire condition of Muslims in India, the
paper went a step further and recurrently depicted Pakistan in idealized
terms, arguing that Pakistan honored the pact and that religious minorities there were better off than their counterparts in India.[61]

Al Jamiat sided with the Pakistani newspapers, which had recently
been its fiercest rivals. We may recall that in 1939, as competition between the nationalist Muslims and Muslim League became vicious, two
Deobandi students murdered the editor of *Al Aman* for his attacks on
the Jamiat Ulama, and that contentious exchanges between Muslim
Leagui and nationalist Muslim papers escalated in the 1940s. But now *Al
Jamiat* praised *Dawn* (relocated to Karachi) for dedicating a column to
the Hindu and Sikh minorities and providing them with a safe space to
express their suffering. The newspapers of India had made no such ges-
ture, continued the editorial, and thus the Muslim press was compelled
to voice the minority's concerns. It added that Pakistan possessed the
unity and leadership required to implement the pact, while India was
torn by opposition, "groupism," and lack of leadership.[62] An editorial that
advanced this unflattering comparison stated:

> [It is] pointless to say that here is a "secular state" [using the English word],
> over there a religious state, here a democracy, over there a dictatorship. This
> discussion is useless for the minorities. What they need is peace and protec-
> tion. It is your business whether you want to establish a secular state or a
> dictatorship or a democracy! The problem of the minorities is solved where
> they do not feel hopeless about their future and do not consider the country's
> majority and government a threat! Beyond that, what does it matter to the
> minority what kind of political system the majority established! . . . If the
> intentions are not good, then no form of government will bear good conse-
> quences. . . . If the minorities in Pakistan are guaranteed their lives, property,
> and honor, and are not discriminated against . . . It is none of their concern
> why Pakistan is an Islamic state, and . . . if Pakistan becomes a secular state![63]

The editorial adds that the world is hiding its brutality and barbarity behind magical words—implying that the democratic and lofty language of India's constitution, passed a few months earlier, is useless for protecting Muslims. It concludes by again comparing the Pakistani newspapers, which have been quick to reform their tone, with the Indian newspapers in Bengal and Delhi, which have not changed a bit and thus impede the agreement and sully India's name in the world.[64] Noteworthy is the writer's claim that the minority has no interest in the form of governance established by the majority, as long as it remains safe. This statement expresses disengagement from the country's political life and decision-making processes, a withdrawal inward into a ghetto. We shall return to this isolationism later in the chapter.

Clearly, *Al Jamiat* stepped up its criticism of the government following the Nehru-Liaquat Pact. Why was the pact such a charged affair? We have seen that various visions of Pakistan in the 1940s addressed the issue of minorities only vaguely, proposing everything from autonomous regions to nation-in-minority status to an independent oversight body.[65] Now the pact brought into sharp relief the hitherto implicit question of minorities' belonging in the new states. The two governments attempted to develop a bilateral framework that made them accountable to each other. This entailed clarifying, in international legal terms, the relationship between each government and the minorities. The pact touched on the vexed question of national belonging and citizenship, and the tension between jus soli and jus sanguinis principles of citizenship.[66]

On the one hand, the pact emphasized that the "allegiance and loyalty of the minorities is to the State of which they are citizens, and that it is to the Government of their own State that they should look for the redress of their grievances."[67] Such a statement is grounded in a conception of citizenship based on one's country of birth (jus soli). Indeed, given that the underlying purpose of the agreement was to stop and even to reverse population transfers, it was anchored in jus soli.[68]

On the other hand, a notion of jus sanguinis, or citizenship based on blood descent, crept into the agreement through the mechanism of accountability that it set in place. In 1948, the Calcutta inter-dominion agreement had given each country's diplomatic representative (the high

commissioner) the power to protect religious minorities in the country where he was posted.[69] The Nehru-Liaquat Pact retreated from this
baldly jus sanguinis arrangement by instead setting up minority commis-
sions in each of the relevant provinces, comprising a minister and representatives of the majority and minority communities, all residents of the
country. But both countries also agreed "to depute two Ministers, one
from each Government, to remain in the affected areas for such period
as may be necessary."[70] A minister from India would continue to monitor the situation in East Pakistan, and vice versa. He was authorized to
participate in or convene meetings of the minority commission and to receive its reports. Thus, while the pact reaffirmed the responsibility of each
state for the minorities in its territory, thereby advancing a territorial conception of nationality and citizenship, it simultaneously recognized that
the other state also had a stake and a voice in their protection, thereby
implying citizenship based on religious affiliation. In essence, India and
Pakistan intimated that minorities were both citizens of their country
of residence and, implicitly, "semi-nationals" of the other country, where
their co-religionists formed a majority.

Pallavi Raghavan points out that the bilateral structure of accountability set up by the Nehru-Liaquat Pact was reminiscent of the League
of Nations' supranational system of minority protection in interwar Europe.[71] I suggest that it also partly echoed the contradictions that inhered
in the earlier system. As Hannah Arendt perceptively observed, the failure of the League of Nations to protect European minorities was not
merely a weakness in implementation, but was structurally ingrained in
the system's logic. When Europe entrusted the protection of minorities
to an international body, it submitted "that millions of people lived outside normal legal protection and needed an additional guarantee of their
elementary rights from an outside body."[72] Furthermore, the operation
of the system inadvertently highlighted extraterritorial loyalties of ethnic
and religious minorities. A notable example is the fervent activism of
Weimar Germany in scrutinizing the condition of German minorities in
East Central and Southern Europe.

Likewise, the Nehru-Liaquat Pact became such a charged issue because it delineated two sets of triangular relationships: first, between each

minority group and the two nation-states—the state where the minority resided and the state where its co-religionists lived; and, second, between each state and the two minority groups—the minority religion residing within its territory and its co-religionist minority residing in the other country. These were triangles of ambiguous affiliation, of tension between jus soli and jus sanguinis conceptions of citizenship. Thus, even before the pact was signed, *Al Jamiat* complained that government leaders who expressed concern for minorities in East Pakistan and Kashmir considered those Hindus brothers and sisters, but did not care about Muslims in their own country.[73] A mirror charge could be leveled at *Al Jamiat*, whose extensive reportage on the oppression of Muslims constructed a discourse of Muslim victimhood, which Pakistan weaponized in its accusations against India, assuming the role of savior of the Muslim minority in India.[74] Such a role had been a central pillar of the Muslim League's justification for Pakistan in the first place (explicitly referencing Germany's protection of Sudeten Germans in Czechoslovakia) and the Nehru-Liaquat Pact seemed to reaffirm it, multiplying doubts about *Al Jamiat's* loyalty in an environment already tending toward suspicion.

The Nehru-Liaquat Pact was an important step in the transition from past expectations to a new reality, but it exemplified the contradictions that accompanied this gradual and painful transition. These contradictions were reflected in *Al Jamiat's* response to the pact—reiterating its loyalty to India while comparing it unfavorably with Pakistan—and in the official response to *Al Jamiat*—treating it as both a nationalist paper and a communal one. The refugee newspapers, to which we now turn, also addressed this contradiction, even as they exchanged verbal blows with the Muslim papers.

THE PUNJABI PRESS TRANSPLANTED TO DELHI

By the late nineteenth century, Lahore had become a pulsating intellectual and political center, bursting with books and newspapers, colleges and libraries, clubs and associations. As historian Farina Mir notes, British policy in Punjab made Urdu the official language of administration and law, and the press followed.[75] With the gradual decline of Urdu in the United Provinces after 1900, "Punjab became the undisputed centre

of Urdu publishing, and by extension of Urdu reading."[76] After partition, much of Lahore's Hindu and Sikh intelligentsia moved to Delhi.
The Delhi CID archives contain bulky files with hundreds of applications
every month for permission to open printing presses, newspapers, and
magazines.[77] They give the impression that the entire Punjabi press was
transplanted to Delhi, and that most of it was in Urdu.

On the whole, the numerous Punjabi proprietors and editors, report-
ers, columnists, writers, poets, and intellectuals who arrived in Delhi
formed a diverse crowd, reflecting the broad ideological spectrum of
late-colonial Punjab—from communists and progressives to Hindu
Mahasabha proponents and Akali Sikhs. We cannot do justice to this
heterogeneity, and we concentrate instead on the most important Hindu
dailies in Lahore, all of which later shifted to Delhi, and all of which engaged in ferocious exchanges with Muslim publications, simultaneously
expressing and intensifying communal polarization.[78] By the late 1920s,
the three most important Hindu dailies in Lahore were the Arya Samaji
Milap and *Pratap*, and the Sanatan Dharmi *Vir Bharat*. A contemporary
joke that played on the names of Lahore's dailies was that the paper that
caused the most discord and rift was *Milap* (Union or Agreement), the
most cowardly one was *Pratap* (Vigor, Courage), and the most conservative one was *Inqalab* (Revolution, a Muslim paper).[79] Daechsel's study of
these publications in the 1930s–1940s finds that they focused on communal tensions and such sensational matter as crime, natural calamities, and
accidents, and that conflict and fear were their defining themes.[80]

Mahashay Krishna launched *Pratap* in March 1919, in the context of
the Gandhian satyagraha against the Rowlatt Act. He named the paper
after the sixteenth-century Rajput Hindu ruler, Maharana Pratap Singh,
who fought the Mughal Akbar. Along with the semantic range of the
word *pratap*—glowing heat, vigor, glory, ardor, and zeal—the name evokes
Hindu masculine heroism. Krishna was a prolific writer who commented
on the burning issues of his time, "a kind of firebrand who simply would
not bow to anybody."[81] He and Lala Kushal Chand, who established the
daily *Milap* four years later in 1923, may have been professional competi-
tors who criticized each other in pungent editorials, but also close associates who went on long walks every evening.[82] Both Krishna's and Kushal

Chand's families took an active part in the nationalist struggle—family members were imprisoned—and their newspapers published nationalist materials deemed objectionable by the government.[83] Their nationalist politics exemplified the politics of Hindus in late-colonial Punjab, where there was an overlap between the Congress and the Hindu Mahasabha in terms of membership and political sentiments.[84]

When the partition riots broke out in Lahore, *Milap*'s office was burned down, and its workers barely escaped under army protection, mirroring the fate of *Dawn* in Delhi. It reopened soon after in Delhi.[85] Likewise, Krishna and his family left Lahore and relocated in Delhi, re-establishing *Pratap* in Panchkuian Road in Paharganj, now a hub of Punjabi presence in the city. Together they became important mouthpieces voicing the concerns and grievances of the city's refugee community. The first piece of information on *Milap*'s relocation is a mention that Kushal Chand was arrested following an "objectionable" speech he delivered in a Hindu Sahayata Samiti public meeting.[86] In subsequent years, both newspapers' relations with the Delhi administration remained tense, as their vocal and confrontational writing was critical of the Congress and closely aligned with the Hindu right.

We should note that this Punjabization of Delhi's press, with its overt Arya Samaji tones, was not entirely new, but built on existing networks. We have seen how Delhi gradually became Hinduized during the latter part of the nineteenth century, a process that ultimately led to the establishment of Birla Mandir, the Hindu Mahasabha Bhavan, and the first RSS branch in the 1930s.[87] Swami Shraddhanand, we noted, was central to spreading the influence of Arya Samaj, with its emphasis on *Shuddhi* (ritual purification reinterpreted as proselytism) and cow protection. He established two daily nationalist newspapers aligned with both the Congress and the Arya Samaj—the Hindi *Vir Arjun*, edited by his son Pandit Indra Vidyavachaspati, and the Urdu *Tej*, which was edited by his follower and local Congress leader Lala Deshbandhu Gupta and engaged in fierce exchanges with the Muslim press. *Milap* and *Pratap* tapped into this Arya Samaji network and extended its presence in the city. The well-connected Deshbandhu Gupta helped Krishna and his family to get a house in New Delhi after partition,[88] and Krishna purchased and revived *Vir Arjun* in 1954, to serve as a Hindi counterpart to the Urdu *Pratap*.[89] These newspapers narrated the refugees' displacement and their experience of Delhi, forging a Punjabi refugee public and staking an assertive moral claim to the city and the nation.

"THIS IS DELHI": THE FORMATION OF A "REFUGEE PUNJABI" PUBLIC IN POST-PARTITION DELHI

As our point of entry into the construction of a refugee public in the city, let us consider the following satirical column, published in *Milap* in July 1948:

> This is Delhi and I am a refugee [*sharanarthi*]. From the very first day I arrived in Delhi, the accountant of *Milap* started to cut taxes from my salary on behalf of the government. The government gave me neither a house nor any other facility. In spite of this, I am considered a refugee and every *Dilliwalla* believes that I am here because of his mercy and that he is my master. . . .
>
> This is Delhi and this is Delhi's Coffee House. Here, the refugees drink coffee and the *Dilliwallas* drink only water. And even water they only drink so they can curse the refugees.[90] One *Dilliwalla* is drinking water and cursing the refugees. The refugees are listening and are keeping quiet. They know very well why the *Dilliwalla* is angry. He doesn't have money for a cup of coffee, so what can he do but curse those who drink coffee. . . .
>
> This is Delhi, this is Paharganj and the *tonga* stand. A ride from Qutab Road costs two annas. Only after I sat down in a *tonga* did I realize that . . . the *tongawalla* was a *Dilliwalla*. When I reached Qutab Road, I gave him two annas. He became angry and demanded four annas. . . . When I started speaking Punjabi, he cooled down and left, saying, "Who will fight with the refugee *goondas* [thugs]."
>
> This is the stand at Qutab Road. The same *tongawalla* stands there. He is not prepared to go for less than four annas, so he doesn't get any passengers. He is sitting in his *tonga* as if it were the Peacock Throne. Within a few minutes, at least ten *tongas* have left the stand with passengers. Still, he looked at

the other *tongawallas* as if saying, "These *kamine* [rascal] refugees have killed my livelihood."

. . .

This is Delhi and this is Connaught Place. I am a newcomer. I am looking for the post office. I ask one *Dilliwalla* for the address. He snaps angrily, "It's in front of you, are you blind?". . . I feel like hitting him on the head, but then I think that I am a refugee, so people will say I am a *goonda*.[91]

The writer of the column, Gopal Mittal, was an Urdu poet and writer who wrote for *Milap* in Lahore and, after partition, in Delhi.[92] He takes us along on a tour of the city, delineating the spatial boundaries of this urban setting as he experiences it. At the center lies Qutab Road, the main road stretching along the railway line, from Sadar Bazar southward through Paharganj to Connaught Place in New Delhi, where the Coffee House is located—the institution that once catered to American soldiers, and where enthusiastic Muslim Leaguers debated the prospects of Pakistan with their Hindu pals. Mittal arranged his daily routine between Sadar Bazar and the Coffee House.

The writer conflates the migrants' wide array of religious, social, regional, and caste identities into the unified social category of "refugee." Notably, this new social actor in the city experiences it as a space of daily friction and hostile encounters. The narrator is bitter, feeling like an unwelcome newcomer in an unfriendly city, whose social landscape is divided in two—the *Dilliwallas* and the refugees.

Ravinder Kaur notes that "Punjabi refugees" has become a monolithic and all-encompassing discursive category. It subsumes, among other distinctions, the various regional identities of migrants under the umbrella name "Punjabis"—referring to the province from which the bulk of refugees came. Conscious efforts at such amalgamation are evident in the contemporary editorials of Ranbir Singh—Lala Kushal Chand's eldest son and editor of *Milap* until his death in 1982. "Ranbir," as he signed his editorials, wrote sardonically in an editorial provocatively entitled "Just Shoot Them with Cannons":

Gandhiji, Pandit Jawaharlalji, and other leaders are sad because of those Punjabis who arrived from Pakistan and are disturbing their life of comfort with stories of destruction. By Punjabis I mean all those Hindus and Sikhs who arrived in India from West Punjab, the frontier, Sindh, or Baluchistan. In terms of race and culture, they are all Punjabis. Their culture is one, their food is one, their customs are one.[93]

These lines attempt to appropriate refugees from other regions, who, in fact, often felt marginalized by the government's Punjabi-centric rehabilitation policy.[94] Similarly, the master narrative about Punjabi refugees conceals class and caste differences that determined strikingly disparate experiences during the journey from Pakistan, absorption into the city, and rehabilitation by the state. As Ian Talbot notes, the experience of the poor masses, "trudging with bullock carts or clinging precariously to train roofs, before huddling together in tented camps," became the dominant image of partition refugees, occluding the more comfortable journeys and living arrangements of the upper classes.[95] In reality, there was a huge difference between those who could transfer money in advance or carry jewelry, and those who arrived destitute; between those who had relatives in the city to host them, those who turned to refugee camps, and those whom the camps could not accommodate and who had to fend for themselves in the streets. Thus, in December 1948, when there were forty-four thousand people in the camps, and there was mounting clamor for admission into the camps because of the harsh winter, almost all applications were flatly refused. Delhi's Relief and Rehabilitation Commissioner expressed embarrassment at the fact that, "Whereas we provide food, clothing, and shelter to refugees in camps we completely ignore the genuine and modest demands for help . . . by those who are in no way being helped by the government."[96]

As Kaur demonstrates, the socioeconomic and caste hierarchies of late-colonial Punjab were preserved and reproduced in Delhi through all stages of rehabilitation. Economic means, connections, and caste determined in what camp, precisely, a refugee family would be accommodated; whether it was housed in a tent or barracks; whether it would be allocated evacuee property or not; and whether it would be permanently settled in a centrally located and spacious colony, such as Nizamuddin Extension, or in a one-room apartment on the city's outskirts, with shared bathrooms, no modern sewage, and no electricity.

FIGURE 4.1 *Rajan Nehru, wife of R. K. Nehru, distributing food to the inmates of the Kingsway refugee camp, 1947. Source: Photo Division, Press Information Bureau, Ministry of Information and Broadcasting, Government of India.*

Judging by the rapidity with which *Milap* and *Pratap* resumed publication after arrival in Delhi, both proprietors left Lahore with sufficient means. Moreover, as mentioned above, they had connections in the city.[97] Yet their writings forged a unified Punjabi refugee category, centered on victimhood and loss, alongside pride, enterprising spirit, and hard work. Parenthetically, their news coverage and editorials throughout 1948 also spoke of refugee Hindus and Sikhs en bloc, as non-Muslim victims of Muslim aggression. This encompassing categorization would start to collapse in 1949 with the rise of Hindu-Sikh tensions in Punjab and attendant controversies between Hindu and Sikh refugee papers.

In addition to refugees as a category, Mittal's satirical column "This Is Delhi" demonstrates a preoccupation with money. The narrator thinks about rupees throughout the day, indicating the state of mind of refugees and, more generally, of a society living in austerity and everyday struggle. Significantly, there is pride in the Punjabi character—hard-working and honest and, no less important, knowing how to enjoy and willing to pay for the small joys of life, such as a cup of coffee. Delhi's people are, by contrast, lazy and arrogant, rude and stingy. Refugees have entrepreneurial spirit—they offer competitive prices for low-margin profits and adapt to changing circumstances. *Dilliwallas*, on the other hand, are inflexible and stuck in the past.

As Kaur notes, the tropes of Punjabi diligence, self-respect, and enterprise have become stereotypes among Hindu and Sikh migrants from West Pakistan—alongside the absence of government assistance when they needed it most.[98] In fact there was significant governmental aid in the form of temporary camps, rationing, job training, and the mass housing projects in "refugee colonies" that expanded Delhi to the west and south.[99] Nevertheless, the column opens with the notion of government uselessness, as the narrator mockingly reports that the government taxes him rather than help him. This assertion of self-reliance, and even of shouldering the collective economic burden, establishes his right to the city. He wishes to shake off the title "refugee," stressing that he lives at the mercy of no one.

Whereas the bitterness that saturates Mittal's satirical column is softened by humor and lightweight tone, it takes on a darker shade elsewhere in the refugee press. Writers directed their anger at three main sources—the Congress government, the Muslim minority, and Delhites in general. By emphasizing the deficiencies of government help, they positioned refugees at the center of a story of loss and injustice that established their moral entitlement to the city at the expense of Muslim residents. The trope of government neglect took shape in close association with the political division between left and right, inside and outside the Congress, especially over the question of Muslims' belonging.

Grievances against the Congress targeted both its past and present misdeeds: the Congress was held responsible both for the disaster of partition and the ruination of Punjab, and for its failure to compensate Punjabis for what was duly theirs. By this logic, rehabilitation was not an expression of the government's goodwill or Delhites' charity, but simply what the government owed the refugees as atonement and compensation for their grave losses, for which it bore responsibility. It is worth explicating this argument by citing a representative editorial, in which Ranbir wrote that Indian leaders and officers

> were sitting in their nice, big bungalows, in their big houses. They have become owners of big factories. And they have become masters of such a huge country. They thought: "The British have gone, so we'll enjoy our life now. We'll draw fat salaries. We'll do a lot of business. And we'll rule with splendor." But then the destroyed Hindus and Sikhs of Punjab, the frontier, and Sindh came to their doorstep like an unexpected disaster. . . . One thing these people forget is that if we have been destroyed, it was not any of our fault, but because the Indian leaders proved incapable of understanding the tricks of the British and the mentality of the Pakistanis. These people were deceived and now they are deceiving us. They accepted Pakistan without asking us and against our own will. They should have known that we would bear the heaviest burden of Pakistan. . . . Then they betrayed us once more. They told us: "You should stay in Pakistan [and] we will protect you." But they had neither a mechanism nor a method to protect us. We were victims of their lack of sense and their deception. And now it is these people who think of us as a problem. These people, who live in huge bungalows, tell us that they don't have any room for us.[100]

As the editorial progresses, it becomes darker:

> These are the same people who came to our doorstep a few months ago like beggars, begging for our votes and support. These are the people who deceived us, saying that Pakistan would be built on their own dead bodies. . . . These are the people whose incompetence and fraud killed not thousands but lakhs of our brothers. . . . It is because of these people that thousands of our sisters and daughters experienced dishonor unlike anything ever seen before. It is because of these people that thousands of our women are caught in the claws of Pakistani animals. And each of these women is forced to become the wife of ten to twenty husbands. It is because of them that our well-settled homes were ruined. . . . These people who sit in grand bungalows and

who have become the guests of big businessmen preach to us the message of *shanti* and *ahimsa* [peace and nonviolence].[101]

The refugee press's coverage of the partition violence in West Pakistan was marked by sensational headings and graphic accounts, laying emphasis on Muslims violating Hindus' and Sikhs' honor by forcing them to eat cows, desecrating their temples, and raping their womenfolk. Refugee papers recurrently utilized emotionally charged images from Indian history, referring to Muslim attackers as "Mahmud of Ghazni," the eleventh-century conqueror who raided and destroyed Hindu temples.[102] They made an explicit connection between what was lost during partition and the refugees' entitlement:

> They did not come here to be treated like beggars and driven away from every place like dogs. Rather, they came here to demand their rights. It is because of you that these people were ruined, and they were ruined so you would get independence, wealth, and comfort. They have as much right to this independence, wealth, and comfort as you do. Actually, they have more right, because they sacrificed so much, more than any Congress leader. They have no need of your sympathy and empty speeches. No need of the messages of *shanti* and *ahimsa*. What they need is their houses, money, businesses, jobs, and factories.[103]

The text makes derisive insinuations about Gandhi's false promise that Pakistan would be established over his dead body, his messages of peace and communal harmony voiced from the comfort of the Birla House—the mansion owned by the leading industrialist, where Gandhi stayed and held his last prayer meetings. Caustic remarks about Gandhi featured prominently in the refugee press in the months before his assassination, right through his fast unto death, as did anger over his protection of the lives and property of Delhi's Muslims.[104] The refugee papers took active part in the struggles over evacuee property, and their rhetoric justified and sustained the violence, drawing a direct connection between refugee compensation and Muslim deprivation:

> These houses, money, businesses, and factories are available in India. Today they are in the hands of your beloved and loyal Muslims. We demand that

> you expel them from here and send them to Pakistan. Give us these houses
> . . . and tell them to go to Pakistan and seize our property. There is no cure
> but this.[105]

Delhi's Muslims, one editorial after another claimed, were Muslim Leagui in disguise, and for the government to appease them was comparable to feeding snakes with milk.[106] Parenthetically, *Al Jamiat* used the image of snakes to depict Hindu nationalists.[107]

Ranbir's editorial is typical of the refugee press—long and emotional, resembling a speech more than a written article. In contrast to the impersonal tone of the mainstream English press, Ranbir does not purport to represent an objective point of view. He presents himself as an involved actor, situated in the local scene, and identified with his readership ("we the Punjabis"). He hammers his point again and again, using repetition as a rhetorical device. Repetition was not confined to single editorials; rather, the same arguments and metaphors were voiced in one editorial after another, cohering into a forceful, even violent refugee discourse, establishing refugees' moral claim to Muslim property and to the space of the city more generally. This discourse is articulated crisply in one of *Pratap*'s texts: "We are not refugees but creditors. As long as the government does not clear our debt, it has no right to be generous to any other community."[108] Or, as Ranbir put it: "You should pay for our loss fully. You should pay compensation for our dead. You should give us the value of our lost property. You should avenge the dishonor of our women. You are the cause of our destruction. You have to pay its price. . . . Whatever we ask is our right [*haq*]."[109]

This discourse dovetailed not only with refugee encroachment into Muslim zones but also with refugees' unauthorized construction and squatting. One focal point was the proliferation of improvised and unauthorized vending stalls. Old inhabitants resented the cramping of streets and pathways. Even Connaught Place, complained Delhi's English-speaking elites, was packed with refugee stalls, resembling the bazaars of the old city. Chandni Chowk, in turn, saw the unprecedented profusion of meat kebab stalls, offensive to the Jain and Hindu mercantile castes.[110]

Shankar Prasad, who was Delhi's chief commissioner during these tense years, later recalled that one of the first "test cases" of his administration was Connaught Place, whose verandahs were completely occupied by squatters. Refugee stall holders refused to move to the new market developed for them on Janpath (which, in due time, would become one of the most profitable markets in the city). Prasad took action to clear Connaught Place overnight, taking advantage of the All-India Congress Committee session, which drew out-of-town ministers and leading Congressmen, ensuring minimal political interference.[111] Another dispute concerned refugees who refused to shift their stalls from the pavements of Chandni Chowk to their allotted shops in Lajpat Rai Market, and squatted in Queen's Gardens instead. When Prasad ordered the police to use force to evict them, refugee leaders complained to Nehru and almost managed to stop the evictions. The administration's effort to clear Ram Lila Ground likewise drew fierce resistance from refugee leaders.

The press harnessed the emphasis on Punjabi self-respect, discussed above, to address these struggles as well. Responding to the decision to evict unauthorized stalls, Ranbir wrote that famine-stricken residents of other regions of India had come to Punjab begging, but Punjabis did not beg when disaster befell them. They worked instead. The "hospitable" residents of Delhi, however, refused to lease them shops, or else demanded extortionate *pugrees* (fee charged illicitly to prospective tenants, see Chapter 3), so Punjabis set up their shops on roads and footpaths. By making very small profits, they managed to compete with big businesses and traders. Then they found out that the Delhi Municipal Committee ordered the police to remove the shopkeepers on the sidewalks. "The excuse is the city's beauty, but the real reason cannot be hidden from anyone."[112]

In the first years after partition, refugees launched numerous campaigns of satyagraha and *hartals* (strikes), including squatting in Queen's Gardens and sit-ins in front of Nehru's residence, to protest evictions and the closing down of camps and to press for speedier construction of housing projects.[113] Such defiance and agitation formed, as Joya Chatterji suggests, "acts of citizenship" that transformed refugees into rights-bearing citizens.[114] These acts were fostered by the editorials' discourse of self-reliance and of compensation as moral rectification. As Ranbir wrote: "This word *sharanarthi* [refugee] irritates me. India's leaders and officers insult us by using this word. We haven't come under the shelter of anyone. We do not beg from anyone."[115] *Milap* often preferred the term *pirit* (oppressed) to the term *sharanarthi*, and by 1954, refugee papers used the carefully chosen word *purusharthi* (manly, vigorous).[116]

Kaur suggests that refugees' adoption of the term *purusharthi*, along with the emphasis on courage, pride, and indomitable spirit, was an attempt to reclaim masculine attributes that had been challenged during the partition violence. In refugee Arya Samaji papers, this shift in terminology also harked back to a Hindu inferiority complex and feeling of vulnerable masculinity that developed during the colonial encounter, and which came to typify Hindu nationalism. The partition violence amplified this underlying anxiety about masculinity and the ability to protect community honor. This politics played out in the acrimonious editorial exchanges between Muslim and refugee newspapers, to which we now turn.

WARS OF WORDS

In the summer of 1952, an interreligious marriage shook Delhi. The groom was Sikander Bakht, a Muslim politician associated with the socialist wing of the local Congress and personal secretary to Delhi's first chief minister, Chaudhary Brahm Prakash. We may recall that he was also part of the Shanti Dal and intervened in struggles over Muslim zones, specifically in the Phatak Habash Khan affair.[117] The bride was Raj Sharma, daughter of a Hindu refugee family. Their decision to get married enraged her father, who managed to obtain a temporary injunction from the court to stop the wedding and applied for a permanent one. Hindu-right organizations and parties, including the Hindu Mahasabha, the recently-formed Bharatiya Jana Sangh, Arya Samaj, and Sanatan Dharam Yuvak Mandal, supported him and organized large protests and processions that converged in front of the district court, where the father's application was heard. They "swelled to a crowd of about 2,500 demonstrators who indulged in hooliganism, smashing window-panes in different courts, removing Gandhi caps from the heads of members of the public and burning these caps on the spot."[118] Stray assaults took place in different parts of the city; seventeen Muslims were wounded, and a young Muslim named Islamuddin died of his injuries. Rioters also attacked local leaders associated with the Congress socialist wing, including Member of Parliament Subhadra Joshi and Chief Minister Brahm Prakash. Subsequent arrests of Hindu demonstrators and leaders, notably Hindu Mahasabha leader and Member of Parliament Vishnu Ganesh Deshpande, led to more demonstrations. It remains unclear whether the stabbing in the same week of a sweeper in Farash Khana was connected with the disturbances, but it precipitated the looting of Muslim shops in the same locality. The agitation both communalized and politicized the marriage, targeting Muslims and socialist Congressmen.

Some political context is in order. The Bharatiya Jana Sangh, a Hindu nationalist party closely aligned with the RSS and forerunner of the Bharatiya Janata Party, was formed the year before. Backed by the city's refugee community, the Jana Sangh would emerge as a serious challenger to Congress hegemony in Delhi, and the city would be the base of this all-India party.[119] Both *Pratap* and *Milap* supported the Bharatiya Jana Sangh in the municipal elections of 1951 and the Delhi state elections of 1952, and Mahashay Krishna was in fact among its founders.[120] However, the Jana Sangh lost the elections, and the socialist wing of the Congress formed the first elected government of Delhi.[121]

The agitation against the marriage of Bakht and Sharma in 1952 was organized by the Jana Sangh and Hindu Mahasabha as part of a political backlash against the ascendancy of Congress socialists. Parliament was in session, and political leaders from all over the country were in the capital—a politically charged time prone to agitations. Members of the local Congress who opposed the socialist wing apparently lent their support to the agitation.[122] Nehru noted that communal forces, who had "received almost a knock-out blow in the elections," were now mobilizing again around two issues—Kashmir and the Bakht-Sharma marriage.[123] Communal trouble was simmering in Delhi, he apprehended, observing a troublingly slack response to the disturbances on the part of some police officers and other officials, who had close relations with the RSS. Subsequent months were indeed rife with communal tensions, minor clashes, reports of "Pakistani spies," and renewed pressure on Muslim houses. Tensions appear to have been connected to an intensified movement of Muslims across the border, perhaps in anticipation of the imminent introduction of the passport system in October.[124]

Unrest around the Bakht-Sharma marriage played on the stereotype of Muslim men as sexual aggressors. This perception resurfaced every summer in the mixed localities of Sadar Bazar and the old city, where Muslims and refugees lived in close proximity. Allegations that Muslims had molested or abducted refugee and other non-Muslim women would trigger small-scale disturbances. Ram Singh, a Hindu Mahasabha leader, told an audience at Gandhi Ground (formerly Queen's Park) that Raj Sharma was not the only girl in danger of being married to a Muslim, and that "girls belonging to fifteen families have been saved and our friends have no courage to arrange their naked dance."[125] The listeners were reportedly moved.

The Urdu press took an active part in this affair, publishing editorials that soon transcended the specific local events, coalesced with arguments about Kashmir, and turned into a debate about the place of the Muslim minority in India. The archive is replete with similar controversies, which were a common feature of the city's vernacular public sphere, fueling tensions in everyday life. Here we delve into one typical controversy, where the Muslim and refugee discourses bitterly clashed.

The exchange started with an editorial in *Pratap*, written by Mahashay Krishna's son, K. Narendra. Narendra claimed that, under the Nehru government, the Muslims received special rights (*khaas huquq*) and status (*rutba*) at the expense of another class (*tabqa*). He warned Muslims that the Nehru government, which made them spoiled children, would not last forever. Muslims, he wrote, called him a communal (*firqa parast*) person and charged him with intentionally ignoring the oath of loyalty (*wafadari*) to India that they had taken. But it was Muslims who were responsible for the grave sin of partition (*taqsim*), for breaking Hindustan into pieces and destroying the Hindus, and it was they who maintained indissoluble family and friendship ties with the Muslims of Pakistan. Narendra continued:

These people are not willing to merge [*mudgham*] themselves with the feelings [*jazbat*] of the great majority [*zabardast aksariyat*] of Hindustan. I will ask them to look at the world's history. In no country can the minority [*aqaliyat*] stay protected by the police, army, or law. Eventually it will have to obtain the approval of the majority. If the minority does not maintain good relations with the majority, if it repeatedly provokes the majority, thinking that because such-and-such ruler supports it, it can do whatever it pleases, then its fate will be exactly what the Muslims fear [*khadsha*]. Take the question of cow slaughter [*gau kashi*]. You should know the law. Isn't it true that the cow is sacred for tens of millions of Hindus who consider her a mother?[126]

The Muslims, Narendra added, insist with pride (*fakhriya*) that cow slaughter is their right. He urged them to be sensible and think about the future, when "Jawaharlal and Azad" would no longer be there for them. They should stop relying on leaders and approach the common Hindus instead. The latter have a justified grudge against them, but they are willing to forgive if the Muslims reform their behavior. If Muslims want to get a sense of the harm that the majority can do to the minority, they should ask Germany's Jews what Hitler did to them, or ask Poland's residents about Stalin. Narendra concluded:

Change your behavior, change your viewpoint, change your mentality, and most important, pacify the Hindus. . . . No Hindu wants you to change your religion by force, your culture is welcome, we don't want to suppress it, but if you want to become happy citizens [*shahri*] of India, then you must accept the culture [*tahzib o sanskriti*] of India. There is no country that would tolerate a minority whose relation with the country is temporary, whose birth was over there. . . . You can think of my words as threats, but this is not how I mean them.[127]

Narendra's long and repetitive editorial is typical of the refugee press. Interestingly, the text is replete with Persian-derived, even Arabic-derived vocabulary, more than Sanskritic words, which refugee editorialists often used. This may have been a calculated decision, because careful vocabulary choices were part of the arsenal of the Urdu press. As Daechsel says of the Urdu public sphere in pre-partition Lahore, "the shared use of the same language actually made matters worse, as the hurling of abuse at an enemy that could fully appreciate the depth of one's contempt became a popular sport."[128] *Sport* indeed seems the right term. Although such controversies touched on the gravest issues of political life in the new nation, their agents undoubtedly enjoyed them; they relished the opportunity to demonstrate their writing skills through direct and personal attacks on their rivals, emotive language, and citations of poems and proverbs. These controversies, it goes without saying, had an entertaining quality, and they boosted sales.

As for its content, the editorial exemplifies an aggressive Hindu majoritarian ideology, marking out the Muslims as outsiders whose loyalty is doubtful and pushing for the minority's assimilation through sinister references to the Nazi "treatment" of Jews. The editorial resounds the words of the RSS leader Madhav Sadashiv Golwalkar, and its conclusion is clear—there is no place for difference in the Indian nation.[129]

Narendra's accusation that Nehru had turned the Muslims into "spoiled children" by granting them special rights gives voice to the Hindu nationalist demand for Muslim assimilation. This demand became pressing after independence, with a renewed RSS campaign against cow slaughter and heated arguments over the proposed Hindu Code Bill to reform Hindu—but not Muslim—personal laws. Small disturbances occasionally broke out in the city over drivers who allegedly sneaked beef into the city or butchers who supposedly sold it.[130] The capital was also recurrently shaken by mass demonstrations organized by Hindu right organizations against the Hindu Code Bill. Refugees reportedly took a prominent role in such protests, and the refugee press advocated them.[131]

Narendra' comments touched on a larger set of dilemmas and tensions surrounding the efforts to establish India as a secular state. Controversies over secularism and what it would mean in practice were bound up with the minority question—the contradictory pulls of minority protection and assimilation. Already prior to partition, the Constitution makers found themselves torn between individual rights and community rights. Many "secularists" sought to relegate religion to the private sphere and to create a democratic polity where the rights-bearing individual would be the basic unit. But they encountered an entrenched colonial legacy that institutionalized the community as the basic unit of representative politics. The Minorities subcommittee initially recommended abolishing separate electorates while retaining for ten years reserved seats in parliament and legislative assemblies for religious minorities and Scheduled Castes and Scheduled Tribes. After partition, however, religious minorities were excluded from the benefit of reservations, which were now deemed barriers that would hinder minorities' integration and the creation of a universal citizenship.[132]

However, while the Constitution denied Muslims political safeguards, it eventually granted them cultural and educational group rights, such as the right to establish religious schools that would be entitled to state aid, the recognition of their religious festivals as public holidays, and support for religious pilgrimage. Taken to its extreme, this logic resulted in the exemption of Muslim personal law from reforms. Eventually, despite opposition from those who wanted to banish religion from public life, the Constitution adopted an expansive definition of the right to religion as religious practice and not merely worship, and enshrined an "equal respect" rather than a "non-concern" position of the state vis-à-vis the country's religions.[133]

This resolution "compromised" the classical model of a secular state as one strictly separating state and religion and providing equal treatment to all individuals irrespective of religion. The compromise emerged, partly, from the need to protect minorities.[134] Nehru and others in the assembly recognized that the imperative to obliterate communal markers in order to secularize the political arena could very easily slide into aggressive assimilation of the minority by the majority. Secularism could slide into majoritarianism.[135]

Yet the problem of unassailable difference continued to haunt Muslim political existence.[136] It lingered not only in the controversies in Parliament and in the public sphere, but also in the conflicting positions taken by individual leaders. A tension between community rights and individual rights emerged, echoing the contradictions besetting the League of Nations' minority protection regime in interwar Europe.[137] Nehru himself was apparently ambivalent: he was convinced that generating confidence among the Muslim minority was crucial for the survival of Indian secular-ism, but he realized that the measures taken simultaneously undermined Indian secularism in hampering the consolidation of a nation-state based on universal citizenship. Nehru defended this policy as morally correct under the specific historical circumstances created by partition.[138]

Hindu nationalist forces have played on this tension. It is no acci-dent that the accusation Narendra levelled against Nehru's "minority appeasement" had more recently been couched in terms of "pseudo-secularism."[139] Narendra's aggressive editorial, in turn, demonstrated the slippery slope between national integration and an intrusive erasure of cultural difference. A dilemma emerged, one that parallels the predica-ment of the government's policy on Muslim zones—namely, that in order to safeguard Muslim life in Delhi, Nehruvian secularist forces resorted to a policy of protective ghettoization, while Hindu nationalist elements pushed to open up localities for mixed habitation.[140] In the case of legal reforms, the secularist government sought to protect Muslims from ag-gressive demands for their assimilation by reinforcing their communitar-ian identity and separateness from the rest of society, overriding the pillar of individual equality before the law.

For their part, *Al Jamiat* and *Nayi Duniya* each published at least three long editorials in response, which prompted *Pratap* to publish an-other article, to which they again responded. While the Muslim press kept referring to the death of Islamuddin in the recent disturbances, it mostly focused on the broader question of the minority's position in India. *Al Jamiat* sarcastically listed the special rights and concessions Muslims received—namely, that after the Nehru-Liaquat Pact, Muslims were killed, their houses burned, and their shops looted, with none of the culprits punished; Muslim children were deprived of their mother tongue, Urdu; bans were placed on slaughter (*zabiha*); writers and editors were free to insult Islam; and employment opportunities were denied to Muslims.[141] Is this the meaning of secularism, *Al Jamiat* asked, using the English term and addressing Nehru—that "the Ganga was flowing in the opposite direction" and, instead of asking Muslims for forgiveness, editors were free to threaten them?[142]

Nayi Duniya's response was even sharper, characteristic of Siddiqui's vigorous writing style. Addressing *Pratap*'s editor directly, and sarcastically calling him "the prince," he contended that Narendra was dissembling when he claimed that he was not threatening Muslims: "What are these then, words of love?" He analyzed the internal contradictions in Narendra's words—that in a single breath he said both that he was warning Muslims and that he wasn't threatening them; both that Muslims had to accept the majority culture and that their own culture and religion were protected. Siddiqui asked Narendra what he meant precisely by the demand that the minority merge with the feelings of the majority and pacify it. If this meant abandoning Islam and becoming Hindus, they would never accept that.

The editorial stressed that Muslims adhered to their religion and culture, and, at the same time, were anchored in the land of India: "Muslims do not live on anyone's charity and mercy, this is their homeland [*watan*] and they obtained the right to live here . . . not because of Jawaharlal or Abul Kalam Azad . . . but because they were born in the land of Hindustan."[143] Listing many Islamic buildings and institutions, including Delhi's Jama Masjid and Qutab Minar, Agra's Taj Mahal, the *imambaras* (Shia mourning halls) of Lucknow, Sufi *dargahs* (shrines), and Aligarh and other universities, Siddiqui claimed that the Muslims had been born in this holy land (interestingly using the adjective *pak*, as in Pakistan) and would die here. Threats would not intimidate them into leaving:

> We have passion [*'ishq*] for the earth and sky of our homeland, for each and every particle of it. Our love could never be extinguished, we are the lovers [*'aziz*] of its mountains, planes, rivers, and desert. We should stay here to protect all this, and no barbarity, oppression, injustice, nor any threats . . . will succeed in preventing us from fulfilling this duty.[144]

The editorial proclaimed the indispensable role that Muslims had played in obtaining independence, listing historical figures such as Siraj-ud-Daulah, who "gave his life for this motherland [*madar-e watan*]"; Tipu Sultan, "whose blood made this land a garden of tulips"; the sons of the last Mughal emperor who in 1857 "gave their heads for independence";

the leaders of the Khilafat movement; the revolutionary Ashfaqulla Khan, "who kissed the gallows"; and Brigadier Mohammad Usman, who was killed in 1948 in the first Indo-Pakistan War in Kashmir.

The emphasis on Muslims' attachment to the motherland was meant to counter the frequent allegation that they were too attached to the holy places of Islam outside India.[145] Additionally, it advanced a territorially based citizenship, one that could encompass myriad religious identities. It thereby resisted the cruel choice between assimilation and expulsion that Narendra offered. It was, in other words, an effort to get out of the trap of minoritization, which the editor of *Pratap* had pushed to its extreme.

Nayi Duniya asserted:

> But we refuse to accept that we are a minority in this country. We are not a minority according to the constitution and law. We are citizens of this country with the same rights as all citizens. You call us a minority and, doing so, you separate us for no reason from the rest of the citizens.[146]

Yet, in the very next sentence, Siddiqui withdrew: "But let us say we accept your words . . . do you put all responsibility on the minority? Should only the minority be aware of its duties? Does the majority have no duty? No responsibility?"[147] *Nayi Duniya* thus tried to transcend the categories of minority and majority and to assert individual rights, but this effort was doomed to fail, and the writer remained trapped in the minority-majority division.

What further exacerbated this controversy about Muslim belonging was the involvement of Delhi's former newspapers, now based in Karachi and representing the *muhajirs*—the Muslims who left Delhi and Muslim-minority provinces for Pakistan. Although these newspapers ceased publication and were even banned in India, under the radar they were regularly sent to Delhi, sold in Ballimaran and other Muslim *mohallas* (neighborhoods), and distributed in Muslim libraries.[148] The management of *Jang* in Karachi and of *Al Jamiat* in Delhi exchanged copies of their papers, and Indian and Pakistani newspapers followed each other closely.

Anjam and *Jang* of Karachi quoted sections of *Pratap*'s editorials, which they found in the pages of *Al Jamiat*, under the headline "If Indian Muslims do not agree to become serfs of Hindus . . . they will be treated as Hitler treated Jews."[149] Subsequently, India's Ministry of External Affairs sent an urgent request to the Delhi secretariat to investigate the veracity of these reports. *Pratap*, for its part, accused the Muslim papers of conspiring with the Pakistani ones to defame India's reputation. For Narendra, it was yet more proof of the unbreakable ties between Indian and Pakistani Muslims, and the loyalty of the former to Pakistan.

The great interest that Pakistani newspapers took in Delhi's editorial controversies attests to the concern that Pakistan's government and society, especially the *muhajir* community in Karachi, felt for the fate of Muslims in India. This triangular dynamic—between the Indian Muslim minority, the Indian government and majority community, and Pakistani government and society—was built into the post-partition state of affairs. It was a response to the minority's anxious position, and was already at play during the Nehru-Liaquat Pact, with *Al Jamiat*'s allegations against the Indian government, and the government's suspicion of it.

Such a reading of the predicament of the Muslim newspapers as the product of profound, unresolved tension is supported by the fact that Nehru himself was perturbed by *Al Jamiat*'s role in these recurrent press controversies. In August 1952, after the Hindi paper *Amrit Patrika* of Allahabad published an insulting representation of the Prophet and a further round of editorial controversy ensued, Nehru sent an angry letter to Maulana Hifzur Rahman, general secretary of the Jamiat Ulama, who had recently been elected to parliament on a Congress ticket. Nehru acknowledged that speeches by Hindu Mahasabha and communal organizations were objectionable, but "to use these Hindu Mahasabha speeches as a basis for communal propaganda on the part of the *Al Jamiat* does not help the cause it is supposed to advance. To make comparisons with conditions in Pakistan and India in regard to minorities indicates either a strange ignorance of these conditions or deliberate perversion of facts."[150] To Maulana Azad he wrote, "the whole tone of *Al Jamiat* was often very wrong and objectionable. The Pakistan papers are continuously quoting from it. The Jamiat-ul-Ulema appears to me to be following a wrong policy which is likely to lead to trouble."[151] Thus it was not only communally minded officials and Jana Sanghi papers that took issue with *Al Jamiat*, but Nehru's own attitude was ambivalent.

Perhaps, at a deeper level, Nehru was annoyed because *Al Jamiat* exemplified the contradictions inherent in the secularism that he himself advanced, between community rights and individual rights, between minorities' ghettoization and assimilation. As discussed above, Nehru's secularism rested on protecting and reassuring the Muslim minority, and this included allowing the Jamiat Ulama to represent Muslims as a group. "I do not particularly fancy our dealing with the Jamiat as an official body representing Muslims," he admitted, "and yet what is the individual Muslim to do. He is frightened of offices and of officers and he has little approach to them. He sends a letter and he gets entangled in the intricacies of the law he does not understand. . . . It is natural, therefore, for him to go to somebody or some organisation which might be able to help him."[152] But the Jamiat Ulama tended to reinforce Muslims' separate religious identity or, as historian Peter Hardy has called it, a "juristic ghetto."[153] Its leaders imagined society as composed of "communities relatively encapsulated in their individual languages, cultures, education, and moral/legal systems."[154] When such isolationism coincided with unfavorable comparison of India's and Pakistan's treatment of minorities, it inadvertently implied extraterritorial affiliation.

Mir Mushtaq Ahmed, a Muslim socialist leader in Delhi, considered the Jamiat a reactionary force, and *Al Jamiat* part of the "communal press" on a par with the refugee dailies *Milap*, *Pratap*, and *Vir Bharat*. As a socialist, Ahmad strove for solidarity on the basis of class, seeing alignment along religious-communal lines as regressive.[155] By contrast, while *Al Jamiat* professed its commitment to secularism (always using the English word), it embodied the idea of cultural encapsulation—it was a Muslim-owned paper, written by and for Muslims, highlighting Islamic ideals, and preoccupied with the concerns of Muslims as a unified and oppressed minority. *Nayi Duniya*, its deep rivalry with *Al Jamiat* notwithstanding, played a similar role.[156]

The long-term implications of this communitarian orientation might be gauged from criticisms of the role played by the Urdu press of Delhi during the 1980s and 1990s, when the contradictions of India's secularism exploded. Urdu scholar Ather Farouqui argues that Muslim journalism failed to play a constructive role in shaping Muslim sensibilities, because it has "more often than not been prone to reinforce a sectarian and emotional outlook among readers"[157] and to "explain the social and economic backwardness which characterizes this community entirely and exclusively in terms of the failure of the Government to protect Muslim interests."[158] Most Urdu newspapers, Farouqui asserts, "deliberately search and compile such material which would push Muslims into pessimism and hopelessness."[159] A. G. Noorani similarly observes that "Muslims' positive contribution to the secular deal, as distinct from protest against injustices, was weak. There were few to counsel them that the politics of protest alone—especially if organized on a communal basis—would aggravate the problem."[160] *Al Jamiat* and *Nayi Duniya* in the years immediately following partition already demonstrated this tendency, showing that it emerged much earlier than scholars have considered—and that it was grounded in the contradictions of minoritization.

Over time, the discourse of grievance declined in the refugee press. As refugees were successfully incorporated into the city and nation, they shed their refugee identity and transformed into rights-bearing citizens. The trope of victimhood continued to dominate the Muslim press, however, indicating Muslims' troubled attempts to integrate into the new India. Their inverted fate is represented spatially in the geographic location of Muslim and refugee papers in contemporary Delhi. Muslim papers did not receive state patronage and remained in the old city or, as in the case of *Nayi Duniya*, moved to Nizamuddin. Refugee papers were allocated space in New Delhi, in the area allotted for newspaper offices after independence—located, ironically, in Bahadur Shah Zafar Marg, named after the last Mughal emperor.

PRINTING CONFLICT AND TAKING THE STATE TO COURT
If the previous chapter looked at the spatial reorganization of the city in the face of partition's dislocations, this chapter examined another space— the public arena of vernacular print media. Taking our cue from Yashpal's realist novel, we explored the importance of Urdu journalism in this period of transition. The Urdu press defied the common relationship between language, nationalism, and the public sphere. Whereas the Hindi public sphere exemplified the consolidation of a national identity around

a shared language, Urdu played the opposite role.[161] As the two Urdu-reading publics grew further and further apart, the Urdu press was the shared space where they played out their bitter separation. Their debates in this shared sphere, however acrimonious and brutal, belonged to a time when complete separation was not conceivable. Thus, the post-partition years were an intriguingly liminal time, when old connections only slowly gave way to total division.

Perhaps what best represents the intermeshing of pre-partition and post-partition logic is the heated debate over Punjab's official language: Hindu refugee newspapers wanted it to be Hindi, while Sikh newspapers advocated Punjabi, but both often presented their arguments on the pages of the Urdu press.[162] The minoritization of Urdu as solely a Muslim language was evident in the content of such controversies—but in their medium and form they still belonged to a time when Urdu was the lingua franca of the Punjabi male intelligentsia. In subsequent years, Urdu's minoritization would be complete, as the younger generation of refugees would cease to learn it. Mahashay Krishna's decision to purchase the Hindi *Vir Arjun* in 1954 and publish his editorials simultaneously in the Urdu *Pratap* and Hindi *Vir Arjun* was part of this transition.[163] While *Milap* and *Pratap* still publish from Delhi today, their readership is extremely limited, confined to elderly Punjabi refugees.[164]

But in these first years, the Urdu press was a reminder of a still unified South Asia. Just as the Nehru-Liaquat Pact, in the very act of working out the separation of India and Pakistan, exposed how interconnected they remained, so too did Delhi's press in its editorial wars conducted in a shared language. Ongoing reportage on these wars by Karachi's newspapers angered Nehru and other Indian officials precisely because they exposed this duality.

The robust and fiery Urdu press was rooted in local affairs and intimately associated with communal tensions. As press officers noted, controversies hiked up sales, so both sides had an interest in inflaming every petty issue out of proportion and keeping the fire burning. These newspapers' sensational headlines, factual distortions, and polemical, even abusive, style of argumentation placed them on the fringes of mainstream journalism. And it was precisely at the fringes that the new state drew and redrew the boundaries between permissible censorship and freedom of the press. Congress, whose nationalist newspapers had faced censorship during colonial times, now found itself having to determine what limits to impose on the papers of the right and left poles of the political map.

Nehru became uneasy with the refugee press early on, writing to Patel that the newspapers that had recently shifted to Delhi were of a very low class, representing "the worst type of journalism that used to prevail in the Punjab. They are poisoning the atmosphere of Delhi and lowering our standards."[165] Gandhi's assassination tilted the scale in favor of Nehru's view, and, along with arresting RSS members, the administration took stern action against the refugee dailies that were deemed communal and indirectly complicit in the assassination.[166] A champion of free speech for decades, the Congress now used the colonial laws at its disposal, mainly the Press Emergency Act (1931), which had been introduced in response to Gandhi's Civil Disobedience movement, and Nehru personally initiated some of the actions taken against these papers.[167] Initially, newspapers took advantage of divisions within the executive branch by pleading their case with one part of the administration against the other.[168] But they soon changed course and started to take the state to court.

Pratap, which apparently had the necessary resources, initiated the first court case concerning the Delhi press after independence, in April 1949. The Punjab High Court decided in its favor, even before the Constitution came into force and rendered colonial-era press laws unconstitutional. While the court made its decision from within the framework of the Indian Press (Emergency Powers) Act 1931, it gave this law as liberal an interpretation as possible, consciously departing from most previous judgments. Moreover, the judges assumed an activist role, pointing to the need, after independence, to change course with regard to press freedom. They reproached the Delhi administration for moving "in the old groove of suspicion and distrust" and for stifling legitimate criticisms in a free country.[169]

While the restraint on the authorities benefited the Muslim papers as well, the main proponents of press freedom in Delhi were the refugee newspapers, especially *Pratap*. The judgment in favor of *Pratap* is instructive for expressing unequivocal sympathy with the refugee discourse of grievance and the demand for compensation: "We see nothing objection-able in these passages. . . . These passages, to our mind, only express the depth of exasperation that the refugees feel on being stigmatised as guilty by persons whom they always held in highest esteem and from whom they least expected such attack."[170] As Chief Commissioner Shankar Prasad noted in a later interview, his orders against *Pratap* and *Milap*, whose "intemperate writings" overburdened law enforcement, were often set aside by the Punjab High Court, "which had a fair sprinkling of refugee judges."[171] In the two court judgements in favor of *Pratap* in 1949, the bench included Justice Achhru Ram, who would be appointed the custodian general later that year and would play a controversial role.[172] Like protests and agitations, taking the state to court and breaking into Muslim houses amounted to "acts of citizenship" through which refugees asserted their rights. In the context of a religious partition, some groups could make their citizenship more substantive than others.

The decade after independence saw an ongoing negotiation between the imperative of law and order and the commitment to free speech.[173] The next chapter will explore the tussle between the authoritarian colonial legacy and the democratization of political life more broadly.

CHAPTER 5

CITIZENS' RIGHTS
Delhi's Law and Order Legacy

Mathur argued excitedly—"Acharya Kripalani was totally right. What revolution was there? Where? Where are Gandhiji's ideals? The slogan 'Victory to Gandhi' became hollow in merely two years. The same old ICS men continue to run governance. These people have not learned to serve but to rule. Their habit is not democracy but bureaucracy. It is the same law and the same rule of police. Not only does detention without trial continue, but . . . the police have become totally unbridled. If the High Court releases people, the police arrest them again. This is shameful." . . .

Tara responded, "Well, the change has not been so radical, but . . . the administrators can govern only according to the policy of those who rule, and those who set the policy have no doubt changed. The foreign rule was replaced by self-rule, and this in itself is a major change."

Marcy expressed her indignation—"What change is it? The situation has become worse. The capitalists have become more powerful. . . . Now even the right to strike has been snatched from the poor laborers. Control [over prices] was removed so the capitalists could make more profits and give more to the Congress."[1]

THIS HEATED ARGUMENT is typical of the many discussions that take place in Delhi among the main characters of the novel *Jhutha Sach*. Born to a lower-middle-class Khatri Hindu family in Lahore, Tara, who is one of the novel's two protagonists, is abducted during the partition violence. She is recovered, and by merit of her intelligence, education, and impressive personality, rebuilds herself in Delhi, gradually climbing to a top position in the secretariat. She is one of the few refugees in this novel for whom the partition crisis eventually provides an opportunity to liberate themselves from the old shackles and gain upward mobility. This is perhaps why, in the conversation above, Tara articulates an optimistic view of the new independent government as entailing transformative capacities. Her socialist and communist friends, on the other hand, echo the declaration issued by the Communist Party of India (CPI) just six months after independence that the transfer of power was false—that it had failed to revolutionize socioeconomic and moral structures, and occasioned more continuity than change. In fact, the very title of the novel (False Truth) gestures towards the CPI's declaration, signaling that the question of continuity versus change in the transition to independence is one of the novel's central themes and was very much on the minds of contemporaries.

The novel details various aspects of continuity—state corruption, poverty, social and gender inequalities, and, most relevant to this chapter, the new government's adoption of the colonial regime's authoritarian measures. Indeed, the Indian Constitution reproduced large parts of the colonial Government of India Act (1935), and the Indian Penal Code of 1860 was retained. The legal, administrative, and policing structures of the colonial state persisted, resulting in "institutional inertia," in the sense that the logic of colonial sovereignty was inscribed into the bureaucratic knowledge, memory, and practices of the postcolonial state.[2] At the same time, independence introduced revolutionary notions and a break with the past by daringly granting a universal franchise, enshrining fundamental rights, and introducing affirmative action and outlawing untouchability in order to uproot caste hierarchy and injustice.[3] As Sudipta Kaviraj notes, after independence, somewhat paradoxically, "the Indian political world saw the simultaneous strengthening of two tendencies . . . the logic of bureaucracy and the logic of democracy."[4] This dynamic, and how it played out in the capital, is at the center of this chapter.

Because of Delhi's status as the national capital, and because it experienced the partition crisis particularly intensely, the city witnessed a particularly forceful confrontation between the colonial authoritarian legacy and the democratization of India's political structures and culture. As the capital city of the new republic, Delhi was the seat of the government and a political nerve center, drawing political leaders, parties, and pressures groups from around the country and witnessing many of the clashes between the government and the opposition. Delhi transformed from a colonial administrative capital to a vibrant political space in this period, as it became the theater in which some of the most important national controversies and movements of the late 1940s and 1950s were staged. In February 1948, the CPI made its False Independence statement, declaring the Congress government a bourgeois regime controlled by Anglo-American and Indian capital.[5] The Congress Socialist Party, founded as a group within the Congress, seceded from it on similar grounds, and prominent leaders of the Delhi Congress, including Aruna Asaf Ali, Mir Mushtaq Ahmed, and B. D. Joshi, were now in the opposition, involved in labor organization.[6] Several months later, in late 1948 and early 1949, the Rashtriya Swayamsevak Sangh (RSS) launched a satyagraha in Delhi and, soon after, the Sikh leader Master Tara Singh, who launched the Punjabi Suba movement, was arrested in Delhi.[7] In the early 1950s, the Hindu right attempted to mobilize support through movements that fused national issues, such as the Hindu Code Bill and Kashmir, with local controversies over evacuee property and the slow pace of refugee rehabilitation, cow protection, and alleged sexual violation of Hindu and Sikh women, as in the uproar over the Sikander Bakht-Raj Sharma inter-religious marriage in 1952.[8]

These agitations became embroiled in the shift to a democratic electoral politics in the first elections to the Lok Sabha and state legislatures under universal franchise in 1951–52. After independence, local politicians increasingly pushed to democratize Delhi's governance.[9] Their efforts partially bore fruit in 1951, when Delhi was declared a Part C State with its own elected legislative assembly and a ministry that would operate with circumscribed powers alongside the chief commissioner, who was

FIGURE 5.1 *The Bharatiya Jana Sangh's campaign truck, Delhi State Assembly elections, 1952. Source: Photo Division, Press Information Bureau, Ministry of Information and Broadcasting, Government of India.*

still in charge of law and order. This partial democratization brought with it political competition, between the left and right within the local Congress itself, and between the Congress and Hindu nationalist parties.[10] The socialist wing took over the Delhi Congress and formed the first elected government of Delhi under Chaudhury Brahm Prakash. Although the Congress would continue to win most elections during the Nehruvian period, the Jana Sangh would become a major competitor to the Congress in Delhi, especially in municipal elections, and its mass movements were part of its mobilization strategies.[11]

Thus, Delhi experienced firsthand the challenges that made "law and order" so appealing. Confronting the era's crises and uncertainties, the government utilized colonial-era measures, including regular surveillance of organizations and leaders, preventive detentions, and restrictions on the press and on political assemblies and processions. Perhaps the most

fundamental measure in the service of law and order was the very decision to retain the authoritarian structure of governance in the capital,
disregarding the clamor of Delhi's local leaders to democratize it. The
democratization that took place in 1952 was both partial, as mentioned
above, and short-lived, as it ended in 1956.[12] As we have seen throughout
this book, India's architects—most overtly Nehru and Patel—were not
only based in Delhi but also controlled its affairs (through the chief commissioner), and, in tackling its challenges, negotiated their own clashing
aspirations. Delhi therefore gives us a vantage point into the fundamental
tension between law and order and democracy, and how it played out in
the transition to independence more broadly.

The following analysis probes the interplay between preexisting structures and historical shifts on the Delhi stage in the early postcolonial
period, focusing on the question of civil liberties. While the tussle between the authoritarian colonial legacy and civil liberties has mostly been
approached from the perspective of legal and constitutional history,[13] this
chapter centers on micropolicing—specifically on intelligence gathering,
surveillance, and preventive detentions. As Ranabir Samaddar notes, intelligence gathering is absent from constitutional documents and interpretations, yet it is "the fulcrum on which reasons of state stand. Intelligence is the close monitoring of human movement, of the body, of the
physical activities—like meeting somebody, writing, talking, seeing, reading, sleeping somewhere—and in this physical form of politics we have
the meeting of the body and reasoning, terror and constitution, violence
and law."[14] Preventive detention was the shape such state violence took.

Focusing on Delhi's Criminal Investigation Department (CID), the
chapter traces the routinization of the colonial logic and practice of monitoring and surveilling, even as subjects became citizens. The CID apparatus emerges as a long-term structure, remaining largely unchanged
from the colonial through the early postcolonial period to the 1970s
Emergency and beyond. It was, if anything, only strengthened. Its surveillance was undergirded by a mode of suspicion that legitimized the
encroachment on people's right to privacy. The chapter goes on to describe how this foundational and latent structure of routine surveillance
was intensified at particular moments to disrupt people's lives with more

severe violations of personal freedoms, including harassment, loss of government employment, and restrictions on movement, most drastically in the form of preventive detention.[15]

In adopting the colonial government's forms of surveillance, the Indian state also adopted its tendency to conflate political risk with security risk, dissent with subversive activity.[16] In the new era of electoral democracy, this meant that surveillance over "suspects" slipped rather easily into watching over political rivals—a tendency that would continue to underlie Delhi's political life for decades, even if silently most of the time.

At the same time, the analysis illuminates the conscious decisions, doubts, debates, and changes that accompanied what seems on the surface to be mere institutional inertia. The chapter traces how this long-term structure was modified by the major events and political shifts of this period—the partition crisis and Muslim minoritization, communist dissent, Hindu right movements, the promulgation of the Constitution. After 1947, restrictive measures did not go unchallenged, which forced the government to think through its actions. In short, the chapter explores change and adaptation within a framework of administrative inertia.

The chapter looks closely at popular politics, finding that political mobilization on the left and right differed sharply in kind and intensity. Socialists and communists mostly engaged in small-scale demonstrations and labor organization. The major threats to law and order came from Hindu right organizations, especially the RSS, which had struck roots in Delhi's society. The Jana Sangh Party, which formed in 1951 and emerged early on as the only effective challenger of the Delhi Congress,[17] relied on the RSS social network and the refugee community to launch large-scale movements. It drew on Gandhian mobilization strategies, but at the same time assumed a disruptive and riotous character, connected to the politics of hatred surrounding partition. Disgruntled refugees engaged in nonviolent satyagraha campaigns of hunger strikes and prolonged encampment outside the prime minister's New Delhi residence, as well as violent attacks on Muslim localities. Nevertheless, it was Muslims, communists, and socialists who were the main targets of suspicion and of routine preventive detentions before the Constitution went into effect.

During these early years, the language of civil liberties came to oc-cupy a central place in political discourse and in people's perceptions and assertions of their rights as citizens. Specifically, both the left and the right rebuked the government for using preventive detentions and ban-ning most demonstrations, emphasizing colonial continuities. Concomi-tantly, key political figures—communists, socialists, Hindu Mahasabha, and Jana Sangh activists—filed habeas corpus petitions and pursued their rights in court. We shall see that although Delhi's self-rule and electoral politics was circumscribed, Nehru and Patel were not immune to politi-cal pressure from below; in many ways, government actions were under greater scrutiny in Delhi. As the national capital, Delhi was a visible the-ater of politics— everything that happened in Delhi was in the limelight, demanding accountability. During the early post-independence period, the balance between law and order and civil liberties was renegotiated and readjusted, and both the left and the right poles of the political map were fundamental to this process.

Accordingly, the analysis pays attention to two major transitions— independence on August 15, 1947, and the promulgation of the Consti-tution on January 26, 1950. Between these dates, India functioned as a British dominion, an intermediate status between imperial colony and independent democratic republic. Rohit De suggests that we must not conflate this period of dominionhood, during which the government's powers went mostly unchecked, with the post-1950 years in arguments about colonial continuities.[18] In Delhi, the years of dominionhood, from 1947 to 1950, indeed emerge as a liminal period that entailed acute crises of law and order and, concomitantly, a more expansive use of emergency provisions to curb civil liberties.[19]

After the Constitution came into force, surveillance and preventive detentions were utilized more cautiously. The clampdown on commu-nists, socialists, and labor agitators declined, as did arrests of Muslims returning from Pakistan. Detentions, which now targeted mostly those involved in communal skirmishes and members of the Hindu right who continued to launch intense agitations, were used relatively moderately, for shorter durations than before.

At the same time—and here our analytical pendulum tilts back to the burden of structure—routine surveillance continued to be prevalent under the radar, covering all political parties and organizations, newspapers, politically active students, and labor organizers. And prolonged detentions still constrained those situated on the fringes of what became acceptable politics in post-partition India—supporters of Sheikh Abdullah on Kashmir and communists supporting China during the Indo-China war. During the Emergency rule of 1975–77, habitual surveillance again came to the surface, and thousands more suddenly found themselves on these fringes and behind bars.

THE CITY AS A SPACE OF SUSPICION: THE CID'S DELHI
When discussing the authoritarian measures that the Indian Constitution retained, scholars often refer to Somnath Lahiri, the sole communist member of the Constituent Assembly, who sarcastically commented that many fundamental rights were "framed from the point of view of a police constable."[20] Indeed, most of the Constitution's framers gave greater weight to considerations of public order and national security than to individual rights, an inclination that developed against the background of postwar restlessness, the partition mayhem, and the daunting tasks of forging a national body and effectuating socioeconomic modernization in a heterogeneous, and overwhelmingly poor and illiterate, society.[21] Two years later, another Lahiri, representing the other end of the political spectrum, made a similar comment on the resilience of colonial authoritarian measures. Ashutosh Lahiri, the Bengali general secretary of the All-India Hindu Mahasabha, now based in the Hindu Mahasabha Bhavan in Delhi's Reading Road, complained to Home Secretary H. V. R. Iengar that a letter from his son in Calcutta had taken ten days to arrive, and that the envelope oddly did not carry any seal from the Delhi post office:

> It is surprising that even domestic letters should be censored like this and withheld from delivery for so long a time. I have instances in which letters of some influential persons relating to my public activities have not been delivered to me at all. As a free citizen of free India, am I not entitled to enjoy

even the basic right of unhampered delivery of my mails? . . . Even under the British regime, I don't remember any of my letters being altogether withheld from delivery, or such domestic letters being censored and delivery being delayed for such a long time.[22]

Internal inquiry with the Delhi CID confirmed that Ashutosh Lahiri's mail was regularly censored, and that a difficulty in finding a Bengali translator had caused the embarrassing and revealing delay. A couple of months later, Lahiri made a speech that the administration deemed "highly intemperate," and he was barred from making further public speeches in Delhi. Lahiri wrote another acerbic letter, this time to Delhi's deputy commissioner:

> Your action is motivated by inexcusable desire to serve the interest of the Congress Party in power. You are still continuing an old British tradition which has no place in democratic India and you have proved yourself unfit to be entrusted with the administration of politically the most important city that Delhi now happens to be.[23]

Taken together, the two Lahiris illustrate that criticism of the Congress's curtailment of civil liberties after independence emerged from the two poles of the political spectrum—the communist left and the Hindu nationalist right. Their sarcastic tone also reveals that postcolonial Delhi was far from a police state: surveillance could be clumsy, and opposition leaders felt at liberty to use strong words in censuring the party in power and the bureaucracy.

The two episodes also represent different levels of political experience: Somnath Lahiri's comment in the Constituent Assembly is a window into the ideological mindsets that clashed during the drafting of the Constitution, as members pondered what fundamental principles would undergird the new republic. Ashutosh Lahiri, on the other hand, takes us from the realm of constitutional philosophies to the realm of the police constable implementing them—in our case, Delhi's CID.

A division of the Delhi Police and part of the all-India network of intelligence set up by the British, the CID became a symbol of the colonial state's intrusion and oppression, channeling anticolonial sentiment.

In 1919, for example, when rumors about the Jallianwala Bagh massacre reached Delhi, a public meeting was held near Jama Masjid, and the agitated crowd started pelting the CID officer and his staff, who were taking notes on the speeches, with stones.[24] Yet, as was the case with most apparatuses left behind by the colonial state, the postcolonial state did not dismantle it. Correspondence from September 1946, after the Interim Government was established, sheds light on how Congress leaders thought about this issue. D. P. Mishra, home minister of Central Province and Berar, wrote to Sardar Patel, the new home member at the center:

> As you are aware there are branches of the Central CID in all the provinces. So far we have looked upon them with suspicion and have been opposed to their existence. Some were of opinion that as soon as a National Government was formed at the Centre these branches should be closed down. I personally feel that as all provinces are not under Congress control, they should continue to exist. . . . It can be great help to us in maintaining peace in the province.[25]

Patel concurred that the CID was "the only useful source of information in some of the truculent provinces."[26]

The voluminous archive produced by the postcolonial Delhi CID demonstrates that the desire for meticulous, daily collection of information on the city and its surroundings did not disappear after independence. The CID inherited a whole apparatus of intelligence, "as is," from its colonial predecessor. Continuity ran through all levels of the CID operation, from its filing system to its methods of intelligence gathering. Indeed, in the archives there is no visible trace of a change in August 1947, as the same kind of information continued to be gathered about the same individuals and institutions in the same ways.

The sentiment underlying the CID apparatus was suspicion, and its main function was surveillance. Accordingly, the urban space that emerges from the CID records, both before and after independence, is one of inherent danger, conceptualized through a dichotomy between public order and an array of threats—subversive activities, undesirable elements, communal frenzy, potential danger, spies, insidious propaganda, and sedition. The transition to independence and the concomitant democratization and proliferation of political life were understood through this lens as threats that required more surveillance. In fact, a series of reorganization schemes expanded the department considerably starting in 1948 and into the 1960s.[27]

The department mapped out the city according to several demographic, spatial, and operational taxonomies, which often overlapped. Thus, its files are divided into several demographic categories—Hindus, Muslims, Sikhs, Communists, Socialists, Labour Unions, Student Organizations, and Volunteer Organizations. This mapping continued colonial-era taxonomy, exemplifying administrative inertia in the transition to independence.

At the same time, the CID was not impervious to the changed political context, and it introduced new categories and reframed some old ones. One new category was Refugees, a response to the mass migration from Pakistan that brought so many unfamiliar faces to the city's streets and transplanted an array of social, political, and criminal networks. CID internal correspondence about refugees reveals its concerns about the extremely anti-Muslim stance many of the migrants held, as well as anxiety about the infiltration of communists, revolutionaries, *goondas* (thugs), and other "bad characters" whose rap sheets had been left behind in Pakistan.[28] The category Foreigners was also added after independence in response to the establishment of foreign embassies, the deepening of the Cold War and of Indo-Pakistani rivalry, and the intertwining of the two in the 1954 U.S.-Pakistan Mutual Defense Assistance Agreement.

Muslims, on the other hand, was an old category that gained a new meaning in the altered context. If, during colonial time, this category had been conceived through the supposedly neutral concern of the colonial state with communal trouble, after independence it was reconceived in light of the minoritization of Indian Muslims and their association with Pakistani espionage and threats to national security. Accordingly, CID surveillance of Muslims after 1947 became part of the bureaucratic web that fixed national citizenship while dispossessing Muslims—interacting with the Custodian of Evacuee Property, the permit system, and the passport system.[29] Furthermore, whereas Muslims were well represented in the colonial CID, most left for Pakistan or were purged from the services after partition, and the staff became overwhelmingly Hindu and Sikh. Hence, after 1947 Muslims were transformed from a state agent of surveillance to purely its target.

Accordingly, from 1949, the CID was ordered to censor all correspondence between Delhi's Muslims and Pakistan—which, in 1951, amounted to roughly 1,700 letters a day.[30] This shows again how a notion of jus sanguinis underwrote the administration's perception and treatment of the Muslim population as inherently suspicious.[31] Whereas the colonial state had surgically targeted surveillance at selected Muslim political figures and organizations, the new nation-state surveilled Muslims en bloc, thus locating them most overtly in the realm of political society, where the state treats its citizens as populations to be managed.[32]

The CID's spatial categories divided Delhi into City—the hub of the old city and the adjacent localities of Karol Bagh, Paharganj, Sabzi Mandi, and Sadar Bazar, where the bulk of the population lived; New Delhi—where political leaders, members of parliament, some party headquarters (Socialist Party, Hindu Mahasabha), labor unions, and foreign embassies were located; and Railways—a politically fraught space, a target of anticolonial sabotage and a hub of labor union activity. After 1948, a Rural section was added to monitor the areas of Mehrauli, Narela, Shahdara, Najafgarh, and Nangloi. Since refugee colonies had not yet been set up, and Delhi's major expansion had just begun, the CID's Delhi before the mid-1950s was still a relatively small world.

These demographic and spatial maps operated alongside the Department's division of labor. The press section scrutinized newspapers and periodicals, transferred objectionable materials for legal action, traced revolutionary and insidious propaganda, and conducted character investigations of those who applied for permits to start presses and newspapers. The censorship staff intercepted letters and telegrams. The personnel in charge of a particular demographic category attended and reported on public meetings, shadowed individuals, and, most important, utilized insiders as informers. In addition, there was a section in charge of interrogation and one in charge of investigating candidates for government employment or existing government employees suspected of subversive affiliations. The CID also conducted all verifications of Muslims applying for permits and passports.[33]

In the next section, we return to mail censorship—which we first encountered through Ashutosh Lahiri—using this practice as a window into structure and change in the work of the CID.

BUREAUCRATIC CONTINUITY, POLITICAL CHANGE

Ashutosh Lahiri, we should state, was not the exception but the rule. Mail censorship in the post-independence period was based on the Indian Post Office Act, 1898. It was pervasive and routine, and appears to have reproduced the colonial government's logic and practices seamlessly, as a matter of inertia. If we were to judge only by whose mail was being intercepted, we would have to say that the transition to democracy brought about no significant change in the relationship between the state and its citizenry. If anything, democratic political life was understood as a threat that required more surveillance over citizens. Yet an uninterrupted continuity is not necessarily a thoughtless or undeliberate one. While bureaucratic and security discourses and practices tend to perpetuate themselves, their reproduction is conditioned by the political context and players.[34] Even as the structure and practices of colonial intelligence were reproduced, the new political rulers made conscious decisions and bent the system to their own purposes.

Continuing mail interception was, like perpetuating the CID, in fact a decision, and thus can give us a glimpse into the dynamic of institutional inertia and change. In February 1947, several months after the establishment of the Interim Government, the British Superintendent of Police CID, F. H. G. Bridgman, wrote a defensive letter, responding to allegations of irresponsible censorship practices in Delhi. Bridgman assured William Christie, the last British chief commissioner of Delhi, that he personally oversaw mail interception. He also wished to convey to the new people in power, through the chief commissioner, the indispensability of mail censorship to intelligence—it revealed crucial information that could not be obtained elsewhere, such as the whereabouts of communists and absconders. If the new Interim Government objected to interception, he emphasized, they should not expect the CID to provide valuable information. Bridgman attached a list of seventy mail addresses that he recommended to continue censoring. Chief Commissioner Christie forwarded the list to Home Secretary A. E. Porter, asking him how to proceed.[35] Porter, who, we may assume, communicated the information to the new Home Member Sardar Patel, confirmed that the policy was to pursue mail censorship, asking for clarification about several students on the list. Thus, regular censorship continued along the suggested lines, and by January 1950, the initial list of 70 addresses had expanded to 166—one of which was the blanket order to intercept all mail between Delhi's Muslims and Pakistan.[36]

It is intriguing that, just days before Attlee's announcement of the impending transfer of power, British bureaucrats were invested in perpetuating the machinery of surveillance they had set up in Delhi. Thus, as Arudra Burra notes, "there is a logic of institutional continuity which is to some extent independent of the logic of control over political power," and which contributed to the persistence of colonial institutions into the postcolonial state.[37] At the same time, it was Home Member Patel who had the final call. In subsequent years, the Home Ministry continued to be a prime agent in approving, amending, and even initiating lists of political suspects to surveil. In so doing, Patel perpetuated the colonial suspicion of a colonized populace, now directed toward citizens of a democratic country. This decision to violate the right to privacy and to compromise political activity was taken despite a lively civil liberties discourse that had become firmly rooted in India over the previous decade, and despite discontent about such measures in the Constituent Assembly.[38]

Continuity is even more glaring when considering whose mail the CID intercepted. The post-1947 lists of addresses approved for regular interception contain many of the political suspects of the late colonial era—the very people who had played a central role in India's struggle for independence and who, after 1947, were prominent figures in Delhi's public life and electoral politics. There is an intriguing overlap between the CID's Who's Who of political suspects and the Who's Who published by Delhi's Municipal Committee.[39]

The mail interception list comprises, first and foremost, the offices of the Communist Party of India and the Indian Socialist Party (both in the Jama Masjid area), as well as the communist commune in Daryaganj and private addresses of local communist and socialist leaders. These include two legends of the Quit India movement, JP Narayan and Aruna Asaf Ali (wife of Congress leader Asaf Ali, India's first ambassador to the United States). Also on the list are Kamaladevi Chattopadhyay and Achyut Patwardhan, who were socialists of national repute; the communists Yag Dutt Sharma, Muqimuddin Farooqi, and Sarla Gupta, all of whom we met when they participated in the 1942 and 1946 anticolonial disturbances;[40] B. D. Joshi, a union leader and later a member of the Legislative Assembly, who was among the special police officers protecting Muslims in 1947; his wife, Subhadra Joshi, who was a member of the local Congress and the Shanti Dal, and later became a member of parliament; and Mir Mushtaq Ahmed, who had been imprisoned for two years during the war and would run for elections after independence. The list also includes leftist students; "nationalist Muslim" leaders of the Jamiat Ulema and Ahrars, including the eminent leader Habibur Rahman, as well as Abdul Sattar and Aziz Hasan Baqai; notable Muslims such as Khawaja Hasan Nizami of the Nizamuddin Dargah; and shadier figures, such as Sadiq Karachiwala, whom we encountered when he colluded with the assistant custodian to forcibly evict poorer Muslims from Katra Shafi.[41] The right wing of the map also figures, with the RSS office in Kamla Nagar (a hub of refugees near Sabzi Mandi), the Hindu Mahasabha Bhavan on Reading Road, Vasant Oak and Hansraj Gupta of the RSS, and V. G. Deshpande and—as we know by now—Ashutosh Lahiri of the Hindu Mahasabha.

Additionally, the list includes employees of the Pakistan High Commissioner's office, the correspondent of the soviet TASS news agency, and the offices of major newspapers and publications, whose mail, as the last British chief commissioner explained, was a source of crucial information: most subversive organizations had contacts in newspaper offices, and government servants were in the habit of writing to newspapers editors, thereby revealing their affiliations with political and communal organizations in contravention of government rules.[42]

FIGURE 5.2 *Socialist leader Mir Mushtaq Ahmed, on the steps of the Jama Masjid, campaigning for the Delhi State Assembly elections, 1952. Source: Photo Division, Press Information Bureau, Ministry of Information and Broadcasting, Government of India.*

While institutional inertia marked mail interception, targeting the same people and organizations before and after independence, surveillance took on a novel political significance in a democracy. Whereas the colonial regime's uppermost levels were wholly external to Indian society, the new rulers were embedded in the sociopolitical landscape. Accordingly, surveillance that had addressed the colonial concern with law and order and its fear of anticolonial resistance now was used to spy on political rivals in the context of a competitive electoral democracy. This is clearly evident in detailed CID reports on internal meetings of Delhi's socialists, communists, the Jana Sangh, and the Hindu Mahasabha, which chart election strategies ahead of the 1952 and 1957 elections.

Leaders and officials were cognizant of this new political role, as evident in their uncertain and shifting approach to surveillance. Initially, after the setup of the Interim Government in September 1946, the two new parties in power—the Congress and the Muslim League—were taken off the mail censorship list, while other parties were retained.[43] But at some point after independence, the Congress was restored to the list.[44] The top Indian Civil Service bureaucrat, H. V. R. Iengar, a repository of administrative memory, experience, and approach, later claimed that he was the one who convinced Patel to do so, telling him, "Sir, how do you know that you know all that is happening within the huge heterogeneous Congress Party of yours? . . . I hear myself of various forces, disparate forces, within the party."[45]

The issue resurfaced in 1952, after Patel's death, when the new home minister, Kailash Nath Katju,[46] learned that mail censorship was targeting socialists and the Congress. When he brought the matter to Nehru's attention, Nehru responded:

> I do not quite know what it means to collect information about a party as such. The Communist Party and like organizations, like the RSP, etc., I can understand because basically their programme is subversive. But I do not think it is generally desirable to track other parties, even though they might be opposed to the Congress. The question therefore of our collecting special information about the Socialist Party or the Congress Party as such does not arise. . . . But it would not be desirable for us to make normally working opposition parties feel that we are tracking them or pursuing them with secret agents. . . . Apart from the Communist Party and the like, it is really individuals about whom we should have information.[47]

Nehru's caution might explain why the Congress, as a separate category of surveillance, appears and disappears from the Delhi CID's fortnightly reports during the 1950s. It seems that information was collected but somewhat hesitantly. Curiously, although the CID structure did not have a separate Congress section, information on the local Congress was collected by the Muslim section.[48]

Clearly, top leaders and bureaucrats were aware that using the state security apparatus to watch over political rivals, outside or inside the party, did not conform to democratic values. Such awareness resulted in a hesitant and inconsistent policy, as leaders—unsurprisingly, Nehru and Patel—did not see eye to eye about the balance between surveillance and civil liberties. Furthermore, Nehru's own approach was internally inconsistent, as he did not rule out surveillance over communists, although by the time he wrote this note in 1952, the CPI had changed course, called off armed struggle, and become a legitimate player in the field of electoral democracy. Theoretically, it should not have been subject to different treatment than other opposition parties. Furthermore, Nehru did not rule out surveillance of individuals, leaving open a wide scope for discretion. And while Nehru himself may have been cautious, such surveillance could be utilized by a less hesitant leader—as it would be during Indira Gandhi's rule. Unsurprisingly, even before the Emergency, after the split in the Congress in 1969, Delhi's CID gathered information on both the rival faction, Congress (O), and Mrs. Gandhi's own party, Congress (R).[49]

QUOTIDIAN SURVEILLANCE, DISRUPTED LIVES

> Everyone knew that Rajaji and Sardar Patel established the communists as "enemy number one." The government deemed those officers who had contact with or sympathy toward the communists as untrustworthy.[50]

The sheer volume of CID correspondence, reports, and dossiers—many of which were never updated, and perhaps not even processed, given the chronic shortage of CID personnel—makes them seem the products of a mechanical, automatic, even harmless collection of information on the city, mere institutional inertia. But on occasion, such routine monitoring intruded into people's lives more aggressively, especially amid the shockwaves of partition.

Of course, shadowing itself had the potential to harass, even if unintentionally. Take, for instance, Ravi Raj Chopra and Naima Qureshi. Both hailed from educated, upper-class families in Lahore. They moved to India in June 1948 and were married by Deputy Commissioner Rand-hawa. People who objected to the interreligious civil marriage spread rumors that Chopra was a communist, that Naima Qureshi was a Pakistani spy, or that he had abducted her during partition. Mridula Sarabhai, who was in charge of recovering abducted women, thoroughly investigated the matter and was convinced that this was not a case of abduction. Randhawa's and Sarabhai's endorsements notwithstanding, and despite the couple's own elite connections, CID men shadowed them and made repeated inquiries with their neighbors and servants, forcing the couple to change residence at least four times. In 1952 Chopra was dismissed from his job at the Indian Council of Agricultural Research with the intimation that he was politically suspect. When Chopra complained, CID Superintendent Rikhi Kesh categorically denied that the CID was persecuting innocent interreligious couples. Yet the CID dossier on the couple is extensive, attesting to the harsh scrutiny they experienced. It details their letters and visits to Pakistan and their association with Delhi's communists, including Aruna Asaf Ali (who had joined the CPI) and A. K. Gopalan (the communist member of parliament). It is noteworthy that these associations took place only after the CPI had turned into a legitimate player in the political field.[51] A similar case is presented by Dr. Duggal, a female Muslim doctor who married a Sikh officer and converted. She was routinely shadowed by the CID and eventually removed from her post at the child welfare center in Palam's IAF station.[52]

Beyond the potential for harassment, CID surveillance was explicitly geared to purge the police, army, and bureaucracy of subversive elements—Muslims of "doubtful loyalty," communists, and RSS members.[53] The CID was the main body in charge of verifying the character, biographies, and antecedents of government servants prior to appointment and, if they came under suspicion, afterward as well. The purging of Muslims from the police had already begun before partition and continued afterward in most government departments.[54] As late as August 1950, the Home Ministry sent an alarmed report about Muslims who had left for Pakistan and later returned to India and secured employment under false names, asking that CID and government departments tighten verification and be alert.[55] Communists were also energetically purged.

Animesh Banerjee, for instance, who was news editor for All India Radio, was fired because of his association with the CPI, and Jugal Kishore at Army Headquarters was under prolonged surveillance, suspected of ties with the Red Communists.[56] RSS members were purged less vigorously, and their removal proved trickier, for reasons we will see while discussing preventive detentions.

EXTREME POLICING UNDER DOMINIONHOOD

Surveillance at times infringed on people's lives and liberties even more harshly, when it led to restraints on physical freedom. The Defence of India Act of 1939, which effectively declared martial law, expired after the end of World War II, but by 1950, almost all the provincial governments had enacted "public safety acts" that empowered them to curb people's liberties without formally declaring an emergency and without suspecting a particular crime, while circumventing the lengthy, cumbersome, and uncertain judicial process.[57] Thus the Punjab Public Safety Act, 1947, and Punjab Public Safety Act, 1949 (extended to Delhi) authorized the administration to impose restrictions on a person's actions, movements, and expression, to extern them or require them to stay in a specific area, and—most radically—to detain them without a trial.

The period of dominionhood was especially turbulent, and this was reflected in numerous arrests and preventive detentions. The Delhi District Jail, which was established after the Great Revolt of 1857 just south of the old city near Delhi Gate, and was designed to hold a population of 677, was crowded with 2,037 inmates in 1948, and authorities were forced to transfer detainees to jails in United Provinces or Punjab.[58] Gandhi's assassination in January 1948 led to a surge of arrests of Hindu nationalists, as did an RSS satyagraha later that year. Meanwhile, the CPI's False Independence declaration in February triggered a wave of arrests of communists. Additionally, many Muslims were arrested and detained for contravening the permit system or acting "suspiciously,"[59] and both Hindus and Muslims were detained upon the occasional flare-up of communal tensions.

The following account of extreme policing in the time of dominionhood reveals differences in the type, intensity, and breadth of political mobilization on the left and right—and in the detentions each group experienced. We will therefore consider the two groups separately, turning first to the left.

False Independence for Communists

Looking back on the years of dominionhood, Chief Commissioner Prasad made an intriguing observation. While the RSS was banned, in Delhi not a single member was behind bars for much of that time. And while the CPI was legal, a large number of Delhi's communists were in detention.[60] Prasad's point is borne out by monthly lists of detainees under the Punjab Public Safety Act in this period, summarized in Table 5.1.

As the table makes clear, there was a temporary hike in the number of RSS detainees during January–April 1949 which, as we shall see, coincided with RSS agitation during those months. Similarly, for a few months in 1949, during an Akali Dal agitation, there were Sikh detainees. Otherwise, the lists confirm Shankar Prasad's recollection that it was mostly communists (and Muslims, in 1948) who faced detention without trial during the period of dominionhood.

The names of Delhi's communists first surface in the CID files during World War II, when most of them were young students who got involved in politics through the All India Students Federation. As noted in Chapter 1, following Germany's invasion of the Soviet Union, the CPI famously changed its policy on World War II, calling it a "people's war." As a result, the party became legal, opened an official office in Urdu bazaar near the Jama Masjid, and started, for the first time, to organize public processions and meetings. Yet, although this dramatic change of policy officially placed the CPI in opposition to the Congress, in practice, Delhi's communists mostly emerged from within the Congress and did not truly part ways with it. Instead, they straddled a delicate balance between supporting the war effort and advancing the Congress's nationalist demands. In fact, most of them were imprisoned for the active part they took in organizing the anticolonial agitations that shook Delhi in 1942 and 1946.

The gap between the Congress and the communists widened after the war. The CPI's armed struggle in Telangana and False Independence

TABLE 5.1 *Monthly lists of detainees in Delhi under the Punjab Public Safety Act, 1948–1950*

	RSS	Hindu Mahasabha	Communists	Muslim League and Allied Activities	Others (goondas)	Akali Sikhs	Total
August 1948	**17** (including 2 students)	**2** (including 1 student)	**34** (including 7 students and 9 trade union workers)	24	84		**161**
September 1948	**8**	**2** (including 1 student)	**17** (including 1 student and 4 trade union workers)	53	41		**121**
October 1948	**6** (including 1 student)	**2** (including 1 student)	**12** (including 1 student and 4 trade union workers)	21	15		**56**
November 1948	**2**	**1**	**8**	5	29 (including 25 socialist-cum labor agitators)		**45**
December 1948	**36** (including 16 students)		**1**	3	2		**42**
January 1949	**162** (including 26 students)		**2** (including 1 trade union worker)	1			**165**
February 1949	**158** (including 39 students)	**2**					**160**
March 1949	**114** (including 19 students)		**7** (including 1 student and 4 trade union workers)		1	12 (including 1 student)	**134**
April 1949	**94** (including 8 students)		**7** (including 1 student and 2 trade union workers)		6	10	**117**

	RSS	Hindu Mahasabha	Communists	Muslim League and Allied Activities	Others (goondas)	Akali Sikhs	Total
May 1949	27 (including 2 students)		7 (including 1 trade union worker)		2	10	46
June 1949	1		8			10	19
July 1949			10		1		11
August 1949			5		2		7
September 1949			5 (including 1 trade union worker)		6		11
October 1949			8 (including 1 trade union worker)		2 (labor agitators)		10
November 1949			8 (including 1 trade union worker)		3 (2 labor agitators and 1 communalist)	23	34
December 1949			7		3 (2 labor agitators and 1 communalist)	20	30
January 1950			18 (including 8 trade union workers)		4 (including 2 labor agitators)	3	25
February 1950			19		4 (including 2 labor agitators)	3	26
March 1950			20 (including 5 trade union workers and 2 students)		1		21

SOURCE: F. CC 70/48-C, Confidential, DSA.
NOTE: The total number of detainees in 1949 was 368. See Deputy Commissioner Rameshwar Dayal to Y. N. Verma, Home Secretary to the chief commissioner, August 29, 1949, F. CC 134/1949-C, Confidential, DSA.

declaration induced a "red scare" in political and bureaucratic circles, and, following the lead of the West Bengal government, provincial governments arrested communists throughout the country, raided provincial CPI offices, and closed down the party's presses.[61] Consequently, the political lives of Delhi's communists look like an unbroken sequence of arrests and detentions under both the colonial and the postcolonial regimes, and their CID dossiers move seamlessly across the 1947 divide. Communist students were also put under CID watch and occasionally faced preventive detentions.[62]

It is worth expounding on some key figures. Many of the political actors in Delhi in this period—communists and others—were migrants from villages and small towns. Muqimuddin Farooqi was born in Ambehta village in Saharanpur district in 1918 to a family that hailed from Delhi, where they had served the Mughal family, and wherefrom they were expelled after the 1857 rebellion. Farooqi was nourished from childhood with stories of 1857 and hatred toward the British. His father died when he was very young, and he moved to Delhi, where he was raised by his elder brother, Abdullah Farooqi, a member of Congress and the Ahrars and a journalist, whom we encountered in the previous chapter. Because of Muqimuddin Farooqi's activities, Abdullah Farooqi's house at 4162 Urdu Bazaar became a hub of the All India Students Federation and the local communists, and hence was under CID watch before and after independence. Muqimuddin Farooqi began his political activity during World War II, when he was a history student at St. Stephens College.[63] He organized a *hartal* (strike) to protest Nehru's arrest in late 1940 and was expelled from his law studies as punishment. He took a leading role in organizing the protests that unleashed the Quit India disturbances, for which he served a year-long prison sentence. After the war he was involved in the Victory Week disturbances of March 1946 and was arrested again for two months. Soon after independence, Farooqi, along with three other communists, was arrested yet again—this time under Section 3 of the Punjab Safety Act, 1947—for organizing a labor strike at the Birla Mills. It is noteworthy that the arrest took place in January 1948, before the False Independence declaration and the wave of arrests that followed. After the declaration, the chief commissioner ordered that

Farooqi's detention be extended, but the directive reached the jail authorities too late. By that time, he had gone underground, moving between hideouts until 1951. In 1954 he married Vimla Kapoor, a party member from Rawalpindi, Punjab, who had arrived in Delhi after partition.

Yag Dutt Sharma, another key figure, was born in Jakhauli village in Rohtak district (today in Sonipat district in Haryana), to educated parents who were both teachers. Like Farooqi, he moved to Delhi in 1930 and lived in Dariba Kalan with his older brother Janardhan, a lawyer who was initially a Congressi involved in labor unions and later a communist. Y. D., as he was called, studied in Ramjas College School in Daryaganj, then in Shri Ram College of Commerce, and in St. Stephens, where he received a master's degree in economics in 1940. There he also met Farooqi, got involved in Congress and student politics, and gradually became attracted to communism.

Y. D. was arrested in early 1940 for distributing antiwar literature. He continued to participate in antiwar activities after his release, took part in the agitations that broke out in August 1942, and condemned the government for the horrid Bengal famine in his speeches. In November 1943, Y. D. was arrested again and detained, along with ten other communists, for disrupting a pro-war public meeting of M. N. Roy's Radical Democratic Party in Karol Bagh's Ajmal Khan Park. When he was finally released over six months later, restrictions on his movement continued, and he was dismissed from Ramjas College, where he was teaching, on the chief commissioner's orders. Consequently, his rented house in Daryaganj (4 Tulsidas Street), which he could no longer keep, became the party's commune for full-time members in Delhi (while the office remained in Urdu Bazaar). Y. D. was arrested again in 1946 for his involvement in the postwar wave of *hartals*. Although he was charged with violating the Defence of India Rules, his trial continued into the post-independence period.[64] In Y. D.'s case, as in Farooqi's, 1947 did not bring much difference. In November 1947, he published an article in the party's organ, *People's Age* (Bombay), blaming Randhawa and Delhi's administration for the September violence against Muslims. The article was deemed objectionable, and both he and the printer were charged under the Punjab Safety Act and the colonial-era Press (Emergency Powers) Act, 1931.[65] Y.

D. absconded and went underground. As he later noted, it was typical of
the twilight period of 1947–50 for the postcolonial administration to suppress legitimate criticism using a colonial law.

In March 1949, Y. D. was captured in his hideout and arrested again
as part of a wave of preventive detentions in anticipation of a general
railway strike across the country. He and fifteen to twenty other workers were detained for six months without trial under the Punjab Public
Safety Act. A habeas corpus petition was filed on behalf of Y. D. and
two other detainees, who were never told why they were being detained
nor informed of their rights, but the judge dismissed the petition.[66] Y.
D. was temporarily released on parole when his first wife, party worker
and Indian People's Theatre Association artist Prem Kumari, died in the
Daryaganj commune, and he immediately went underground until 1951.[67]

Others remained in prison for several more months, including Mohammad and Sara Yamin. Their case epitomizes the additional pressures
put on Muslim communists at the time. Mohammed Yamin, whose family house and shop were in Sadar Bazar, is remembered by Delhi's communists as a true *Dilliwallah*, possessing an impressive persona, haughty
face, and sturdy body. Like many others, he got involved in politics during
his student days, which he spent at the Anglo-Arabic College at Ajmeri
Gate.[68] He was among the communists arrested in 1943 for disrupting M.
N. Roy's pro-war meeting, and he was sentenced to nine months' imprisonment. After his release, he continued to organize workers and simultaneously agitated for the release of Congress leaders, and consequently he
was barred from taking part in processions and public assemblies.

Yamin married Sara Mookerji, a Bengali Hindu and a prominent
party worker, and they lived in the party commune in Daryaganj. His
family left for Pakistan in 1947–48, but Sara and Mohammad were attached to the Delhi party and decided to stay. During the red scare that
followed the party's False Independence declaration, they went underground, but they were caught and detained during 1949–50, when the
habeas corpus petition was filed on their behalf and rejected. Eventually,
despite their reluctance, they left through Dhaka for Karachi with their
child in January 1951. The departure was meant to be a temporary family visit, but one of the many Muslim CID men who had moved from

Delhi to Karachi spotted Yamin, and the couple was detained again, this time in Karachi. After their release, they tried to return to Delhi, but neither the Pakistani nor the Indian government was willing to approve the move, and they were forced to stay in Pakistan and abandon any political activity.[69]

Preventing Labor Strikes

It is worth noting that the CPI's official line during this period was violent insurrection, and it thus positioned itself outside the parameters of acceptable politics and made itself a legitimate target of state repression—even though it was not officially banned in Delhi. Nevertheless, Delhi's communists were not involved in actual violence. Farooqi, Y. D., and other leaders were arrested for their condemnation of government policy, or in connection with their efforts to organize labor to improve working conditions. Indeed, labor union activities emerge as a key target of the exceptional measure of preventive detentions in this period.

Khem Raj, who was born in Hassanpur village (Gurgaon district), settled in Delhi's Sabzi Mandi and worked in the Birla Mills. He was detained under the Punjab Public Safety Act for six months in 1948. After his release he was restricted from public speaking and publishing, and several months later, he was convicted and sentenced to nine months of rigorous imprisonment. His arrests and prolonged detentions were not grounded on any allegations of violence. Rather, the CID files describe his efforts to organize labor: urging fellow workers to stage a demonstration during a visit from the mill's owner, encouraging them to attend the Adjudicators Court when their dispute with the mill was being heard, exhorting them to declare a *hartal*, and standing at the gate of the Birla Mills to prevent workers from entering—a form of picketing that was common during Quit India.[70] Significantly, what justified his arrests was a restriction under the Punjab Public Safety Act against addressing public meetings or publishing anything without permission. Thus, almost any action he took was in defiance of this law and grounds for a new arrest.

Khem Raj's case is typical of many less well-known labor activists, socialists, and communists who were active in Delhi in this early period and who were placed under restriction and detained. Another example is Janardhan Sharma, Y. D.'s brother, whose detentions before independence and after—for eleven months in 1949, and soon after for three more months—were all connected with his labor organizing among employees of the Central Public Works Department.[71] Let us consider the list of detainees in Table 5.1. While socialists do not feature as a separate category, details on the table in the file clarify that the ambiguous, catchall category of Others (*goondas*) was often used as a synonym for socialist labor union activities. This belies a prevalent assumption that socialists, who did not declare an armed insurrection like the CPI, and were not banned like the RSS, were therefore not subjected to preventive detentions.[72]

Mir Mushtaq Ahmed, the prominent socialist leader of Delhi, was arrested in November 1948 for fomenting labor unrest and detained for a week.[73] The other important socialist leader, B. D. Joshi (husband of Subhadra Joshi), who was also vice president of the Textile Mazdoor Sangh, faced a longer detention as well as restrictions on his movements. In April 1949, during a dispute between management and labor at the Birla Mills over the arrangement of shifts, Joshi and several other socialists "instigated" the laborers to go on strike and were arrested. Their arrest, according to the chief commissioner, "brought about a more sober outlook . . . and the majority of the workers returned to work."[74] Joshi filed a habeas corpus petition and was released before his case was heard in court.[75] Soon after, he applied for the deputy commissioner's permission to hold a demonstration in front of the Delhi Cloth Mills' management office and was flatly refused. Demonstrations of all kinds, clarified the deputy commissioner, went against existing orders; he intimated that disobeying the ban would lead to another arrest.[76]

Joshi's experience illuminates two points. First, the transitional government often detained the same people over and over again by using the Punjab Public Safety Act. Second, the administration relied in tandem on Section 144 of the Criminal Procedure Code, which enabled it to ban demonstrations altogether without prior permission. Both the Punjab Public Safety Act and Section 144 were also used to restrict individuals' movements and to prevent them from attending and speaking at public meetings. Any violation of such restrictive orders could serve as grounds for arrest, enabling the administration to treat almost every act of political organizing as a potential threat to public safety. Section 144 thus effectively curbed labor organization.

On the Right Side

A more complicated picture emerges when we turn to consider the RSS, its protests during the dominion years, and the government's response. The RSS, as we have seen, was actively involved in the ethnic cleansing of Delhi's Muslims in September 1947, and conflict within the political leadership and bureaucracy resulted in an equivocal and feeble reaction.[77] It was only in response to Gandhi's assassination that the government outlawed the RSS. In Delhi, roughly 280 RSS and Hindu Mahasabha members were arrested, and the government clamped down on newspapers associated with these organizations.[78]

Yet, as Clement Six has found, while these first steps were decisive, subsequent measures were half-hearted and inconsistent, grounded in profound disagreements within the government about the meaning of secularism and the nature of the RSS; Patel in particular took a conciliatory approach to the RSS.[79] He sought to channel what he considered enthusiastic patriotism into constructive channels by integrating the RSS into Congress.[80]

The Home Ministry's lack of political will did not exist in a vacuum, but represented deep currents within society. Thus, it appears that the government's scope of action was also constrained by how rooted the RSS had become in society, especially among sections of Delhi's refugees, but also among government employees and students. It was simply not feasible to ban the organization as a whole. Even Chief Commissioner Prasad, an impartial bureaucrat with secular leanings, considered the ban on the RSS unsustainable. Prasad thought the Delhi government should have followed the British colonial example and suppressed only the top leadership. As he later pointed out, "If an entire organization such as the Congress were to be declared illegal, every four-anna member would be liable to arrest."[81]

This became obvious when, on December 9, 1948, the RSS launched an all-India satyagraha against the ban. Roughly 60,000 people across the country defied the ban and took part in the agitation. In Delhi, RSS propaganda was conspicuous, and several dozen new volunteers appeared every day, wearing vermillion marks on their foreheads, shouting slogans, and courting arrest. Tens of thousands of people were arrested across India, including RSS leader M. S. Golwalkar, and in Delhi more than 2,000 people were arrested and 233 detained. Nevertheless, the protests continued. Prasad recalled that Nehru pressed him to deal harshly with the movement, and, while Patel was annoyed as usual with Nehru's intervention in his sphere of authority, he exerted pressure to contain the movement just as adamantly.[82]

As Prasad pointed out to Patel, given the RSS's financial resources and the three thousand hardcore volunteers that it commanded, the satyagraha could last for months. Furthermore, RSS leaders strategically used Gandhian popular mobilization techniques. Nehru was perturbed by the RSS's employment of the Gandhian term *satyagraha*, calling it a cloak for violence and secret activities.[83] Yet there is no denying that the agitation was conducted on nonviolent lines and drew on Gandhian political culture, challenging the Congress at its own game—and thus limiting the administration's scope for reaction. Newspapers supporting the RSS depicted conditions in jail poignantly, claiming that the political prisoners were treated like common criminals.[84] As Hindu right leaders and media increasingly adopted a civil liberties discourse in their criticism of the government, there was less room for a full show of force. Prasad's recollections of the dilemma this posed confirm that the government was not oblivious to such critiques. Prasad eventually did resort to some stern measures—arresting the movement's financers, confiscating property, and driving the slogan-shouting volunteers to the outskirts of the city, where they were given "a ducking" in the freezing Yamuna.[85] Various organizations protested against these unconstitutional measures, but the movement fizzled out. Meanwhile, Patel pushed to lift the ban on the RSS, release the "top-class" RSS detainees, and cancel fines imposed on agitators. In July 1949, the ban on the RSS was indeed lifted.[86]

Only a few months later, the RSS was again involved in mass agitation, which this time turned violent. No other political agitation in the city neared it in scope and intensity. In December, while parliament debated the Hindu Code Bill, which would reform Hindu personal law,

RSS workers joined the Hindu Mahasabha, the Akhil Bharatiya Hindu Sangh, Ram Rajya Parishad, and the All-India Mahila Samaj in mobilizing Delhi's public against the bill.[87] Roughly sixteen thousand people in Delhi signed a "satyagraha pledge," and several thousand people attended a public meeting at Ramlila Ground. There, local Hindu Mahasabha leader Ram Singh[88] and RSS leader Vasant Oak, among others, delivered forceful speeches condemning the gross interference in Hindu religion, claiming that, if the proposed reform went through, wives and husbands would separate, brothers and sisters would sue each other, and the Hindu family, the backbone of Hindus' strength, would be broken. They maintained that parliament had no mandate to enact such far-reaching legislation. This argument was not unfounded; until the 1952 elections, members of parliament were not elected but nominated by provincial legislatures, which had themselves been elected before independence on a narrow franchise of 14 percent. The speakers went further, claiming that India's leaders were not entitled to speak on behalf of Hindus—not Nehru, who had given his daughter to a non-Hindu, not Ambedkar, who had married in a civil marriage and announced himself a non-Hindu, and not Sir Sultan Ahmad, who was Muslim. They repeatedly compared the bill to the hated Rowlatt Act, which had spurred the first Gandhian mass movement after World War I. They called for a *hartal* and a public demonstration in front of parliament.

Reports from the chief commissioner, the CID, and Shanti Dal note that, while inspiration for the demonstration and *hartal* came largely from extremist elements in the Mahasabha, it was the RSS that printed, pasted, and distributed posters throughout the city, arranged meetings and *prabhat pheris* (morning walks) in the various neighborhoods, and popularized the demonstration in refugee business areas such as Lajpat Rai Market—all overnight. Clearly, despite the prolonged ban, the RSS had the grassroots-level network to carry out a mass protest.

Gandhi had developed a language of resistance whose strength lay in part in its resonance with Hindu ritual traditions, and the RSS now consciously drew on this language—as in the *prabhat pheris*, whereby groups of people would walk around the city at daybreak, singing patriotic songs and playing music.[89] At the same time, the movement expressed not just outrage but also hatred. On the day after the demonstration, there was an almost complete *hartal* in the city's business area. A couple of hundred protesters, many of them refugees, demonstrated on the lawn near the southern gate of parliament, shouting slogans against the bill and against the Congress and Nehru's "police raj," "dictatorship," and "Hitlerism." While the police managed to stop most of the protesters from breaking into the premises, many women entered the grounds and assembled in front of the building's main gate. Outside, as the crowd swelled, women walked in front, copying traditional Congress methods. The men, meanwhile, threw stones and shoes at the police and played football with a steel helmet they had snatched from one policeman. When the Kashmiri leader Sheikh Abdullah's car entered the gate, demonstrators surrounded and stoned it and pulled off its license plate. Effigies of Nehru and Ambedkar were beaten with shoes and burned. High-level RSS leaders reportedly acted as silent spectators and guides throughout.

At some point the crowd moved freely into the precincts of the Assembly grounds, performed a mock funeral of Nehru, and grabbed Gandhi caps from the heads of passers-by. After the police managed to push them out, the hostile crowd paraded an effigy of Nehru on Raisina Road and burned the Gandhi caps as they walked toward the old city through Ajmeri Gate. When they reached Hauz Qazi, they encountered police and assaulted them with brickbats. An outraged Chief Commissioner Prasad noted that the leaders who had given intemperate speeches were conspicuous in their absence, having left the scene for the younger, more hot-headed elements to indulge in acts of hooliganism.[90]

The demonstrators condemned police brutality—namely, effecting a *lathi* (wooden baton) charge and injuring allegedly peaceful demonstrators. The CID and Chief Commissioner Prasad argued that, given the extreme provocation and attacks on police personnel and vehicles, the police showed commendable restraint. The Shanti Dal, which, we may recall, was headed by Mridula Sarabhai and was aligned with leftist forces in the Congress, went a step further, hinting that the police showed too much restraint, on orders from above. In his later interview, Prasad submitted that instructions from the Home Ministry hampered efforts to restrain the crowds.[91] Only twelve people were arrested, and some were detained but released soon afterward. In fact, while Hindu right organizations engaged in violence in and around parliament, communists were the ones to find themselves behind bars in January–February 1950, as we shall soon see.

To recap, whereas Hindu right agitations posed a greater challenge to law and order, it was communists, socialists, and labor organizers who were routinely targeted by preventive detention. Both the left and the right, in any event, sharply criticized the practice of preventive detention, as well as the extensive use of Section 144 to restrict people all across the political map and to arrest them when they exercised their rights of assembly and movement.[92] The entwined working of these two practices became a focal point of criticism across the country, for this was a period when the future state of Indian democracy was argued in the government, Constituent Assembly, and civil society.[93] In the capital city, the confrontation between popular mobilization and state control gained national resonance, both because so many high-profile opposition leaders were present and because the central government directly controlled the city. Criticism of "police atrocities," denial of judicial relief, and oppressive conditions in jail came from both the right and the left, pressuring Patel and Nehru respectively. Political prisoners, it was frequently argued, were treated like common criminals—a charge that resonated with Congress leaders, who had been high-profile political prisoners under colonial rule, and who had enjoyed certain privileges even while benefitting from an aura of sacrifice. If Patel was concerned about RSS inmates and pressed for their release, Nehru was anxious about the socialists. These criticisms contributed to more moderation in the use of preventive detentions after dominionhood ended.

The arrest, in May 1949 of eminent socialist leader Ram Manohar Lohia and his supporters, for leading a procession in New Delhi in defiance of Section 144, is a case in point.[94] Nehru worried because socialists made allegations of a *lathi* charge during their arrest and ill treatment in prison. Embarrassed, Nehru urged the Delhi administration to exercise particular care in the treatment of political prisoners, especially those of note, not merely for humanitarian reasons but also for political ones, because anything that happened in Delhi received great publicity and influenced public opinion.[95] His apprehension about imprisonment during the hot Delhi summer resulted in his secretary visiting Lohia and bringing some mangoes, and his daughter Indira sending an electric fan to the inmates.[96] In fact, both the RSS detainees and, after their release, the socialists, were given the "European Ward," with the prison's best facilities.[97] Lohia and the socialists were released within a month, and the fines imposed on them were canceled. The government clearly ascribed importance to the case, as the chief commissioner held a press conference, and the Home Ministry urged the radio station to include a "press note" in its evening news bulletin announcing the prisoners' release and defending Section 144.[98] Public criticism, therefore, contributed to more moderation in the use of preventive detentions after dominionhood ended.

CONSTITUTION AS TURNING POINT?

India became a fully independent republic when its Constitution was promulgated on January 26, 1950, exactly twenty years after the Congress announced complete independence (*purna Swaraj*) as its goal. The birth of the republic was celebrated solemnly with a thirty-one-gun salute. President Rajendra Prasad and more than three thousand army men paraded through Kingsway and Connaught Place with a column of IAF aircraft above. Enthusiastic crowds lined the parade route, and the city's streets and buildings were decorated with bunting, flowers, and flags.[99]

Sardar Patel said in his speech that day, "Although we obtained independence on August 15, 1947, it was not complete in the sense of the pledge that we took. Today, by the grace of god, that pledge has been completely fulfilled."[100] Yet Hans Raj Rahbar, a communist and a progressive Urdu writer, remembers the day very differently, for he spent it in prison.[101] Like other communists, his political experience of the state went unchanged across the 1947 juncture. Back in Lahore, Rahbar was president of the Congress Socialist Party. For his participation in the Quit India movement, he was imprisoned for two years, during which he was exposed to Marxist thought, and he joined the CPI after his release. When riots broke out in Lahore in March 1947, Rahbar left for East Punjab and then Delhi, where he became the news editor of the party weekly *Naya Daur* (New Generation) and later ran the party's office near Jama

Masjid. In 1950, before the awaited celebrations, Rahbar and other communist workers were arrested and detained for a month as a preventive measure.[102] Among the detainees were students from the black lists of the CID and Director of Education, demonstrating the ties between routine surveillance and more drastic curtailment of civil liberties.[103]

An Intelligence Bureau informant reported that communists were secretly planning an anti-Constitution procession on January 26, starting in Connaught Place's Regal Cinema. They were going to parade the streets with stones tied to their bodies—most likely to convey the message that this was a slave constitution. Communist students arrived from other states, and the CID prepared to watch them closely. Posters in Urdu, Hindi, and English were posted in several parts of the city, reiterating the False Independence argument and criticizing the Nehru-Patel government for showing off its pomp and power to foreign countries at the expense of the laborers' blood and sweat. The Indian republic, these posters claimed, was a police state that infringed on basic civil liberties and imprisoned people without a trial. Tellingly, the CID file is suffused with panic over rumors that communists were planning to foment trouble during the big procession in honor of India's first president, in line with the disturbances that had taken place during the British Victory Week celebrations in March 1946. A telegram from the Home Ministry noted that, possibly, nothing would actually happen, but that it was desirable to prepare in order to prevent a breach of the peace—and that this included preventive detentions.[104] Thus, there was a gap between the lofty speeches made on January 26 in the capital, and communists' experience of that day.

Yet in hindsight, the formation of the republic proved a turning point. In the decade after the Constitution was promulgated, India's government attempted a delicate dance between civil liberties and the imperatives of law and order. After they withdrew their proclaimed insurgency, communists found their relationship with the state began to change. Afterward, and especially in the election of 1952, many communists who had been imprisoned or gone underground ran for office.[105] The mainstreaming of Delhi's communists is evident in the trajectories of Muqimuddin Farooqi, who ran in the municipal elections; Vimla Kapoor (Farooqi after

FIGURE 5.3 *The Communist Party's election camp in Karol Bagh. It carries in Urdu the name of Vimla Kapoor, the party candidate for the Delhi State Assembly from this constituency, along with the slogan "Hindustan demands bread, clothing, and housing." Source: Photo Division, Press Information Bureau, Ministry of Information and Broadcasting, Government of India.*

she married Muqimuddin), who ran in the Delhi State Assembly elections from Karol Bagh, a refugee-majority constituency; and Sarla Gupta (Sharma after she married Y. D.), who won a seat in the municipal committee in 1954 and the municipal corporation in 1958.[106] For this reason, Y. D. Sharma retrospectively treats the declaration of the republic as a watershed. Justifiably, he also draws a favorable comparison between the mainstreaming of communists in India and their total crushing in Pakistan.

Yet the Congress government did not simply discontinue old practices. Instead, we will see that it gradually reined in its most extreme policing practices—without giving up its power to use them.

Restricting the Police: Preventive Detentions in the Republic

The Constitution introduced fundamental rights that rendered some existing laws unconstitutional, and the courts struck them down in highly publicized press censorship cases. In response, in 1951 the government enacted the First Amendment to the Constitution, broadening its power to restrict speech, and the Press (Objectionable Matters) Act.[107] Likewise, as provincial Public Safety Acts lapsed or were challenged in court, the Home Ministry initiated a rapid enactment of the Preventive Detention Act in 1950, mainly to thwart the release of communist detainees. The act was initially presented as a temporary, one-year measure to address the extraordinary aftermath of partition and independence, but it was extended repeatedly for almost two decades, briefly allowed to lapse in 1969, and reintroduced a mere two years later through the Maintenance of Internal Security Act, 1971. After all, the Constitution itself explicitly provided for preventive detention in the Fundamental Rights section. It thus ensured the constitutionality of such measures, even though the Preventive Detention Act denied political detainees most of the judicial safeguards granted to ordinary criminals and delimited the justifications for detention only in general and vague terms.[108]

Evidence from Delhi suggests that continuing protest against the act and its repeated extensions, by communists, socialists, and the Jana Sangh, contributed to government restraint.[109] The Home Ministry asked the Delhi administration to compile monthly lists of detainees to assist it in refuting "irresponsible criticism" from the press and the public.[110] The promulgation of the Constitution did not effect immediate relief for communists, who, we recall, were either underground or behind bars during the Republic Day celebrations, but the lists of detainees from April 1950 onward show a noticeable decline in the number of all detainees, including communists.[111]

Table 5.2 shows that, for most of 1950, there were no communist, Muslim League, RSS, or Sikh detainees. It is not clear what the vague category "others" denotes, but it seems not to refer to labor union organizers, because fortnightly labor reports for 1951 feature labor agitation activities with no reference to arrests. The "others" might be connected with criminal activity and clampdown on gangs of *dacoits* (bandits) during this period.[112]

The few detainees in these months belonged to the Hindu Mahasabha, and their detentions were connected with the minority crisis in

TABLE 5.2 *Monthly lists of detainees under the Preventive Detention Act, April 1950–May 1951*

	RSS	Hindu Mahasabha	Communists	Muslim League and Allied Activities	Others	Akali Sikhs	Total
April 1950		1	1		1		3
May 1950		1	1		1		3
June 1950		1			1		2
July 1950		1			1		2
August 1950					1		1
September 1950		3			1		4
October 1950		3			1		4
November 1950		3			1		4
December 1950		3			1		4
January 1951		3			1		4
February 1951		3			1		4
March 1951		3					3
April 1951					5		5
May 1951					3		3

SOURCE: Files CC 70/48-C and CC 44/1951-C, Confidential, DSA.

Bengal, which spilled over into Delhi. Ashutosh Lahiri and other Hindu Mahasabha leaders were detained in reaction to inflammatory speeches that allegedly contributed to the breakout of communal riots in Delhi on March 19, 1950. The Supreme Court dismissed the habeas corpus petitions and affirmed the Preventive Detention Act's constitutionality,[113] but the judges submitted that the drastic measure of preventive detention aroused suspicions of bad faith and implored the administration not to misuse the extraordinary powers vested in it.[114] Such frequent appeals to the courts—and the legal discussion they animated—helped to enshrine the language of civil liberties, further pressuring the government.

Thereafter, the administration occasionally resorted to preventive detentions when communal tensions in the city were on the rise. In August 1951 it issued detention orders against eight Hindus following violent attacks on Muslims suspected of selling beef.[115] Several months later, following the violent agitations against the interreligious marriage of Raj

Sharma and Sikander Bakht, eleven Hindus, including Mahasabha leaders Ram Singh and Balraj Khanna, were arrested and detained under the Preventive Detention Act. Significantly, the detainees were released after three days, indicating a more restrained use of this measure.[116]

Throughout the 1950s, the challenge to law and order continued to come almost exclusively from Hindu nationalists—a development that was commensurate with the growing influence of the Jana Sangh as a political force in Delhi. In 1953 the Jana Sangh and Hindu Mahasabha joined forces with Kashmir's Praja Parishad (People's Party) to criticize Kashmir's special status and to declare a satyagraha demanding its full integration into India. Volunteers arrived in Delhi from all parts of India, and the CID described "a wave of communalism let loose in the Capital."[117] By the end of April, thirteen hundred people had been arrested. When Jana Sangh leader Syama Prasad Mukherjee went to Kashmir, disobeying an order prohibiting him from entering the state, he was arrested. His health deteriorated, and he died in jail on June 22. His outraged followers called for revenge and clashed with police near Ajmeri Gate. The atmosphere in the capital became especially charged when Mukherjee's ashes arrived in the capital.

When the government asked Chief Commissioner Prasad whether the Jana Sangh movement should be treated as a conspiracy against the secular character of the state, based on intimations from Mridula Sarabhai that preparations were underway for large-scale violence, Prasad clarified that the CID had no information on imminent violence, that the Jana Sangh was a legal party operating openly, and that the Constitution did not permit political warfare.[118] Government restraint was also evident once the satyagraha was called off in July, as the Home Ministry under Katju quickly released all detainees, canceled all externment orders, remitted all fines, and released all those awaiting trial or already convicted for disobeying orders related to the agitation, except those accused of violence. Home Minister Katju emphasized the need to withdraw cases against those below twenty-one years of age.[119] Throughout the 1950s, the government continued using Section 144 and preventive detention, but the latter much more cautiously.

The Improbable Detainee: Kashmiri Politics and the Limits of Restraint
One significant exception to government restraint was the case of Mridula Sarabhai. It is somewhat ironic that Sarabhai, who advocated stern action against the Jana Sangh's Kashmir agitation, found herself behind bars several years later in connection with her own involvement in Kashmir. A follower of Gandhi, and Nehru's right hand in the struggle against communal elements, Sarabhai has surfaced multiple times throughout this book, as she was a formidable activist during the turmoil of partition, working vigorously to recover abducted women and to rehabilitate refugees and Muslims. As head of the Shanti Dal, we may recall, she was at loggerheads with Patel, Randhawa, and Hindu right groups in the city. Shanti Dal's workers and informers produced a voluminous collection of intelligence reports on sociopolitical developments in the city, and Sarabhai, in her efforts to strengthen secular forces, duly transferred these to Nehru and the officers in power. Home Minister Katju once told Chief Commissioner Prasad that he was afraid of only two people in Delhi, Mridula Sarabhai being one of them.[120]

Nehru, we know from his correspondence, defended Sarabhai's honesty and dedication when complaints about her constant intervention came his way. Yet, when Sarabhai was eventually detained, it was under Nehru's watch. Her active involvement in Kashmir began in December 1952, when she established a Friends of New Kashmir Committee in Delhi, along with Shanti Dal members Subhadra Joshi, Shah Nawaz Khan, and Sikander Bakht, and Delhi communists Shakil Ahmad and Muqimuddin Farooqi. After Sheikh Mohammad Abdullah was arrested in August 1953, Sarabhai was a lone voice in his support, and she found herself increasingly marginalized and isolated. Nehru cut off contact with her and refused to receive her letters. She was asked to vacate the Constitution House in New Delhi and to relinquish her responsibilities in connection with the recovery of abducted women, the United Council for Relief and Welfare, and the Shanti Dal, which dissolved in 1954. Henceforth, she devoted all her energies to publicizing Abdullah's point of view and supporting his family. Her house became a refuge for Kashmiris in Delhi and was under constant CID watch.

Finally, in 1958, Sarabhai was detained under the Preventive Detention Act and held for a year without trial in the new premises Delhi's Tihar Jail. The grounds for her detention were propaganda calculated to cause hatred and contempt for the national government and the government of Jammu and Kashmir; advocacy for Sheikh Abdullah and his followers, who had allegedly sought to overthrow the government of Jammu and Kashmir with support from Pakistan; circulars she issued that were published in the Pakistani press and compromised India's security; and close association with people conspiring to overthrow Kashmir's government and to annex it to Pakistan. The Advisory Board rejected her appeal, and the Supreme Court dismissed her subsequent petition for a writ of habeas corpus.[121]

Sarabhai later expressed that "detention and internment through the hands of those one thought belonged to the same ideology was an experience terribly painful and shocking."[122] Nehru, for his part, defended the decision to detain her, clarifying that he did not doubt Sarabhai's motives and loyalty, but

> under an unfortunate set of circumstances, her courage and her capacity is
> being utilized and exploited for wrong and dangerous purposes. She got far
> greater publicity in Pakistan than in India. This is no argument, I know; but
> I merely say that her whole activity—not that she meant it—became so anti
> national, so harmful to India that it became rather difficult to leave it where
> it was.[123]

Nehru's concern with Sarabhai's propaganda playing into the hands of Pakistan echoes the anxiety surrounding Muslim newspapers whose words circulated in the Pakistani public sphere.[124] Nehru immediately qualified this statement ("This is no argument, I know"), yet we can clearly see how India's relations with Pakistan became the most vexed issue for the nation-state, the point at which freedom of expression and civil liberties reached their limit. Like Delhi's Muslims, who traversed the boundaries between the two states in myriad ways (physically, through family relations, or through the public sphere), Kashmir became a region where partition was not hermetically sealed. Any objectionable article or action was a matter of both internal and external security.

In Delhi—always in the spotlight—public criticism led to a more measured use of preventive detentions after 1950. But Kashmir—a trouble zone on India's periphery—would experience the state's more authoritarian face. In Sarabhai's case, the logic governing Kashmir was transplanted into Delhi.

BETWEEN THE LOGICS OF BUREAUCRACY
AND DEMOCRACY

In 1951, Home Minister Chakravarti Rajagopalachari addressed a meeting of the states' CIDs and the central Intelligence Bureau's officials in New Delhi, stating that these organizations were "the watch-dog of our Republic."[125] He acknowledged the public's distrust of the CID, explaining that its prejudice emerged from the history of British rule, as people had not yet grasped the true function and role of the CID in the changed context. "We do not want an OGPU [Soviet Union secret police] or a gestapo in India," he declared, but even in a democracy, antisocial elements would always operate, and the intelligence bodies were "absolutely essential to watch, catch and help the State to put down such anti-social elements." Attempting to distance the CID from its recent colonial functions, Rajagopalachari referred to the classic Tamil text *Kural*, emphasizing that spies were not a modern evil but an essential institution of ancient India.

The following day, the *Hindustan Times* commented on the Home Minister's speech with a cartoon carrying the title "Beware of the Dog!" It depicts a baby named Republic sleeping in a cradle, guarded on one side by the Home Minister, who gently rocks the cradle, and on the other by a fierce watchdog whose collar carries the name tag C.I.D.[126] The cartoon captures the dilemma of early postcolonial India. By portraying the republic as a baby, it captures the temporal colonial logic that still resounded in the Home Minister's rhetoric—the idea that Indian society was still immature, and hence the British must defer the transfer of power until their civilizing mission was complete, continued to resonate in the early postcolonial years. As legal scholar David Bayley observed at the twilight of the Nehruvian period, "One of the most puzzling questions confronting the statesmen of the newly developing nations is: to what

extent may a government arrogate to itself in the name of democratic tu-
telage the power to regulate the rules of political interaction without, by
this very action, jeopardizing the long-run development of democracy?"[127]

Of course, both the Home Minister's defensive speech and the cartoon demonstrate, like many other examples in this chapter, that the
pedagogic state did not go unchallenged. India was indeed far from a
"gestapo state," as the scope of criticism in the public sphere, parliament,
and the street makes clear. This chapter has demonstrated the vibrancy
of political mobilization on the streets of Delhi and the centrality of civil
liberties to public discourse in the early 1950s—both of which forced the
government to be more transparent and cautious in utilizing extreme
measures.

Yet the structure of surveillance, along with its blurred boundaries
between political opponents and security threats, persisted. Communists,
socialists, and members of the Jana Sangh and Hindu Mahasabha—all

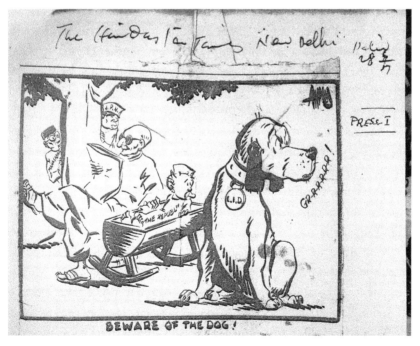

FIGURE 5.4 *"Beware of the Dog!" from the* Hindustan Times, *April 28, 1951.*
Source: F. 435, Delhi Police Records, Eighth Installment, NMML.

players in the field of electoral democracy—were under regular surveillance, with reports routinely produced about their movements and meetings. And if, as Samaddar notes, intelligence is "the fulcrum on which reasons of state stand," it can be used during times of crisis to infringe on people's liberties more overtly. After all, the massive and rapid arrests of leaders, activists, and students, on the left and the right, that took place in the capital following the declaration of Emergency on June 25, 1975, were enabled by a repository of dossiers and reports produced over the previous three decades by the local CID.

Let us revisit Delhi's communist worker and Urdu poet Hans Raj Rahbar, whom we first met in jail during the Republic Day celebrations of 1950. Rahbar was arrested twice under British rule and then five times after independence.[128] When the CPI split over the Soviet-China schism and the Sino-India War, Rahbar joined the pro-China CPI(M) and was elected its general secretary in Delhi. Thus, while Delhi's communists were gradually mainstreamed, Rahbar positioned himself outside the boundaries of acceptable Indian politics, much like Sarabhai. The government raided the party's office, and Rahbar and other leaders were arrested and detained in Tihar Jail for sixteen months (December 1964–April 1965). Later, as the Naxalite movement gathered momentum and was repressed by the CPI (M) government in West Bengal, the CPI (M) itself split, and Rahbar, again disillusioned, joined the new CPI (ML) faction in 1969. He was arrested again during the 1971 war in Bangladesh and, along with Jammat-e Islami members, was detained for a month or so, until the war's end. His fifth arrest took place on the night of June 25, 1975, when the Emergency was declared, and he was imprisoned for twenty-one months. But this time he was not alone. In Ambala Central Jail, Rahbar shared a long barracks with members of all political stripes. On one side, the Jana Sangh people held classes on the Gita and recited the *Ramayana*. On the other side, the Jammat-e Islami and Muslim League read the Quran and performed *namaz* prayers five times a day. In between, Rahbar and a socialist read and played chess.

While the Indian government may have exercised restraint in applying preventive detentions, it opened the way to abuse by repeatedly extending the Preventive Detention Act without clarifying what constituted a security risk. "In the days of political jockeying, infighting, and striving which are sure to come with the death of Mr. Nehru, will his successors be able to resist his towering example?" asked Bayley prophetically in 1962. "Has a precedent been set for the by-passing of the judiciary, the circumscription of fundamental rights, and the deprivation of the suspected from due process of law?" Unfortunately, he concluded, "India's political leaders have gradually come to the realization that for them emergency is a way of life."[129] In 1975 political leaders, activists, and students spanning the spectrum suddenly found themselves, alongside Rahbar, outside the parameters of acceptable politics and inside prison walls.

IN DECEMBER 2019, the Indian parliament passed the controversial Citizenship Amendment Act (CAA). The act promises an expedited path to Indian citizenship to Hindu, Sikh, Buddhist, Jain, Parsi, and Christian migrants from Pakistan, Bangladesh, and Afghanistan who entered India before 2015. The implication is that Muslim migrants from these or other countries would continue to be treated as illegal immigrants.[1] The act, as political scientist Niraja Gopal Jayal argues, breaks new ground by introducing religious identity into India's legal definition of citizenship. It consummates the gradual erosion of the principle of jus soli in favor of jus sanguinis since the 1980s. The act is coupled with the provocative proposal by the ruling Bharatiya Janata Party to implement a National Register of Citizens across the country to distinguish legal citizens from illegal immigrants. Together, the act and the projected register inherently discriminate on the basis of religion, targeting Muslim migrants while legalizing all others.[2] Furthermore, since many people, especially at the lower socioeconomic strata of society, do not possess identity documentation, there is widespread fear among Muslims that the new citizenship law and national register will be used to harass, disenfranchise, and even dispossess Muslim citizens born in India.

Indeed, the Citizenship Amendment Act precipitated persistent, widespread protests. Agitations erupted in Assam[3] and quickly spread to cities and university campuses across the country. Delhi became a center of the protests, starting with a demonstration at the Jantar Mantar and in the Muslim area of Jamia Nagar, where the Delhi police reportedly forced its way into the Jamia Millia Islamia University campus and used *lathi* (wooden baton) charges, tear gas, and extreme force to quell the student protests. Over the next few months, protests were held in multiple locations in Delhi, the most famous being Shaheen Bagh, a Muslim locality in south Delhi, where a sit-in by women attracted tens of thousands of visitors as well as media attention and became a symbol of the anti-CAA movement.[4] Another high-profile protest was held by Dalit activist and Bhim Army Chief Chandrashekhar Azad "Ravan," who, violating Section 144 and evading the police, arrived with his supporters at the steps of the Jama Masjid after Friday prayers in solidarity with the Muslim minority.[5]

Events took a grim turn in late February 2020, when clashes between supporters and opponents of the act degenerated into intense communal violence in northeast Delhi, the gravest that Delhi had witnessed in decades, with fifty-three people killed, hundreds wounded, and property burned and destroyed. While two-thirds of the casualties were Muslims, the police filed charges against mostly Muslim student leaders, activists, and protestors, in what it tagged as "the Delhi riots conspiracy case," under the Unlawful Activities (Prevention) Act (UAPA), and protest leaders were in judicial custody for six months.[6]

While COVID-19 lockdowns subdued the anti-CAA agitation, another wave of mass protests was underway. Hundreds of thousands of farmers, afraid that agricultural reforms will render them easy prey for corporations, launched a "Dilli Chalo" (On to Delhi) protest, marched to Delhi and were in effect besieging the city. During a tractor rally on Republic Day, January 26, 2021, some of the protesters digressed from their preapproved route, drove through barricades, clashed with police, marched to the symbolic Red Fort, and hoisted flags atop it.[7] The farmers' protest has attracted support from global celebrities and activists, and when a toolkit prepared by Indian activists to advance the farmers' campaign was tweeted, the government launched an investigation into an alleged conspiracy against the Indian state and ultimately arrested climate activist Disha Ravi.[8] Additionally, several sedition cases were filed against journalists who covered the Republic Day events. Commentators have criticized the government's intolerance of dissent and clampdown on the media, with some calling it "an undeclared emergency."[9]

These recent events show how the structural tensions surrounding citizenship and civil liberties, which inhered in the intertwining of decolonization and partition, persist and burden Delhi, which is at one and the same time a paradigmatic "partition city," and a capital city where national controversies are staged. The protests and violence surrounding the Citizenship Amendment Act demonstrate the lingering clash between a secular and a Hindu majoritarian view of the nation and the state. The act was passed after the Bharatiya Janata Party won sweeping reelection under Narendra Modi, a testimony to his overwhelming popularity and unprecedented consolidation of power in recent years, bringing about an accelerated Hinduization of the Indian state. Two issues that centered the partition politics in Delhi—as we saw throughout this book—have taken particularly brutal form. One is the protection of cows, involving lynching of Muslims and Dalits accused of smuggling, killing, or consuming cows. The second issue is the protection of Hindu women from so-called "love jihad"—that is, from Muslim men who allegedly lure or force vulnerable Hindu women to marry them and convert to Islam.[10]

In August 2019 the constitutional autonomy of Jammu and Kashmir was repealed, and almost at the same time, the Supreme Court granted the site of the sixteenth-century Babri Masjid—demolished by Hindus in 1992—to Hindu appellants for building a Ram temple. As Hindu identity is imposed ever more comprehensively on Indian nationalism, India comes closer to the model of ethnic democracy epitomized by Israel, at least de facto.[11] The Citizenship Amendment Act gives this shift a de jure stamp, echoing Israel's citizenships laws, which are based purely on ethnic-religious criteria.[12]

India's recent tilt to the Israeli model of ethnic democracy, despite the strikingly different choices made by the two countries' founding figures,[13] leads to a key historiographical question that I have grappled with throughout this book: which is more powerful in shaping history—contingency and human agency or deep structures? On the one hand, we saw that self-determination meant different things to different historical players during the twilight of British rule, and did not have to bring about a territorial partition and population exodus. We also observed how individual players—most notably Nehru and Patel—influenced the trajectory of the Indian state. Nehru's undisputed power, after 1950, certainly helped curb Hindu nationalist visions of Delhi and the nation. On the other hand, the secular republic was in fact established through territorial partition, resulting in a deep contradiction that even the most secular voices—Nehru included—could not escape. This led to the protective and well-intentioned ghettoization of Delhi's Muslims, to Nehru's ambivalence to Delhi's Muslim newspapers, and to the Nehru-Liaquat Pact's implicit affirmation of India's responsibility to the Hindus of Pakistan. In these early decisions, a jus sanguinis notion of citizenship remained latent. Decades later, it finds overt expression in the Citizenship Amendment Act—giving force to a structural, almost deterministic interpretation of history.

Recent events also show that India continues to negotiate between authoritarian instincts and democratic aspirations, and that Delhi continues to be a major theater for this confrontation. It is no surprise that protesting farmers chose to converge on the borders of the capital, or that the most dramatic scenes from this movement took place on Republic Day at the Red Fort—a symbolic time and location that appeared in this book time and again. In this case, as well, the classical question of structure versus change and agency looms large. On the one hand, we advanced a structural reading of the authoritarian legacy of colonial rule by demonstrating that, their differences notwithstanding, India's architects maintained the colonial system of surveillance as well as its curbs on civil liberties—Section 144, the law of sedition, and preventive detentions. Thus, it was Nehru of all people who sanctioned the detention without trial of Mridula Sarabhai. The authoritarian burden of the past, which resurfaced brutally during the Emergency, is again ascendant, as the government shut down the Internet in protest sites, employed Section 144 to ban demonstrations, arrested and detained students and activists, and filed sedition cases against journalists.[14]

At the same time, we saw that such authoritarian measures did not go unchallenged, and in fact met with robust criticism during the early postcolonial period. Recent events intimate that such a democratic and liberal sense of empowerment has only deepened in India's civil society. It is emblematized in the image of Chandrashekhar Azad "Ravan" at the Jama Masjid steps, brandishing a copy of the Constitution with a picture of Dalit leader and architect of the Constitution Bhimrao Ambedkar on its cover. Many others held a copy of the Constitution and read out its Preamble. Thus, colonial rule and partition brought about a vulnerable yet promising democracy, encapsulated in the constraints and possibilities of the current moment.

NOTES

INTRODUCTION

1. Husain, *Chiraghon Ka Dhuan* (1999), 22.
2. Frykenberg, "Study of Delhi" (1992 [1986]), 1.
3. Frykenberg, "Study of Delhi," (1992 [1986]), 4.
4. Gupta, *Delhi between Two Empires* (1981), 54.
5. "... if one is more accurate, something much closer to fourteen distinct cities, concentrated in three main areas of urban population density, can be identified. Of these, the 'seven cities' are in reality only the successive citadels (or 'cities') which were built during medieval times." Frykenberg, "Study of Delhi" (1992 [1986]), 6.
6. Rajagopalan, *Building Histories* (2017), 119–51.
7. Dehlvi, *Dilli Ki Bipta* (2010 [1950]), 63.
8. For Hakim Ajmal Khan, see Metcalf, "Nationalist Muslims in British India" (1985).
9. Ehlers and Krafft, "Islamic Cities in India?" (2003 [1993]), 16. For the main architectural principles and features of Shahjahanabad, see also Blake, "Cityscape of an Imperial Capital" (1992); Pernau, *Ashraf into Middle Class* (2013).
10. Ehlers and Krafft, "Islamic Cities in India?" (2003 [1993]), 19. For the *havelis* and their transformation under the pressures of colonial rule, see Hosagrahar, "Mansions to Margins" (2003).
11. For the Revolt of 1857 and its aftermath, see Gupta, *Delhi between Two Empires* (1981); Farooqui, *Besieged* (2010); Hosagrahar, *Indigenous Modernities* (2005); Pernau, *Ashraf into Middle Class* (2013); Dalrymple, *The Last Mughal* (2007).
12. Pritchett, *Nets of Awareness* (1994).
13. Gupta, *Delhi between Two Empires* (1981), 116, 120–21, 214–16.
14. The Municipal Committee was headed by the British commissioner and his deputy, and consisted of ex-officio and nonofficial Europeans and members of the Indian loyalist elite who were nominated. With time, the representation of elected Indians increased. For a historical survey of municipal governance in Delhi, see Oldenburg, *Big City Government in India* (1976), 269–85. For a recent study of Delhi municipality during 1858–1911, see Kishore, *(Un)Governable City* (2020).
15. Gupta, *Delhi between Two Empires* (1981), 61–66; Hosagrahar, *Indigenous Modernities* (2005), 119–42.
16. For the architecture of Town Hall and new civic buildings, see Hosagrahar, *Indigenous Modernities* (2005), 53–55; Gupta, *Delhi between Two Empires* (1981), 84–86.

17. Until the completion of New Delhi, the Civil Lines functioned as the temporary location of the Imperial Government. For New Delhi, see Irving, *Indian Summer* (1981); Metcalf, *Imperial Vision* (1989).

18. Hosagrahar, *Indigenous Modernities* (2005), 149. For the intimate connections between the seemingly distinct spaces under colonial governmental rationalities, see Legg, *Spaces of Colonialism* (2007).

19. Pritchett, *Nets of Awareness* (1994), 21.

20. The elegy is quoted as an epigraph in Gupta, *Delhi between Two Empires* (1981).

21. Ali, *Twilight in Delhi* (2007 [1940]). For the literary strategies employed in this novel and its relationship with the *shahr-e ashob* genre, see Sadana, *English Heart, Hindi Heartland* (2012), 33–40; Joshi, *In Another Country* (2002), 205–27.

22. Ali, *Twilight in Delhi* (2007 [1940]), xix–xx. See also Hasan, *Legacy of a Divided Nation* (1997), 126–27.

23. Dehlvi, *Ujra Dayar* (1967).

24. Dehlvi, *Dilli Ki Bipta* (2010 [1950]), 23.

25. Metcalf, *Islamic Revival in British India* (1982); Jones, *Socio-Religious Reform Movements* (1989); Dalmia, *The Nationalization of Hindu Traditions* (1996).

26. For representative studies of colonial governmentality and its impact on identity politics, see Cohn, "Census, Social Structure and Objectification" (1987); Appadurai, "Number in the Colonial Imagination" (1993); Kaviraj, "Imaginary Institution of India" (1992); Pandey, *The Construction of Communalism* (1990). For an account focused on the emergence of Muslims as a political community in the later part of the nineteenth century, see Hardy, *The Muslims of British India* (1972), 116–46.

27. The Lucknow Pact of 1916 between the Congress and the Muslim League, which was facilitated by Muhammad Ali Jinnah, and the post–World War I Khilafat Movement are considered two milestones of Hindu-Muslim cooperation. For an approach that underscores such cooperation and the role of Muslims in the nationalist Congress movement, see Mushirul Hasan's studies, e.g., *India's Partition: Process, Strategy, and Mobilization* (2013 [1993]) and *M. A. Ansari: Gandhi's Infallible Guide* (2010 [1987]).

28. For a study that places the rise of the Gandhian nationalist movement in the global context of World War I and the disillusionment in its aftermath, see Manela, *The Wilsonian Moment* (2007).

29. Brubaker, "Aftermaths of Empire" (1995); Diner, *Cataclysms* (2008 [1999]), 153–98. For a volume that places India's partition within this larger context, see Panayi and Virdee, eds., *Refugees and the End of Empire* (2011).

30. Weitz, "From the Vienna to the Paris System" (2008), 1314.

31. For a genealogy of the language of minorities and majorities and its transformation by the 1860s into a terminology attached to ethnicities or nationalities, mainly in the Habsburg Empire, see Weitz, "From the Vienna to the Paris System" (2008), 1329–30.

32. Arendt, *Origins of Totalitarianism* (1979 [1951]), 273. See also Mazower, "Minorities and the League of Nations" (1997).

33. Tejani, *Indian Secularism* (2008), Chapter 3.

34. Mufti, *Enlightenment in the Colony* (2007).

35. Jalal, *The Sole Spokesman* (1994 [1985]). Farzana Shaikh analyzes this insistence on a national rather than a minority status through a theological lens, identifying the difference between Islamic and liberal approaches to political representation. Shaikh, "Muslims and Political Representation" (1986).

36. Gilmartin, "Partition, Pakistan, and South Asian History" (1998). For the vagueness of Pakistan, see also Devji, *Muslim Zion* (2013); Pandey, *Remembering Partition* (2001); Khan, *The Great Partition* (2007).

37. More recently, Venkat Dhulipala has sought to refute this thesis in his study of the politics of Pakistan in the United Provinces, claiming that Pakistan was in fact envisioned in great detail and clarity. But the materials that Dhulipala presents reveal, to the contrary, that even though Pakistan was continuously discussed and debated, territorially speaking it remained fuzzy. I will discuss this in greater detail in Chapter 1. Dhulipala, *Creating a New Medina* (2015).

38. Dubnov and Robson, "Drawing the Line, Writing Beyond It" (2019), 1–2.

39. For the federal alternatives to the nation-state imagined at the twilight of empire, see Collins, "Decolonisation and the 'Federal Moment'" (2013); Cooper, *Citizenship between Empire and Nation* (2014). For a critique of this exercise as oblivious to the racial hierarchy inherent in imperial federalism, see Moyn, "Fantasies of Federalism" (2015).

40. Devji, *Muslim Zion* (2013); Dubnov, "Notes on the Zionist Passage to India" (2016).

41. See Chapter 2.

42. Shaikh, *Making Sense of Pakistan* (2009), 44.

43. Ansari, *Life after Partition* (2005); Ansari and Gould, *Boundaries of Belonging* (2020); Chatterji, *The Spoils of Partition* (2007); Kaur, *Since 1947* (2007); Zamindar, *The Long Partition* (2007); Khan, *The Great Partition* (2007); Talbot, *Divided Cities* (2006); Chattha, *Partition and Locality* (2011); Roy, *Partitioned Lives* (2012); Sen, *Citizen Refugee* (2018); Sherman, *Muslim Belonging in Secular India* (2015); Purushotham, *From Raj to Republic* (2021).

44. Kaur, *Since 1947* (2007); Pandey, "Folding the National into the Local" (2001); Zamindar, *The Long Partition* (2007). Exceptions are Mehra, "Planning Delhi Ca. 1936–1959" (2013); Bhardwaj Datta, "Genealogy of a Partition City" (2019); Legg, "A Pre-Partitioned City?" (2019); Nazima Parveen's *Contested Homelands* (2021) came out as I was in the final stages of writing, precluding an extended engagement with its findings, though I refer to it here and in several other relevant places below.

45. Chopra, *Delhi Gazetteer* (1976); Rao and Desai, *Greater Delhi* (1965), 25–35.

46. Rao and Desai, *Greater Delhi* (1965), vii.

47. Chopra, *Delhi Gazetteer* (1976), 127.

48. The migration from Pakistan was overwhelmingly urban, and as refugee colonies were established in the periphery of the city—mainly to its west and south but also north of the university campus—the city expanded at the expense of the surrounding villages. This and subsequent waves of expansion are beyond the scope of this book, which concentrates on the original urban areas.

CHAPTER 1

1. A secret government report on the Quit India disturbances in Delhi, August 14, 1942, cited in Chopra, ed., *Quit India Movement* (1986), 18. Research toward this chapter has received funding from the European Research Council (ERC) under the European Union's Seventh Framework Programme (FP7/2007–2013)/ERC Grant Agreement Number 340124: "JudgingHistories: Experience, Judgement, and Representation of World War II in an Age of Globalization."

2. Siddiqi, *Smoke without Fire* (2011), 152.

3. For historicity as an experience of temporality, see Koselleck, *Futures Past* (2004).

4. Siddiqi, *Smoke without Fire* (2011), 157. For an in-depth study of the complex socio-economic and sectarian composition of Delhi's Muslim elites, and the growing significance of religious community as a marker of their identity in the late nineteenth and early twentieth centuries, see Pernau, *Ashraf into Middle Class* (2013).

5. Siddiqi, *Smoke without Fire* (2011), 158. The Khilafat movement was organized in the aftermath of World War I by Indian Muslims who sought to protect the position of the Ottoman sultan as the *chalif* of the Islamic world. They joined forces with Mahatma Gandhi's Noncooperation Movement. See Minault, *Khilafat Movement* (1982). For accounts focused on Delhi, see Gupta, *Delhi between Two Empires* (1981), 186–221; Metcalf, "Nationalist Muslims in British India" (1985); Hasan and Pernau, eds., History of the Non-Cooperation and Khilafat Movements in Delhi" (2005).

6. Siddiqi, *Smoke without Fire* (2011), 159.

7. More on the Congressi Muslims below.

8. Siddiqi, *Smoke without Fire* (2011), 159.

9. Kamtekar, "The End of the Colonial State in India" (1988), 5. The account of the crisis in the next paragraphs draws on Kamtekar's analysis.

10. Hutchins, *Illusion of Permanence* (1976).

11. Chopra, "Delhi Gazetteer" (1976), 120–21. Rao and Desai, *Greater Delhi* (1965), 55–56.

12. The civilian population of the cantonment, which stood at 8,798 in 1939, rose by the end of July 1944 to 27,920. In addition, an estimated 7,000 laborers, living outside the cantonment, arrived in the Central Depot Ordnance every day. See Fortnightly report for the second half of July 1944, F. CC 1/44-C, Confidential, DSA. For population increase and the spatial expansion of Delhi during World War II, see Mehra, "Planning Delhi ca. 1936–1959" (2013); Bhardwaj Datta, "Genealogy of a Partition City" (2019). For congestion in the interwar period and the failed housing extension schemes, see Sharan, *In the City, Out of Place* (2014), 118–46.

13. In May–June 1943, 9,280 acres of mortgaged land were redeemed, according to the revenue authorities, involving the total payment of over two lakhs of rupees. "For such a small area as the Delhi province, where the total land revenue is not much more than three lakhs a year, these are big figures." Between September 1942 and June 1943, the cooperative societies returned Rs. 534,437 out of Rs. 946,953 taken on loan. See Fortnightly report for the second half of June 1943, F. CC 1/43-C, Confidential, DSA.

14. For the differential economic impact of World War II on different classes in India, see Kamtekar, "A Different War Dance" (2002).

15. The INA trials will be discussed further below.

16. For the palace's transformation in the aftermath of the revolt, see Rajagopalan, *Building Histories* (2017), 27–57.

17. Copies of the pamphlet are in F. DC 381/1942, DSA. Although the pamphlet is not dated, it was probably published sometime in August 1942, like all other documents in this file.

18. In the months preceding Quit India, Gandhi used strong words about the sexual violation of Indian women. Khan, *The Raj at War* (2015), 150. For the centrality of rape and violation of women's honor in the Quit India movement, see Hutchins, *India's Revolution* (1973); Greenough, "Political Mobilization and the Underground Literature of the Quit India Movement" (1999).

19. Kamtekar, "The Shiver of 1942" (2002).

20. Churchill, *The Second World War, Volume 4* (1985 [1950]), xiii.

21. Kamtekar, "The Shiver of 1942" (2002), 82; Voigt, *India in the Second World War* (1987).

22. Bayly and Harper, *Forgotten Armies* (2005), 154.

23. Kamtekar, "The Shiver of 1942" (2002), 84, emphasis in original. See also Khan, *The Raj at War* (2015), 93–121.

24. For Delhi newspapers' harsh criticism of the British Army's blunders, and its total neglect of India's defense, see F. CC 75/1942, Confidential, DSA; Fortnightly reports for February–April 1942, F. CC 1/42-C, Confidential, DSA.

25. Unless stated otherwise, the following paragraphs draw on fortnightly reports for the year 1942 in F. CC 1/42-C, Confidential, DSA (henceforth CC 1/42-C)

26. Siddiqi, *Smoke without Fire* (2011), 207.

27. Abbas, *Let India Fight for Freedom* (1943), 68.

28. F. CC 70/1942, Confidential, DSA.

29. Bose, *His Majesty's Opponent* (2011), 213, 25.

30. Fortnightly report for the first half of June, F. CC 1/42-C. For the tour, which ironically was meant to boost morale, see Khan, *The Raj at War* (2015), 173.

31. For complaints about the Americans' responsibility for Delhi's *tongawallas'* expensive fares, see "Trudging Along," *Dawn*, November 1, 1942.

32. Extract from military Force H.Q. orders, August 14, 1942, in F. DC 380/1942, DSA.

33. Siddiqi, *Smoke without Fire* (2011), 220. Delhi's eminent historian, Percival Spear, who taught at St. Stephens and served in the Information and Propaganda Department during the war, likewise recalls the arrival of American soldiers in April 1942 and the enthusiasm they aroused. Spear and Spear, *India Remembered* (2010 [1981]).

34. Siddiqi, *Smoke without Fire* (2011), 219.

35. Raghavan, *India's War* (2016), 227.

36. Moore, *Churchill, Cripps, and India* (1979).

37. "Covering Cripps," April 12, 1942, in Abbas, *I Write as I Feel* (1948), 26–29.

38. The park was named Jahanara in the Mughal period, after Shahjahan's daughter. It was known in the early British period as Company Bagh and later renamed Queen's Gardens. After independence it would be renamed Mahatma Gandhi Park.

39. Fortnightly report for the second half of May, CC 1/42-C.

40. Report for August 1942, in F. CC 1/42-C; Chopra, ed., *Quit India Movement* (1986), 96.

41. Hindi *Vir Arjun* reports and official correspondence, in F. CC 40(N)1942, Special Press Adviser, DSA.

42. Fortnightly report for the first half of March, in F. CC 1/42-C.

43. Fortnightly report for the second half of July, in F. CC 1/42-C.

44. Chopra, ed., *Quit India Movement* (1986), 13. For Delhi's communists and Quit India, see Gupta, *Dilli Ki Communist Party Ka Itihas* (2007), 197–98.

45. The following account draws mainly on "A brief diary of events in connection with the Congress Civil Disobedience campaign," F. CC 1/42-C; "City's Magistrate's report," August 12, 1942, F. DC 381/1942, DSA.

46. Chopra, ed., *Quit India Movement* (1986), 13.

47. Section titled "Students" in untitled report for August 1942, F. CC 1/42-C.

48. Protesters in Chandni Chowk threw stones at an American military lorry carrying petrol. The driver was injured and lost control, the lorry overturned, and the crowd set it on fire. The driver and travelers were rescued at the last minute.

49. Legg, *Spaces of Colonialism* (2007), 118.

50. Chopra, ed., *Quit India Movement* (1986), 14.

51. F. CC 128/1942, Confidential, DSA. It was a large and impressive building known as Pili Kothi. A Muslim subinspector of police was killed while trying to stop the crowd. According to the CID, this was a rare case, because the crowds mostly refrained from attacking Indian officers, specifically targeting British ones. F. CC 128/1942, Confidential, DSA, 49. J. N. Sahni remembers the building as one of the first seven-story buildings in the city: Interview with J. N. Sahni, No. 203, CSAS.

52. F. CC 123/1942, Confidential, DSA.

53. F. CC 123–1/1942, Confidential, DSA.

54. Intelligence reports cited in Chopra, ed., *Quit India Movement*, 16, 48.

55. Jugal Kishore Khanna, who held the key position of general secretary of the Delhi Pradesh Congress Committee, returned to the city from Bombay only after the initial outbreak was contained. Interview with Jugal Kishore Khanna, Oral History Transcript No. 177, NMML, 113–14. Interview with Jugal Kishore Khanna, No. 207, CSAS, 26–27.

56. The Delhi Muslim League leaders called on the Muslim public to stay away from the Quit India movement. See reports on speeches in F. 16, Delhi Police Records, (henceforth DPR), Third Installment, NMML.

57. For example, among the twenty-five people found guilty of taking part in burning Pili Kothi, eleven were Muslims. F. CC 128/1942, Confidential, DSA. Siddiqi remembers that a young man from his *mohalla* was shot dead in the disturbances in Chandni Chowk. Siddiqi, *Smoke without Fire* (2011), 212.

58. For seminal work analyzing crowd violence as a political language of resistance, see Guha, *Elementary Aspects of Peasant Insurgency in Colonial India* (1999 [1983]). For the Quit India disturbances in different parts of India and their political language, see Pandey, *The Indian Nation in 1942* (1988); Hutchins, *India's Revolution* (1973).

59. Interview with Jugal Kishore Khanna, No. 207, CSAS, p. 29.

60. Mainly of Ramjas College, Hindu College, and Indraprastha College for women. Delhi's administration threatened to withdraw its financial support of universities unless they disciplined the troublemakers. F. CC 123/1942, Confidential, DSA; F. CC 123–1/1942, Confidential, DSA; Bhargava and Dutta, *Women, Education, and Politics* (2005), 84–94.

61. Arrested leaders included, among others, F. H. Ansari, Dr. Yudhvir Singh, Nuruddin Behari, Shatrughan, Radha Raman, Brij Kishan Chandiwala, Satyavati, and Mir Mushtaq Ahmed. Phool Chand Jain was arrested in September. See reports on arrests in F. CC 1/42-C. The government took legal steps to seize control of absconders' houses and confiscated all movable property, including furniture, bedding, clothes, books, and even children's toys. Deshbandhu Gupta, who lived in a big house on Keeling Road and owned the nationalist Urdu daily *Tej*, could not sustain government pressure on his property and surrendered early on. Interview with Jugal Kishore Khanna, Oral History Transcript No. 177, NMML.

62. For Aruna Asaf Ali's activities in Delhi, where she stayed until the end of February 1943, see Chopra, ed., *Quit India Movement* (1986), 298, 306–16 passim. For her importance in Quit India, see also Khan, *The Raj at War* (2015).

63. Jain, *Civil Disobedience* (2010); Interview with Jugal Kishore Khanna, Oral History Transcript No. 177, NMML.

64. Interview with Jugal Kishore Khanna, Oral History Transcript No. 177, NMML, 95, 104–5. For the help from government officials, including policemen, see also: Interview with J. N. Sahni, No. 203, CSAS.

65. Report of March 17, 1943, cited in Chopra, ed., *Quit India Movement* (1986), 298. Fortnightly reports for August and November 1942, F. CC 1/42-C.

66. Fortnightly report for the second half of November, F. CC 1/42-C.

67. Chopra, ed., *Quit India Movement* (1986), 307–8.

68. Fortnightly report for the second half of September and CID notes of October 4 and 8, 1943, in F. CC 1/43-C, Confidential, DSA.

69. Growing discontent with the authorities' failure to control landlords was prominent in the older parts of Delhi, where the New Delhi House Rent Control order of 1939 did not apply. Fortnightly reports for the first half of January and first half of February 1944, F. CC 1/44-C, Confidential, DSA.

70. For rationing in wartime Delhi, see fortnightly reports for 1944 in F. CC 1/44-C, Confidential, DSA; Sriraman, *In Pursuit of Proof* (2018), 1–44.

71. Factory workers saw their wages rise, but other laborers did not. There were demands for higher wages and threats of mass resignation among employees of the Controller of Supply Accounts, the Railway Clearing Accounts, and the Delhi Joint Water and Sewage Board.

72. Interview with Chaudhury Brahm Prakash, Oral History Transcript No. 503, NMML.

73. Even the joint invasion by Japan and Bose's INA into Assam in March 1944 would not arouse much excitement. It was camouflaged by British propaganda and ended in a Japanese retreat. As Yasmin Khan claims, the military crisis was passing, but the domestic fallout of the war was just heating up. Khan, *The Raj at War* (2015), 289.

74. From late 1942 to the end of the war the Delhi secretariat's fortnightly reports repeatedly comment on the public's loss of interest in the war front and its preoccupation with economic hardships. F. CC 1/42-C; F. CC 1/43-C; F. CC 1/44-C; F. CC 1/45-C, Confidential, DSA.

75. For a concise discussion of the shift in Muslim politics from defining the Muslims as a minority to defining them as a nation, see Shaikh, *Making Sense of Pakistan* (2009), 14–45.

76. Siddiqi, *Smoke without Fire* (2011), 134–38. For the increasing significance of religion as a marker of identity and the escalation of conflicts between religious communities in Delhi during the 1820s–1830s, see Pernau, *Ashraf into Middle Class* (2013).

77. Jones, *Arya Dharm* (1976); Jaffrelot, *The Hindu Nationalist Movement in India* (1993), 12–25.

78. For Shraddhanand's role in the Noncooperation movement, see Nair, *Changing Homelands* (2011), Chapter 3. On the 1924 riots, see Gupta, *Delhi between Two Empires*, 218–19. For the *Shuddhi-Tabligh* controversy, see Interview with Imdad Sabri, Oral History Transcript No. 722, NMML, 92–93. For Shraddhanand's assassination and Abdul Rashid's execution, see Jones, "Organized Hinduism in Delhi and New Delhi" (1992 [1986]); Interview with Phool Chand Jain, Oral History Transcript No. 479, NMML, 82–84; Legg, *Spaces of Colonialism* (2007), 125–26. See the latter, more generally, for an analysis of communal riots in Delhi, focusing on colonial governmentality and security schemes.

79. Jones, "Organized Hinduism in Delhi" (1992 [1986]), 216–7.

80. Nair, *Changing Homelands* (2011); Gupta, "The Indian Diaspora of 1947" (1991); Jaffrelot, *The Hindu Nationalist Movement in India* (1993), 291–92. For this entanglement in the United Provinces Congress, see Gould, *Hindu Nationalism and the Language of Politics* (2004).

81. Interview with Jugal Kishore Khanna, Oral History Transcript No. 177, NMML, 39. Delhi Congress leader Phool Chand Jain reconstructs the atmosphere in *Vir Arjun*, where he worked as a journalist. Interview with Phool Chand Jain, Oral History Transcript No. 479, NMML, 52–57; Daechsel, *The Politics of Self-Expression* (2006), 43.

82. Jaffrelot, "The Hindu Nationalist Movement in Delhi" (2011).

83. For the financing of the Hindu Mahasabha Bhavan in Delhi by Birla, see "Hindu Mahasabha Bhavan," *Hindustan*, May 15, 1940.

84. In a house owned by Mohammad Mahasabha Punjabi of Ballimaran. Mazhar Uddin, the editor of the Urdu daily *Al Aman*, which operated from Turkman Gate, was instrumental in this move.

85. For detailed intelligence reports on the establishment of the local branch, see F. 14, DPR, Third Installment, NMML.

86. Jalal, *The Sole Spokesman* (1994 [1985]), 15–17.

87. Several contemporary commentators and later historians see the experience of the Congress ministries as crucial for the emergence of the Pakistan demand in the Muslim minority provinces, especially in the United Provinces. Coupland, *The Indian Problem*, Vol. 2 (1944); Moore, "Jinnah and the Pakistan Demand" (1983); Hasan, "Nationalist and Separatist Trends in Aligarh, 1915–1947" (1985); Brennan, "The Illusion of Security" (2013 [1993]).

Hasan describes a "carefully-orchestrated campaign" by the Muslim League against the Congress from 1937 onwards. Hasan, *Legacy of a Divided Nation* (1997), 82. William Gould, who analyzes the political language of the United Provinces Congress, provides the episode with historical depth. Gould, *Hindu Nationalism and the Language of Politics*. Likewise, Sandria Freitag traces changes in the pattern of riots after the 1920s, with Muslims developing an increasingly defensive symbolism. Freitag, *Collective Action and Community* (1989), 197–248.

88. Interview with Jugal Kishore Khanna, Oral History Transcript No. 177, NMML.

89. On the eve of Independence, the Municipal Committee consisted of forty-three members, twenty-eight of whom were elected, half Hindu, half Muslim. The city was divided into fourteen wards, each electing through separate electorates one Hindu and one Muslim. Chopra, *Delhi Gazetteer* (1976), 716. For the growing pressure by Delhi's Muslim elites to implement weightage and separate electorates in the Municipal Committee, see Gupta, *Delhi between Two Empires* (1981), 149, 152, 217.

90. For the high representation of Muslims in the pre-partition police force, see chapter 2, passim and footnote 81. It was also customary that 50 percent of appointments made by the Delhi Municipality were of Muslims. "Muslims in Irwin Hospital," [Letter to the Editor], *Dawn*, December 20, 1945.

91. In the aftermath of the Great Revolt of 1857, the mosque was confiscated and sold to Lala Chunna Mal. It was returned to the Muslims in 1877, put under a Muslim managing committee, and became an important arena for religious debates. It was patronized by the Punjabi Muslim community within the walled city and in Sadar Bazar, and hence formed a link between the city and the localities to its west. Gupta, *Delhi between Two* (1981), 54; Pernau, *Ashraf into Middle Class* (2013), 281 and passim.

92. Adjacent to the western wall of the mosque was the property known as Sarai Bangash, a later construction by Muslims from Kohat, in today's Khyber Pakhtunkhwa. It was confiscated in 1858 and transferred to a Hindu banker, Lala Chunna Mal, along with the mosque. Around 1934 the firm of Lala Chunna Mal sold the property to another Hindu firm, which then sold it to Seth Gadodia. Gadodia demolished the old building and undertook construction of what is now known as the Gadodia Market.

93. For the dispute, see files CC 65/1938; CC 49/1940; CC 41/1941; CC 41/1942, Confidential, DSA.

94. Report of the Fatehpuri Managing Committee, in F. CC 65/1938, Confidential, DSA.

95. CID reports in F. 14, DPR, Third Installment, NMML.

96. The core group of nationalist Muslims in Delhi, who founded the Jamia Millia Islamia University, had been Mufti Kifayatullah of the Jamiat Ulama; Hakim Ajmal Khan, the famous doctor of traditional Muslim medicine from Ballimaran in Delhi; the medical doctor Mukhtar Ahmed Ansari, who was close to Gandhi; and barrister Asaf Ali, whose house in Daryaganj became the venue for Congress meetings. Faruqi, *The Deoband School and the Demand for Pakistan* (1963); Metcalf, "Observant Muslims, Secular Indians" (2007); Metcalf, "Nationalist Muslims in British India"; Hasan, *M. A. Ansari: Gandhi's Infallible Guide* (2010 [1987]). Ajmal Khan and M. A. Ansari had both died by the end of the 1930s.

97. In their public meetings over the Fatehpuri-Gadodia dispute, Muslim League leaders tagged Congressi Muslims as traitors who turn the Muslim away from the Kaaba to Wardha, referring to the Congress "Wardha Scheme" for primary education, formulated by Dr. Zakir Husain of Jamia Millia Islamia University. The proposal was presented as an attack on Islamic education. One of the important members of the managing committee attacked by the League was Mufti Kifayatullah of the Jamiat. For recollections of this dispute, see Interview with Maulana Abdullah Farooqi, Oral History Transcript No. 634, NMML.

98. Siddiqi, *Smoke without Fire* (2011), 135.

99. Almost eight hundred people, apparently Hindus, were arrested in connection with the Shiv Mandir movement. For the controversy and ensuing riots, see F. CC 47/1938, Confidential, DSA; F. CC 34/1938, Confidential, DSA. For an analysis, see Vanaik, *Possessing the City* (2019), chapter 7.

100. Siddiqi, *Smoke without Fire* (2011), 138.

101. F. CC 98/1940, Confidential, DSA.

102. For example, a Muslim delegation to the chief commissioner, including the imam of the Jama masjid and Muslim League leader Shuja-ul-Haq Gotewala, disowned Haji Rashid Ahmad, who had previously negotiated the matter, claiming he was a Congressi who did not represent Muslim interests.

103. The Majlis-e Ahrarul-Islam Party was established in Punjab in 1931. For the influence of the Ahrars in Delhi, see Interview with Maulana Abdullah Farooqi, Oral History Transcript No. 634, NMML. The Jama Masjid was restored to the Muslims in 1862 on condition that it not serve as a venue for political gatherings, but the Ahrars totally disregarded these rules, complained the managing committee. F. CC 21/1939, Confidential, DSA; F. CC 109/1940 Confidential, DSA.

104. The murder took place in the context of the annual session of the Jamiat Ulama-e Hind. *Al Aman* and *Wahdat* had been embroiled in communal tensions in the city since the riots of the mid-1920s. They were responsible for "frequently publishing unfounded, exaggerated, alarming and mischievously distorted news calculated to cause disturbances and disaffection." CID report on Al Aman and Wahdat, September 25, 1940, F. CC 137/1940, Confidential, DSA. In 1935 the papers became advocates of the Muslim League and, in 1937, the editor Mazhar Uddin was a prime agent in the formation of the Delhi branch of the party.

105. F. CC 40–5/1939, Confidential, DSA.

106. Recruitment to the Muslim League's Muslim National Guards started in early 1938 when, during a procession in honor of Jinnah, Delhi Muslim League president Shuja-ul-Haq Gotewala decorated 200 to 300 volunteers with badges of white cloth bearing the words, "Allah o Akbar, Muslim National Guard, Muslim League Delhi." Muslim League leaders Sheikh Habibur Rahman (Magistrate), and Abdul Salam (Member of Municipal Committee) were said to have enlisted "bad characters" to the volunteer organization. F. 14 and 15, DPR, Third Installment, NMML. For the All India Muslim National Guards, see Hasan, *Legacy of a Divided Nation* (1997), 87–91.

107. CID reports from August 1939, F. 15, DPR, Third Installment, NMML.

108. Extract from City CID Daily Report, April 10, 1939, F. 42, DPR, Second Install-ment, NMML.

109. Siddiqi, *Smoke without Fire* (2011), 152. *Zindabad* is a common political slogan; the chant meant "Long live Mr. Jinnah! Long live the Muslim League!" For Deliverance Day in Delhi, see CID report in F. 15, DPR, Third Installment, NMML.

110. "The A.I.M.L.'s resolution, March 23, 1940," cited in Jalal, *The Sole Spokesman* (1994 [1985]), 58.

111. Moore, "Jinnah and the Pakistan Demand" (1983); Jalal, *Self and Sovereignty* (2000), 388–400.

112. For contemporary discussions of the intentional ambiguity of Pakistan in Muslim League discourse, see Ambedkar, *Thoughts on Pakistan* (1941); Coupland, *The Indian Prob-lem*, Vol. 3 (1944), 80; Prasad, *India Divided* (1946). For this claim among later historians, see Jalal, *The Sole Spokesman* (1994 [1985]); Gilmartin, "Partition, Pakistan, and South Asian History" (1998). Devji emphasizes the Muslim League's geographically indifferent attitude to Pakistan. Devji, *Muslim Zion* (2013), 25–30, 38.

113. Dubnov, "Notes on the Zionist Passage to India" (2016). Devji also points to the multinational model of the Soviet Union as an inspiration. Devji, *Muslim Zion* (2013), 25–33.

114. Iqbal's presidential address to the All-India Muslim League on December 29, 1930, in Pirzada, ed., *Foundations of Pakistan* (1970). For analysis of Iqbal's political vision, see Devji, "From Minority to Nation" (2019).

115. The scheme is ascribed to Mian Kifayat Ali and was financed by Nawab Shahn-awaz Khan of Mamdot. Prasad, *India Divided*, 176–81. For surveys of the different schemes, see also Coupland, *The Indian Problem*, Vol. 2 (1944), 197–207; Durrani, *The Meaning of Pakistan* (1944); Gauba, *The Consequences of Pakistan* (1946), 53–67; Jalal, *Self and Sovereignty* (2000), 388–400.

116. For Haroon's recommendations, see Coupland, *The Indian Problem*, Vol. 2 (1944), 251; Prasad, *India Divided* (1946), 199–204, 223–24; Moore, "Jinnah and the Pakistan De-mand" (1983), 551.

117. "Bharat men tin swatantra rajya," *Hindustan*, March 29, 1940. Khaliquzzaman's in-terpretation conformed with his earlier suggestions to create three or four British domin-ions coordinated at the center in matters of defense. Dhulipala, *Creating a New Medina* (2015), 218–19.

118. Cited in Dhulipala, *Creating a New Medina* (2015), 205–6.

119. The other was Bhimrao Ambedkar's scheme.

120. Prasad, *India Divided* (1946), 188. The three other Muslim zones are the northwest block, northeast block, and a Deccan block centered around Hyderabad.

121. The scheme is included as an appendix in Hasan, "Nationalist and Separatist Trends in Aligarh." The map of the scheme is in F. 42, DPR, Second Installment, NMML. Hyderabad would join with Berar and Karnataka to form an autonomous state.

122. As Jalal notes, "Given the difficulties in equating 'nationhood' with 'statehood,' Muslims and non-Muslims had to remain linked to a larger Indian whole, albeit radi-cally rearticulated in form and substance by virtually independent self-governing parts.

Outright secession was clearly not an option for minority-province Muslims." Jalal, *Self and Sovereignty* (2000), 396.

123. The latter rejected Latif's scheme on the basis of its federal character and unity with India, as well as the impracticality of the large exchange of populations it contemplated. See appendix in Hasan, "Nationalist and Separatist Trends in Aligarh, 1915–1947" (1985), 32–33.

124. Moore, "Jinnah and the Pakistan Demand" (1983), 543; Dhulipala, *Creating a New Medina* (2015), 227–28.

125. Jinnah raised this idea in an interview in the *New York Times* in 1942: Dhulipala, *Creating a New Medina* (2015), 229. He raised it again in 1946 and 1947, as we shall see in the next chapter.

126. Dhulipala, *Creating a New Medina* (2015), 405–6.

127. For Anis Al Din's scheme and map, see Dhulipala, *Creating a New Medina* (2015), 194–204, 77.

128. The maps are in Ali, *Pakistan* (1946), 247, 72.

129. Musavvir also assumed a continued British presence in the foreseeable future. Dhulipala, *Creating a New Medina*, 249.

130. For a history of the Anglo-Arabic College, see Pernau, *The Delhi College* (2006); Gupta, "The Halcyon Yesterdays of Delhi College" (1998).

131. Siddiqi, *Smoke without Fire* (2011), 223.

132. Siddiqi, *Smoke without Fire* (2011), 153.

133. Siddiqi, *Smoke without Fire* (2011). For a similar leap of faith among the United Provinces Muslims, see Qazi Jaleel Abbasi's memoir, cited in Naim, "The Muslim League in Barabanki" (2010).

134. Parveen, *Contested Homelands* (2021), 85–89.

135. Ikramullah, *From Purdah to Parliament* (1998 [1963]), 133–34.

136. Singh, "Dehlviyat," (2014), 216.

137. The marked shift toward the agenda of Pakistan in Delhi's Muslim League meetings is evident in CID reports in F. 15, DPR, Third Installment, NMML.

138. Siddiqi, *Smoke without Fire* (2011), 154.

139. See Chapter 2.

140. F. DC 276/1941, DSA. The Urdu park is adjacent to the Edward Park, which was renamed Netaji Subhash Park after independence.

141. Interview with Jugal Kishore Khanna, Oral History Transcript No. 177, NMML, 130, 136; Interview with Maulana Abdullah Farooqi, Oral History Transcript No. 634, NMML, 13; Jain, *Civil Disobedience* (2010), 64.

142. See, e.g., the assistance given to the Muslim League by the Delhi secretariat in organizing the April 1943 All-India Muslim League annual session. F. DC 93/1943, DSA.

143. CID report on Pakistan Day, March 23, 1941, F. 15, DPR, Third Installment, NMML.

144. As the chief commissioner reported on Pakistan Day in 1942, the procession "made a halt apparently deliberately in front of Sisganj Gurdwara in the Chandni Chowk—provocative act of a kind which the Muslims have generally left to the Sikhs in

Delhi." F. CC 1/42-C Confidential, DSA. See the CID report on the procession in F. 16, DPR, Third Installment, NMML.

145. Freitag, *Collective Action and Community* (1989), 201.

146. CID report on the Pakistan Day, in F. 17, DPR, Third Installment, NMML. Unfortunately, there is no trace of the placards or Pakistan map presented at the procession.

147. Fortnightly report for first half of May 1945, F. CC 1/45-C, Confidential, DSA.

148. Siddiqi, *Smoke without Fire* (2011), 228.

149. Negotiations commenced with the Shimla Conference in July 1945, convened by India's Viceroy Archibald Wavell.

150. Penderel Moon cited in Sarkar, "Popular Movements and National Leadership" (1982), 679.

151. Reports of "Recruiting Headquarters" in Delhi for 1946, F. CC 24/1946, Confidential, DSA.

152. For the Muslim League election campaign in the Punjab, see Talbot, "The Role of the Crowd in the Muslim League Struggle for Pakistan" (1993); Gilmartin, "A Magnificent Gift" (1998). For the United Provinces, see Dhulipala, *Creating a New Medina* (2015), 390–461.

153. See, e.g., official reports stating that the excitement over the election campaigns of Muslim League and Congress reached the rural areas surrounding Delhi, even to isolated villages which had hitherto remained untouched by the politics of the two parties. F. CC 24/1946, Confidential, DSA.

154. Including the Deobandi Ulama (notably Maulana Shabbir Usmani) who had recently joined the League.

155. CID reports on Dehli Muslim League for the end of September 1945, in F. 17, DPR, Third Installment, NMML.

156. Siddiqi, *Smoke without Fire* (2011), 247. For Azad's political analysis of the condition of Indian Muslims undergirding his rejection of Pakistan, see Mufti, *Enlightenment in the Colony* (2007), 154–76.

157. Gilmartin, "A Magnificent Gift" (1998).

158. The pamphlets are included in F. 17, DPR, Third Installment, NMML.

159. "Jamiat-Ul-Ulema-I-Hind," *Dawn*, December 22, 1945.

160. "Jamiat-Ul-Ulema-I-Hind," *Dawn*, December 22, 1945.

161. Report on Muslim League public meeting of February 11, 1946, in F. 18, DPR, Third Installment, NMML. Unfortunately, there is no way to know what the Pakistan map presented looked like.

162. The three officers were Shah Nawaz Khan, Prem Kumar Sahgal, and Gurbaksh Singh Dhillon.

163. Kamtekar, "The End of the Colonial State in India," (1988), 100–101.

164. Others included Asaf Ali, Sir Tej Bahadur Sapru, Bhulabhai Desai, and Kailash Nath Katju. Jugal Kishore Khanna was in charge of setting up the Defence Committee office. Interview with Jugal Kishore Khanna, No. 207, CSAS.

165. Green, "The Indian National Army Trials" (1948).

166. Khan, *The Raj at War* (2015), ix–x.

167. Ram, *Two Historic Trials in Red Fort* (1946). For the INA-related publications in Delhi, see F. CC 130/1945, DSA; F. DC 643/1946; F. DC 651/1946; F. DC 656/1946; F. DC 658/1946, DSA.

168. Nehru to Cripps, January 27, 1946, cited in Kamtekar, "The End of the Colonial State in India" (1988), 102.

169. Green, "The Indian National Army Trials" (1948), 62; Alpes, "The Congress and the INA Trials" (2007).

170. Delhi's communists made conscious efforts at the time to link up with young and progressive members of the Delhi Muslim League, such as Anis Hashmi, and change its orientation from the inside, by "planting" Muslim communist workers in the League. The strategy failed. Gupta, *Dilli Ki Communist Party Ka Itihas* (2007), 199–200.

171. CID reports, F. 18, DPR, Third Installment, NMML.

172. Report and note of February 18, 1946, F. 18, DPR, Third Installment, NMML.

173. Letter of March 5, 1946, F. CC 60/1946, Confidential, DSA. The report refers to Lala Shankar Lal, who led Subhas Chandra Bose's Forward Block in Delhi.

174. See a poster signed by the Student Federation calling students to join a black flag cycle procession, in F. CC 110/1946, Confidential, DSA. The charge sheets in this file also show the prominence of Delhi's communists—Muqimuddin Farooqi, Santosh Chatterji, Mohammed Yamin, *inter alia*. See also Gupta, *Dilli Ki Communist Party Ka Itihas* (2007), 185–86, 370–78.

175. Marston, *The Indian Army and the End of the Raj* (2016), 146.

176. F. CC 47/1946; F. CC 110/1946, Confidential, DSA. The charge sheets mention more cases of arson, targeting buses, post offices, electric substations and poles, and banks.

177. F. CC 110/1946 Confidential, DSA.

178. Sarkar, "Popular Movements and National Leadership" (1982), 682.

179. F. CC 48/1946, Confidential, DSA. The Delhi police was three thousand men strong.

180. F. CC 110/1946 Confidential, DSA.

181. See in Chapter 5.

182. Siddiqi, *Smoke without Fire* (2011), 224.

183. For Qureshi's recollections of the growing split on campus, see Qureshi, "A Case Study of the Social Relations between the Muslims and the Hindus, 1935–47" (1970). For the history and recollections of St. Stephen's College, see Baker, "St. Stephen's College, Delhi, 1991–1997" (1998); Spear and Spear, *India Remembered* (2010 [1981]).

184. Siddiqi, *Smoke without Fire* (2011), 236–37.

CHAPTER 2

1. Siddiqi, *Smoke without Fire* (2011), 262–63.

2. Siddiqi, *Smoke without Fire* (2011), 280–81.

3. Dehlvi, *Dilli Ki Bipta* (2010 [1950]), 29–30.

4. Khurshid Ahmad Khan to R. N. Banerjee, Fortnightly Report for the First Half of September 1947, CC 1/47-C, Confidential, DSA. For mass conversions of Muslims in the

rural areas, see CC 21/49, Confidential, DSA; Kidwai, *In Freedom's Shade* (2011), 176–80, 194–95, 209, 233–41.

5. Daily reports in *Hindustan* and *Hindustan Times*, September 6–15, 1947. Fortnightly Report for the First Half of September 1947, CC 1/47-C, DSA.

6. Pandey, *Remembering Partition* (2001), 130; Dehlvi, *Dilli Ki Bipta* (2010 [1950]), 38.

7. Jawaharlal Nehru to Rajendra Prasad, September 17, 1947, Selected Works of Jawaharlal Nehru (henceforth SWJN) Vol. 4, 82. Foreign correspondents' reports cited in Malik, *The Tragedy of Delhi* (1948).

8. "Sikhs Slaughter Muslim Students in Delhi: Over Fifty Killed," *Dawn*, September 7, 1947, in DC 15/1947, Press Advisor, DSA; Dehlvi, *Dilli Ki Bipta* (2010 [1950]), 32; Pandey, *Remembering Partition* (2001), 129.

9. Kidwai, *In Freedom's Shade* (2011), 22. For the impact of partition on Jamia Millia, see also Talib, "Jamia Millia Islamia" (1998), 176–86; Gautier, "A Laboratory for a Composite India?" (2020).

10. Barelvi, "Such a Strange Maidan" (1994).

11. Interview with Jugal Kishore Khanna, Oral History Transcript No. 177, NMML, 133; Dehlvi, *Dilli Ki Bipta* (2010 [1950]), 36.

12. Dehlvi, *Dilli Ki Bipta* (2010 [1950]), 34.

13. Kidwai, *In Freedom's Shade* (2011), 119.

14. Jain, *Civil Disobedience* (2010), Chapter 4.

15. Interview with Phool Chand Jain, Oral History Transcript No. 479, NMML, 91–92 (my translation).

16. Jain, *Civil Disobedience* (2010), 58.

17. Qureshi, "A Case Study of the Social Relations between the Muslims and the Hindus, 1935–47" (1970).

18. Gupta, "The Indian Diaspora of 1947" (1991), 89.

19. Interview with Jugal Kishore Khanna, Oral History Transcript No. 177, NMML, 134.

20. Interview with Jugal Kishore Khanna, Oral History Transcript No. 207, Centre of South Asia Studies Archive, Cambridge, 40.

21. Interview with Jugal Kishore Khanna, Oral History Transcript No. 177, NMML, 137–38.

22. "Ruthless War against Evil-Doers," *Hindustan Times*, September 10, 1947.

23. Gandhi, *Delhi Diary* (1948).

24. Pandey, *Remembering Partition* (2001), 89–91; Talbot and Singh, *The Partition of India* (2009), 61–62.

25. Gupta, "The Indian Diaspora of 1947," 88; Interview with Jugal Kishore Khanna, Oral History Transcript No. 177, NMML, 133.

26. Malik, *The Tragedy of Delhi* (1948), 24.

27. "Big Haul of Arms in Paharganj," *Hindustan Times*, September 13, 1947; "Stray Stabbing and Sniping Incidents," *Hindustan Times*, September 17, 1947.

28. Bayly and Harper, *Forgotten Armies* (2005), 337–38.

29. Kidwai, *In Freedom's Shade* (2011), 35–71; Zamindar, *The Long Partition* (2007), 34–39.

30. The Muslim population was 304,501 at the time of the 1941 census, or 33.2 percent of the total population. Based on Delhi's population growth rate in this decade, in March 1947, Muslims numbered an estimated 424,000. In the 1951 census, the Muslim population had dwindled to 99,501, or 5.71 percent of the population. See Chopra, *Delhi Gazetteer* (1976), 130; Rao and Desai, *Greater Delhi* (1965), 55.

31. Naimark, *Fires of Hatred* (2001), 3; Lieberman, "'Ethnic Cleansing' Versus Genocide?" (2010).

32. Gilmartin, "Partition, Pakistan, and South Asian History" (1998), 1087. For a comparison of "traditional" communal riots and the purificatory and genocidal elements of partition violence, see Talbot and Singh, *The Partition of India* (2009), 65–68.

33. Fortnightly Report for the First Half of September 1947, F. CC 1/1947, Confidential, DSA.

34. For instance, Menon, *The Transfer of Power in India* (1957), 424–31; SWJN Vol. 4, 54, editor's footnote no. 2. These features mark standard nationalist Indian and Pakistani narratives on the partition violence in other places: Talbot and Singh, *The Partition of India* (2009), 62–65.

35. Interview with R. N. Banerjee, Oral History Transcript No. 366, NMML, 116–17.

36. Chopra, *Delhi Gazetteer* (1976), 111.

37. Pandey, "In Defence of the Fragment" (1991), 563–64; Pandey, "The Prose of Otherness" (1994), 199.

38. "Situation in Capital Under Control," *Hindustan Times*, September 10, 1947.

39. For a critique of the concept of riots in contemporary India as concealing what are essentially pogroms, see Brass, *Forms of Collective Violence* (2006).

40. "Dilli ki sampradayik sthiti men sudhar," *Hindustan*, September 10 1947; "Two Stabbed in Delhi," *Hindustan Times*, September 3, 1947.

41. "Dr. Joshi ki hatya," *Hindustan*, September 10, 1947; "Nehru ji dwara Dilli ke updravgrast ilaqon ka daura," *Hindustan*, September 7, 1947; "Arson and Stabbing in Delhi," *Hindustan Times*, September 5, 1947; "City Now Near Normal," *Hindustan Times*, September 12, 1947. For rules concerning coverage of communal riots, see Sethi, *Wars over Words* (2019), 182–86.

42. "Nayi Dilli men sthiti swabhavik," *Hindustan*, September 12, 1947.

43. "Large Arms Haul in Delhi," *Hindustan Times*, November 20, 1947.

44. For the use of machine guns by a numerical minority in battles, see Diner, *Cataclysms* (2008 [1999]), 27–31.

45. Fortnightly Report for the First Half of September 1947. *Arain* were Muslim gardeners. Social tensions between the Muslim gardeners and the Hindu *bania* (trader caste) in the fruit and vegetable wholesale market of Sabzi Mandi had been imbued with religious feelings from the mid-nineteenth century: Pernau, *Ashraf into Middle Class* (2013), 194.

46. Guha, "The Prose of Counter-Insurgency" ([1983] 1988).

47. Khosla, *Stern Reckoning* (1989 [1949]), 282.

48. Khosla, *Stern Reckoning* (1989 [1949]), 283.

49. The shooting of Dr. Joshi was a highly publicized case: F. CC 69/1947, Confidential, DSA; Interview with Shankar Prasad, Oral History Transcript No. 494, NMML; "Joshie

Murder Case," *Hindustan Times*, December 18, 1947; "Qureshi Sentenced to Death," *Hindustan Times*, January 7, 1948.

50. Khosla, *Stern Reckoning* (1989 [1949]), 284.

51. Menon, *The Transfer of Power in India* (1957), 419–21; Shankar, *My Reminiscences of Sardar Patel, Vol. 1* (1974), 98–100; Interview with R. N. Banerjee, Oral History Transcript No. 366, NMML.

52. Gupta, "The Indian Diaspora of 1947" (1991); Pandey, "Folding the National into the Local" (2001); Zamindar, *The Long Partition* (2007), 19–27.

53. Pandey, *Remembering Partition* (2001), 49–51.

54. Pandey, "In Defence of the Fragment" (1991), 559.

55. Gilmartin, "Partition, Pakistan and South Asian History" (1998); Chatterji, "New Directions in Partition Studies" (2009).

56. Detailed analyses have been conducted with regard to partition violence in other regions: Aiyar, "'August Anarchy'" (1995); Brass, "The Partition of India and Retributive Genocide" (2003); Talbot, *Divided Cities* (2006); Chatterji, *Bengal Divided* (1994), 232–40.

57. Jalal, *The Sole Spokesman* (1994 [1985]), 209–10.

58. For the Great Calcutta Killing, see Das, *Communal Riots in Bengal* (1991), Chapter 6; Chatterji, *Bengal Divided* (1994), 232–40; Mukherjee, *Hungry Bengal* (2015), Chapter 7.

59. "Absolute Pakistan the Only Solution: Exchange of Population Must Be Considered," *Dawn*, November 15, 1946; Banerjea, "Exchange of Population" (1946); Khosla, *Stern Reckoning* (1989 [1949]), 219–20.

60. For a recent revisionist account of the Interim Government, see Ankit, *India in the Interregnum* (2019).

61. Extract from urban CID daily report, April 10, 1946, F. 18, Delhi Police Records (henceforth DPR), Third Installment, NMML.

62. Chief Commissioner Christie to H. C. Prior, April 27, 1946, F. CC 62/46-C, Confidential, DSA.

63. Parveen, *Contested Homelands* (2021), 110–13.

64. CID reports on the Muslim League meeting in Urdu Park on June 6, 1946, in F. 18, DPR, Third Installment, NMML.

65. Report on the proceedings of a meeting of the Delhi Provincial Muslim Students Federation, August 18, 1946, F. 18, DPR, Third Installment, NMML.

66. *Dawn* issue of August 16, 1946, included in F. DC 601/1946, DSA.

67. For clippings of Delhi's main newspapers in August–November 1946, see F. DC 598/1946, DSA; F. DC 601/1946, DSA; F. DC 652/1946, DSA; F. DC 655/1946, DSA.

68. Special police report, in F. CC 108/1946, Confidential, DSA.

69. Extract from a CID source report, September 4, 1946, F. 18, DPR, Third Installment, NMML.

70. F. CC 91/1946, Confidential, DSA.

71. For the disturbances of November 1946, see F. CC 113/46, Confidential, DSA; F. CC 26/1947, Confidential, DSA; F. DC 628/1946, DSA; F. 5/44/46-Police, Home Department, Political (I), NAI. For analysis of the disturbances through the lens of colonial policing, see Legg, *Spaces of Colonialism* (2007), 146–47.

72. Sharan, *In the City, Out of Place* (2014), 84–100.

73. Reports in F. DC 628/1946, DSA.

74. Specifically, the violence in Garhmukhteshwar in the western United Provinces. See Randhawa's report in F. DC 628/1946, DSA. For the violence in Garhmukhteshwar, see Pandey, *Remembering Partition* (2001), 92–120.

75. CID Reports for September–October 1946, F. 19, Third Installment, DPR, NMML; "Repeated Police Firing in Delhi on Friday," *Dawn*, November 15, 1946.

76. Aiyar, "'August Anarchy'" (1995); Brass, "The Partition of India and Retributive Genocide" (2003); Talbot, *Divided Cities* (2006).

77. This information was compiled along with other intelligence documents in a report on the activities of the RSS between 1946 and 1949: Inspector-General of Police S. R. Chaudhri to CC Shankar Prasad, March 3, 1949, D.O. No. 1595 E.M., F. CC 48/1949, Confidential, DSA.

78. W. Christie to A. E. Porter, Fortnightly Report for the Second Half of December 1946, F. CC 1/47, Confidential, DSA. For the strengthening of the RSS in Delhi during this period, see also Six, *Secularism, Decolonisation, and the Cold War* (2018), 94–97. For the disorganization of the National Guards, see reports in F. 64 and 65, DPR, Fifth Installment, NMML.

79. Ankit, *India in the Interregnum* (2019).

80. F. 5/44/46-Police, Home Department, Political (I), NAI. I am grateful to Rakesh Ankit for pointing me to this file.

81. In December 1946 Patel asked for a report on the composition of the Delhi Police high officials. The report reveals that among the top 12 officers there were 7 Europeans or Anglo-Indians, 4 Muslims, and 1 Hindu. Among the 21 inspectors were 10 Muslims, 4 Europeans or Anglo-Indians, and 7 "others" (Hindus and Sikhs). Patel pressed the chief commissioner to increase Hindu and Sikh representation and asked for monthly reports on progress. By the end of August 1947, officers of and above the rank of inspector included 14 Hindus, 6 Sikhs, 7 Anglo-Indians, 1 Christian, and only 7 Muslims. See F. CC 27/47, Confidential, DSA. For an analysis of this point, drawing a comparison to Hyderabad, which was also the responsibility of Patel in his capacity as Minister of States, see Gould, Sherman, and Ansari, "The Flux of the Matter" (2013), 250–51. For efforts to change the communal composition of the lower ranks of the Delhi police, see F. CC 51/47, Confidential, DSA. According to the latter, in May 1947, the force consisted of 2,500 policemen.

82. Gandhi, *Mohandas* (2006), 597. For Punjabi Hindus' support of the province's partition, see Nair, *Changing Homelands* (2011).

83. For an analysis of the role of the crowd in Muslim League politics, with a focus on Punjab, see Talbot, "The Role of the Crowd in the Muslim League Struggle for Pakistan" (1993).

84. CID reports for January–February 1947, F. 20, DPR, Third Installment, NMML; Fortnightly Report for the Second Half of February 1947, F. CC 1/47, Confidential, DSA. For students' participation, see Zaidi, ed., *Quaid-I-Azam Mohammad Ali Jinnah Papers*, First Series Volume I Part 2, Appendices (1993), 290.

85. Fortnightly Report for the First Half of March 1947, F. CC 1/47, Confidential, DSA; Chief Commissioner Christie to Home Secretary Porter, D.O. 447 ST/CC, April 28, 1947, in F. CC 36/47-C, Confidential, DSA.

86. Fortnightly reports for the second half of February and the first half of March, F. CC 1/47, Confidential, DSA.

87. Stolte, "'The Asiatic Hour'" (2014).

88. CID Reports for March 1947, F. 21, DPR, Third Installment, NMML.

89. The account of the disturbances on Pakistan Day (March 23, 1923) and in the following weeks is based on F. CC 36/47-C, Confidential, DSA.

90. Chief Commissioner Christie to Home Secretary Porter, D.O. 447 ST/CC, April 28, 1947, in F. CC 36/47-C, Confidential, DSA.

91. For English-language and vernacular newspaper coverage of the events, see F. DC 7/1947, Press Advisor, DSA.

92. For the growing presence of Sikhs in Delhi from March 1947, and their responsibility for the outbreak of violence on March 23, see F. CC 36/47 C, Confidential, DSA; Home Member Patel to Mountbatten, June 27, 1947, in F. 28/5/47, Home, Political (I), NAI. I am grateful to Rakesh Ankit for pointing me to this latter file.

93. Chief Commissioner Christie to Home Secretary Porter, D.O. 447 ST/CC, April 28, 1947, in F. CC 36/47-C, Confidential, DSA. For the Muslims' grave apprehensions about the Sikh *kirpans*, see CID reports on the Muslim League in F. 21, DPR, Third Installment, NMML.

94. Fortnightly Report for the Second Half of March 1947, F. CC 1/47, Confidential, DSA.

95. Letter of Himmat Ali to Home Member Patel, March 28, 1947; SSP Lal to DC Randhawa, D.O. No. 428/S-11, April 12, 1947, in F. CC 36/47-C, Confidential, DSA.

96. Note by Chief Commissioner Christie to SSP and DC about a deputation of the Muslim League, March 25, 1947, in F. CC 36/47, Confidential, DSA.

97. W. Christie to R. N. Banerjee, Fortnightly Report for the First Half of May 1947, F. CC 1/47, Confidential, DSA.

98. Extract from CID Daily Report, May 10–11, 1947 and Casual Source Report, May 21, 1947, F. 62, DPR, Fifth Installment, NMML; Reports of May 12 and 19, 1947, F. 109, DPR, Fifth Installment, NMML.

99. The AIML intervened, and it was decided to hold fresh elections to the Provincial Muslim League Committee. CID source reports for April–May 1947, F. 21, DPR, Third Installment, NMML. It is noteworthy that the "extremist elements" were those who, as discussed in the previous chapter, were involved in the anticolonial agitations of 1946–47 against the call of the old guard. Anis Hashmi was close to communist workers in Delhi.

100. "Extract from Monthly Report on Volunteer Organizations in the Delhi Province for April 1947," F .63, DPR, Fifth Installment, NMML.

101. W. Christie to Banerjee, Fortnightly Report for the second half of April 1947; Inspector-General of Police S. R. Chaudhri to CC Shankar Prasad, March 3, 1949, D.O. No. 1595 F.M., F. CC 48/49, Confidential, DSA.

102. Most probably this was a reference to Jugal Kishore Birla, who was closely associated with the Hindu Mahasabha and who, in a meeting of the Mahasabha in March 1944, called on Hindus to arm themselves. Fortnightly report for the second half of March 1944, F. CC 1/44, Confidential, DSA.

103. CC Christie to R. N. Banerjee, May 26, 1947, F. CC 51/1947, Confidential, DSA; F. 28/5/47, Home, Political (I), NAI.

104. Jawaharlal Nehru to Sardar Patel, October 6, 1947, SWJN Vol. 4, 126.

105. Nair, *Changing Homelands* (2011).

106. "Note by Mumtaz Fateh Ali on the Administrative Set-Up of Pakistan," April 28, 1947, F. 918/202–204 in Zaidi, ed., *Quaid-I-Azam Mohammad Ali Jinnah Papers*, First Series, Volume I, Part 1 (1993), 615.

107. Ali Asadullah Khan to Jinnah, "Manifesto of the Muslim League Left Wing," April 30, 1947, in Zaidi, ed., *Quaid-I-Azam Mohammad Ali Jinnah Papers*, First Series, Volume I, Part 1 (1993), 666.

108. Muhammad Yamin Khan to Jinnah, May 28, 1947, F. 10/22–23, in Zaidi, ed., *Quaid-I-Azam Mohammad Ali Jinnah Papers*, First Series, Volume I, Part 1 (1993), 903.

109. Siddiqi, *Smoke without Fire* (2011), 249.

110. Police "Secret Abstract of Intelligence" reports, May 2 and 9, 1947, F. 21, DPR, Third Installment, NMML.

111. Police "Secret Abstract of Intelligence" reports, May 2 and 9, 1947, F. 21, DPR, Third Installment, NMML; Extract from CID Daily Report, May 28, 1948, and Source Report, June 6, 1947, F. 22, DPR, Third Installment, NMML.

112. Jalal, *The Sole Spokesman* (1994 [1985]), 277–78. Jinnah had spoken earlier about a corridor in an interview to the BBC in April 1946: Prasad, *India Divided* (1946), 394–95. For the notion of a corridor in Muslim League circles at this time, tantamount to a "middle Pakistan province" that would consist of large chunks of Bihar and United Provinces, including Agra, Aligarh, Moradabad, Meerut, and Delhi, see Ali Asadullah Khan to Jinnah, "Manifesto of the Muslim League Left Wing," April 30, 1947, in Zaidi, ed., *Quaid-I-Azam Mohammad Ali Jinnah Papers*, First Series, Volume I, Part 1 (1993), 665.

113. W. Christie to Banerjee, Fortnightly Report for the Second Half of May 1947.

114. Siddiqi, *Smoke without Fire* (2011), 254.

115. Siddiqi, *Smoke without Fire* (2011), 255. This is how Jinnah famously responded to Congress leader C. Rajagopalachari's offer in 1944: Jalal, *The Sole Spokesman* (1994 [1985]), 121.

116. W. Christie to A. E. Porter, Fortnightly Report for the First Half of June 1947, CC 1/47-C, Confidential, DSA.

117. This and following paragraph are based on CID reports for June 1947, in F. 62, DPR, Fifth Installment, NMML; F. 22, DPR, Third Installment, NMML.

118. Siddiqi, *Smoke without Fire* (2011), 262–63.

119. Siddiqi, *Smoke without Fire* (2011), 263.

120. "Jinnah Wishes Hindustan Peace and Prosperity," *Dawn*, August 8, 1947; W. Christie to A. E. Porter, Fortnightly Report for the Second Half of July 1947 and Khur-

shid Ahmad Khan to R.N. Banerjee, Fortnightly report for the first half of October, CC 1/1947-C, Confidential, DSA; Noorani, ed., *The Muslims of India* (2003), chapter 1.

121. Interview with Jugal Kishore Khanna, Oral History Transcript No. 177, NMML, 135–36; "Delhi Municipality Demand for a New President," *Hindustan Times*, January 29, 1948.

122. Azad, *India Wins Freedom* (2009 [1988]), 226–27.

123. Khan, *The Great Partition* (2007), 92; Dhulipala, *Creating a New Medina* (2015), 469–70.

124. Siddiqi, *Smoke without Fire* (2011), 271. For the disillusionment of many of the Muslim League supporters in the United Provinces, see Dhulipala, *Creating a New Medina* (2015), 476–77.

125. Siddiqi, *Smoke without Fire* (2011), 271.

126. For a reconstruction of the Independence Day celebrations, see Kudaisya, *A Republic in the Making* (2017), 2–8.

127. "80,000 Refugees in Delhi Now," *Hindustan Times*, August 5, 1947; "Refugees Pouring into Delhi," *Hindustan Times*, August 21, 1947; Dehlvi, *Dilli Ki Bipta* (2010 [1950]), 27–28.

128. Dehlvi, *Dilli Ki Bipta* (2010 [1950]), 32–33.

129. "Refugees Pouring into Delhi," *Hindustan Times*, August 21, 1947; "Problems of Refugees in Delhi," *Hindustan Times*, September 4, 1947.

130. Talbot, *Divided Cities* (2006), 49–50; Kaur, *Since 1947* (2007), 65–69, 128. As Joya Chatterji finds with regard to the partition exodus in Bengal, the wealthiest were the first to leave, usually in a more organized manner, transferring some assets in advance and bringing along some property. It was the poorest who stayed behind and left only when there was no other choice, embarking on a dangerous journey that not all survived: Chatterji, *The Spoils of Partition* (2007), 105–208.

131. Inspector General of Police S. R. Chaudhri to CC Shankar Prasad, March 3, 1949, D.O. No. 1595 E.M., F. CC 48/1949, Confidential, DSA.

132. Dehlvi, *Dilli Ki Bipta* (2010 [1950]), 32–33.

133. Editorial: "Keep the Peace," *Hindustan Times*, August 30, 1947; "Problems of Refugees in Delhi," *Hindustan Times*, September 4, 1947.

134. Khurshid Ahmad Khan to R. N. Banerjee, Fortnightly Report for the First Half of August 1947, F. CC 1/1947, Confidential, DSA. For the violence perpetrated on the Meos, see Mayaram, *Resisting Regimes* (1997); Ankit, "In the Hands of a 'Secular State'" (2019).

135. Dehlvi, *Dilli Ki Bipta* (2010 [1950]), 42.

136. Jain, *Dilli, Shahr Dar Shahr* (2009), 70.

137. For this being a general feature of cities torn apart by the partition violence across north India, see Talbot and Singh, *The Partition of India* (2009), 70.

138. Interview with Phool Chand Jain, Oral History Transcript No. 479, NMML, 91–92 (my translation).

139. Pandey, *Remembering Partition* (2001), 69; Talbot, "The Role of the Crowd in the Muslim League Struggle for Pakistan" (1993).

140. Chatterji, *Bengal Divided* (1994), 232–40.

141. "80,000 Refugees in Delhi Now," *Hindustan Times*, August 5, 1947. For RSS refugee relief efforts in Delhi prior to partition, see also Six, *Secularism. Decolonisation, and the Cold War* (2018), 102–3. The RSS-sponsored organization for refugee relief, Hindu Sahayata Samiti, and other offices were located in Kamla Nagar, Sabzi Mandi, a hub of refugees: F. DC 162/1948, DSA.

142. Interview with Jugal Kishore Khanna, Oral History Transcript No. 177, NMML. The Muslim League of Delhi certainly pinpointed Sikhs as the main perpetrators of the violence: Malik, *The Tragedy of Delhi* (1948).

143. Jawaharlal Nehru to Sardar Patel, September 30, 1947, in Singh, ed., *Nehru–Patel* (2010).

144. F. CC 51/47, Confidential, DSA.

145. Interview with R. N. Banerjee, Oral History Transcript No. 366, NMML.

146. Patel to Nehru, October 12, 1947, in Singh, ed., *Nehru–Patel* (2010); Menon, *The Transfer of Power in India* (1957), 420. A list of the personnel employed in the Delhi police after 1948 reveals the almost total elimination of Muslims from the force: There is not a single Muslim name among the 6 superintendents, 10 deputy superintendents, and 25 inspectors. There are 2 Muslims among 88 subinspectors, and 2 among 154 assistant subinspectors. F. CC 43/1948, Confidential, DSA.

147. Khurshid Ahmad Khan to R. N. Banerjee, Fortnightly Report for the First Half of September 1947; Azad, *India Wins Freedom* (2009 [1988]), 229; B. D. Joshi's report on Sadar Bazar, F. 26-37-47-Police, MHA Political, NAI.

148. V. Shankar's note, June 10, 1947, Patel to Mountbatten, June 27, 1947, F. 28/5/47-Poll.I, MHA, NAI. Quoted in Ankit, *India in the Interregnum* (2019), 137.

149. Das, "Official Narratives, Rumour and the Social Production of Hate" (1998).

150. Cited in Mufti, *Enlightenment in the Colony* (2007), 166. Mufti's bracketed references to the original Urdu have been deleted.

151. Pritchett, *Nets of Awareness* (1994), 21.

152. Dehlvi, *Dilli Ki Bipta* (2010 [1950]), 61.

CHAPTER 3

1. Rakesh, *Andhere Band Kamre* (1961); Yashpal, *Jhutha Sach, Vol. 2* (2007 [1960]) An earlier version of this chapter was published as Geva, "The Scramble for Houses" (2017). I thank the editor and anonymous reviewers for their input.

2. For property exchanges between upper class Muslims, Hindus, and Sikhs, see Ravinder Kaur, *Since 1947* (2007), 134.

3. Similarly, Liaquat Ali Khan, Pakistan's first prime minister, exchanged his land in rural Delhi with Indian government official Datar Singh, who had land in West Punjab: F. CC 104/48 Confidential, DSA.

4. Rotting corpses were found in a pile of garbage two months afterward. See "Stray Assaults in Delhi," *Hindustan Times*, November 4, 1947.

5. Kaur, "Claiming Community through Narratives" (2005).

6. Anis Kidwai, *In Freedom's Shade* (2011), 163. For the occupation and destruction of mosques and graves, see also Taneja, *Jinnealogy* (2018).

7. Dehlvi, "Man: Dilli Ath Mahine Ba'd," in *Dilli Ki Bipta* (2010 [1950]); Sobti, "Abhi Dilli Dur Hai" (1995); Sahni, "Abhi Dilli Dur Hai" (1995); Yashpal, *Jhutha Sach, Vol. 2* (2007 [1960]).

8. "Registration of Refugees in Delhi to Stop," *Hindustan Times*, January 8, 1948; "Delhi Can't Take Any More Refugees," *Hindustan Times*, January 24, 1948; "Delhi's Hospitality Reaches Saturation Point," *Hindustan Times*, April 5, 1948; DC M. S. Randhawa to CC Khurshid Ahmad Khan, Fortnightly Report for the Second Half of December 1947, F. CC 1/47-C, Confidential, DSA.

9. Situation reports by congress S.P.O.s in F. 26-37-47-Police, MHA Political, NAI. By 1955, refugees formed 36 percent of households in Delhi: Rao and Desai, *Greater Delhi* (1965), 107.

10. For the rise in crime, see fortnightly reports for the year 1948, in F. CC 1/48-C, Confidential, DSA.

11. Fortnightly Report for the Second Half of October 1947, F. CC 1/47-C; Dehlvi, "Man: Dilli Ath Mahine Ba'd," in *Dilli Ki Bipta* (2010), 66.

12. Fortnightly reports for November 1947–January 1948, F. CC 1/47-C, and F. CC 1/48-C, Confidential, DSA.

13. Kidwai, *In Freedom's Shade* (2011), chapter 2; Jain, *Dilli Shahr Dar Shahr* (2009), 77.

14. Fortnightly Report for the Second Half of November 1947, F. CC 1/47-C; "Objection to Quran Recitation," *Hindustan Times*, October 31, 1947; Jain, *Civil Disobedience* (2010), 66–67.

15. For the pledges signed by political leaders, bureaucrats, and police officers, see F. CC 68/48-C, Confidential, DSA.

16. For violence during the fast against Congress peace volunteers and Muslims, see F. CC 68/48, Confidential, DSA; "Police Ki Ghaflat," *Al Jamiat* May 1, 1948. For resentment of Gandhi's blackmail, see editorials in the refugee Urdu daily *Milap* throughout January 1948; Fortnightly reports for January 1948, F. CC 1/48-C.

17. "Do sau communiston aur socialiston ka daftar-e Milap par hamla," *Milap*, February 4, 1948; "Dehli Men Rashtriya Sangh ke akhbar ke daftar par police ka chhapa," *Milap*, February 4, 1948; "Delhi Crowds Dispersed," *Times of India*, February 2, 1948.

18. F. DC 162/48, DSA; Khan, "Performing Peace" (2011); Ansari and Gould, *Boundaries of Belonging* (2020), 26–36.

19. Jayal, *Citizenship and Its Discontents* (2013).

20. This understanding builds on scholarship that has emphasized the need to move away from abstract conceptualizations and toward concrete study of the ways in which the state functions and is experienced in everyday life: Fuller and Bénéï, eds., *The Everyday State and Society* (2001); Hansen and Stepputat, eds., *States of Imagination* (2001); Gould, *Bureaucracy, Community and Influence in India* (2011). Clement Six, who has studied the ambivalent attitude in political circles toward the RSS in post-partition Delhi, reaches a similar conclusion: Six, *Secularism, Decolonisation, and the Cold War* (2018), 90, 104.

21. Tarlo, "Welcome to History" (2000); Hansen, *Wages of Violence* (2001); Chatterjee, *The Politics of the Governed* (2004).

22. Azad, *India Wins Freedom* (2009 [1988]), 231.

23. V. Shankar, Sardar Patel's private secretary in that period, provides a detailed account of this affair from Patel's point of view: Shankar, *My Reminiscences of Sardar Patel, Vol. 1* (1974), 144–79.

24. For the speech in Lucknow, excerpts from other speeches Patel made at the time, and the controversy surrounding them, see Shankar, *My Reminiscences of Sardar Patel, Vol. 1* (1974), 140–53, 60.

25. For the ideological tensions within the Congress leadership and party, see Hasan, *Legacy of a Divided Nation* (1997), Chapter 5; Jaffrelot, *The Hindu Nationalist Movement in India* (1993), 80–107. For an examination of this suspicion in Hyderabad, see Sherman, *Muslim Belonging in Secular India* (2015).

26. For a convincing exposition of this argument, see Pandey, "Can a Muslim Be an Indian?" (1999). For a close reading demonstrating that Patel did not anticipate the large-scale population transfer that took place, see Chatterji, "South Asian Histories of Citizenship" (2012).

27. Azad, *India Wins Freedom* (2009 [1988]), 232.

28. For Nehru's and Patel's dispute over their division of responsibility, see correspondence included in Singh, ed., *Nehru-Patel* (2010), 274–80. For ICS officers' accounts of this dispute, see Shankar, *My Reminiscences of Sardar Patel, Vol. 1* (1974), 144–79; Interview with H. V. R. Iengar, Oral History Transcript No. 303, NMML; Interview with Shankar Prasad, Oral History Transcript No. 494, NMML, 165.

29. Shankar, *My Reminiscences of Sardar Patel, Vol. 1* (1974), 99.

30. For his niece and relatives in Pakistan, see Zamindar, *The Long Partition* (2007), 89.

31. Jawaharlal Nehru to Sardar Patel, October 6, 1947, Selected Works of Jawaharlal Nehru (SWJN), vol. 4, 127–28.

32. Sardar Patel to Jawaharlal Nehru, October 12, 1947, in Singh, ed. *Nehru-Patel* (2010), 93.

33. A copy of the poster, entitled "Mahatma Gandhi aur wazarat-e Indian Union se Dehli ka musalman kya chahta hai? ("What Does the Delhi Muslim Want from Mahatma Gandhi and the Ministry of the Indian Union?"), is included in F. CC 8(1)/48, Home-Press, DSA.

34. Interview with Jugal Kishore Khanna, Oral History Transcript No. 177, NMML, 137; Azad, *India Wins Freedom* (2009 [1988]), 231–32.

35. Jawaharlal Nehru to Sardar Patel, September 30, 1947; Jawaharlal Nehru to Sardar Patel, October 11, 1947; Jawaharlal Nehru to Sardar Patel, October 6, 1947, SWJN, vol. 4, 110–14, 135–36, 126–28; Sardar Patel to Jawaharlal Nehru, October 12, 1947, in Singh, ed., *Nehru-Patel* (2010), 93.

36. Zamindar, *The Long Partition* (2007), 91.

37. Randhawa, *Out of the Ashes* (1954).

38. Interview with Shankar Prasad, Oral History Transcript No. 494, NMML, 165.

39. See section 18 of the Police Act (1861), cited in: letter by G. V. Bedekar, Deputy Secretary to Home Ministry, October 14, 1947, F. 26-37-47-Police, MHA Political, NAI.

40. See coverage of Patel's report on the process in parliament: "Large Arms Haul in Delhi," *Hindustan Times*, November 20, 1947.

41. Many political parties and public bodies in Delhi encouraged their members to join, including Jamiat Ulama, DPCC, RSS, and Sikh organizations: Gould, Sherman, and Ansari, "The Flux of the Matter" (2013), 255.

42. Patel to Nehru, September 28, 1947, in Singh, ed., *Nehru-Patel* (2010), 238.

43. Jawaharlal Nehru to Patel, September 30, 1947, SWJN, vol. 4, 110–14. For Muslim residents' complaints, see the above-mentioned poster in F. CC 8(1)/48, Home-Press, DSA. In response, Patel gave a detailed breakdown of Special Police officers and magistrates, claiming that Randhawa had accepted all the names recommended by the DPCC and was responsible for barely a third of the selection. Patel stated that out of 1,304 Special Police officers, 574 were Congress nominees, all recommended by the DPCC. See Sardar Patel to Jawaharlal Nehru, October 12, 1947, in Singh, ed., *Nehru-Patel* (2010), 93.

44. "Delhi Situation Reports from 1st to 5th Oct. 47," and "Report of Ch. Sher Jang S.M. and Chief of Congress SPOs, Town Hall Area," F. 26-37-47 Police, MHA Political, NAI.

45. Kidwai, *In Freedom's Shade* (2011), 108. For his biographical details, see Gupta, *Dilli Ki Communist Party Ka Itihas* (2007), 251–55; F. 107, Eighth Installment, Delhi Police Records (henceforth DPR), NMML.

46. V. Shankar, Private Secretary to the Home Minister to Home Secretary R. N. Banerjee, October 27, 1947; D. I. G. Mehra to Deputy Secretary, Home Ministry, October 29, 1947, F. 26-37-47-Police, MHA Political, NAI.

47. The conflicting reports appear in F. 26-37-47-Police, MHA Political, NAI.

48. For Nehru's high regard for Sher Jung, see Jawaharlal Nehru to Sardar Patel, October 11, 1947, SWJN, vol. 4, 136. The Home Ministry filed a revised petition against Sher Jung, which was dismissed on February 13, 1950.

49. F. CC 43/48-C, Confidential, DSA. For the removal of RSS members of the police and Special Police, see also: Gould, Sherman, and Ansari, "The Flux of the Matter" (2013), 256–57.

50. F. DC 311/48, DSA; F. CC 77/48, Confidential, DSA.

51. Delhi's Chief Commissioner Office to R. N. Banerjee, Fortnightly Report for the First Half of November 1947, F. CC 1/47-C.

52. Pandey, *Remembering Partition* (2001), 123; "Purana Qila Closed," *Hindustan Times*, October 24, 1947.

53. Khurshid Ahmad Khan to R. N. Banerjee, Fortnightly Report for the Second Half of October 1947, F. CC 1/47-C.

54. Jawaharlal Nehru to Sardar Patel, October 6, 1947, SWJN, vol. 4, 128; Jawaharlal Nehru to Sardar Patel, October 9, 1947, SWJN, vol. 4, 133.

55. Shankar, *My Reminiscences of Sardar Patel, Vol. 1* (1974), 104.

56. "A Foul Crime," *Hindustan Times*, October 21, 1947; Khurshid Ahmad Khan to R. N. Banerjee, Fortnightly Report for the Second Half of October 1947; "Situation Reports" in F. 26-37-47-Police; CID Source Report dated May 15, 1948, in F. CC 55/48-C, Confidential, DSA.

57. Jawaharlal Nehru to Sardar Patel, November 21, 1947, SWJN, vol. 4, 185; Khurshid Ahmad Khan to R. N. Banerjee, Fortnightly report for the second half of September 1947, F. CC 1/47-C; Zamindar, *The Long Partition* (2007), 29.

58. Subhadra Joshi's estimate is cited in Tan and Kudaisya, *The Aftermath of Partition* (2000), 199.

59. Rationing authorities estimate, quoted in "Influx of Refugees Continues," *Hindustan Times*, November 17, 1947. Chief Commissioner Khurshid Ahmad Khan claimed that, since the United Provinces government had forbidden any further entry of refugees into its province, the entire brunt of the Punjab's population movement was being borne by Delhi: Khurshid Ahmad Khan to R. N. Banerjee, Fortnightly report for the second half of November 1947, F. CC 1/47-C.

60. For example, "a mob of 800 non-Muslims visited a Muslim mohalla and wanted the residents of that place to vacate their houses for them," in "CID report for the second half of December 1947," F. CC 1/48-C; Zamindar, *The Long Partition* (2007), 33.

61. "More Muslims Leave Delhi," *Hindustan Times*, November 14, 1947; "25,000 Refugees in Humayun's Tomb Camp," *Hindustan Times*, November 26, 1947; "CID reports January-February 1948," F. CC 1/48-C; Kidwai, *In Freedom's Shade* (2011), chapter 4.

62. The legislation had a retaliatory character—every restriction enacted by Pakistan was introduced into the Indian legislation, and vice versa, reflecting the unresolved negotiations between the two countries over the question of compensation. India claimed that the aggregate property left behind by non-Muslims in Pakistan was much larger than the property left by Muslims in India and, accordingly, compensation should be settled at the governmental level and should involve Pakistan paying the difference to India. Pakistan, for its part, insisted that the property on both sides was more or less equal in value, and that compensation should be arranged privately by individuals selling or exchanging their properties. Schechtman, "Evacuee Property in India and Pakistan" (1951), 407. For a detailed comparison of the difference, calculated by the Indian government, see Das Gupta, *Indo-Pakistan Relations* (1958), 188–89. The evacuee property legislation in South Asia originated from, yet significantly modified, the World War II–era British Trading with the Enemy Act. It was then adopted and further modified in the Israeli absentee property legislation: Kedar, "Expanding Legal Geographies" (2014).

63. Zamindar, *The Long Partition* (2007), 145–46; "Notes on the new evacuee property ordinance," No. 14(57)Cus/49, 18 October 1949, in F. CC 126/49, Confidential, DSA.

64. Chatterji, "South Asian Histories of Citizenship" (2012), 1066. For the refusal of the Custodian Department to accept interference from the Delhi civil courts, see V. D. Dantyagi (Ministry of R&R) to Khurshid Ahmad Khan, D.O. No. 484-JS/48, April 14, 1948, F. CC 41/48, Confidential, DSA.

65. By September 1948, more than 3,000 cases came before the courts of the Custodian. Of these, only 6 were decided in favor of Muslim applicants, 566 were decided against them, and about 2,500 cases remained pending—the result of repeated delays by the custodian. This is according to Sultan Yar Khan, the lawyer appointed by the Muslim Relief Committee of Jamiat Ulama to provide legal representation to Delhi's Muslim

residents. See Report of the Jama'at-e Islah-e Custodian, F. 26, DPR, Second Installment, NMML.

66. "Demand for Muslim Zones," *Hindustan Times*, November 29, 1947; Fortnightly report for the first half of December 1947, F. CC 1/47-C; CID report for the first half of December 1947, F. CC 1/48-C.

67. Kidwai, *In Freedom's Shade* (2011), 200.

68. For Zamindar's assumption that Muslim zones were outside the jurisdiction of the Custodian Department, grounded in the Constituent Assembly debates, see Zamindar, *The Long Partition* (2007), 132–36.

69. A copy of the Urdu report, summing up the complaints prepared by the Jama'at-e Islah-e Custodian, is located in F. 26, DP R, Second Installment, NMML.

70. The 1948 list estimates that Nawabganj was a Muslim pocket of 2,400 people. On refugees trying to break into sealed houses in Nawabganj, see SP of Police City Report on the Political Situation of Delhi, August 14, 1948, in F. 371, DPR, Eighth Installment, NMML.

71. For attacks on Pul Bangash, see Urdu poster in F. CC 8(1)/48-Home, Home-Press, DSA; SP of Police City Report on the Political Situation of Delhi, August 14, 1948, in F. 371, DPR, Eighth Installment, NMML.

72. For allotment of houses in Pul Bangash, see also: "15 Arrested in Khari Baoli," *Hindustan Times*, January 10, 1948. For the Custodian Department allotment of Houses in Beri Wala Bagh, see CID report of August 18, 1948, in F. 371, DPR, Eighth Installment, NMML.

73. Sardar Patel to K. C. Negoy, December 21, 1947, in Singh, ed., *Nehru-Patel* (2010), 256. See also Sardar Patel to Jawaharlal Nehru, October 11, 1947; Sardar Patel to Jawaharlal Nehru, November 22, 1947, in Singh, ed., *Nehru-Patel* (2010), 87–88, 256–57; Jawaharlal Nehru to Sardar Patel, November 21, 1947, SWJN, vol. 4, 184.

74. Kidwai, *In Freedom's Shade* (2011), 107–8.

75. Siddiqi, *Smoke without Fire* (2011), 294–95.

76. M. S. Randhawa to Khurshid Ahmad Khan, Fortnightly report for the first half of January 1948, F. CC 1/48-C; Daily reports on Phatak Habash Khan by City Superintendent of Police Jagan Nath, F. CC 21/48, Confidential, DSA. The military barracks in Bela Road and Anand Parbat were opened as temporary shelters for Hindu and Sikh refugees as a result of the disturbances in Phatak Habash Khan.

77. A report by SP Police City Jagan Nath, January 8, 1948, F. CC 21/48.

78. Oldenburg, *Big City Government in India* (1976), 76; Krafft, "Contemporary Old Delhi" (2003 [1993]), 116–17; Zamindar, *The Long Partition* (2007), 142.

79. "Refugees Pouring into Delhi," *Hindustan Times*, August 21, 1947; Jawaharlal Nehru to Sardar Patel, October 6, 1947, SWJN, vol. 4, 128.

80. Kidwai, *In Freedom's Shade* (2011), 111, 202.

81. M. S. Randhawa to Khurshid Ahmad Khan, Fortnightly Report for the Second Half of May 1948, F. CC 1/48-C, Confidential, DSA; F. 21/48-C, CC Files, Confidential, DSA.

82. Basu, *Mridula Sarabhai* (1996); Menon and Bhasin, *Borders & Boundaries* (1998).

83. For Nehru's positive view of Sarabhai, see Nehru to B. C. Roy, May 7, 1950, SWJN, vol. 14II, 167. For Patel's dislike of her, associating her with "Nehru's camp," see Shankar Prasad, Oral History Transcript No. 494, NMML, 153–54; Shankar, *My Reminiscences of Sardar Patel, Vol. 1* (1974), 160, 171, 183.

84. Sarabhai's report in F. CC 54/48, Confidential, DSA.

85. Sixty-five vigilance committee members were divided among ten police *thanas* in Delhi: Mridula Sarabhai's letter of June 14, 1948, F. CC 54/48, Confidential, DSA.

86. Interview with Shankar Prasad, Oral History Transcript No. 494, NMML, 153–54

87. A letter by Mridula Sarabhai, September 20, 1948, in F. S/EST/2 - 1948–54, Mridula Sarabhai Papers (henceforth MSP), NMML.

88. For Joshi's claim that Karachiwala was "a formerly notorious Muslim Leaguer," see "Statement submitted to police authorities," in F. CC 55/1948, Confidential, DSA. For Sadiq Karachiwala's Muslim League links prior to partition, see CID reports in files 17 and 19, Third Installment, DPR, NMML; F. 311, Eighth Installment, DPR, NMML.

89. Jawaharlal Nehru to Mridula Sarabhai, September 12, 1948, SWJN, vol. 7, 49–50. My reconstruction of the case is based on reports, meeting protocols, and correspondence included in Mridula Sarabhai Papers, the Chief Commissioner collection, and the CID collection: F. S/Ind. Pro/7 1948–53, MSP; F. CC 55/48, Confidential, DSA; F. 371, DPR, Eighth Installment, NMML; F. 26, DPR, Second Installment, NMML.

90. Rajendra Prasad to Mridula Sarabhai, September 24, 1948, F. S/Ind. Pro/7 1948–53, MSP; Mridula Sarabhai to Rajendra Prasad, September 28, 1948, F. RW/S/4-1/D, MSP; Vallabhbhai Patel to Rajendra Prasad, October 14, 1948, included in Kidwai, *In Freedom's Shade* (2011), 266.

91. Sarabhai's letters of September 13 and 20, 1948, in F. S/EST/2 - 1948–54, MSP.

92. Chatterjee, *The Politics of the Governed* (2004).

93. Tarlo, *Unsettling Memories* (2003).

94. "Note on Predominantly Muslim Areas Regarding Government Policy," F. No. S/EST/1 – 1948, MSP; Subhadra Joshi to Jawaharlal Nehru, February 21, 1951, F. No. S/EST/6 - 1949–52, MSP.

95. Mridula Sarabhai to Shankar Prasad, September 20, 1948, F. No. S/EST/2 - 1948–54, MSP. For the temporary authorization of private exchange and sales in Karachi Inter-Dominion Agreement of January 1949, see Zamindar, *The Long Partition* (2007), 125–40; Joint Secretary (Ministry of R&R) to CC of Delhi, No. 8(2)Cus/48, November 26, 1948, F. CC 41/1948-C, Confidential, DSA. For public discussions of this authorization in anticipation of the decision, see "Transfer of Evacuee Property," *Hindustan Times*, April 2, 1948.

96. General Secretary, Jamiat Ulama, to Delhi's CC, DC and SP CID, June 6, 1949, in F. 96, DPR, Fifth Installment, NMML; "Extract from CID Daily Diary, 20–21.8.49," in F. 27, DPR, Second Installment, NMML.

97. Jawaharlal Nehru to Mohanlal Saksena, April 11, 1950, SWJN, vol. 14II, 162. On the riots of 1950s in Uttar Pradesh, see Brass, *The Production of Hindu-Muslim Violence* (2003), 76; Hasan, *Legacy of a Divided Nation* (1997), chapter 6. About 135,000 Muslims fled across the western border: Zamindar, *The Long Partition* (2007), 169.

98. IB Report on Vacant Muslim Houses, May 4, 1950, F. 98, DPR, Sixth Installment, NMML. For Muslim exodus from Delhi in 1950, see also F. CC 97/1950, Confidential, DSA; F. CC 159/1950, Confidential, DSA.

99. "Custodian Ka Taza Insaf," *Al Jamiat*, May 8, 1950.

100. This and following paragraphs are based mainly on the reports of a Shanti Dal informer inside Phatak Habash Khan from February 1950, in F. RW/S/3/D "Shanti Dal: Reports from Workers on the Delhi Situation, 1950," MSP. For tenants' complaints against the Custodian Department's collection of arrears in lump sums, exceedingly high rent, or charging rent twice from the same tenant, see "Yah Custodian Office Hai," *Al Jamiat*, July 27, 1949; "Ten Important Resolutions of Ahrar General Council," August 8, 1949, F. CC 37/49-C Vol. II, Confidential, DSA; Zamindar, *The Long Partition* (2007), 142.

101. Custodian-General Achhru Ram was believed to be biased against the Muslims: De, "Evacuee Property" (2018), 100. For his close relationship with the All India Refugee Association, which strongly protested his removal: CID fortnightly report for first half of October 1951, F. CC 1/51-C, Confidential, DSA.

102. Gupta, *Delhi between Two Empires* (1981), ix.

103. Raghavan, *Animosity at Bay* (2020), 47–72. For an analysis of the pact, see chapter 4.

104. Jawaharlal Nehru to Mohanlal Saksena, April 14, 1950, SWJN, vol. 14II, 163–64; Jawaharlal Nehru to Mohanlal Saksena, April 14, 1950, SWJN, vol. 14II, 163.

105. Note to the Minister of Rehabilitation, May 29, 1950, SWJN, vol. 14II, 177.

106. Interview with Ajit Prasad Jain, Oral History Transcript No. 291, NMML.

107. India finally removed the "intending evacuees" clause from the legislation in 1953: Zamindar, *The Long Partition* (2007), 131.

108. Jawaharlal Nehru to A. P. Jain, November 27, 1953, SWJN, vol. 24, 459–61.

109. Jawaharlal Nehru to Mohammad Ali, March 6, 1954, SWJN, vol. 25, 346–52; Jawaharlal Nehru to Mohammad Ali, May 7, 1954, SWJN, vol. 25, 353–54; Jawaharlal Nehru to Mohammad Ali, November 9, 1954, SWJN, vol. 27, 177.

110. Jawaharlal Nehru to Mehr Chand Khanna, May 25, 1955, SWJN, vol. 28, 561.

111. Note to the Minister for Home Affairs, June 19, 1954, SWJN, vol. 26, 197.

112. CID Fortnightly Reports, January–August 1956, F.CC 34/56, Confidential, DSA.

113. Jawaharlal Nehru to A. P. Jain, September 23, 1952, SWJN, vol. 19, 162; Mridula Sarabhai to Jawaharlal Nehru, "Note Regarding the Sealed Houses in the Muslim Locality of Delhi," November 25, 1953, RW/S/4-1/D, MSP.

114. Note to the Home Ministry, September 26, 1955, SWJN, vol. 30, 235; Fortnightly Reports for July–August 1956, F. CC 34/56, Confidential and Cabinet, DSA.

115. For a strikingly parallel dynamic in 1948 Israel, see Yfaat Weiss's analysis of the geographical concentration of Haifa's Arabs in Wadi Nisnas, and the subsequent encroachment on this locality: Weiss, *A Confiscated Memory* (2011), chapter 2.

116. Jawaharlal Nehru to Mohanlal Saksena, April 14, 1950, SWJN, vol. 14II, 164.

117. SP of CID Rikhi Kesh to Deputy Director of IB Handoo, May 25, 1950, F. 118, DPR, Sixth Installment, NMML.

118. Zamindar cites CID statistics suggesting that 16,350 Muslims returned to Delhi between March and August 1948. Since about 4,450 left, the increase in the Muslim popu-

lation in the city amounted to only 11,900, much lower than newspaper estimates: Zamindar, *The Long Partition* (2007), 86–88.

119. For a collection of vernacular newspaper cuttings from July 1948, all reporting on the infiltration and arrests of "Pakistani spies," see F. CC 8 (59A) 1948, Home-Press, DSA. For arrests of Muslims suspected of arriving "with the intention of creating communal trouble," see F. CC 56/48-C, Confidential, DSA; F. 371, DPR, Eighth Installment, NMML. Muslim newspaper *Al Jamiat* argued, on the contrary, that these were harmless Muslims detained without a trial: "Jasuson Ki Giraftari," *Al Jamiat*, July 19, 1948, in F. CC 8 (59A) 1948, Home-Press, DSA.

120. Zamindar, *The Long Partition* (2007); "Notes on the New Evacuee Property Ordinance," No. 14(57)Cus/49, October 18, 1949, in F. CC 126/49, Confidential, DSA.

121. Correspondence in F. 96, DPR, Fifth Installment, NMML. For the difficulties in administering the permit system, see also Chatterji, "South Asian Histories of Citizenship" (2012).

122. Note to B. N. Kaul, Principal Private Secretary to the Prime Minister, 22 September 1952, SWJN, vol. 19, 162.

123. Dehlvi, "Man: Dilli Aath Mahine Ba'd," in *Dilli Ki Bipta* (2010), 69.

124. The letter was submitted via M. N. Masud, Maulana Azad's private secretary. It is included in F. CC 37/49-C Vol. II, Confidential, DSA.

125. In a similar vein, as mentioned above, Subhadra Joshi of the Shanti Dal emphasized that Sadiq Karachiwala had been a notorious Muslim Leaguer. See note 88 above.

126. Oldenburg, *Big City Government in India* (1976), 159–60.

127. Krishna, "Communal Violence in India, Part 2" (1985).

128. Jamil, *Accumulation by Segregation* (2017); Author's interview with Shahid Siddiqui, June 13, 2011, New Delhi.

129. Jamil, *Accumulation by Segregation* (2017), 6–7; Tarlo, *Unsettling Memories* (2003).

130. Prakash, *Emergency Chronicles* (2019), 290–96. For Joshi's subsequent political career in the local Congress, see Puri, *Party Politics in the Nehru Era* (1993).

131. Interviews cited in Jamil, *Accumulation by Segregation* (2017), 42–43.

CHAPTER 4

1. Hindi is written in the Devanagari script and generally draws on Sanskrit vocabulary. Urdu is written in the Perso-Arabic script and draws on Persian and Arabic vocabulary. The two languages emerged, however, from the same dialect of Khari Boli, spoken in Delhi and its vicinity, and hence share the same syntax and basic vocabulary. While scholars debate the exact period and causes of the differentiation and growing rivalry between Hindi and Urdu, all agree that by the late nineteenth century, they were rival standardized languages, around which competing Hindu and Muslim publics mobilized. Rai, *A House Divided* (1984); Faruqi, "A Long History of Urdu Literary Culture, Part 1" (2003); King, *One Language, Two Scripts* (1994); Dalmia, *The Nationalization of Hindu Traditions* (1996).

2. Shackle and Snell, *Hindi and Urdu since 1800* (1990), 22. See also Trivedi, "The Progress of Hindi, Part 2" (2003), 966.

3. For the Constituent Assembly debates on the language question see Austin, *The Indian Constitution* (2013 [1966]), 330–83; Das Gupta, *Language Conflict and National Development* (1970), 127–58; Hasan, *Legacy of a Divided Nation* (1997), 156–60; Austin, *Indian Constitution* (2013 [1966]), Chapter 12. For a survey of Hindi-Urdu differentiation and a critical reading of Gandhi and Nehru's stances on the language question see Mufti, *Enlightenment in the Colony* (2007), 131–53.

4. Das Gupta, "Practice and Theory of Language Planning" (1976).

5. Farouqi, ed., *Redefining Urdu Politics in India* (2006). For language policy in Uttar Pradesh, see Hasan, *Legacy of a Divided Nation*, 148, 57–60; Das Gupta, *Language Conflict and National Development* (1970), 141. For Urdu's marginalization in Hyderabad, see Sherman, *Muslim Belonging in Secular India* (2015), 147–73.

6. Faruqi, "A Long History of Urdu Literary Culture, Part 1" (2003).

7. The total population of Muslims was 155,453. Those who identified Urdu as their mother tongue numbered 153,247: Chopra, *Delhi Gazetteer* (1976), 142.

8. Sadana, *English Heart, Hindi Heartland* (2012); Sharma, "Architecture of Intellectual Sociality" (2016); Vanshi, ed., *Dilli Tea House* (2009).

9. Trivedi, "The Progress of Hindi, Part 2" (2003), 961–62.

10. Chopra, *Delhi Gazetteer* (1976), 125.

11. According to a 1951 CID report, the English daily *Hindustan Times*, owned by the leading capitalist Birla and edited by Mahatma Gandhi's son Devdas Gandhi, had a circulation of 26,000. The equivalent Hindi daily, *Hindustan*, had a circulation of 15,000. The Hindi daily *Nav Bharat Times*, which was part of the Bennett Coleman Group that also published the English daily *Times of India*, had a circulation of 28,335. CID report in F. 89, Delhi Police Records (henceforth DPR), Second Installment, NMML. For the newspaper business structure and the concentration of the press in the hands of monopoly capitalists, see Jeffrey, *India's Newspaper Revolution* (2000), Chapter 5; Sahni, *Truth About the Indian Press* (1974).

12. For rough information on the circulation of Urdu newspapers in the early 1950s, see two CID press files: F. 468, DPR, Eighth Installment, NMML; F. 89, DPR, Second Installment, NMML. According to file 468: *Vishwa Miter* (5,000), *Vir Bharat* (8000), *Tej* (10,000), *Ranjit Nagara* (2,000). According to file 89: Bande Mataram (11,550), *Milap* (8,000), *Pratap* (14,000), *Vir Bharat* (2,000), *Al Jamiat* (5,000). Discrepancies between the two files indicate the unreliable nature of information on newspaper circulation, as discussed in Jeffrey, "Punjabi: 'The Sub-Liminal Charge'" (1997), 445; Farouqi, "The Emerging Dilemma of the Urdu Press in India" (1995).

13. Author's Interview with Aslam Parvez, June 29, 2011, New Delhi.

14. Ahmad, *Lineages of the Present* (2000), 103. See also Naim, "The Consequences of Indo-Pakistani War for Urdu Language and Literature" (2004).

15. Ahmad, *Lineages of the Present*, 120–21. Emphasis in original.

16. For the progressive writers, see Gopal, *Literary Radicalism in India* (2005); Ahmed, *Literature and Politics in the Age of Nationalism* (2009). For the literary circles of Hindi, Urdu, and Punjabi writers in 1950s Delhi, see Sahni, *Aaj Ke Atit* (2003), 172–73.

17. As mentioned in chapter 1. For Gopi Nath Aman's biography, see F. CC 40/S/1942, Special Press Adviser, DSA; *Rajdhani Weekly Supplement* (1953), 118.

18. "Proceedings of a meetings of editors with Chief Commissioner Shankar Prasad on December 11, 1948," F. CC. 8(081)/48, Home-Press, DSA.

19. Zamindar, *The Long Partition* (2007), 140.

20. Daechsel, *The Politics of Self-Expression* (2006), 15.

21. Ansari and Gould, *Boundaries of Belonging* (2020), 13.

22. See Chapters 1–2.

23. Siddiqi, *Smoke without Fire* (2011), 268; "Freedom and After: About Ourselves," *Dawn*, August 15, 1947.

24. Karaka, *Betrayal in India* (1950), 33.

25. Siddiqi, *Smoke without Fire* (2011), 277.

26. "Painful Realities," *Dawn*, August 18, 1947.

27. F. DC 15/1947, Press Advisor, DSA.

28. Congress newspapers and later memoirs framed this arson as counterinsurgency, a response to a shooting from *Dawn's* office: "Patel Visits Riots Areas," *Hindustan Times*, September 14, 1947; "Shops in New Delhi Re-open," *Hindustan Times*, September 24, 1947; Khosla, *Stern Reckoning* (1989 [1949]), 283.

29. Siddiqi, *Smoke without Fire* (2011), 286; Malik, *The Tragedy of Delhi* (1948), 16. For banning the entry of *Dawn* into India: Letter by Press Officer Gopi Nath Aman, September 22, 1948, F. DC 7/1947 Vol. I, Press Advisor, DSA.

30. See correspondence and *Jang's* news clips deemed objectionable in F. DC Press Advisor 22/1947, DSA.

31. F. CC 8(145) 1952, Home-Press, DSA.

32. For the stark change that took place in the demography of Delhi's printing and publishing world: Annual Report of the Registrar of Newspapers for India," (1956), 374–403. For the ransacking of the library of the Urdu literature association Anjuman-e Taraqqi-e Urdu in Daryaganj and its ultimate division between India and Pakistan see Amstutz, "A Partitioned Library" (2020).

33. Author's interview with Shahid Siddiqui, the founder's son, subsequently the editor of *Nayi Duniya*, and a former member of the Rajya Sabha, June 13, 2011, New Delhi. Abdul Waheed Siddiqui worked as an editor at *Al Jamiat* until 1951, when he launched *Nayi Duniya*. On the bitter rivalry between *Nayi Duniya* and *Al Jamiat* see F. CC 9(47)/54, Home Department, DSA.

34. F. CC 19(47)/54 and F. CC 19(50)/54, Home Department, DSA; F. CC 8(137)/52, Home-Press, DSA; Files 106 and 274, DPR, Eighth Installment, NMML.

35. See *Hurriyat's* article of September 8, 1946, in F. DC 600/1946, DSA. Baqai also published slanderous attacks on Maulana Usmani, who supported the Muslim League, see Dhulipala, *Creating a New Medina* (2015), 385. On Baqai, see Interview with Jugal Kishore Khanna, Oral History Transcript No. 177, NMML.

36. The letters are in Aziz Hasan Baqai papers, File No. 18, Private Papers Collection, DSA.

37. For the hardships the family faced after partition, see an editorial written by Aziz Hasan Baqai's son, Anis Hasan Baqai, when he relaunched *Hurriyat* in 1959: "Hurriyat ke band hone ki 'abratnak kahani," *Hurriyat*, August 2, 1959, in F. 508, DPR, Eighth Installment, NMML. For CID surveillance on the Baqai family and *Hurriyat*: Files 2 and 468, DPR, Eighth Installment, NMML.

38. F. CC 8(1)/48-Home, Home-Press, DSA; Files. 2, 468 and 504, DPR, Eighth Installment, NMML; Interview with Maulana Abdullah Farooqi, Oral History Transcript No. 634, NMML. Farooqi was the elder brother of local communist leader Muqimuddin Farooqi, who appears in Chapters 1 and 5.

39. *Al Jamiat* was first published as a biweekly in 1924: F. CC 266/1943, Special Press Adviser, DSA.

40. Khurshid Ahmad Khan to R. N. Banerjee, "Fortnightly Report for the Second Half of October 1947." F. CC 1/47-C, Confidential, DSA.

41. For the resolution, see Noorani, ed., *The Muslims of India* (2003), 73–80; "Bombay men Jamiat Ulema-e Hind ka tarikhi ijlas khatam," *Al Jamiat*, May 2, 1948. For its political and social policies after independence see Hasan, *Legacy of a Divided Nation* (1997), 210–14; Sherman, *Muslim Belonging in Secular India* (2015), 19–55, 130–46; Mayaram, *Resisting Regimes* (1997), 8, 234–42.

42. CID Report on *Al Jamiat*, May 11, 1950, F. 98, DPR, Sixth Installment, NMML; Press Officer Rajendra Nath Shaida to Ram Lal Varma, August 24, 1954, F. CC 3(8)/1954, Home-Press, DSA. For recognition of *Al Jamiat* for the purpose of placing government ads, a crucial economic benefit that was not extended to any other Muslim-owned paper in Delhi, see F. CC 4 (30)/1951, Passport & Political, DSA.

43. "Note on the Tone of *Al Jamiat*," January 3, 1951, F. CC 4-A (5)/50, Passport & Political Department, DSA.

44. Note on *Al Jamiat*'s use of fictitious letters, forwarded by SP of Police CID Rikhi Kesh, September 29, 1950, F. 97, DPR, Sixth Installment, NMML.

45. "Musalman kya karen?," *Al Jamiat*, December 12, 1948.

46. "Tum darya ke kinare ho," *Al Jamiat*, February 3, 1949.

47. F. 89, DPR, Second Installment, NMML; F. 106, DPR, Eighth Installment, NMML.

48. The speech was given at Mohammed Ali Park in Calcutta on January 28, 1949, in a mass meeting organized by the Jamiat Ulama-e Hind.

49. See Chapter 3.

50. For letters sent to *Al Jamiat*'s office and intercepted by the CID, see files 98 and 100, DPR, Sixth Installment, NMML.

51. "Hamari Dehli," *Al Jamiat*, August 19, 1948.

52. For the incidents that took place between May and October 1949 over mango sales, see Chief Commissioner Shankar Prasad's reports in F. CC 127/49-C, Confidential, DSA. "Ishte'al Angezi," *Al Jamiat*, July 6, 1949.

53. "Minor Clash in Old Delhi," *Times of India*, July 4, 1949; "The Rest of the News," *Times of India*, July 5, 1949.

54. "Mazlumon ki imdad," *Al Jamiat*, July 2, 1949; "Dharam ki iste'mal," *Al Jamiat*, July 6, 1949.

55. "Musalman kyon ja rahe hain?," *Al Jamiat*, May 5, 1950. I write "purported" because the CID doubted the authenticity of readers' letters. CID report on *Al Jamiat*'s objectionable tone, May 11, 1950, F. 98, DPR, Sixth Installment, NMML; CID Report on *Al Jamiat*, September 16, 1950, F. 97, DPR, Sixth Installment, NMML.

56. "Musalman kyon na jae?," signed by Fazul Rahman Azhar, Delhi. *Al Jamiat*, May 7, 1950.

57. "Firqawar gadagari," *Al Jamiat*, September 2, 1950; "Railway men ishte'al angezi," *Al Jamiat*, March 8, 1950.

58. Cited in Raghavan, *Animosity at Bay* (2020), 187.

59. Cited in Raghavan, *Animosity at Bay* (2020), 190.

60. "Euphemisms Hide Delhi Pact Violations," *Times of India*, October 11, 1950; Jaffrelot, *The Hindu Nationalist Movement in India* (1993), 96–98.

61. See, e.g., letter to the editor from one Jiwan Nizami of Bara Hindu Rao, Delhi: "Yah kya ho raha hai?," *Al Jamiat*, May 19, 1950.

62. "Aman aur e'timad," *Al Jamiat*, May 3, 1950.

63. "Aqaliyaton ka itminan," *Al Jamiat*, May 15, 1950.

64. For *Al Jamiat*'s criticism of Indian newspapers, and its praise for Pakistani ones, see also "Musalman kyon ja rahe hain?," *Al Jamiat*, May 5, 1950; "Kamyab ya nakam," *Al Jamiat*, May 22, 1950; "Akhir kab tak?," *Al Jamiat*, June 4, 1950; "Mo'ahida-e Dehli ke bad," *Al Jamiat*, June 4, 1950; "Hamare akhbarat," *Al Jamiat* July 13, 1950.

65. See Chapter 1.

66. Discussed in Chapter 3.

67. Raghavan, *Animosity at Bay* (2020), 188., Appendix I.

68. Such efforts to reverse population migrations also stemmed from practical constraints—the limited resources at the hands of provincial governments to accommodate refugees from the other country. For the political tensions between locals and refugees in the regions absorbing them, see Ansari, *Life after Partition* (2005); Chatterji, *The Spoils of Partition* (2007); Zamindar, *The Long Partition* (2007), chapter 5.

69. Chatterji, "South Asian Histories of Citizenship" (2012), 1059–60.

70. Raghavan, *Animosity at Bay* (2020), 190.

71. Raghavan, *Animosity at Bay* (2020), 57–60. For the League of Nations minority protection regime and its limitations, see Fink, "The League of Nations and the Minorities Questions" (1995); Mazower, "Minorities and the League of Nations" (1997).

72. Arendt, *Origins of Totalitarianism* (1979 [1951]), 274–75.

73. "Dilon ko tatolo," *Al Jamiat*, March 13, 1950.

74. For Pakistani newspapers and broadcasts citing *Al Jamiat*, see CID press reports on *Al Jamiat*, May 11 and 17, 1950, F. 98, DPR, Sixth Installment, NMML; Delhi secretariat press office report, January 3, 1951, F. CC 4-A (5)/50, Passport & Political, DSA.

75. Mir, *The Social Space of Language* (2010), 31. See also Jones, *Arya Dharm* (1976); Jalal, *Self and Sovereignty* (2000), Chapter 2.

76. Daechsel, *The Politics of Self-Expression* (2006), 13.

77. Under colonial law, which remained in effect after independence, printers and publishers had to apply for government approval before they could start a newspaper or printing press. Their applications were transferred to the CID press division for verification of the applicant's identity, political inclinations, financial situation, and criminal or political record. For monthly applications received by the Delhi CID, see files 9, 11, 274, 277, DPR, Eighth Installment, NMML.

78. For the embittered exchanges, editorial and tract wars between Arya Samaji and Muslim publications in Lahore from the late nineteenth century until the 1940s, see Jones, *Arya Dharm* (1976), 193–202; Jalal, *Self and Sovereignty* (2000), 160–65, 297–99, passim; Gilmartin, "Democracy, Nationalism and the Public" (1991); Nair, "Beyond the 'Communal' 1920s" (2013); Stephens, "The Politics of Muslim Rage" (2014); Scott, "Aryas Unbound" (2015).

79. Interview with Hansraj Rahbar, Oral History Transcript No. 629, NMML, 71–72.

80. Daechsel, *The Politics of Self-Expression* (2006), 142. For *Pratap* and *Milap* in Lahore, see also Rahbar, "Abhi Dilli Dur Hai" (1995); Jalal, *Self and Sovereignty* (2000), passim.

81. Rahbar, "Abhi Dilli Dur Hai" (1995) 29, 31.

82. Rahbar, "Abhi Dilli Dur Hai" (1995), 31.

83. Lala Kushal Chand's eldest son, Ranbir Singh, was convicted in the second Lahore Conspiracy Case: Author's Interview with Navin Suri, grandson of Lala Kushal Chand and editor of *Milap*, May 3, 2011, New Delhi. On the arrest of Mahashay Krishna's son, K. Narendra, see "Habeas Corpus Plea Rejected," *Times of India*, October 24, 1942.

84. Nair, *Changing Homelands* (2011); Jalal, "Nation, Reason and Religion" (1998), 2186; Gupta, "The Indian Diaspora of 1947" (1991); Jaffrelot, "The Hindu Nationalist Movement in Delhi" (2011).

85. Author's Interview with Navin Suri, May 3, 2011, New Delhi.

86. "Milap Proprietor Released on Bail." *Hindustan Times*, August 28, 1947. The Hindu Sahayata Samiti (committee for assisting Hindus), associated with the RSS, was established in April 1947. Jaffrelot, *The Hindu Nationalist Movement in India* (1993), 75–76.

87. See Chapter 1.

88. The connection between the two families is described by Mahashay Krishna's son K. Narendra in a booklet commemorating Deshbandhu Gupta, published by his family: *Through Freedom's Battle: Deshbandhu Gupta 1901–1951, a Recollection*. I thank Deshbandhu Gupta's son, Vishwa Bandhu Gupta, for giving me a copy.

89. CID report on *Vir Arjun*, March 27, 1954, F. 501, DPR, Eighth Installment, NMML.

90. The writer's joke about the stinginess of Delhi's residents plays on a common proverb: "Pani pipi kar ke gali dena," meaning, he curses so much that his throat gets dry, and he constantly needs to drink water between the abuses he utters.

91. "Yah Dilli hai," *Milap*, July 26, 1948.

92. Author's interview with Gopal Mittal's son, Prem Gopal Mittal, June 30, 2011, New Delhi; Mittal, *Lahore Ka Jo Zikr Kiya* (2000).

93. "Top Se ura dijiye inhen," *Milap*, January 30, 1948.

94. Kaur, *Since 1947* (2007), 138.

95. Talbot, *Divided Cities* (2006), xxv.

96. Fortnightly report for the first half of December 1948, Office of Relief and Reha-bilitation, Wavell Canteen, F. CC 1/48-C.

97. Both newspapers had Delhi editions before partition. Daechsel, *The Politics of Self-Expression* (2006), 14.

98. Kaur, "Claiming Community through Narratives" (2005); Datta, "Panjabi Refugees and the Urban Development of Greater Delhi" (1986).

99. For a study of refugee rehabilitation in Delhi from the perspective of gender, see also Bhardwaj Datta, "'Useful' and 'Earning' Citizens?" (2019).

100. "Kan khol kar suniye," *Milap*, October 19, 1947. The editorial was placed in two files about *Milap*'s objectionable tone: F. CC 8(29)/48 and F. CC 8(178)/48, Home-Press, DSA.

101. "Kan khol kar suniye," *Milap*, October 19, 1947.

102. "Qasur aur Chunian," *Pratap*, December 27, 1947; "Riyasat Bahawalpur men," *Pratap*, December 22, 1947. *Pratap*'s riot-related news stories are in F. CC 8 (11) /48, Home-Press, DSA. For *Milap*'s clippings, see F. CC 8 (178) /48, Home-Press, DSA.

103. "Kaa khol kar suniye," *Milap*, October 19, 1947.

104. "Bapu ab to hamari halat par rahm karo," *Pratap*, December 21, 1947, in F. CC 8(11)/48, Home-Press, DSA; "Brat khatam hua," *Milap*, January 21, 1948; "Gandhi ji par bam," *Milap*, January 23, 1948; "Apil kijiye sarkar," *Milap*, January 30, 1948.

105. "Kan khol kar suniye," *Milap*, October 19, 1947.

106. Kushal Chand's editorial "Barhta hua asantosh," *Milap*, July 31, 1948, in F. CC 8(178)/48, Home-Press, DSA; "Tamasha dekhte jaiye," *Milap*, October 18, 1947.

107. "Akhir kab tak?," *Al Jamiat*, June 4, 1950.

108. "Ek dukhi dil," *Pratap*, May 6, 1948. Included in F. CC 8(11)/48, Home-Press, DSA.

109. "Top se ura dijiye inhen," *Milap*, January 30, 1948.

110. "Pavement Shops to Be Abolished," *Hindustan Times*, November 5, 1947; "Rs. 10 Lakhs Loss to Delhi Municipality," *Hindustan Times*, December 11, 1947; "Public Sale of Cooked Food to Be Stopped," *Hindustan Times*, April 1, 1948. For refugee squatters, see Sharan, *In the City, Out of Place* (2014), 147–50.

111. Interview with Shankar Prasad, Oral History Transcript No. 494, NMML, 197.

112. "Top se ura dijiye inhen," *Milap*, January 30, 1948. For Punjabis' extension of help to other provinces, see also "Ai khanman barbad Logo!" *Milap*, July 28, 1948.

113. CID reports in Files 26, 27, and 28, DPR, Second Installment, NMML.

114. Chatterji, "South Asian Histories of Citizenship" (2012), 1061.

115. "Top se ura dijiye inhen," *Milap*, January 30, 1948.

116. Similarly, by 1951 several refugee associations carried the name *purusharthi*: CID List of refugee associations in F. 89, DPR, Second Installment, NMML.

117. See Chapter 3. Sikander Bakht later joined the Janata Party and, when it fell apart, the BJP: "Sikander Bakht: BJP's Best Known Muslim Face," *India Outlook*, February 23, 2004.

118. Johnson to Iengar, "Fortnightly Report for the Second Half of May 1952," F. CC 1/52-C, Confidential, DSA. For Home Minister Kailash Nath Katju's statement, see "Delhi Disorder Details," *Times of India*, June 3, 1952.

119. Puri, *Bharatiya Jana Sangh* (1980); Oldenburg, *Big City Government in India* (1976); Puri, *Party Politics in the Nehru Era* (1993); Gupta, "The Indian Diaspora of 1947" (1991); Jaffrelot, "The Hindu Nationalist Movement in Delhi" (2011); Krishna, "Communal Violence in India, Part 2" (1985), 118.

120. Puri, *Bharatiya Jana Sangh*, 27. Shankar Prasad to H. V. R. Iengar, "Fortnightly report for the first half of June 1951," F. CC 1/51-C, Confidential, DSA.

121. For the partial democratization of Delhi's administrative setup and the 1952 elections, see Chapter 5. For the rise of Congress socialists in Delhi see Puri, *Party Politics in the Nehru Era* (1993); Interview with Chaudhury Brahm Prakash, Oral History Transcript No. 503, NMML.

122. Shanti Dal's "Reports from the workers on Delhi situation 1952," F. No. S/EST/6-1949–52, MSP; F. S/Ind.Pro./6 Sikander Bakht & Raj Sharma, MSP; F. RW/s/5–1/D, MSP.

123. Nehru to Minister of Home Affairs, Kailash Nath Katju, June 21, 1952, Selected Works of Jawaharlal Nehru (SWJN) Vol. 18, 351; Nehru's note to K. N. Katju, May 27, 1952, SWJN Vol. 18, 211.

124. Fortnightly reports for the year 1952 in F. CC 1/52-C, Confidential, DSA; F. CC 113/1952-C, Confidential, DSA; F. CC 105/1952-C, Confidential, DSA. F. 66/1952-C, Confidential, DSA.

125. CID report on Ram Singh's speech on June 1, 1952, F. CC 8(145)/1952, Home-Press, DSA.

126. "Bharatiya Musalmanon se do baten," *Pratap*, June 2, 1952. This and other editorials relating to this controversy are located in F. CC 8(145)/1952, Home-Press, DSA.

127. "Bharatiya Musalmanon se do baten," *Pratap*, June 2, 1952.

128. Daechsel, *The Politics of Self-Expression* (2006), 15.

129. For Golwalkar's *We, or Our Nationhood Defined* (1939), including his selective drawing on Nazi ideology, see Jaffrelot, *The Hindu Nationalist Movement in India* (1993), 55–62. For the influence of nineteenth-century German nationalism on him, see Hansen, *The Saffron Wave* (1999), 80–84.

130. SP Police and CID reports, F. 371, DPR, Eighth Installment, NMML; F. CC 73/1951-C, Confidential, DSA. For the politics of cow protection in post-partition Delhi, see Parveen, *Contested Homelands* (2021), 164–84.

131. For the violent protests in December 1949, see Chapter 5. For the Hindu Code Bill, see Newbigin, *The Hindu Family and the Emergence of Modern India* (2013).

132. For analyses of the Constituent Assembly debates about safeguards for minorities, see Tejani, *Indian Secularism* (2008), chapter 6; Bajpai, "Constituent Assembly Debates and Minority Rights" (2000); Jha, "Secularism in the Constituent Assembly Debates, 1946–1950," (2002); Jha, "Rights Versus Representation" (2003).

133. Jha, "Secularism in the Constituent Assembly Debates, 1946–1950," (2002).

134. For Donald Smith's analysis of the deviation of Indian secularism from the classical model, and for a criticism of Smith, see Smith's and Bhargava's chapters in Bhargava, ed., *Secularism and Its Critics* (1998).

135. Bhargava, "Democratic Vision of a New Republic" (2000), 41.

136. Prakash, "Secular Nationalism, Hindutva, and the Minority" (2007); Mufti, *Enlightenment in the Colony*.

137. Weitz, "From the Vienna to the Paris System" (2008), 1330.

138. Ahmad and Kaviraj, "Indian Democracy and the World's Largest Muslim Minority" (2018), 207–8; Sherman, *Muslim Belonging in Secular India* (2015), 14; Jaffrelot, *The Hindu Nationalist Movement in India* (1993), 102–4.

139. Chatterjee, "Secularism and Toleration" (1994).

140. See Chapter 3.

141. "Ilzamat aur dhamkiyan," *Al Jamiat*, June 1952, in F. CC 8(145)/1952, Home-Press, DSA.

142. "Dhamkiyon ka yah tufan," *Al Jamiat*, June 4, 1952, in F. CC 8(145)/1952, Home-Press, DSA.

143. "Bharatiya Musalmanon ka jawab," *Nayi Duniya*, June 4, 1952.

144. "Bharatiya Musalmanon ka jawab," *Nayi Duniya*, June 4, 1952.

145. Savarkar, *Hindutva* (1969), 113.

146. "Ye pyar ki baten hain pyare," *Nayi Duniya*, June 7, 1952.

147. "Ye pyar ki baten hain pyare," *Nayi Duniya*, June 7, 1952.

148. CID report No. D/S 9342 Press-23, October 13, 1948, F. 100, DPR, Sixth Installment, NMML; SP of CID Rikhi Kesh to Home Secretary to the Chief Commissioner, No. 1380, September 5, 1951, F. CC 100/1951-C, Confidential, DSA; F. 8(196)/48, CC Files, Home-Press, DSA.

149. "Bharatiya Musalman Hinduon ki ghulami razi na hue to unke sath 'abratnak suluk kiya jaega," *Jang*, June 4, 1952; Letter from Madan Lal Mehta, Under Secretary, Ministry of External Affairs, No. D. 3596-P.III/52, June 3, 1952. Both are in F. CC 8(145) 1952, Press, DSA.

150. Nehru's Note to Private Secretary, New Delhi, August 9, 1952, SWJN, Vol. 19, 543.

151. Nehru to Maulana Azad, August 16, 1952, SWJN, Vol. 19, 547–48. For the controversy surrounding the *Amrit Patrika* article, see fortnightly reports for August 1952, F. CC 1/52-C, Confidential, DSA.

152. Nehru to A. P. Jain, September 22, 1951, SWJN, Vol 16. Part 2, 476–77.

153. Hardy, *The Muslims of British India* (1972), 194.

154. Metcalf, "Observant Muslims, Secular Indians" (2007), 109.

155. Mir Mushtaq Ahmed to Ashoka Mehta, June 19, 1952, Mir Mushtaq Ahmed Papers, NMML.

156. For Nayi Duniya's editorials, which exemplify this tendency, see F. CC 19 (47) 1954, Home, DSA; F. 106, DPR, Eighth Installment, NMML.

157. Farouqui, "The Emerging Dilemma of the Urdu Press in India" (1995), 91.

158. Farouqui, "The Emerging Dilemma of the Urdu Press in India" (1995), 95.

159. Masoom Moradabadi cited in Farouqui, "The Emerging Dilemma of the Urdu Press in India" (1995), 97.

160. Noorani, ed., *The Muslims of India* (2003), 9 (emphasis in original). See also Hasan, *Legacy of a Divided Nation* (1997), 213–14; Mayaram, *Resisting Regimes* (1997), 237–48.

161. The prevalent assumption is that nationalism relies on the emergence of national publics of readership, centered on print culture in one standardized language; see Anderson, *Imagined Communities* (1991). For the emergence of a Hindi public sphere, see Dalmia, *The Nationalization of Hindu Traditions* (1996); Orsini, *The Hindi Public Sphere 1920–1940* (2002).

162. Das Gupta, *Language Conflict and National Development* (1970), 151; Fortnightly report for the first half of February 1951, F. CC 1/51-C, Confidential, DSA.

163. See this practice in clips of *Pratap* and *Vir Arjun* in F. CC 14 (13) 1954, Press, DSA. The marginalization of Urdu in the 1960s is evident in the trajectory of Lala Jagat Narain, a refugee from Lahore and founder of the Hind Samachar Group, who, although more comfortable in the Urdu script, founded the Hindi daily *Punjab Kesari* in 1965. See Jeffrey, "Hindi: 'Taking to the Punjab Kesari Line'" (1997), 79.

164. Author's interview with Navin Suri, May 3, 2011, New Delhi; Farouqui, "The Emerging Dilemma of the Urdu Press in India" (1995); Jeffrey, "Punjabi: 'The Sub-Liminal Charge'" (1997), 444.

165. Jawaharlal Nehru to Sardar Patel, October 27, 1947, in Singh, ed., *Nehru-Patel* (2010), 30–31. See also Jawaharlal Nehru to Sardar Patel, October 6, 1947, in Singh, ed., *Nehru-Patel* (2010), 247.

166. Chief commissioner's comments on the role of the press in F. CC 8 (81) 1948, Press, DSA; Fortnightly report on the press for the first half of February 1948, F. CC 1/48-C, Confidential, DSA; F. 100, DPR, Sixth Installment, NMML; F. CC 8 (15) 1948, Press, DSA.

167. Dharma Vira to R. N. Banerjee, May 4, 1948, F. CC 8 (11) 1948, Press, DSA.

168. *Milap* appealed to Sardar Patel in February 1948, hoping he would cancel the order imposed by Chief Commissioner Khurshid Ahmad Khan to temporarily ban the paper; see F. CC 8 (29) Press, DSA.

169. *Narendra v. The Crown* ILR (1949) 1 P&H 348.

170. *Narendra v. The Crown* ILR (1949) 1 P&H 348.

171. Interview with Shankar Prasad, Oral History Transcript No. 494, NMML.

172. See Chapter 3.

173. For the renegotiation of press censorship and freedom after independence: Austin, *Working a Democratic Constitution* (1999), 38–53; Sethi, *Wars over Words* (2019), 175–245; Rook-Koepsel, "Dissenting against the Defence of India Rules" (2018); Burra, "Freedom of Speech and Constitutional Nostalgia" (2017).

CHAPTER 5

1. Yashpal, *Jhutha Sach, Vol. 2* (2007 [1960]), 301. Research for this chapter was supported by the Israel Science Foundation (grant No. 887/20).

2. For administrative continuity, see Potter, *India's Political Administrators, 1919–1983* (1996); Burra, "The Indian Civil Service" (2010). For drafting of the Constitution, see Austin, *The Indian Constitution* (2013 [1966]). For "institutional inertia" in the transition from colonial to postcolonial regimes, see Baruah, "Routine Emergencies" (2014); Jensen, "The Battlefield and the Prize" (2001).

3. Bhargava, "Democratic Vision of a New Republic" (2000). For the role played by the elections bureaucracy in institutionalizing democratic values, see Shani, *How India Became Democratic* (2018). For the Constitution's liberating effect for subaltern populations, see De, *A People's Constitution* (2018).

4. Kaviraj, "A State of Contradictions" (2010), 222–23.

5. This move was occasioned by the rise of the hardliner Bhalchandra Trimbak Ranadive to party leadership; by the onset of the Cold War and a global shift in the international communist movement; by the communist-led, armed peasant insurgency in Telangana; and by disappointment with Congress conservatism on labor issues. "Political Thesis (Adopted at the second Congress, 28 February to 6 March 1948)" in Rao, ed., *Documents of the History of the Communist Party of India* vol. VII (1960). See also Alam, "State and the Making of Communist Politics in India" (1991); Sharma, "'Yeh Azaadi Jhoothi Hai!'" (2014).

6. Sharma, "'Yeh Azaadi Jhoothi Hai!'" (2014); Zachariah, *Nehru* (2004), 180–85. For the split within the Delhi Congress, see Puri, *Party Politics in the Nehru Era* (1993), 59; Saini and Andersen, "The Congress Split in Delhi" (1971), 1087.

7. Master Tara Singh was arrested in February 1949 at the Narela railway station to prevent him from entering the city and presiding over a mass political meeting in defiance of government orders. His followers were arrested in Delhi. F. CC 43/1949-C, Confidential, DSA; Grewal, *Master Tara Singh in Indian History* (2018), 438–50; Das, ed., *Sardar Patel's Correspondence, 1945–50 Vol. 9* (1974), 116–72.

8. See Chapter 4.

9. Delhi's Congress leader, Deshbandhu Gupta, was the most vocal proponent of democratizing Delhi's governance. Deshbandhu Gupta, *Constituent Assembly Debates*, July 30–31, 1947; November 8, 1948; August 1–2, 1949. For Gupta, see also Chapter 1.

10. Initially the eminent right-wing leader Lala Deshbandhu Gupta ran for the position of Delhi's chief minister, supported from outside Congress by the Jana Sangh and refugee papers, especially his friend Mahashay Krishna's *Pratap*. "Reports from Workers on the Delhi Situation, Sep–Dec 1951," Reel 21 RW/S/4-1/D, MSP, NMML. Gupta died an untimely death in late 1951.

11. In the 1951 elections to the Municipal Committee the Jana Sangh won 7 seats as against 42 by the Congress, out of a total of 62. Yet its vote share was more impressive: 25 percent of votes as against 33 percent by the Congress. In the 1952 elections to the Delhi State Assembly, the Jana Sangh ran candidates for 31 of 48 seats and won only 4, polling 22 percent of the vote share. Those it won or almost won were mainly of Hindu refugee constituencies. In the 1954 elections to the Municipal Committee, the Jana Sangh increased its share of seats to 17, while the Congress declined to 28. By 1958, when the Municipal Corporation was established, the Jana Sangh's powerful organizing was apparent, and its performance was impressive. Puri, *Bharatiya Jana Sangh* (1980), 138–46, 149.

12. The legislative assembly and ministry were abolished in 1956 when the States Reorganization Act constituted Delhi as a Union Territory. The central government established a metropolitan council in 1966 to function as a representative body. An elected legislative assembly and a cabinet were restored in 1991. Puri, *Party Politics in the Nehru Era* (1993), 146–72; Oldenburg, *Big City Government in India* (1976), 22–28.

13. Austin, *Working a Democratic Constitution* (1999); Mehta, "Indian Constitutionalism" (2007).

14. Samaddar, "Law and Terror" (2006), 18.

15. For the deployment of preventive measures and other security schemes to curb nationalist agitations in interwar Delhi, see Legg, *Spaces of Colonialism* (2007), 96–119.

16. For the conflation of political risk with security risk in the colonial emergency regulations, and the bureaucratic mechanisms for population control, see Berda, "Managing 'Dangerous Populations'" (2020).

17. The Delhi Congress's electoral successes during the Nehruvian period rested on Nehru's charismatic appeal and on the organizational skills of local leader Bram Prakash, who successfully assembled a heterogeneous support base comprised of Muslims, Scheduled Castes, Other Backward Castes, and Sikhs, as well as some sections of the upper-caste Hindu and business communities through links with their traditional leaders. Prakash also built a strong network in Delhi's rural areas. The Jana Sangh's support base was more homogenous, concentrated in the urban areas, and confined to the refugee community and upper-caste Hindu petty traders and shopkeepers. Puri, *Bharatiya Jana Sangh* (1980); Puri, *Party Politics in the Nehru Era* (1993).

18. While accepting that the Indian Constitution granted enormous powers to the state and, as compared with the U.S. Constitution, curbed individual freedoms, De nonetheless emphasizes that it also empowered a judiciary that regularly blocked the Congress government's decisions. De, "Between Midnight and Republic" (2019), 1216.

19. Indeed, De submits that the Congress leaders accepted a dominion status, despite vehement opposition to it in the past, precisely because of the "flexible, centralized and authoritarian constitutional framework" that such a status provided them. De, "Between Midnight and Republic" (2019), 1216.

20. Somnath Lahiri, *Constituent Assembly Debates*, April 29, 1947, cited in Dasgupta, "'A Language Which Is Foreign to Us'" (2014), 237.

21. Brass, "The Strong State and the Fear of Disorder" (2000); Mehta, "Indian Constitutionalism" (2007); Prakash, *Emergency Chronicles* (2019), 38–74. For the "passive revolution" in India as an imperative for a strong and centralized state that could effectuate socioeconomic transformation, see Kaviraj, "A Critique of the Passive Revolution" (1998); Chatterjee, *Nationalist Thought and the Colonial World* (1986).

22. Ashutosh Lahiri to H. V. R. Iengar, March 17, 1949, F. CC 37/49-C Vol. II, Confidential, DSA.

23. Ashutosh Lahiri to Delhi's Deputy Commissioner, September 1, 1949, F. CC 37/49-C Vol. II, Confidential, DSA.

24. Interview with Jugal Kishore Khanna, Oral History Transcript No. 177, NMML, 32; Gupta, *Delhi between Two Empires* (1981), 208. For examples from other provinces, see Samaddar, "Law and Terror" (2006), 23.

25. D. P. Mishra to Sardar Patel, September 9, 1946, D. P. Mishra Papers, Installments I and II, NMML. I thank Rakesh Ankit for sharing this correspondence.

26. Sardar Patel to D. P. Mishra, September 11, 1946, D. P. Mishra Papers, Installments I and II, NMML. In fact, already during 1937–39, Congress provincial governments

collaborated cordially with Indian Civil Service bureaucrats and the police, and used the CID and colonial emergency laws against political opposition. Sardar Patel to B. G. Kher, April 10, 1939, in Singh, ed., *Nehru-Patel* (2010), 48. See also Arnold, *Police Power and Colonial Rule* (1986), 210–29; Ramnath, "ADM Jabalpur's Antecedents" (2016), 228–30; Burra, "What Is 'Colonial" About Colonial Laws?" (2016), 148–50.

27. The files consulted here are located at the Delhi Police Records, NMML. For the development of the colonial information order and the pervasive anxiety about not truly knowing Indian society, see Bayly, *Empire and Information* (1996). For the history of the CID, see Popplewell, *Intelligence and Imperial Defence* (1995); Silvestri, "The Thrill of 'Simply Dressing Up'" (2001).

28. Of special concern were the Lal (Red) Communists from Punjab. Files 34–35, Delhi Police Records (henceforth DPR), Fifth Installment, NMML; Gupta, *Dilli Ki Communist Party Ka Itihas* (2007), 435–36.

29. See Chapter 3.

30. See a 1951 note on the workings of the censor staff, CID Delhi, F. 89, DPR, Second Installment, NMML.

31. See Chapters 3–4.

32. Chatterjee, *The Politics of the Governed* (2004).

33. F. CC 80/1951-C, Confidential, DSA. For a late case, see a 1959 CID report on Mohammad Abdul Rafi, who applied for a visa to visit a relative in Delhi and was denied. F. 1, DPR, Eighth Installment, NMML. For the CID's internal structure and reorganization schemes, see F. CC 83/1955-C, Confidential, DSA; F. 89, DPR, Second Installment, NMML; Files 46 and 47, DPR, Seventh Installment, NMML.

34. Berda, "Managing 'Dangerous Populations'" (2020).

35. F. CC 29/1947-C, Confidential, DSA.

36. F. CC 82/1948-C, Confidential, DSA; F. CC 71/1949, Confidential, DSA.

37. Burra, "What Is 'Colonial,' About Colonial Laws?" (2016), 141. Burra's larger point is to challenge arguments about colonial continuity, claiming that "colonial" is not precise or helpful as an analytical category, because colonial rule entailed both authoritarian and liberal legacies.

38. For the emergence in India of a language of civil liberties—or freedoms attributed to citizens—already by the late 1930s, see Kalyani Ramnath's study of the Indian Civil Liberties Union, which Nehru formed in 1936. Ramnath, "Adm Jabalpur's Antecedents" (2016), 227–38.

39. Compare the CID's "Who's Who" political suspects series, spanning the 1930s–1950s in files 107, 197, 311, 313, 318–20, 362, Eighth Installment, DPR, NMML, with *Rajdhani Weekly Supplement: Delhi State* (1953).

40. See Chapter 1.

41. See Chapter 3.

42. F. CC 29/1947-C, Confidential, DSA.

43. Chief Commissioner W. Christie to Secretary of Home Department, A. E. Porter, February 11, 1947, F. CC 29/1947-C, Confidential, DSA.

44. The Delhi Muslim League, as mentioned in Chapter 2, dissolved by then.

45. Interview with H. V. R. Iengar, Oral History Transcript No. 303, NMML, 202.

46. After a brief stint in office by Chakravarti Rajagopalachari.

47. Nehru to K. N. Katju, July 15, 1952, Selected Works of Jawaharlal Nehru (SWJN) Vol. 18, 296.

48. F. 89, DPR, Second Installment, NMML.

49. Fortnightly reports in F. CC 1/71-C, Confidential, DSA.

50. Yashpal, *Jhutha Sach, Vol. 2* (2007 [1960]), 335.

51. F. CC 44/1953-C, Confidential, DSA.

52. F. CC 44/1953-C, Confidential, DSA; Mridula Sarabhai to H. M. Patel, November 30, 1952, REEL NO-19(36), MSP.

53. For an analysis of the purging of the police and government offices, see Gould, Sherman, and Ansari, "The Flux of the Matter" (2013).

54. For the police see Chapter 2. For purging Muslims from government offices, see F. CC 95/1948-C, Confidential, DSA; Gould, Sherman, and Ansari, "Flux of the Matter" (2013); Zamindar, *The Long Partition* (2007); Ankit, "G. A. Naqvi" (2018).

55. F. CC 129/1950-C, Confidential, DSA.

56. F. CC 37/49-C Vol. II, Confidential, DSA; F. 149, DPR, Fifth Installment, NMML.

57. Kalhan et al., "Colonial Continuities" (2006), 131; Austin, *Working a Democratic Constitution* (1999), 54.

58. Judges in habeas corpus cases often forbade the transfer of detainees to jails in Uttar Pradesh and Punjab. F. CC 25/1949-C, Confidential, DSA; Shankar Prasad to H. V. R. Iengar, June 17, 1949, F. 110/1949-C, Confidential, DSA. In 1958 the jail moved to larger premises in Tihar village, and the old building was incorporated into the Maulana Azad Medical College. Chopra, *Delhi Gazetteer* (1976), 668.

59. F. 371, DPR, Eighth Installment, NMML.

60. Interview with Shankar Prasad, Oral History Transcript No. 494, NMML, 165.

61. Proceedings of a conference between Home Minister Patel and the chief ministers on the CPI, August 20, 1950, in. F. CC 137/1950, Confidential, 1950. For the repression of communists in West Bengal, see Bandyopadhyay, ed., *Decolonization in South Asia* (2009).

62. See correspondence spanning 1950–52 in F. CC 30/1952-C, Confidential, DSA.

63. For Farooqi's biography, see Gupta, *Dilli Ki Communist Party Ka Itihas*, 192–201. His CID dossier is in F. 107, Eighth Installment, DPR, NMML.

64. For Y. D.'s biography, see Gupta, *Dilli Ki Communist Party Ka Itihas* (2007), 179–88. Interview with Yag Dutt Sharma, Oral History Transcript No. 777, NMML. His CID dossier is in F. 107, Eighth Installment, DPR, NMML.

65. F. 4, DPR, Eighth Installment, NMML. Interview with Yag Dutt Sharma, Oral History Transcript No. 777, NMML, 133–34.

66. *Virendra Kumar Tripathi v. The Crown*, 1951 CriLJ 3.

67. He later married Sarla Gupta, a Delhi party worker. Interview with Sarla Sharma, Oral History Transcript No. 71, NMML.

68. On Mohammad Yamin, see Gupta, *Dilli Ki Communist Party Ka Itihas* (2007), 189–91.

69. Interview with Yag Dutt Sharma, Oral History Transcript No. 777, NMML, 144. Mohammed and Sara Yamin's arrest and detention in Karachi is corroborated in his CID

dossier in F. 319, DPR, Eighth Installment, NMML. For the clampdown on communists in Pakistan, see Ali, "The Enemy Within" (2018).

70. "Khem Raj," in F. 107, Eighth Installment, DPR, NMML.

71. Janardhan Sharma's CID dossier in F. 107, Eighth Installment, DPR, NMML. See the similar case of Santosh Chatterjee, in F, 107.

72. Austin, *Working a Democratic Constitution* (1999), 54.

73. Mir Mushtaq Ahmed's CID dossier in F. 318, DPR, Eighth Installment, NMML. For his subsequent political career in Delhi, see Puri, *Party Politics in the Nehru Era* (1993).

74. Shankar Prasad to H. V. R. Iengar, fortnightly report for the first half of April 1949, F. CC 37/49-C Vol. I, Confidential, DSA.

75. F. CC 145/1949-C, Confidential, DSA.

76. Deputy Commissioner Rameshwar Dayal to B. D. Joshi, December 1, 1949, F. CC 37/49-C Vol. II, Confidential, DSA.

77. See Chapters 2 and 3.

78. DC Randhawa's fortnightly report for the second half of January 1948, F. CC 1/48-C, Confidential, DSA. 35/48-C, DSA; F. DC 162/48, DSA.

79. Six, *Secularism, Decolonisation, and the Cold War* (2018), 103–23.

80. In October 1948 Patel proposed to lift the ban on the RSS, and Nehru rejected the idea. Nehru to Patel, October 27, 1948, JN (SG) Papers, File No. 14.

81. Interview with Shankar Prasad, Oral History Transcript No. 494, NMML, 165.

82. Interview with Shankar Prasad, Oral History Transcript No. 494, NMML, 166.

83. Nehru to the Home Ministry, December 5, 1948, JN (SG) Papers, File No. 16 Pt.-I.

84. "Jailon ki halat," *Pratap* (Delhi), January 5, 1949.

85. For fines of RSS supporters and confiscation of their property, see CID Fortnightly report for the second half of December 1948, F. CC 1/48-C, Confidential, DSA.

86. H. V. R. Iengar to Shankar Prasad, May 25, 1949, and correspondence regarding Amrit Rai and RSS detenus, Files CC 37/49-C Vol. II and CC 162/1948-C, Confidential, DSA. For the negotiations taking place behind the scenes between Golwalkar and Patel, see Ankit, "How the Ban on the RSS Was Lifted" (2012); Jaffrelot, *The Hindu Nationalist Movement in India* (1993), 87–90.

87. For reports and correspondence on this agitation, see F. CC 155/1950-C, Confidential, DSA. For the controversy over the Hindu Code Bill, see Chapter 4.

88. Local Hindu Mahasabha leader Ram Singh was born to a rich *bania* family in Farmanah village, Rohtak (today in Haryana's Sonipat District). He obtained an MA degree from D. A. V. College in Lahore and moved to Delhi, where he worked as a teacher in Sanatan High School, Ajmer Gate. He was a staunch Arya Samaji, joined the Hindu Mahasabha, and took an active role in the Shiv Mandir agitation, in "anti-Pakistan" demonstrations before partition, and in agitations against the Congress and Gandhi after it. He was prominent in Hindu right politics in the 1950s. See his CID dossier in F. 197, DPRecords, Eighth Installment, NMML.

89. Masselos, "Controlling Prabhat Pheris" (2007). For *prabhat pheris* in nationalist agitations in Delhi, see Legg, "Gendered Politics and Nationalised Homes" (2003), 21.

90. Shankar Prasad to V. Shankar, December 15, 1949, F. CC 155/1950-C, Confidential, DSA.

91. Interview with Shankar Prasad, Oral History Transcript No. 494, NMML. Specifically, Prasad accused Iengar, claiming that he acted without Patel's knowledge. Given Prasad's deep personal resentment of Iengar, which runs throughout his interview, and the many years that elapsed between the events and the interview, we shall leave this issue open.

92. Section 144 was used against Ram Singh of the Hindu Mahasabha in 1948, the socialist leader Ram Manohar Lohia, Master Tara Singh and the Akali Sikhs who held a mass meeting in February 1949 without a permit, numerous RSS volunteers during the satyagraha, communist leaders and labor agitators, and students who walked in procession within the university to get their exams postponed and reportedly attacked the university office. See Ram Singh's CID dossiers in Files 197 and 313, DPR, Eighth Installment, NMML; F. CC 110/1949-C, Confidential, DSA; Deputy Commissioner's report in F. CC 134/1949-C, Confidential, DSA.

93. See Kalyani Ramnath's analysis of the All India Civil Liberties Conference in July 1949. Ramnath, "Adm Jabalpur's Antecedents," 238–39. For the backlash against the continued use of Section 144 in Madras, see Kumar, *Police Matters in South India, 1900–1975* (2021), chapter 5.

94. Lohia led a procession to the Nepalese embassy to protest the Rana Rule in Nepal F. CC 110/1949-C, and F. CC 112/1949-C, Confidential, DSA.

95. Nehru's private secretary A. V. Pai to Home Secretary H. V. R. Iengar, June 6, 1949; A. V. Pai to Shankar Prasad, June 8, 1949. Both are in F. CC 110/1949-C, Confidential, DSA.

96. The gestures leaked to the press and received political color, as right-wing and refugee newspapers saw in the affair evidence of Nehru's partiality toward socialists. "Khush qismat qaidi," *Pratap*, June 10, 1949, in F. CC 110/1949-C. Congress socialists, for their part, complained of the Home Ministry's partiality to the RSS.

97. Shankar Prasad to Iengar, June 17, 1949, F. CC 110/1949-C.

98. See U. K. Ghosal, Ministry of Home Affairs, to Chief Commissioner Shankar Prasad, July 3, 1949, F. CC 112/1949-C, Confidential, DSA.

99. Kudaisya, *A Republic in the Making* (2017), 76. For an analysis of the Republic Day parades, see Roy, *Beyond Belief* (2007), 66–104.

100. Patel on January 26, 1950, cited in Roy, *Beyond Belief* (2007), 70.

101. For Rahbar's recollections, see Hansraj Rahbar, "Dilli Ab Dur Nahin," in Vanshi, ed., *Dilli Tea House* (2009); Interview with Hansraj Rahbar, Oral History Transcript No. 629, NMML. His CID dossier is in F. 107, Eighth Installment, DPR, NMML.

102. The account in this and the following paragraph is based on CID and IB reports in F. 13, DPR, Fifth Installment, NMML.

103. See dossiers of Jaidev Sethi, Tilak Raj Nijhowne, and Harish Chander Agarwal, F. 107, Eighth Installment, DPR, NMML; F. CC 30/1952-C, Confidential, DSA.

104. Telegram No. 7/6/50-Poll, January 17, 1950, from Ministry of Home Affairs, F. 13, DPR, Fifth Installment, NMML. For security arrangements in anticipation of the Republic Day celebrations, see F. CC 59/1950-C, Confidential, DSA.

105. Interview with Yag Dutt Sharma, Oral History Transcript No. 777, NMML.

106. Muqimuddin Farooqi ran in elections from Matiya Mahal, and Sarla Gupta ran and won from Ballimaran constituency—both Muslim-majority constituencies.

107. See Chapter 4; Austin, *Working a Democratic Constitution* (1999), 38–50.

108. Detainees were not completely deprived of protections. The act required the authorities to inform detainees of the grounds of their detention within five days, and authorized courts to intervene in this matter and to examine whether the information furnished was sufficient for detainees to make representation. Additionally, detention orders were to be examined within ten weeks by the quasi-judicial Advisory Boards. Bayley, "The Indian Experience with Preventive Detention" (1962); Tripathi, "Preventive Detention" (1960); Kalhan et al., "Colonial Continuities" (2006), 134–35; Austin, *Working a Democratic Constitution* (1999), 53–68.

109. For protests against the act in Delhi, see fortnightly reports for October 1951, F. CC 1/51-C, Confidential, DSA; Fortnightly reports for July and August 1952, F. CC 1/52-C, Confidential, DSA.

110. U. K. Ghoshal, Deputy Secretary, Home Ministry, No. 57/188/50-Poll, August 11, 1950, in F. 70/1948-C, Confidential, DSA.

111. Table 5.2 buttresses legal scholar David Bayley's assessment that, with the exception of 1957, the number of people detained under the act declined each year throughout the 1950s, and that overall both state and central governments administered the act in a moderate and cautious manner. Bayley, "The Indian Experience with Preventive Detention" (1962), 104, 10.

112. Fortnightly reports for 1951 in F. CC 1/51-C, Confidential, DSA.

113. The Supreme Court had just validated the constitutionality of the Preventive Detention Act in the famous *A. K. Gopalan v. State of Madras* judgment, which rejected the communist leader's arguments.

114. Specifically, the judges explained that the ordinary law (Section 144) was sufficient to extern Lahiri from Delhi and prevent the meetings he sought to organize. *Ashutosh Lahiri v. The State of Delhi*, AIR 1953 SC 451; *Ram Singh v. The State of Delhi*, AIR 1951 SC 270.

115. F. CC 73/1951-C, Confidential, DSA.

116. For the violent agitation, see Chapter 4. For the arrests, see Fortnightly Report for the Second Half of May 1952, F. CC 1/52-C, Confidential, DSA; dossiers of Balraj Khanna, Mauli Chander Sharma, Har Dayal Singh, and Vir Pirja in F. 197, DPR, Eighth Installment, NMML.

117. F. 90, DPR, Second Installment, NMML. Files CC 57/1953-C, CC 82/1953-C, CC 94/1953-C, Confidential, DSA; Guha, *India after Gandhi* (2008), 242–60.

118. F. CC 82/1953-C, Confidential, DSA.

119. By the end of July, 11 detention orders had been revoked, 40 externment orders were canceled, 106 undertrials were released, 192 convicts were released, and fines worth a total of 140,100 rupees were remitted. Thirty-five people involved in the violence had not yet been released by the end of July, but by mid-August Home Minister Katju urged the release of all but the ringleaders and those who had taken a particularly prominent part in the violence, in order to secure conviction of these more culpable offenders. See correspondence in F. CC 94/1953-C, Confidential, DSA.

120. The other was Speaker of the Lok Sabha. Interview with Shankar Prasad, Oral History Transcript No. 494, NMML, 153–54.

121. F. CC 11(7) 1958, Home, DSA; Basu, *Mridula Sarabhai* (1996), 154–229.

122. Mridula Sarabhai to Rao Saheb Patwardhan, June 29, 1967, cited in Basu, *Mridula Sarabhai* (1996), 222.

123. Lok Sabha Debates, Nehru's speech, December 9, 1958, cited in Basu, *Mridula Sarabhai* (1996), 207. For Nehru's growing impatience with Sarabhai, see his correspondence from 1956 in SWJN, Vol. 34, 253–55.

124. See Chapter 4.

125. "No Gestapo in India: Govt. Essentially Democratic," *Hindustan Times* (Delhi), April 27, 1951.

126. "Beware of the Dog," *Hindustan Times*, April 28, 1951.

127. Bayley, "The Indian Experience with Preventive Detention" (1962), 99.

128. Interview with Hansraj Rahbar, Oral History Transcript No. 629, NMML; Rahbar, "Abhi Dilli Dur Hai" (1995).

129. Bayley, "The Indian Experience with Preventive Detention" (1962), 114.

EPILOGUE

1. Jayal, "Reconfiguring Citizenship in Contemporary India" (2019), 36.

2. The CAA is partly an effort by the ruling government to address the results of the Register of Citizens already conducted in Assam, which identified a large number of Hindus among the illegal immigrants there.

3. The nature of resistance to the CAA in Assam is unique, grounded in historical Assamese objection to immigration of Bengalis and, after partition, of Bangladeshis—both Hindu and Muslim. Baruah, *In the Name of the Nation* (2020), 47–75.

4. Mustafa, ed., *Shaheen Bagh and the Idea of India* (2020).

5. Ananya Bhardwaj, December 21, 2019, "How Azad's Anti-CAA Protest Turned into a 13 Hour Stand-Off with Delhi Police" https://theprint.in/india/13-hours-of-pakdam-pakdai-how-azad-dodged-arrest-by-delhi-police-during-anti-caa-protest/338968/.

6. Vijayta Lalwani, October 8, 2020, "Backgrounder: What Is Delhi Police's Riots Conspiracy Case?" https://scroll.in/article/974904/backgrounder-what-is-delhi-polices-riots-conspiracy-case.

7. Vijayta Lalwani and Supriya Sharma, "'Delhi Is Our Capital Too': A Blow-by-Blow Account of the Farmers' Tractor Rally on Republic Day," January 26, 2021, https://scroll.in/article/985160/delhi-is-our-capital-too-a-blow-by-blow-account-of-the-farmers-tractor-rally-on-republic-day; Ananya Bhardwaj, "3 Reasons Why Delhi Police Failed to Stop Farmers from Storming the Heart of the Capital," January 27, 2021, https://theprint.in/india/governance/3-reasons-why-delhi-police-failed-to-stop-farmers-from-storming-the-heart-of-the-capital/592734/.

8. Apurva Vishwanath, "Conspiracy, Sedition: Ruling in Disha Ravi Case Raises Bar for State," February 24, 2021, https://indianexpress.com/article/explained/conspiracy-sedition-ruling-in-disha-ravi-case-raises-bar-for-state-7201885/.

9. "It's Like An Undeclared Emergency: Media Bodies On Sedition Charges Against Journalists," January 31, 2021, https://www.outlookindia.com/website/story/india-news-living-at-a-time-of-undeclared-emergency-media-bodies-condemn-sedition-charges-against-journalists/372766.

10. Hindu nationalist activists exert enormous pressure on Hindu women to renounce their decision to marry Muslims, file false charges against them of rape and abduction, and marry Hindu men instead. Jaffrelot, "A De Facto Ethnic Democracy?" (2020). In Uttar Pradesh, the fight against "love jihad" has received a legal fillip with the Prohibition of Unlawful Religious Conversion Ordinance, 2020.

11. Jaffrelot, "De Facto Ethnic Democracy?" (2020). For ethnic democracy see Smooha, "Ethnic Democracy" (1997).

12. The Law of Return (1950) "guarantees immediate right of entry to every Jew who comes to Israel and expresses a wish to settle there," and the Nationality Law (1952) "grants every person admitted under the Law of Return Israeli citizenship from the day of arrival in the country." Peled, "Ethnic Democracyand the Legal Construction of Citizenship" (1992), 435. See also Robinson, *Citizen Strangers* (2013).

13. The notion of transfer was much more present in Zionist thinking, than in the expectations of Indian Hindu and Muslim leaders in the early 1940s. Additionally, India formalized an inclusive territorial citizenship in its progressive Constitution, unlike Israel, which never wrote a constitution and formalized an exclusive form of citizenship through the Law of Return. I am developing this comparison in a separate article.

14. "Home Ministry Holds Security Meet Amid Protests Against Citizenship Act," December 19, 2019, https://www.ndtv.com/india-news/amit-shah-to-chair-meeting-on-nationwide-protests-against-citizenship-act-2151391.

BIBLIOGRAPHY

ARCHIVES

Centre of South Asian Studies, Cambridge
Jugal Kishore Khanna Oral History Transcript

Delhi State Archives, Delhi
Aziz Hasan Baqai Papers
Chief Commissioner Files
Deputy Commissioner Files

National Archives of India, Delhi
Ministry of Home Affairs

Nehru Memorial Museum and Library, Delhi
Delhi Police Records
D. P. Mishra Papers
Jawaharlal Nehru Papers
Mir Mushtaq Ahmed Papers
Mridula Sarabhai Papers
Abdullah Farooqi Oral History Transcript
Ajit Prasad Jain, Oral History Transcript
Chaudhury Brahm Prakash Oral History Transcript
Hansraj Rahbar Oral History Transcript
H. V. R. Iengar Oral History Transcript
Imdad Sabri Oral History Transcript
Jugal Kishore Khanna Oral History Transcript
Phool Chand Jain Oral History Transcript
R. N. Banerjee Oral History Transcript
Shankar Prasad Oral History Transcript
Yag Dutt Sharma, Oral History Transcript

NEWSPAPERS
Al Jamiat (Urdu daily)
Dawn (English daily)
Milap (Urdu daily)
Nayi Duniya (Urdu daily)

Pratap (Urdu daily)
Hindustan (Hindi daily)
Hindustan Times (English daily)
Times of India (English daily)

COURT JUDGMENTS
Ashutosh Lahiri v. The State of Delhi, AIR 1953 SC 451.
Narendra v. The Crown ILR (1949) 1 P&H 348.
Ram Singh v. The State of Delhi, AIR 1951 SC 270.
Virendra Kumar Tripathi v. The Crown, 1951 CriLJ 3

PUBLISHED PRIMARY AND SECONDARY SOURCES
Abbas, Khwaja Ahmad. *I Write as I Feel*. Bombay Hind Kitab, 1948.
———. *Let India Fight for Freedom*. Bombay: Sound Magazine, 1943.
Ahmad, Aijaz. *Lineages of the Present: Ideology and Politics in Contemporary South Asia*. London: Verso, 2000.
Ahmad, Hilal, and Sudipta Kaviraj. "Indian Democracy and the World's Largest Muslim Minority." In *Democratic Transition in the Muslim World: A Global Perspective*, edited by Alfred Stepan. New York: Columbia University Press, 2018.
Ahmed, Akbar S. *Jinnah, Pakistan and Islamic Identity: The Search for Saladin*. London: Routledge, 1997.
Ahmed, Talat. *Literature and Politics in the Age of Nationalism: The Progressive Writers' Movement in South Asia, 1932–56*. New Delhi: Routledge, 2009.
Aiyar, Swarna. "'August Anarchy': The Partition Massacres in Punjab, 1947." *South Asia: Journal of South Asian Studies* 18, no. special issue (1995): 13–36.
Alam, Javeed. "State and the Making of Communist Politics in India, 1947–57." *Economic & Political Weekly* 26, no. 45 (1991).
Ali, Ahmed. *Twilight in Delhi: A Novel*. New Delhi: Rupa, 2007 [1940]
Ali, Choudhary Rahmat. *Pakistan: The Fatherland of the Pak Nation*. Cambridge: Pakistan National Liberation Movement, 1946.
Ali, Kamran Asdar. "The Enemy Within: Communism and the New Pakistan State." In *The Postcolonial Moment in South and Southeast Asia*, edited by Gyan Prakash, Michael Laffan, and Nikhil Menon. New York: Bloomsbury, 2018.
Alpes, Maybritt Jill. "The Congress and the Ina Trials, 1945–1950: A Contest over the Perception of 'Nationalist' Politics." *Studies in History* 23, no. 1 (2007).
Ambedkar, B. R. *Thoughts on Pakistan*. Bombay: Thacker, 1941.
Amstutz, Andrew. "A Partitioned Library: Changing Collecting Priorities and Imagined Futures in a Divided Urdu Library, 1947–49." *South Asia: Journal of South Asian Studies* 43, no. 3 (2020): 505–21.
Anderson, Benedict R. O'G. *Imagined Communities: Reflections on the Origin and Spread of Nationalism*. New York: Verso, 1991.
Ankit, Rakesh. "G. A. Naqvi: From Indian Police (up), 1926 to Pakistani Citizen (Singh), 1947." *Journal of the Royal Asiatic Society* 28, no. 2 (2018): 295–314.

———. "How the Ban on the RSS Was Lifted." *Economic & Political Weekly* 47, no. 16 (2012): 71–78.

———. "In the Hands of a 'Secular State': Meos in the Aftermath of Partition, 1947–49." *Indian Economic and Social History Review* (2019).

———. *India in the Interregnum: Interim Government, September 1946–August 1947*. New Delhi: Oxford University Press, 2019.

"Annual Report of the Registrar of Newspapers for India." New Delhi: Ministry of Information and Broadcasting, Government of India, 1956.

Ansari, Sarah F. D. *Life after Partition: Migration, Community and Strife in Sindh, 1947–1962*. New York: Oxford University Press, 2005.

Ansari, Sarah, and William Gould. *Boundaries of Belonging: Localities, Citizenship and Rights in India and Pakistan*. Cambridge: Cambridge University Press, 2020.

Appadurai, Arjun. "Number in the Colonial Imagination." In *Orientalism and the Postcolonial Predicament: Perspectives on South Asia*, edited by Carol Breckenridge and Peter van der Veer. Philadelphia: University of Pennsylvania Press, 1993.

Arendt, Hannah. *Origins of Totalitarianism*. New York: Harcourt Brace, 1979 [1951].

Arnold, David. *Police Power and Colonial Rule, Madras, 1859–1947*. Delhi: Oxford University Press, 1986.

Austin, Granville. *The Indian Constitution: Cornerstone of a Nation*. New Delhi: Oxford University Press, 2013 [1966].

———. *Working a Democratic Constitution: The Indian Experience*. New Delhi: Oxford University Press, 1999.

Azad, Abul Kalam. *India Wins Freedom: The Complete Version*. New Delhi: Orient Blackswan 2009 [1988].

Bajpai, Rochana. "Constituent Assembly Debates and Minority Rights." *Economic & Political Weekly* 35, no. 21/22 (2000): 1837–45.

Baker, David. "St. Stephen's College, Delhi, 1991–1997: An 'Alexandria on the Banks of the Jamuna'?". In *Knowledge, Power & Politics: Educational Institutions in India*, edited by Mushirul Hasan. New Delhi: Roli Books, 1998.

Bandyopadhyay, Sekhar, ed. *Decolonization in South Asia: Meanings of Freedom in Post-Independence West Bengal, 1947–52*. London: Routledge, 2009.

Banerjea, B. N. "Exchange of Population: Lessons from Recent History." *Indian Journal of Political Science* 8, no. 2 (1946): 697–702.

Barelvi, Ebadat. "Such a Strange Maidan." *Seminar* 420, Special Issue on Partition (1994): 36–37.

Baruah, Sanjib. *In the Name of the Nation: India and Its Northeast*. Stanford, CA: Stanford University Press, 2020.

———. "Routine Emergencies: India's Armed Forces Special Powers Act." In *Civil Wars in South Asia: State, Sovereignty, Development*, edited by Aparna Sundar and Nandini Sundar. New Delhi: Sage, 2014.

Basu, Aparna. *Mridula Sarabhai: Rebel with a Cause*. Delhi: Oxford University Press, 1996.

Bayley, David H. "The Indian Experience with Preventive Detention." *Pacific Affairs* 35, no. 2 (1962): 99–115.

Bayly, C. A. *Empire and Information: Intelligence Gathering and Social Communication in India, 1780–1870*. Cambridge: Cambridge University Press, 1996.

Bayly, Christopher, and Tim Harper. *Forgotten Armies: Britain's Asian Empire and the War with Japan*. London: Penguin, 2005.

Berda, Yael. "Managing 'Dangerous Populations': How Colonial Emergency Laws Shape Citizenship." *Security Dialogue* 51, no. 6 (2020): 557–78.

Bhardwaj Datta, Anjali. "Genealogy of a Partition City: War, Migration and Urban Space in Delhi." *South Asia: Journal of South Asian Studies* 42, no. 1 (2019): 152–69.

———. "'Useful' and 'Earning' Citizens? Gender, State, and the Market in Post-Colonial Delhi." *Modern Asian Studies* 53, no. 6 (2019): 1924–55.

Bhargava, Meena, and Kalyani Dutta. *Women, Education, and Politics: The Women's Movement and Delhi's Indraprastha College*. New Delhi: Oxford University Press, 2005.

Bhargava, Rajeev. "Democratic Vision of a New Republic: India, 1950." In *Transforming India: Social and Political Dynamics of Democracy*, edited by Francine R. Frankel, Zoya Hasan, Rajeev Bhargava, and Palveer Arora. New Delhi: Oxford University Press, 2000.

———, ed. *Secularism and Its Critics*. Themes in Politics Series. Delhi: Oxford University Press, 1998.

Blake, Stephen P. "Cityscape of an Imperial Capital: Shahjahanabad in 1739." In *Delhi through the Ages: Selected Essays on Urban History, Culture and Society*, edited by R. E. Frykenberg. Delhi: Oxford University Press, 1992.

Bose, Sugata. *His Majesty's Opponent: Subhas Chandra Bose and India's Struggle against Empire*. Cambridge, MA: Belknap Press, 2011.

Brass, Paul R. *Forms of Collective Violence: Riots, Pogroms and Genocide in Modern India*. New Delhi: Three Essays Collective, 2006.

———. "The Partition of India and Retributive Genocide in the Punjab, 1946–7: Means, Methods, and Purposes." *Journal of Genocide Research* 5, no. 1 (2003): 71–101.

———. *The Production of Hindu-Muslim Violence in Contemporary India*. New Delhi: Oxford University Press, 2003.

———. "The Strong State and the Fear of Disorder." In *Transforming India: Social and Political Dynamics of Democracy*, edited by Francine R. Frankel, Zoya Hasan, Rajeev Bhargava, and Palveer Arora. New Delhi: Oxford University Press, 2000.

Brennan, Lance. "The Illusion of Security: The Background to Muslim Separatism in the United Provinces." In *India's Partition: Process, Strategy, and Mobilization*, edited by Mushirul Hasan. New Delhi: Oxford University Press, 2013 [1993].

Brubaker, Rogers. "Aftermaths of Empire and the Unmixing of Peoples: Historical and Comparative Perspectives." *Ethnic and Racial Studies* 18, no. 2 (1995): 189–218.

Burra, Arudra. "Freedom of Speech and Constitutional Nostalgia." *Seminar* 697 (2017).

———. "The Indian Civil Service and the Nationalist Movement: Neutrality, Politics and Continuity." *Commonwealth & Comparative Politics* 48, no. 4 (2010): 404–32.

———. "What Is 'Colonial' About Colonial Laws?" *American University International Law Review* 31, no. 2 (2016): 137–69.

Chatterjee, Partha. *Nationalist Thought and the Colonial World: A Derivative Discourse*. London: Zed Books, 1986.

———. *The Politics of the Governed: Reflections on Popular Politics in Most of the World*. New York: Columbia University Press, 2004.

———. "Secularism and Toleration." *Economic and Political Weekly* 29, no. 28 (1994): 1768–77.

Chatterji, Joya. *Bengal Divided: Hindu Communalism and Partition, 1932–1947*. Cambridge: Cambridge University Press, 1994.

———. "New Directions in Partition Studies." *History Workshop Journal*, no. 67 (Spring 2009): 213–20.

———. "South Asian Histories of Citizenship, 1946–1970." *Historical Journal* 55, no. 4 (2012): 1049–71.

———. *The Spoils of Partition: Bengal and India, 1947–1967*. Cambridge: Cambridge University Press, 2007.

Chattha, Ilyas. *Partition and Locality: Violence, Migration, and Development in Gujranwala and Sialkot, 1947–1961*. Karachi: Oxford University Press, 2011.

Chopra, P. N., ed. *Quit India Movement: Secret British Documents*. New Delhi: Interprint, 1986.

Chopra, Prabha. *Delhi Gazetteer*. New Delhi: Gazetteer Unit, Delhi Administration, 1976.

Churchill, Winston S. *The Second World War Volume 4: The Hinge of Fate*. New York: Houghton Mifflin, 1985 [1950].

Cohn, Bernard S. "The Census, Social Structure and Objectification in South Asia." In *An Anthropologist among the Historians and Other Essays*. Delhi: Oxford University Press, 1987.

Collins, Michael. "Decolonisation and the 'Federal Moment.'" *Diplomacy & Statecraft* 24 (2013): 21–40.

Cooper, Fredrick. *Citizenship between Empire and Nation: Remaking France and French Africa, 1945–1960*. Princeton, NJ: Princeton University Press, 2014.

Coupland, R. *The Indian Problem: Report on the Constitutional Problem in India*. Oxford: Oxford University Press, 1944.

Daechsel, Markus. *The Politics of Self-Expression: The Urdu Middle-Class Milieu in Mid-Twentieth Century India and Pakistan*. New York: Routledge, 2006.

Dalmia, Vasudha. *The Nationalization of Hindu Traditions: Bharatendu Harischandra and Nineteenth-Century Banaras*. Delhi: Oxford University Press, 1996.

Dalrymple, William. *The Last Mughal: The Fall of a Dynasty, Delhi 1857*. New Delhi: Penguin, 2007.

Das, Durga, ed. *Sardar Patel's Correspondence, 1945–50*, Vol. 9. Ahmedabad: Navajivan, 1974.

Das, Suranjan. *Communal Riots in Bengal, 1905–1947*. New York: Oxford University Press, 1991.

Das, Veena. "Official Narratives, Rumour, and the Social Production of Hate.". *Social Identities* 4, no. 1 (1998): 109–30.

Das Gupta, Jyoti Bhusan. *Indo-Pakistan Relations, 1947–1955*. Amsterdam: Djambatan, 1958.

Das Gupta, Jyotirindra. *Language Conflict and National Development: Group Politics and National Language Policy in India.* Berkeley: University of California Press, 1970.

———. "Practice and Theory of Language Planning: The Indian Policy Process." In *Language and Politics,* edited by William O. O'Barr and Jean F. O'Barr. The Hague: Mouton, 1976.

Dasgupta, Sandipto. "'A Language Which Is Foreign to Us': Continuities and Anxieties in the Making of the Indian Constitution." *Comparative Studies of South Asia, Africa and the Middle East* 34, no. 2 (2014): 228–42.

Datta, V. N. "Panjabi Refugees and the Urban Development of Greater Delhi." In *Delhi through the Ages: Essays in Urban History, Culture, and Society,* edited by Robert Eric Frykenberg. Delhi: Oxford University Press, 1986.

De, Rohit. "Between Midnight and Republic: Theory and Practice of India's Dominion Status." *International Journal of Constitutional Law* 17, no. 4 (2019): 1213–34.

———. "Evacuee Property and the Management of Economic Life in Postcolonial India." In *The Postcolonial Moment in South and Southeast Asia,* edited by Gyan Prakash, Michael Laffan, and Nikhil Menon. New York: Bloomsbury, 2018.

———. *A People's Constitution: The Everyday Life of Law in the Indian Republic.* Princeton, NJ: Princeton University Press, 2018.

Devji, Faisal. "From Minority to Nation." In *Partitions: A Transnational History of Twentieth-Century Territorial Separatism,* edited by Arie Dubnov and Laura Robson. Stanford, CA: Stanford University Press, 2019.

———. *Muslim Zion: Pakistan as a Political Idea.* Cambridge, MA: Harvard University Press, 2013.

Dhulipala, Venkat. *Creating a New Medina: State Power, Islam, and the Quest for Pakistan in Late Colonial North India.* Delhi: Cambridge University Press, 2015.

Dehlvi, Shahid Ahmad. *Dilli Ki Bipta.* Karachi: Shahrzad, 2010 [1950].

———. *Ujra Dayar.* Karachi: Daniyal, 1967.

Diner, Dan. *Cataclysms: A History of the Twentieth Century from Europe's Edge.* Madison: University of Wisconsin Press, 2008 [1999].

Dubnov, Arie. "Notes on the Zionist Passage to India, Or: The Analogical Imagination and Its Boundaries." *Journal of Israeli History* 35, no. 2 (2016): 174–214.

Dubnov, Arie, and Laura Robson. "Drawing the Line, Writing Beyond It: Toward a Transnational History of Partitions." In *Partitions: A Transnational History of Twentieth-Century Territorial Separatism,* edited by Arie Dubnov and Laura Robson, 1–27. Stanford, CA: Stanford University Press, 2019.

Durrani, F. K. *The Meaning of Pakistan.* Lahore: Sh. Muhammad Ashraf, 1944.

Ehlers, Eckart, and Thomas Krafft. "Islamic Cities in India? Theoretical Concepts and the Case of Shahjahanabad/Old Delhi." In *Shahjahanabad/Old Delhi: Tradition and Colonial Change,* edited by Eckart Ehlers and Thomas Krafft. Delhi: Manohar, 2003 [1993].

Farooqui, Mahmood. *Besieged: Voices from Delhi 1857.* New Delhi: Penguin Viking, 2010.

Farouqui, Ather. "The Emerging Dilemma of the Urdu Press in India: A Viewpoint." *South Asia: Journal of South Asian Studies* 18, no. 2 (1995): 91–103.

———, ed. *Redefining Urdu Politics in India*. New Delhi: Oxford University Press, 2006.

Faruqi, Shamsur Rahman. "A Long History of Urdu Literary Culture, Part 1: Naming and Placing a Literary Culture." In *Literary Cultures in History: Reconstructions from South Asia*, edited by Sheldon Pollock. Berkeley: University of California Press, 2003.

Faruqi, Ziya-ul-Hasan. *The Deoband School and the Demand for Pakistan*. London: Asia Publishing House, 1963.

Fink, Carole. "The League of Nations and the Minorities Questions." *World Affairs* 157, no. 4 (1995): 197–205.

Freitag, Sandria B. *Collective Action and Community: Public Arenas and the Emergence of Communalism in North India*. Berkeley: University of California Press, 1989.

Frykenberg, Robert Eric. "The Study of Delhi: An Historical Introduction." In *Delhi through the Ages: Essays in Urban History, Culture, and Society*, edited by Robert Eric Frykenberg. Delhi: Oxford University Press, 1992 [1986].

Fuller, C. J., and Véronique Bénéï, eds. *The Everyday State and Society in Modern India*. London: Hurst, 2001.

Gandhi, M. K. *Delhi Diary, Prayer Speeches from 10-9-47 to 30-1-48*. Ahmedabad: Navajivan, 1948.

Gandhi, Rajmohan. *Mohandas: A True Story of a Man, His People and an Empire*. New Delhi: Penguin, 2006.

Gauba, K. L. *The Consequences of Pakistan*. Lahore: Lion, 1946.

Gautier, Laurence. "A Laboratory for a Composite India? Jamia Millia Islamia around the Time of Partition." *Modern Asian Studies* 54, no. 1 (2020): 199–249.

Geva, Rotem. "The Scramble for Houses: Violence, a Factionalized State, and Informal Economy in Post-Partition Delhi." *Modern Asian Studies* 51, no. 3 (2017): 769–824.

Gilmartin, David. "Democracy, Nationalism and the Public: A Speculation on Colonial Muslim Politics." *South Asia: Journal of South Asian Studies* 14, no. 1 (1991): 123–40.

———. "A Magnificent Gift: Muslim Nationalism and the Election Process in Colonial Punjab." *Comparative Studies in Society and History* 40, no. 3 (1998): 415–36.

———. "Partition, Pakistan, and South Asian History: In Search of a Narrative." *Journal of Asian Studies* 57, no. 4 (1998): 1068–95.

Gopal, Priyamvada. *Literary Radicalism in India: Gender, Nation and the Transition to Independence*. New York: Routledge, 2005.

Gould, William. *Bureaucracy, Community, and Influence in India: Society and the State, 1930s-1960s*. New York: Routledge, 2011.

———. *Hindu Nationalism and the Language of Politics in Late Colonial India*. Cambridge: Cambridge University Press, 2004.

Gould, William, Sherman C. Taylor, and Sarah Ansari. "The Flux of the Matter: Loyalty, Corruption and the 'Everyday State' in the Post-Partition Government Services of India and Pakistan." *Past and Present* 219, no. May (2013).

Green, L. C. "The Indian National Army Trials." *Modern Law Review* 11, no. 1 (1948): 47–69.

Greenough, Paul R. "Political Mobilization and the Underground Literature of the Quit India Movement, 1942–44." *Social Scientist* 27, no. 7/8 (1999): 11–47.

Grewal, J. S. *Master Tara Singh in Indian History: Colonialism, Nationalism and the Politics of Sikh Identity*. New Delhi: Oxford University Press, 2018.

Guha, Ramachandra. *India after Gandhi: The History of the World's Largest Democracy*. Pan Macmillan, 2008.

Guha, Ranajit. *Elementary Aspects of Peasant Insurgency in Colonial India*. Durham, NC: Duke University Press, 1999 [1983].

———. "The Prose of Counter-Insurgency." In *Selected Subaltern Studies*, edited by Ranajit Guha and Gayatri Chakravorty Spivak, 45–84. New York: Oxford University Press, [1983] 1988.

Gupta, Anand. *Dilli Ki Communist Party Ka Itihas*. Delhi: Communist Party Prakashan, 2007.

Gupta, Dipankar. "The Indian Diaspora of 1947: The Political and Ethnic Consequences of Partition with Special Reference to Delhi." In *Communalism in India: History, Politics, and Culture*, edited by K. N. Panikkar. New Delhi: Manohar, 1991.

Gupta, Narayani. *Delhi between Two Empires, 1803–1931: Society, Government and Urban Growth*. Delhi: Oxford University Press, 1981.

Gupta, Nina Dey. "The Halcyon Yesterdays of Delhi College: A Chequered History." In *Knowledge, Power & Politics: Educational Institutions in India*, edited by Mushirul Hasan. New Delhi: Roli Books, 1998.

Hansen, Thomas Blom. *The Saffron Wave: Democracy and Hindu Nationalism in Modern India*. Princeton, NJ: Princeton University Press, 1999.

———. *Wages of Violence: Naming and Identity in Postcolonial Bombay*. Princeton, NJ: Princeton University Press, 2001.

Hansen, Thomas Blom, and Finn Stepputat, eds. *States of Imagination: Ethnographic Explorations of the Postcolonial State*. Durham, NC: Duke University Press, 2001.

Hardy, Peter. *The Muslims of British India*. London: Cambridge University Press, 1972.

Hasan, Mushirul, ed. *India's Partition: Process, Strategy, and Mobilization*. New Delhi: Oxford University Press, 2013 [1993].

———. *Legacy of a Divided Nation: India's Muslims since Independence*. London: Hurst & Co., 1997.

———. *M. A. Ansari: Gandhi's Infallible Guide*. New Delhi: Manohar, 2010 [1987].

———. "Nationalist and Separatist Trends in Aligarh, 1915–1947." *Indian Economic and Social History Review* 22, no. 1 (1985): 1–33.

Hasan, Mushirul and Margrit Pernau, eds. "History of the Non-Cooperation and Khilafat Movements in Delhi." In *Regionalizing Pan-Islamism: Documents on the Khilafat Movement*, edited by Mushirul Hasan and Margrit Pernau, 1–54. New Delhi: Manohar, 2005.

Hosagrahar, Jyoti. *Indigenous Modernities: Negotiating Architecture and Urbanism*. New York: Routledge, 2005.

———. "Mansions to Margins: Modernity and the Domestic Landscape of Historic Delhi, 1847–1910." *Journal of the Society of Architectural Historians* 60, no. 1 (2001): 26–45.

Husain, Intizar. *Chiraghon Ka Dhuan: Yadon Ke Pachas Bars*. Lahore: Sang-e Meel Publications, 1999.

Hutchins, Francis G. *The Illusion of Permanence*. Princeton, NJ: Princeton University Press, 1976.

———. *India's Revolution: Gandhi and the Quit India Movement*. Cambridge, MA: Harvard University Press, 1973.

Ikramullah, Shaista Suhrawardy. *From Purdah to Parliament*. Revised and expanded ed. Karachi: Oxford University Press, 1998 [1963].

Irving, Robert Grant. *Indian Summer: Lutyens, Baker, and Imperial Delhi*. New Haven, CT: Yale University Press, 1981.

Jaffrelot, Christophe. "A De Facto Ethnic Democracy? Obliterating and Targeting the Other, Hindu Vigilantes, and the Ethno-State." In *Majoritarian State: How Hindu Nationalism Is Changing India*, edited by Angana P. Chatterji, Thomas Blom Hansen, and Christophe Jaffrelot. London: Hurst, 2020.

———. "The Hindu Nationalist Movement in Delhi: From 'Locals' to Refugees and Towards Peripheral Groups?". In *Religion, Caste, and Politics in India*. New York: Columbia University Press, 2011.

———. *The Hindu Nationalist Movement in India*. New York: Columbia University Press, 1993.

Jain, L. C. *Civil Disobedience: Two Freedom Struggles, One Life*. New Delhi: Book Review Literary Trust, 2010.

Jain, Nirmala. *Dilli, Shahr Dar Shahr*. New Delhi: Rajkamal Prakashan, 2009.

Jalal, Ayesha. "Nation, Reason and Religion: Punjab's Role in the Partition of India." *Economic and Political Weekly* 33, no. 32 (1998): 2183–90.

———. *Self and Sovereignty: Individual and Community in South Asian Islam since 1850*. New York: Routledge, 2000.

———. *The Sole Spokesman: Jinnah, the Muslim League, and the Demand for Pakistan*. Cambridge: Cambridge University Press, 1994 [1985].

Jamil, Ghazala. *Accumulation by Segregation: Muslim Localities in Delhi*. New Delhi: Oxford University Press, 2017.

Jayal, Niraja Gopal. *Citizenship and Its Discontents: An Indian History*. Cambridge, MA: Harvard University Press, 2013.

———. "Reconfiguring Citizenship in Contemporary India." *South Asia: Journal of South Asian Studies* 42, no. 1 (2019): 33–50.

Jeffrey, Robin. "Hindi: 'Taking to the Punjab Kesari Line.'" *Economic & Political Weekly* 32, no. 3 (1997): 77–83.

———. *India's Newspaper Revolution: Capitalism, Politics and the Indian-Language Press, 1977–99*. London: Hurst, 2000.

———. "Punjabi: 'The Sub-Liminal Charge'." *Economic & Political Weekly* 32, no. 9–10 (1997): 443–5.

Jensen, Steffen. "The Battlefield and the Prize: ANC's Bid to Reform the South African State." In *States of Imagination: Ethnographic Explorations of the Postcolonial State*, edited by Thomas Blom Hansen and Finn Stepputat. Durham, NC: Duke University Press, 2001.

Jha, Shefali "Rights Versus Representation: Defending Minority Interests in the Constituent Assembly". *Economic & Political Weekly* 38, no. 16 (2003): 1579–83.

———. "Secularism in the Constituent Assembly Debates, 1946–1950." *Economic & Political Weekly* 37, no. 30 (2002): 1579–83.

Jones, Kenneth W. *Arya Dharm: Hindu Consciousness in 19th-Century Punjab*. Berkeley: University of California Press, 1976.

———. "Organized Hinduism in Delhi and New Delhi." In *Delhi through the Ages: Essays in Urban History, Culture, and Society*, edited by Robert Eric Frykenberg. Delhi: Oxford University Press, 1992 [1986].

———. *Socio-Religious Reform Movements in British India*. Cambridge: Cambridge University Press, 1989.

Joshi, Priya. *In Another Country: Colonialism, Culture, and the English Novel in India*. New York: Columbia University Press, 2002.

Kalhan, Anil, Gerald P. Conroy, Mamta Kaushal, Sam Scott Miller, and Jed S. Rakoff. "Colonial Continuities: Human Rights, Terrorism and Security Laws in India." *Columbia Journal of Asian Law* 20, no. 1 (2006): 92–233.

Kamtekar, Indivar. "A Different War Dance: State and Class in India, 1939–1945." *Past and Present* 176 (2002): 187–221.

———. "The End of the Colonial State in India, 1942–1947." PhD diss., Churchill College, University of Cambridge, 1988.

———. "The Shiver of 1942." *Studies in History* 18, no. 1 (2002).

Karaka, D. F. *Betrayal in India*. London: Victor Gollancz, 1950.

Kaur, Ravinder. "Claiming Community through Narratives: Punjabi Refugees in Delhi." In *The Idea of Delhi*, edited by Romi Khosla. Mumbai: Marg, 2005.

———. *Since 1947: Partition Narratives among Punjabi Migrants of Delhi*. New Delhi: Oxford University Press, 2007.

Kaviraj, Sudipta. "A Critique of the Passive Revolution." In *State and Politics in India*, edited by Partha Chatterjee. Delhi: Oxford University Press, 1998.

———. "The Imaginary Institution of India." In *Subaltern Studies Vol 7*, edited by Partha Chatterjee and Gyanendra Pandey, 1–39. Delhi: Oxford University Press, 1992.

———. "A State of Contradictions: The Post-Colonial State in India." In *The Imaginary Institution of India: Politics and Ideas*. New York: Columbia University Press, 2010.

Kedar, Alexandre. "Expanding Legal Geographies: A Call for a Critical Comparative Approach." In *The Expanding Spaces of Law: A Timely Legal Geography* edited by Irus Braverman, Nicholas Blomley, David Delaney, and Alexandre Kedar. Stanford, CA: Stanford University Press, 2014.

Khan, Yasmin. *The Great Partition: The Making of India and Pakistan*. New Haven, CT: Yale University Press, 2007.

———. "Performing Peace: Gandhi's Assassination as a Critical Moment in the Consolidation of the Nehruvian State." *Modern Asian Studies* 45, no. 1 (2011): 57–80.

———. *The Raj at War: A People's History of India's Second World War*. London: Bodley Head, 2015.

Khosla, G. D. *Stern Reckoning: A Survey of the Events Leading up to and Following the Partition of India*. Delhi: Oxford University Press, 1989 [1949].

Kidwai, Anis. *In Freedom's Shade*. Translated by Ayesha Kidwai. New Delhi: Penguin, 2011.

King, Christopher R. *One Language, Two Scripts: The Hindi Movement in the Nineteenth Century North India*. Bombay: Oxford University Press, 1994.

Kishore, Raghav. *The (Un)Governable City: Productive Failure in the Making of Colonial Delhi, 1858–1911*. Hyderabad: Orient BlackSwan, 2020.

Koselleck, Reinhart. *Futures Past: On the Semantics of Historical Time*. Translated by Keith Tribe. New York: Columbia University Press, 2004 [1985].

Krafft, Thomas. "Contemporary Old Delhi: Transformation of an Historical Place." In *Shahjahanabad/Old Delhi: Tradition and Colonial Change*, edited by Eckart Ehlers and Thomas Krafft. Delhi: Manohar, 2003 [1993].

Krishan, Gopal. "Mahashay Krishna." *Vidura* 7 (1970).

Krishna, Gopal. "Communal Violence in India: A Study of Communal Disturbance in Delhi, Part 2." *Economic & Political Weekly* 20, no. 3 (1985): 117–31.

Kudaisya, Gyanesh. *A Republic in the Making: India in the 1950s*. New Delhi: Oxford University Press, 2017.

Kumar, Radha. *Police Matters: The Everyday State and Caste Politics in South India, 1900–1975*. Ithaca, NY: Cornell University Press, 2021.

Latif, Syed Abdul. *The Muslim Problem in India: Together with an Alternative Constitution for India*. Bombay: Times of India Press, 1939.

Legg, Stephen. "Gendered Politics and Nationalised Homes: Women and the Anti-Colonial Struggle in Delhi, 1930–47." *Gender, Place, and Culture* 10, no. 1 (2003): 7–27.

———. "A Pre-Partitioned City? Anti-Colonial and Communal Mohallas in Inter-War Delhi." *South Asia: Journal of South Asian Studies* 42, no. 1 (2019): 170–87.

———. *Spaces of Colonialism: Delhi's Urban Governmentalities*. Malden, MA: Blackwell, 2007.

Lieberman, Benjamin. "'Ethnic Cleansing' Versus Genocide?" In *The Oxford Handbook of Genocide Studies*, edited by Donald Bloxam and Dirk A. Moses. Oxford: Oxford University Press, 2010.

Malik, D. M. *The Tragedy of Delhi (through Neutral Eyes)*. Delhi: Provincial Muslim League, 1948.

Manela, Erez. *The Wilsonian Moment: Self-Determination and the International Origins of Anticolonial Nationalism*. Oxford: Oxford University Press, 2007.

Marston, Daniel. *The Indian Army and the End of the Raj*. Cambridge: Cambridge University Press, 2016.

Masselos, Jim. "Controlling Prabhat Pheris." In *The City in Action: Bombay Struggles for Power*, 221–41. New Delhi: Oxford University Press, 2007.

Mayaram, Shail. *Resisting Regimes: Myth, Memory, and the Shaping of a Muslim Identity*. Delhi: Oxford University Press, 1997.

Mazower, Mark. "Minorities and the League of Nations in Interwar Europe." *Daedalus* 126, no. 2 (1997): 47–63.

Mehra, Diya. "Planning Delhi Ca. 1936–1959." *South Asia: Journal of South Asian Studies* 36, no. 3 (2013): 354–74.

Mehta, Uday S. "Indian Constitutionalism: The Articulation of a Political Vision." In *From the Colonial to the Postcolonial: India and Pakistan in Transition*, edited by Dipesh Chakrabarty, Rochona Majumdar, and Andrew Sartori, 13–30. New Delhi: Oxford University Press, 2007.

Menon, Ritu, and Kamla Bhasin. *Borders & Boundaries: Women in India's Partition*. New Delhi: Kali for Women, 1998.

Menon, V. P. *The Transfer of Power in India*. Princeton, NJ: Princeton University Press, 1957.

Metcalf, Barbara Daly. *Islamic Revival in British India: Deoband, 1860–1900*. Princeton, NJ: Princeton University Press, 1982.

———. "Nationalist Muslims in British India: The Case of Hakim Ajmal Khan." *Modern Asian Studies* 19, no. 1 (1985): 1–28.

———. "Observant Muslims, Secular Indians: The Political Vision of Maulana Husain Ahmad Madani, 1938–57." In *From the Colonial to the Postcolonial: India and Pakistan in Transition*, edited by Dipesh Chakrabarty, Rochona Majumdar, and Andrew Sartori. New Delhi: Oxford University Press, 2007.

Metcalf, Thomas R. *An Imperial Vision: Indian Architecture and Britain's Raj*. Berkeley: University of California Press, 1989.

Minault, Gail. *The Khilafat Movement: Religious Symbolism and Political Mobilization in India*. New York: Columbia University Press, 1982.

Mir, Farina. *The Social Space of Language: Vernacular Culture in British Colonial Punjab*. Berkeley: University of California Press, 2010.

Mittal, Gopal. *Lahore Ka Jo Zikr Kiya*. New Delhi: Modern Publishing House, 2000.

Moore, R. J. *Churchill, Cripps, and India, 1939–1945*. Oxford: Oxford University Press, 1979.

———. "Jinnah and the Pakistan Demand." *Modern Asian Studies* 17, no. 4 (1983): 529–61.

Moyn, Samuel. "Fantasies of Federalism." *Dissent* 62, no. 1 (2015): 145–51.

Mufti, Aamir. *Enlightenment in the Colony: The Jewish Question and the Crisis of Postcolonial Culture*. Princeton, NJ: Princeton University Press, 2007.

Mukherjee, Janam. *Hungry Bengal: War, Famine and the End of Empire*. London: Hurst, 2015.

Mustafa, Seema, ed. *Shaheen Bagh and the Idea of India: Writings on a Movement for Justice, Liberty and Equality*. New Delhi: Speaking Tiger, 2020.

Naim, C. M. "The Consequences of Indo-Pakistani War for Urdu Language and Literature: A Parting of the Ways?" In *Urdu Texts and Contexts: The Selected Essays of C. M. Naim*. New Delhi: Permanent Black, 2004.

———. "The Muslim League in Barabanki: A Suite of Five Sentimental Scenes." *India Institute of Advanced Study* (2010).

Naimark, Norman M. *Fires of Hatred: Ethnic Cleansing in Twentieth-Century Europe*. Cambridge, MA: Harvard University Press, 2001.

Nair, Neeti. "Beyond the 'Communal' 1920s: The Problem of Intention, Legislative Prag-matism and the Making of Section 295a of the Indian Penal Code." *Indian Economic and Social History Review* 50, no. 3 (2013): 317–40.

———. *Changing Homelands: Hindu Politics and the Partition of India.* Cambridge, MA: Harvard University Press, 2011.

Newbigin, Eleanor. *The Hindu Family and the Emergence of Modern India: Law, Citizenship and Community.* Cambridge: Cambridge University Press, 2013.

Noorani, Abdul Gafoor Abdul Majeed, ed. *The Muslims of India: A Documentary Record.* New Delhi: Oxford University Press, 2003.

Oldenburg, Philip. *Big City Government in India: Councilor, Administrator, and Citizen in Delhi.* Tucson: University of Arizona Press, 1976.

Orsini, Francesca. *The Hindi Public Sphere 1920–1940: Language and Literature in the Age of Nationalism.* New Delhi: Oxford University Press, 2002.

Panayi, Panikos, and Pippa Virdee, eds. *Refugees and the End of Empire: Imperial Col-lapse and Forced Migration in the Twentieth Century.* New York: Palgrave Macmillan, 2011.

Pandey, Gyanendra. "Can a Muslim Be an Indian?". *Comparative Studies in Society and History* 41, no. 4 (1999): 608–29.

———. *The Construction of Communalism in Colonial North India.* New Delhi: Oxford University Press, 1990.

———. "In Defence of the Fragment: Writing About Hindu-Muslim Riots in India To-day." *Economic & Political Weekly* 26, no. 11/12 (1991): 559–72.

———, ed. *The Indian Nation in 1942.* Calcutta: Centre for Studies in Social Sciences, 1988.

———. "The Prose of Otherness." In *Subaltern Studies Vol. 8,* edited by David Arnold and David Hardiman. Delhi: Oxford University Press, 1994.

———. *Remembering Partition: Violence, Nationalism, and History in India.* Cambridge: Cambridge University Press, 2001.

Parveen, Nazima. *Contested Homelands: Politics of Space and Identity.* New Delhi: Blooms-bury, 2021.

Peled, Yoav. "Ethnic Democracy and the Legal Construction of Citizenship: Arab Citizens of the Jewish State." *American Political Science Review* 86, no. 2 (1992): 432–43.

Pernau, Margrit. *Ashraf into Middle Class: Muslims in Nineteenth-Century Delhi.* New Delhi: Oxford University Press, 2013.

———, ed. *The Delhi College: Traditional Elites, the Colonial State, and Education before 1857.* New Delhi: Oxford University Press, 2006.

Pirzada, Syed Sharifuddin, ed. *Foundations of Pakistan: All India Muslim League Documents, 1906–1947,* Vol. II. Karachi: National Publishing House, 1970.

Popplewell, Richard James. *Intelligence and Imperial Defence: British Intelligence and the Defence of the Indian Empire, 1904–1924.* Portland, OR: Frank Cass, 1995.

Potter, David C. *India's Political Administrators, 1919–1983.* Oxford: Clarendon, 1996.

Prakash, Gyan. *Emergency Chronicles: Indira Gandhi and Democracy's Turning Point*. Princeton, NJ: Princeton University Press, 2019.

———. "Secular Nationalism, Hindutva, and the Minority." In *The Crisis of Secularism in India*, edited by Anuradha Dingwaney Needham and Rajeswari Sunder Rajan. Durham, NC: Duke University Press, 2007.

Prasad, Rajendra. *India Divided*. Bombay: Hind Kitabs, 1946.

Pritchett, Frances W. *Nets of Awareness: Urdu Poetry and Its Critics*. Berkeley: University of California Press, 1994.

Puri, Geeta. *Bharatiya Jana Sangh, Organisation and Ideology: Delhi, a Case Study*. New Delhi: Sterling, 1980.

Puri, Yogesh. *Party Politics in the Nehru Era: A Study of Congress in Delhi*. New Delhi: National Book Organisation, 1993.

Purushotham, Sunil. *From Raj to Republic: Sovereignty, Violence, and Democracy in India*. Stanford, CA: Stanford University Press, 2021.

Qureshi, I. H. "A Case Study of the Social Relations between the Muslims and the Hindus, 1935–47." In *The Partition of India: Policies and Perspectives, 1935–1947*, edited by C. H. Philips and Mary Doreen Wainwright. London: Allen & Unwin, 1970.

Raghavan, Pallavi. *Animosity at Bay: An Alternative History of the India-Pakistan Relationship, 1947–1952*. New York: Oxford University Press, 2020.

Raghavan, Srinath. *India's War: The Making of Modern South Asia 1939–1945*. London: Allen Lane, 2016.

Rahbar, Hansraj. "Abhi Dilli Dur Hai." In *Abhi Dilli Dur Hai*, edited by Rajendra Yadav. New Delhi: Pravin Prakashan, 1995.

———. "Dilli Ab Dur Nahin." In *Dilli Tea House: Arddhashati Ki Sahityik Halchal*, edited by Baldev Vanshi. New Delhi: National Publishing House, 2009.

Rai, Amrit. *A House Divided: The Origin and Development of Hindi/Hindavi*. Delhi: Oxford University Press, 1984.

Rajagopalan, Mrinalini. *Building Histories: The Archival and Affective Lives of Five Monuments in Modern Delhi*. Chicago: University of Chicago Press, 2017.

Rajdhani Weekly Supplement: Delhi State. Delhi: Rajdhani Weekly, 1953.

Rakesh, Mohan. *Andhere Band Kamre*. New Delhi: Rajkamal Prakashan, 1961.

Ram, Moti. *Two Historic Trials in Red Fort: An Authentic Account of the Trial by a General Court Martial of Captain Shah Nawaz Khan, Captain P. K. Sahgal and Lt. G. S. Dhillon; and the Trial by a European Military Commission of Emperor Bahadur Shah*. New Delhi: Roxy, 1946.

Ramnath, Kalyani. "ADM Jabalpur's Antecedents: Political Emergencies, Civil Liberties and Arguments from Colonial Continuities in India." *American University International Law Review* 31, no. 2 (2016).

Randhawa, M. S. *Out of the Ashes: An Account of the Rehabilitation of Refugees from West Pakistan in Rural Areas of East Punjab*. Punjab: Public Relations Department, 1954.

Rao, M. B., ed. *Documents of the History of the Communist Party of India, Vol. VII, 1948–1950*. New Delhi: People's Publishing Press, 1960.

Rao, V. K. R. V., and P. B. Desai. *Greater Delhi: A Study in Urbanisation, 1940–1957.* Delhi: Planning Commission, Government of India, 1965.

Robinson, Shira. *Citizen Strangers: Palestinians and the Birth of Israel's Liberal Settler State.* Stanford, CA: Stanford University Press, 2013.

Rook-Koepsel, Emily. "Dissenting against the Defence of India Rules: Emergency Regulations and the Space of Extreme Government Action." *South Asia: Journal of South Asian Studies* 41, no. 3 (2018): 642–57.

Roy, Haimanti. *Partitioned Lives: Refugees, Migrants, Citizens in India and Pakistan, 1947–65.* Oxford: Oxford University Press, 2012.

Roy, Srirupa. *Beyond Belief: India and the Politics of Postcolonial Nationalism.* Ranikhet: Permanent Black, 2007.

Sadana, Rashmi. *English Heart, Hindi Heartland: The Political Life of Literature in India.* Berkeley: University of California Press, 2012.

Sahni, Bhisham. *Aj Ke Atit.* New Delhi: Rajkamal Prakashan, 2003.

———. "Abhi Dilli Dur Hai." In *Abhi Dilli Dur Hai*, edited by Rajendra Yadav. New Delhi: Pravin Prakashan, 1995.

Sahni, J. N. *Truth About the Indian Press.* Bombay: Allied, 1974.

Saini, Mahender Kumar, and Walter Andersen. "The Congress Split in Delhi: The Effects of Factionalism on Organizational Performance and System Level Interactions." *Asian Survey* 11, no. 11 (1971): 1084–100.

Samaddar, Ranabir. "Law and Terror in the Age of Colonial Constitution Making." *Diogenes* 53, no. 4 (2006): 18–33.

Sarkar, Sumit. "Popular Movements and National Leadership, 1945–47." *Economic & Political Weekly* 17, no. 14/16, Annual Number (1982): 677–89.

Savarkar, Vinayak Damodar. *Hindutva: Who Is a Hindu?* Bombay: Veer Savarkar Prakashan, 1969.

Schechtman, Joseph B. "Evacuee Property in India and Pakistan." *Pacific Affairs* 24, no. 4 (1951): 406–13.

Scott, Barton J. "Aryas Unbound: Print Hinduism and the Cultural Regulation of Religious Offense." *Comparative Studies of South Asia, Africa, and the Middle East* 35, no. 2 (2015): 294–309.

Sen, Uditi. *Citizen Refugee: Forging the Indian Nation after Partition.* Cambridge: Cambridge University Press, 2018.

Sethi, Devika. *Wars over Words: Censorship in India, 1930–1960.* Cambridge: Cambridge University Press, 2019.

Shackle, C., and Rupert Snell. *Hindi and Urdu since 1800: A Common Reader.* New Delhi: Heritage, 1990.

Shaikh, Farzana. *Making Sense of Pakistan.* New York: Columbia University Press, 2009.

———. "Muslims and Political Representation in Colonial India: The Making of Pakistan." *Modern Asian Studies* 20, no. 3 (1986): 539–57.

Shani, Ornit. *How India Became Democratic: Citizenship and the Making of the Universal Franchise.* Cambridge: Cambridge University Press, 2018.

Shankar, V. *My Reminiscences of Sardar Patel, Vol. I*. Delhi: Macmillan, 1974.

Sharan, Awadhendra. *In the City, Out of Place: Nuisance, Pollution, and Dwelling in Delhi, C. 1850–2000*. New Delhi: Oxford University Press, 2014.

Sharma, Ravikant. "Architecture of Intellectual Sociality: Tea and Coffee Houses in Post-Colonial Delhi." *City, Culture and Society* 7 (2016): 275–81.

Sharma, Shalini. "'Yeh Azaadi Jhoothi Hai!': The Shaping of the Opposition in the First Year of the Congress Raj." *Modern Asian Studies* 48, no. 5 (2014): 1358–88.

Sherman, Taylor C. *Muslim Belonging in Secular India: Negotiating Citizenship in Postcolonial Hyderabad*. Cambridge: Cambridge University Press, 2015.

Siddiqi, Abdul Rahman. *Smoke without Fire: Portraits of Pre-Partition Delhi*. Delhi: Aakar Books, 2011.

Silvestri, Michael. "The Thrill of 'Simply Dressing Up': The Indian Police, Disguise, and Intelligence Work in Colonial India." *Journal of Colonialism and Colonial History* 2, no. 2 (2001).

Singh, Neerja, ed. *Nehru-Patel, Agreement within Differences: Select Documents and Correspondences 1933–1950*. New Delhi: National Book Trust, 2010.

Singh, Nishtha. "Dehlviyat: The Making and Un-Making of Delhi's Indo-Muslim Urban Culture, C. 1750–1900." PhD diss., Princeton University, 2014.

Six, Clemens. *Secularism, Decolonisation, and the Cold War in South and Southeast Asia*. New York: Routledge, 2018.

Smooha, Sammy. "Ethnic Democracy: Israel as an Archetype." *Israel Studies* 2, no. 2 (1997): 198–241.

Sobti, Krishna. "Abhi Dilli Dur Hai." In *Abhi Dilli Dur Hai*, edited by Rajendra Yadav. New Delhi: Pravin Prakashan, 1995.

Spear, Percival, and Margaret Spear. *India Remembered*. Hyderabad: Orient Blackswan, 2010 [1981].

Sriraman, Tarangini. *In Pursuit of Proof: A History of Identification Documents in India*. Oxford: Oxford University Press, 2018.

Stephens, Julia. "The Politics of Muslim Rage: Secular Law and Religious Sentiment in Late Colonial India." *History Workshop Journal* 77, no. 1 (2014): 45–64.

Stolte, Carolien. "'The Asiatic Hour': New Perspectives of the Asian Relations Conference, New Delhi 1947." In *The Non-Aligned Movement and the Cold War: Delhi - Bandung - Belgrade*, edited by Nataša Mišković, Harald Fischer-Tiné, and Nada Boškovska. New York: Routledge, 2014.

Talbot, Ian. *Divided Cities: Partition and Its Aftermath in Lahore and Amritsar, 1947–1957*. Karachi: Oxford University Press, 2006.

———. "The Role of the Crowd in the Muslim League Struggle for Pakistan". *Journal of Imperial and Commonwealth History* 21, no. 2 (1993): 307–33.

Talbot, Ian, and Gurharpal Singh. *The Partition of India*. Cambridge: Cambridge University Press, 2009.

Talib, Mohammad. "Jamia Millia Islamia: Career of Azad Talim." In *Knowledge, Power & Politics: Educational Institutions in India*, edited by Mushirul Hasan. New Delhi: Roli Books, 1998.

Tan, Tai Yong, and Gyanesh Kudaisya. *The Aftermath of Partition in South Asia*. New York: Routledge, 2000.

Taneja, Anand Vivek. *Jinnealogy: Tines, Islam, and Ecological Thought in the Medieval Ruins of Delhi*. Stanford, CA: Stanford University Press, 2018.

Tarlo, Emma. *Unsettling Memories: Narratives of the Emergency in Delhi*. London: C. Hurst, 2003.

———. "Welcome to History: A Resettlement Colony in the Making." In *Delhi: Urban Space and Human Destinies*, edited by Véronique Dupont, Emma Tarlo, and Denis Vidal. New Delhi: Manohar, 2000.

Tejani, Shabnum. *Indian Secularism: A Social and Intellectual History, 1890–1950*. Bloomington: Indiana University Press, 2008.

Tripathi, Pradyumna K. "Preventive Detention: The Indian Experience". *American Journal of Comparative Law* 9, no. 2 (1960): 219–48.

Trivedi, Harish. "The Progress of Hindi, Part 2: Hindi and the Nation." In *Literary Cultures in History: Reconstructions from South Asia*, edited by Sheldon I. Pollock, 958–1022. Berkeley: University of California Press, 2003.

Vanaik, Anish. *Possessing the City: Property and Politics in Delhi, 1911–1947*. Oxford: Oxford University Press, 2019.

Vanshi, Baldev, ed. *Dilli Tea House: Arddhashati Ki Sahityik Halchal*. New Delhi: National Publishing House, 2009.

Voigt, Johannes H. *India in the Second World War*. New Delhi: Arnold-Heinemann, 1987.

Weiss, Yfaat. *A Confiscated Memory: Wadi Salib and Haifa's Lost Heritage*. New York: Columbia University Press, 2011.

Weitz, Eric D. "From the Vienna to the Paris System: International Politics and the Entangled Histories of Human Rights, Forced Deportations, and Civilizing Missions." *American Historical Review* 113, no. 5 (2008): 1313–43.

Yashpal. *Jhutha Sach, Volume 2: Desh Ka Bhavishya*. Allahabad: Lokbharati Prakashan, 2007 [1960].

Zachariah, Benjamin. *Nehru*. London: Routledge, 2004.

Zaidi, Z. H., ed. *Quaid-I-Azam Mohammad Ali Jinnah Papers: Prelude to Pakistan, 20 February–2 June 1947*, First Series, Volume I, Parts 1 and 2. Islamabad: National Archives of Pakistan, 1993.

Zamindar, Vazira Fazila-Yacoobali. *The Long Partition and the Making of Modern South Asia: Refugees, Boundaries, Histories*. New York: Columbia University Press, 2007.

INDEX

Page numbers in italics refer to figures and tables.